# WHAT IT TOOK
## TO WIN

# WHAT IT TOOK
# TO WIN

## A HISTORY OF THE
# DEMOCRATIC
# PARTY

## MICHAEL KAZIN

FARRAR, STRAUS AND GIROUX

*New York*

Farrar, Straus and Giroux
120 Broadway, New York 10271

Library of Congress Cataloging-in-Publication Data
Names: Kazin, Michael, 1948– author.
Title: What it took to win : a history of the Democratic Party / Michael Kazin.
Description: First Edition. | New York : Farrar, Straus and Giroux, [2022] |
    Includes bibliographical references and index. | Summary: "A history of the
    Democratic Party from Andrew Jackson to Joe Biden" —Provided by publisher.
Identifiers: LCCN 2021044929 | ISBN 9780374200237 (Hardcover)
Subjects: LCSH: Democratic Party (U.S.)—History. | Political parties—United
    States—History. | United States—Politics and government.
Classification: LCC JK2316 .K379 2022 | DDC 324.2736/09—dc23/eng/20211109
LC record available at https://lccn.loc.gov/2021044929

Our books may be purchased in bulk for promotional, educational, or business use.
Please contact your local bookseller or the Macmillan Corporate and Premium Sales
Department at 1-800-221-7945, extension 5442, or by email at
MacmillanSpecialMarkets@macmillan.com.

www.fsgbooks.com
www.twitter.com/fsgbooks • www.facebook.com/fsgbooks

1  3  5  7  9  10  8  6  4  2

For Danny and Maia

# CONTENTS

## PREFACE: TO PROMOTE THE GENERAL WELFARE

*What the people want is very simple. They want an America*
*as good as its promise.*
—BARBARA JORDAN, CONGRESSWOMAN FROM TEXAS, 1977[1]

*There are members of the Democratic Party that really have no*
*business being in the same party together. I think maybe the thing*
*that would tether us together is . . . a belief that people are more*
*important than property and individual wealth.*
—JEREMIAH ELLISON, MEMBER OF THE MINNEAPOLIS
CITY COUNCIL, 2020[2]

*Parties exist to win elections.*
—JAMES WOOD, CRITIC[3]

This book tells the story of how the oldest mass party in the world
contended for power and what its leaders did with it when they won.
The aims and methods of Democrats have evolved, inevitably, over
the past two centuries. But one theme has endured: they have insisted that the economy should benefit the ordinary working person,
whether farmer or wage earner, and that governments should institute policies to make that possible—and to resist those that do not.
Of course, Democrats argued about and for many other causes. Yet
who gains and who loses in the competition for vital resources has
been a constant theme in the history of every nation and people.
When Democrats made a convincing appeal to the economic interests of the many, they usually celebrated victory at the polls.

It took a hideously long time for the self-proclaimed "party of the people" to welcome the support and fight for the needs of Americans whose skin was not white and whose gender was not male. For the first century of its existence, the Democratic Party was in fact, if not official doctrine, an organization that solicited the votes of white men only and neglected or disparaged everyone else. During the nineteenth century, its leaders carried out the forced removal of Native Americans from their ancestral lands, defended slavery and allowed it to expand, did their best to sabotage Reconstruction, and constructed the brutal Jim Crow order that followed. They also lagged behind Republicans in endorsing woman suffrage. Not until the 1930s did the party, at the national level, begin, tentatively, to embrace an interracial constituency. The change was a long time in coming and did not result in the passage of strong civil rights laws until almost three decades later. The liberal journalist Michael Tomasky sums up this benighted record: "The Pre-FDR Democrats: A Horrible Party."[4]

Yet throughout their history, Democrats won national elections and were competitive in most states when they articulated an egalitarian economic vision and advocated laws intended to fulfill it—first only for white Americans but eventually for every citizen. Even when they defended racial supremacy and instituted brutal policies that devastated the lives of Black Americans and other people of color, Democrats swore by Jefferson's maxim of "equal rights to all and special privileges to none."

"Moral capitalism" is a useful way to describe both that ideal and the policies it helped inspire. Only programs designed to make life more prosperous, or at least more secure, for ordinary people proved capable of uniting Democrats and winning over enough voters to enable the party to create a governing majority that could last for more than one or two election cycles. Party leaders understood that most voters saw no alternative to the system of markets and wages, and they did not try to offer one. But they also believed, quite accurately, that the capitalist order failed to produce the utilitarian ideal of the greatest good for the greatest number.

Most Democrats repudiated their racist heritage in the final four decades of the twentieth century. But securing equal rights under the law gave Black people little relief from the injuries of poverty and de facto segregation. To put political muscle and government funding behind the Constitution's vow "to promote the general Welfare" has been and remains the best way to unify Democrats and win their candidates enough votes to make possible the creation of a more caring society. Such universal programs as Social Security, the GI Bill, and Medicare were popular when Democratic congresses enacted them and Democratic presidents signed them. Altered to help Americans of all races, they have become impregnable pillars of state policy since then.

I borrow the term "moral capitalism" from a fine book by the historian Lizabeth Cohen, which describes how, in the 1930s, Chicago workers both Black and white elected New Deal Democrats and flocked to the new unions of the Congress of Industrial Organizations. Cohen coined the term to describe "a form of political economy . . . that promised everyone, owner or worker, a fair share." During the 1930s, "a fair share" meant a modest redistribution of wealth through higher wages secured by the labor movement. More recently, Joseph Kennedy III, the grandson of Robert F. Kennedy and a representative from Massachusetts, defined it as a system "judged not by how much it produces, but how broadly it empowers, backed by a government unafraid to set the conditions for fair and just markets."[5]

But Democrats have been talking about essentially the same idea since the party began. A thread of moral capitalism stretches from Andrew Jackson's war against the Second Bank of the United States to Grover Cleveland's attack on the protective tariff, from William Jennings Bryan's crusade against the "money power" to FDR's assault on "economic royalists" to the full-employment promise embedded in the Humphrey-Hawkins Act of 1978. Democrats picked up the thread again after the Great Recession of 2008. Barack Obama declared it was "a make-or-break moment for the middle class, and for all those who are fighting to get into the middle class." In his 2020 bid for the presidency, Bernie Sanders vowed to tax the "extreme wealth" of billionaires "and invest in working people." Elizabeth Warren, another 2020 contender, declared, "I support markets . . . But markets without rules . . . that's corruption, that's capture of our government by the richest and most powerful around us." A few weeks before his inauguration, Joe Biden vowed he would be "the most pro-union president you've ever seen.[6]

In all these iterations, moral capitalism would be a system that balanced protection for the rights of Americans to accumulate property, start businesses, and employ people with an abiding concern for the welfare of those with little or modest means who increasingly worked for somebody else. When Democrats restricted their egalitarianism to whites only, they still espoused the ideal, even as they betrayed it in practice.

The ideal itself combines what have been two different and, at times, competing tendencies. The first is a harsh critique of concentrated elite power—"monopoly," whether of high finance or manufacturing or a corrupt alliance between private wealth and public officials. It envisions a society of small proprietors or at least of a government that strictly regulates larger ones and often requires them to redistribute part of their wealth, usually through progressive taxation. Racists could embrace the anti-monopoly cause quite comfortably because it did not threaten their desire for an economy run for and by white people.

The second tendency of moral capitalism attacks the oppression of Americans in the workplace, whether by poor working conditions, bad wages, insecure employment, a ban on union organizing, or other indignities. Its defenders seek to unite wage earners and their sympathizers in every region—and to look more kindly on those employers, no matter how large and powerful, who are willing to respect the rights and raise the pay of their employees while spurring economic growth.

The two tendencies are not, in theory, mutually exclusive. One can criticize monopolies for dominating the marketplace and damaging consumers as well as for paying low wages to their workers and refusing to recognize their unions. But, historically, which theme Democrats emphasized led them to construct a particular kind of coalition.

The anti-monopoly theme was the dominant one through the first century of the party's history—from Andrew Jackson's rise in the 1820s to the Great Depression in the 1930s. It helped make Democrats a national party, while either ignoring the rights and needs of non-white people, most of whom were of course workers, or seeking to keep them in bondage and, after emancipation, in a manifestly unequal status. Anti-monopoly had a very long run because it was able to unite such disparate social forces as Southern planters and Irish Catholic immigrant workers behind a shared animosity toward Northern industrialists, high tariffs, and Wall Street speculators.

The pro-labor theme largely replaced the anti-monopoly one in the 1930s and defined the party's message and animated the key members of its coalition through the 1960s. It is hardly a coincidence that the change occurred just when Southern Democrats became, for the first time, a minority of the Democratic caucus in Congress.

On occasion, the pro-labor vision of moral capitalism verged on becoming an American version of social democracy, although this was the case more in rhetoric than in policy. In his 1944 State of the Union Address, Franklin D. Roosevelt proposed his ambitious Economic Bill of Rights, which included the right to a job, the right to a home, and the right to medical care. But the powerful alliance between Southern Democrats and Republicans in Congress prevented any of these rights from being turned into realities.

Most Democrats continued to praise unions and sought ways to increase their membership, as long as doing so did not threaten the stability of the economy overall. They also pursued ideas for reducing and regulating corporate power—in alliance with movements of small farmers, wage earners, and progressive intellectuals. This required striking a balance between class-aware populist rhetoric and policies that often fell short of their promise.

Shaping the ideology of moral capitalism and an electoral coalition animated by it proved to be the most fruitful strategy for Democrats over time, despite all the changes that have taken place in the nation during the past two centuries. In fact, eras when the Democrats argued persuasively about their commitment to make the economy serve ordinary people were the only periods when the party gained durable majorities: from the late 1820s to the mid-1850s and again from the 1930s to the late 1960s. The historian Richard Hofstadter wrote midway through the twentieth century, "It has been the function of the liberal tradition in American politics, from the time of Jeffersonian and Jacksonian democracy down through Populism, Progressivism, and the New Deal, at first to broaden the numbers of those who could benefit from the great American bonanza and then to humanize its workings and help heal its casualties." Democrats were the most consistent upholders of this tradition, shot through as it was with the hypocrisy and cruelty of white and male domination.[7]

In 1914, one of the party's harsher critics paid a backhanded compliment to its stubborn longevity. In the first issue of *The New Republic*, the progressive Republican Herbert Croly scoffed that the Democratic Party "has the vitality of a low organism. It can not only subdivide without losing the continuity of its life, but it can temporarily assume almost any form, any color or any structure without ceasing to recognize itself and without any apparent sacrifice of collective identity." Two years later, the ability of that humble creature (or rather the Congress it controlled) to pass laws to regulate big business and improve the lives of some hard-pressed white wage earners had improved Croly's opinion enough that he endorsed the reelection of President Woodrow Wilson.[8]

An appealing ideology promoted by what we now call "messaging" is hardly enough to win national elections consistently. Although Democrats tended to prosper when they framed an economic critique and alternative proposals in moral terms, ethical behavior has not been a requirement for those skilled in the strategies and tactics of campaigns. As those warfighting metaphors suggest, political operatives have to analyze the strengths and weaknesses of an adversary and inspire their own forces to dominate the field of battle.

To win, Democrats had to construct and, after painful losses, reconstruct an efficient, cleverly led organization made up of intersecting parts. The builders of such an organization were seldom presidents; some, like Eleanor Roosevelt and the labor leader Sidney Hillman, were not elected officials at all. But they understood what it took to recruit candidates who could appeal to a demographically diverse coalition. They also had the ability to co-opt or absorb the demands and energies of rising social movements. When political institutions are managed by shrewd and practical men and women who know how to exploit opportunities but are also motivated by empathy for ordinary people, they have nudged the United States along a path to social decency if not yet to become a truly democratic or egalitarian society.

The focus of this book is admittedly selective; I trace a theme about how the large, protean universe of officials, candidates, and voters thought and behaved—on both the national and local levels—from the rise of Martin Van Buren, the first party builder, to Nancy Pelosi, the first woman to serve as Speaker of the House. In 1928, the journalist Frank Kent introduced his own volume on this subject with a sober acknowledgment: "To attempt a complete history of the Democratic party, the oldest continuously existing political instrumentality in America, would be an appalling job. Volumes could be and have been written about its particular periods and around its outstanding personalities. To expect adequately to give the whole story in a single book is not reasonable." My ambition is more modest; the historian Jill Lepore has put it well: "To write history is to make an argument by telling a story."[9]

This book springs from a fascination with and concern about the current state of American politics. I began research the month Donald Trump became president—as Democrats clashed with one another about how their nominee could have lost to a man who, until he ran for the office, had been famous only for being arrogant, flamboyant, and very rich. Trump's 2016 victory provoked a sense of crisis and dread for millions of Democrats. But one could also view it as a consequence of the long devolution of the major parties from the time when their legitimacy, if not their merit, was taken for granted. A few weeks after Joe Biden's inauguration, a Gallup poll reported that half of American adults considered themselves to be political independents—the highest percentage ever recorded. At the same time, only a tiny percentage of voters were truly willing to venture out of their partisan trenches. In the 2020 election, Biden carried 224 of the nation's congressional districts; Democratic candidates for the House won 222 of them.[10]

For most of the past six decades, through thick and thin, I have usually done what I could to advance the partisan cause. At the age of twelve, I spent part of every fall Saturday handing out leaflets for

John F. Kennedy on the streets of my suburban hometown in northern New Jersey—at the time a Republican bastion. I have canvassed or made calls for the Democratic nominee in every presidential election since then—except in 1968, when I couldn't stomach Hubert Humphrey's cheerleading for the war in Vietnam, and in 1980, when Jimmy Carter's hapless record drove me to cast a ballot for a marginal left-wing party.

To be sure, my commitment to the Democrats is an ambivalent one, alloyed with regret and caution. The party's history is rife with missteps and outrages. Yet for all their—for all *our*—faults, the Democrats remain the only electoral institution in twenty-first-century America able to help solve the serious problems facing the United States and, to a degree, the rest of humanity as well. "Great history," the political philosopher George Sabine wrote in 1945, "is the product of social crisis . . . because it is one means by which an age becomes conscious of what it is doing, in the light of what it has done and what it hopes to do." The crises we face are quite different from those that Americans confronted at the end of World War II. But resolving them will require institutions willing to address popular discontents and the demands of progressive social movements. I hope my book can explain how the Democratic Party sought to do that in the past, with both successes and failures—and might do better in the future. To paraphrase Bertolt Brecht's remark about the world, "Change the party; we need it."[11]

# WHAT IT TOOK
## TO WIN

.

# PROLOGUE: A USEFUL MYTH

*If I could not get to heaven but with a party,*
*I would not go there at all.*
—THOMAS JEFFERSON, 1789[1]

*The Republicans are the* nation. *The last hope of human liberty*
*in the world rests on us. We ought, for so dear a stake, to sacrifice*
*every attachment and every enmity.*
—THOMAS JEFFERSON, 1810[2]

*He believed, as we believe, that men are capable of their own*
*government, and that no king, no tyrant, no dictator can govern*
*for them as wisely as they can govern for themselves.*
—FRANKLIN D. ROOSEVELT, AT THE DEDICATION OF THE
JEFFERSON MEMORIAL, 1943[3]

The temple consecrated to the memory of Thomas Jefferson sits in one of the loveliest and most spacious corners of the nation's capital. Ringed by cherry trees planted along the rim of the Tidal Basin, the pantheon, begun in 1938 and dedicated in 1943, shares space with no other structure. In contrast, the Lincoln Memorial, the only other presidential shrine in D.C. designed in the grand neoclassical style, nearly abuts the dark wall containing the names of the Americans who died in the disastrous conflict in Vietnam. The soaring columns and massive statue of the sixteenth president honor a victorious war that kept the nation together. In its sorrowful elegance, the Wall bears witness to the tragedy of a lost war that tore it apart.

But the Jefferson Memorial seems to transcend thoughts of bloodshed in any cause, whether noble or misguided. In the quotations that crowd its walls, the third president declares that "institutions must advance . . . to keep pace with the times," defends the freedom to worship any religion or none at all, and preaches the equality of mankind—while briefly condemning the "despotism" of slavery. Unmentioned is the fact that the writer owned hundreds of Black people whose labors turned his hilltop estate in central Virginia into a marvel of architectural and agricultural innovation. Jefferson's words etched in stone encourage visitors to be inspired by an "Apostle of Freedom." His legacy, wrote the historian Richard Hofstadter, was not limited to the realm of "economics or politics" or "even a political party." It was "an imperishable faith expressed in imperishable rhetoric."[4]

Nowhere in the Jefferson Memorial is there any hint that it was conceived and financed by members of the party that dominated every elected branch of the federal government from 1933 until the onset of the Cold War almost fifteen years later. A House Democrat chaired the committee that planned it, a Democratic Congress appropriated the $3 million to construct it (the equivalent of roughly $55 million today), and a Democratic president spoke at all three stages of the process of building it: the groundbreaking, the laying of the cornerstone, and the final dedication.

Such favoritism struck few people as odd at the time. After all, the Lincoln Memorial had been planned and built under Republican administrations. And for decades, Democratic politicians and journalists had routinely referred to the master of Monticello as the "founder" of their party. Democrats from every region and ideological persuasion quoted Jefferson in their speeches and named their magazines and annual fund-raising dinners for him (later, those occasions honored Andrew Jackson, too). Although the populist-talking William Jennings Bryan won three Democratic nominations for president, conservatives in his party never ceased to loathe him. Yet they would not have dared to disagree with Bryan's statement, in 1912, that "Jefferson's motto of equal rights to all and privileges to none is the fundamental law that governs legislation and the administration of government." One could quarrel over how to interpret the messiah's creed; only an infidel would deny its eternal truth.[5]

But the Democrats' abiding veneration of Jefferson required them to believe in two myths about his political views that turned a figure limited by the beliefs of his time into an icon for all ages. Jefferson did not, in fact, create the mass, fiercely competitive party that figures from Jackson to Bryan to FDR to Obama would lead. Neither was the slave-owning grandee the apostle of individual freedom and mass democracy that the selected, albeit inspirational, words inside his memorial suggest.

Like all the eminent, mostly wellborn figures who steered the public affairs of the new American nation, Thomas Jefferson actually detested competitive political parties and mistrusted anyone who sought to create them. Two opposing groups of notable citizens did arise from the sharp debates he and James Madison had with Alexander Hamilton during the mid-1790s over such issues as the need for a central bank and whether to sympathize with or oppose the revolution in France. But these were factions composed of men who made or hoped to make government policy. They were not the kind of parties that would become familiar to Americans in the middle of the nineteenth century and that, for all their flaws, continue to thrive today.

The followers of Hamilton dubbed themselves Federalists; Jefferson's allies adopted the name Democratic-Republicans, which they usually shortened to Republicans. But neither band favored a political order shaped by permanent organizations that would contest election after election for every office from alderman to president. "Men who have been intimate all their lives cross the streets to avoid meeting," reported Jefferson from Philadelphia in 1797. They "turn their heads another way, lest they should be obliged to touch their hats." He looked forward to a restoration of comity between such gentlemen. Jefferson twice ran for the presidency against John Adams, the Federalist from Massachusetts; the tone of their 1800 campaign was particularly bitter. But they had worked closely together during the Revolution and resumed their friendship after the Virginian left office.[6]

Jefferson did claim legitimacy for just one political faction: his own. Only Republicans, he believed, had the interests of "the people" at heart. As he declared in his 1801 Inaugural Address, they believed in a "wise and frugal" government that would allow "the middling sort" (whose whiteness was assumed) to "regulate their own pursuits of industry and improvement." Unlike the monarchies that ruled nearly everywhere else in the world, the American state should "not take from the mouth of labor the bread it has earned." In the late 1790s, Jefferson denounced the Federalists then in power for passing laws that essentially made it a crime to criticize their administration. He charged that, as would-be aristocrats, they would substitute their own wisdom and connections for the sovereignty and opinions of ordinary citizens. Such a high-handed cabal had no place in a nation dedicated to the principle of self-government. As president in 1802, Jefferson vowed, "I shall . . . by the establishment of republican principles . . . sink federalism into an abyss from which there shall be no resurrection for it." He got his wish a decade later when the Federalists' intense opposition to the War of 1812 with Great Britain stamped them with the mark of treason.[7]

Nearly all the Republicans who articulated the anti-elitist message belonged to various segments of the national elite themselves. In the Middle Atlantic states, Jeffersonians proliferated among evangelical ministers and freethinking lawyers who resented the Federalist leanings of the more established churches. Local merchants and bankers from the region charged that Hamilton's Bank of the United States rewarded its friends and hoped to starve everyone else of vital capital. Artisans in New York City and Philadelphia rallied to the Republican cause, too. The embryonic machine of Tammany Hall was their bailiwick in New York, whose population of nearly 100,000 in 1810 made it the largest city in the nation. But such uneducated men rarely edited a newspaper or wrote a pamphlet stuffed with their visions and resentments.

The Republicans were able to gain hegemony in American politics because they dominated in the South. Jefferson, Madison, and Monroe—successive presidents from the faction that emerged from the conflicts of the 1790s—were all wealthy planters from Virginia, where the main route to high status was to own a large plot of land and inherit or purchase large numbers of Black people to do the work.

The contradiction that would bedevil Democrats until the final decades of the twentieth century was thus imbedded in the identities of its putative founders: the party of "the people" could get a chance to govern the nation only if it acquiesced to a realm of unfreedom south of the Mason-Dixon Line. Without the advantage of the three-fifths clause that Southern delegates were able to wedge into the Constitution, Jefferson would have lost the presidency to John Adams in 1800. In that contest, the "aristocratic" Federalist candidate carried nearly every state that had either abolished slavery or was in the process of doing so. Jefferson's popularity in the South netted him fourteen more electoral votes than he would have received if only free men were counted. As the political theorist Danielle Allen puts it, "You can't actually have freedom for all unless most people have equal standing in relationship to each other."[8]

The "democracy" the Virginian was supposed to have invented had another major deficit: during his political career, only a minority of adult men, even white ones, enjoyed the right to vote. Not until the 1820s did most states do away with all or most of the property qualifications that had been universal during the colonial era. In Jefferson's own state, it took the War of 1812 to persuade legislators to extend the franchise to landless militiamen who chafed at fighting for a government whose representatives they had not had the ability to choose. Even the minority of men who did enjoy the franchise showed little interest in the national contests that mattered so much to elite Americans. In 1800, fewer than 10 percent of eligible men turned out to vote for either Adams or Jefferson. The total of sixty-seven thousand who did was smaller than the population of Philadelphia at the time.[9]

Most state elections drew appreciably larger numbers to the polls. But many of those contests pitted local gentlemen of wealth and standing against others of their class "for the honor of serving their districts." Ideological distinctions often mattered less than personal rivalries. Uncounted numbers of "middling men" came to curry favor with those on whose goodwill and largesse their livelihoods depended. Nearly everywhere, a voter had to state his choice out loud, in the presence of his peers.[10]

 

The fact that Jefferson neither created the Democratic Party nor practiced the egalitarian ideals he so eloquently professed does not mean that those who believed in the myth were either fools or conscious hypocrites. Myths have power when they stir politicians, activists, and voters to act as if they were true; that helps explain why the mass party that was beginning to form at the time of Jefferson's death in 1826 became so successful after he was gone.

As it happens, the Democratic politicians who did the most to turn the idea of a Jefferson shrine into a monument in marble and bronze embodied rather precisely the two key and often interlocking aspects of the party's ideology from its beginnings into the 1930s: defending racial hierarchy and representing the interests of ordinary white farmers and workers. Chairing the five-man Memorial Commission was John Joseph Boylan, an Irish-Catholic congressman from New York City, who devoted himself more to the cause of honoring Jefferson than to any other task he performed during his fifteen years in Congress. At the same time, Boylan, a former postal clerk and stalwart of Tammany Hall, voted reliably for every significant element of the New Deal agenda—to create public jobs for the unemployed, protect union organizers, give government pensions to the elderly, and provide free health care to military veterans. He would have concurred with Senator Alben Barkley, a Kentucky Democrat, who told an audience in 1937 that Jefferson "was the real inventor of the New Deal," and that the antagonism toward "his efforts at progress make the similar clamor at President Roosevelt seem mild indeed."[11]

The commission's secretary, in contrast, represented the antithesis of FDR's modern liberal order. Congressman Howard Worth Smith, who hailed from a district in northern Virginia, was a relentless scourge of the same industrial unions Boylan supported. In 1940, he also pushed through Congress a law, the Smith Act, under which leftists were jailed for advocating the overthrow of the government. Perhaps he had never read or had forgotten Jefferson's rhetorical question: "What country can preserve its liberties if their rulers are not warned from time to time that their people preserve the spirit of resistance?" Later, as chair of the powerful Rules Committee, Smith fought hard against every attempt to pass a civil rights bill. He stated flatly, "The Southern people have never accepted the colored race as a race of people who had equal intelligence and education and social attainments." That Boylan and Smith, in the 1930s, both sincerely regarded themselves as Jeffersonian Democrats underscores how vital, if contested, their icon's legacy remained.[12]

Speaking at the memorial's dedication, Franklin Roosevelt paid tribute to his predecessor's acute relevance to the ongoing war, the bloodiest in history. Jefferson, he said, had established the U.S. government "as a democracy and not as an autocracy." His example ought to inspire Americans who were "playing a tremendous part in the battle for the rights of man all over the world." The president avoided mentioning the Virginian's deep mistrust of a federal bureaucracy that could override the powers of individual states. Nor in his six-minute address did FDR say anything about either race or slavery. His silence on those subjects probably bothered few if any of the five thousand people in attendance on that April afternoon in 1943. Like nearly every other official gathering in the capital at the time, it was segregated; surviving photos show nothing but white faces on the rostrum and in the crowd.[13]

In the twenty-first century, few Democrats still subscribe to the myth that stimulated their forerunners to ennoble Jefferson with a nineteen-foot-tall statue inside a temple of polished stone. They still hold fund-raising dinners, of course. But nearly all the organizers have scrapped the tribute to Jefferson and Jackson and renamed their annual celebrations after one or more contemporary figures unsullied by the Democrats' racist traditions. Yet they continue to struggle with the paradoxes in the legacy of a man who did not want to lead a party but did shape, in vital ways, the political future of a nation quite different from the one he had known.[14]

# 1

## CREATING THE DEMOCRACY, 1820–1848

*No free country can exist without political parties.*
—MARTIN VAN BUREN[1]

*Do I contradict myself?*
*Very well then I contradict myself;*
*(I am large, I contain multitudes).*
—WALT WHITMAN, DEMOCRAT

The rising politician from America's largest state certainly knew how to make a first impression. In 1813, a few days past his thirtieth birthday, Martin Van Buren strolled to his seat in the New York state senate dressed, according to one witness, in "a green coat, buff breeches, and white topped boots." Several years later, he walked into the U.S. Senate, to which he had recently been elected, wearing a coat the color of dark brown snuff, an orange tie, white trousers, and bright yellow gloves. Van Buren was a self-taught lawyer who had imbibed political talk while helping out at his father's prosperous inn and tavern in the village of Kinderhook, New York, outside Albany. He routinely competed against gentlemen of greater wealth and status. To bear himself as their equal, even their sartorial superior, was essential to earning their respect. His choice of clothes signaled that he wanted, at the same time, to transform the political order and to rise within it.[2]

The tavern keeper's son went on to have an illustrious political career, if not always a triumphant one. Following service in the New

York state legislature and Congress, Van Buren became President Andrew Jackson's secretary of state, then his vice president. In 1836, he was narrowly elected to the White House himself, only to lose four years later to William Henry Harrison—like Old Hickory, a former military hero. In 1844, John C. Calhoun, tribune of the planter slaveocracy, deftly prevented Van Buren from winning another presidential nomination. But the pol from Kinderhook got revenge of a sort in 1848 when he ran again for the nation's top office as the candidate of a short-lived party that demanded an end to the expansion of slavery.

Midway through the next decade, Van Buren retreated across the ocean to a villa overlooking the Bay of Naples to write his memoirs. He boasted, rather awkwardly, that he was "one, who, without the aid of powerful family connexions, and with but few of the adventitious facilities for the acquisition of political power had been elevated by his Countrymen to a succession of official trusts, not exceeded, perhaps, either in number, in dignity or in responsibility by any that have ever been committed to the hands of one man."[3]

Yet the self-made son of upstate New York never sought power for himself alone. The figure inside those gaudy costumes became one of the first and most successful party builders in American history. Van Buren's ambition was to create and then consolidate the supremacy of an organization that would represent "the People" (a noun he often capitalized) in their never-ending battle with anyone who schemed to use the elected government to advance the selfish interests of a few.

How did Van Buren, together with several close friends and a swelling number of political allies, create the institution that became known as the Democratic Party? They started with an ideological vision, recruited a corps of talented leaders who knit together a coalition of regional and social diversity, and slowly constructed an organization that could publicize and defend itself—and mount a series of winning campaigns. The project began in the 1820s and did not fully mature until twenty years later. But it depended on an explicit embrace of competitive parties, which the founders of the republic had warned against. Parties were, wrote James Madison, Jefferson's close ally, in 1787, in the *Federalist Papers*, "united and actuated by some common impulse of passion, or of interest, adverse to the rights of other citizens, or to the permanent and aggregate interests of the community."[4]

Van Buren and his fellow Democrats disagreed. "The spirit of party," declared their Albany organ, was "the vigilant watchman over the conduct of those in power." Mass parties, they argued, cultivated the habits of democracy. They encouraged the civic-minded to work constructively with their peers, sharpening collective appeals to voters and preventing any individual from forging a tyranny over his fellow citizens, such as existed in the monarchies and empires that spanned most of the globe. Van Buren allowed that "excesses frequently attend [parties] and produce many evils." Yet if the mass of men stayed faithful to "the principles and objects" of their organization, they would advance the welfare of the republic far better than any tiny clique of the haughty and wellborn could ever do.[5]

In building this party of a new type, Van Buren did not mean to bestow legitimacy on any parties created by his opponents. He believed, as had Jefferson, that "aristocrats" would perpetually seek to thwart the desires of "democrats"; the opposition party was run by the same elitist cabal, whether it went under the name of Federalist, Whig, or Republican. "They glory," he charged in 1840, "in the supposition . . . that the mass of the people are every where too fickle in their opinions, too little informed in public affairs + too unstable in their views for the enjoyment of self Government." Not until after the Civil War, when the party of Lincoln reigned supreme, did Democrats begin to acknowledge that their rivals might enjoy an enduring popular base of their own.[6]

Like libertarians today, antebellum Democrats believed the federal state should refrain from intervening in most aspects of economic life—from chartering banks to financing public works to taxing income. But unlike twenty-first-century conservatives, they based their adherence to laissez-faire doctrine on a populist suspicion: an interventionist federal government would *always* benefit the rich and the well-connected. Economic growth was a splendid thing, so long as Washington insiders were not able to direct it to selfish ends. What one historian calls "the glorious absence of a powerful state" also appealed to many European-born newcomers who had fled monarchies that impressed them into armies, stripped taxes from the poor, and crushed them when they protested. It was also in sync with the emerging liberal doctrine across the Atlantic, where workers, shopkeepers, and intellectuals were demanding a role in governing nations ruled by landed gentry who repressed the speech and activism of the "popular classes."[7]

Democrats appealed to voters who worried more about what a powerful national state could do to harm them than about how it might protect their liberties and further their economic welfare. They favored such measures as low tariffs, free immigration, and an end to prison for debtors, and sympathized with early labor unions against courts that blasted them as "criminal conspiracies" to restrain trade. The fear of statism, coupled with the creed of white supremacy, also led Northern Democrats to condemn abolitionists as dangerous meddlers with the rights of agrarian property-owners. Van Buren and his allies defended the practice of reserving public jobs for the party faithful (which their Whig opponents vehemently derided) as a way to ensure that governments would heed the wishes of ordinary people instead of those of their social superiors.

Not every Democrat agreed with each policy that flowed from this moralistic ideology, but it played a major role in binding together the coalition that surged into national power with Andrew Jackson and held on to it, with brief interruptions, until the last election before the Civil War. In the South, most big planters and yeomen farmers shared a mistrust of a central state that might take the side of well-placed Northerners in battles over the tariff and the expansion of slavery. They made common cause with artisans and shopkeepers in Eastern cities and on the Midwestern frontier who considered wealthy bankers and financiers to be "based . . . upon fraud and corruption," as John S. Bagg, a Democratic newspaper editor from Detroit, put it. "Our government is based upon equal rights," declared the journalist. Banks and the speculators they funded were "unequal in their practices; a bundle of . . . hypocrisy and incongruity, from their commencement to their death."[8]

With these resentments—and ideals—Democrats brought together working-class radicals from Manhattan and Dixie planters whose ownership of hundreds of slaves and acres of land made them the richest Americans of the era. In Tammany Hall, they built the first urban political machine; by the 1830s, it was winning most local elections and ensuring that Van Buren's party would be competitive in New York State. Democrats won votes from subsistence farmers and from merchants whose warehouses bulged with goods from Europe; most of the native-born Americans who worshipped at well-established Episcopalian churches were Democrats, but so were most Catholics, the majority of whom had been born abroad. For most of the 1840s, both Walt Whitman and Jefferson Davis were ardent Democrats; the budding young poet edited a party organ in Brooklyn and spoke at election rallies, while the future president of the Confederacy canvassed in Mississippi for the party's presidential nominees and ran for a seat in the House of Representatives.

From the 1820s through the following decade, Van Buren played the pivotal role in constructing this organization of unlikely partners. It went by different names—the Jackson Party, the Republicans, the Democratic-Republicans. Not until 1840 did partisans settle on calling themselves simply Democrats or, with a grandiose touch, "the Democracy."

But what they accomplished was unique in world history. The Democrats were the first political body to attract masses of voters, the first to hold nominating conventions on a regular basis, the first to organize a network of partisan newspapers, the first to establish a national committee and a congressional caucus, and the first not merely to acquiesce in the reality of competition among parties of the new type but also to celebrate it. With this potent apparatus, the Democrats dominated national politics during the antebellum era, winning all but two presidential elections from 1828 until 1856 and controlling both houses of Congress for nearly that entire span.

The only constituency that party officials and activists made no effort to attract was African Americans. Until the Civil War, Democrats in every region protected slavery where it already existed and sought to exclude free Blacks from participating in politics at all. Fear of racial competition drove most white workers to view abolitionists as a threat to their livelihood. Urban merchants and manufacturers did a fine business supplying Southern plantations with clothing, machinery, and luxury goods. And Democrats, like most Americans, took it for granted that only white people were worthy and capable of governing themselves. Thus, at its creation, the self-styled "party of the people" was a contradiction in terms, albeit a remarkably heterogeneous one. Van Buren himself had grown up in a household with six enslaved people and continued to hire Black men and women owned by others when he served as vice president and president.[9]

For a century, the Democrats would waver little from their racist convictions. Electorally, this turned out to be both a boon and a burden. Except during the Civil War, white Southerners were the most reliable and stable voting bloc in the nation; without their support, Democrats would have struggled to ever take the presidency or enough seats to control either house of Congress. The doctrine of racial supremacy also helped the party win over those white small farmers and wage earners who feared competition from Blacks, and later Chinese immigrants, too. On the one hand, Democrats vowed to fight for their interests against a wealthy elite that allegedly used dark-skinned hands to damage the prospects of paler ones. On the other hand, politicians who talked this way developed habits that stamped them as immoral and reactionary when slavery was abolished, and non-white Americans gradually exercised the power of their numbers at the polls and in the larger civic culture.

Van Buren and his allies were able to build their broad yet all-white party by taking advantage of a transformation of American society that was gathering speed during the second quarter of the nineteenth century. Drawing from both native-born and immigrant streams, the nation's population expanded by a remarkable 240 percent between 1820 and 1850; new states came into being across the continent—from Maine to Florida and from Missouri to Oregon and California. Those new Americans fueled a huge domestic market, which artisans, farmers, and entrepreneurs equipped with new technologies and rushed to exploit. Canals and railroad lines linked factory towns to food producers and made the efficient delivery of mail a commercial necessity. Steam presses increased the speed and lowered the price of printing, turning an increasingly literate public into regular readers of newspapers and magazines. Banks sprouted up in rural and metropolitan America alike to finance some new enterprises and, inevitably, to ruin others. Artisans formed trade unions in big cities and factory towns to wrest from their bosses a share of the profits and control on the job.

The United States remained a largely agrarian society through the remainder of the nineteenth century. But it was becoming one full of urban enterprises and national institutions stamped indelibly, as Whitman sang about the railroads, as "Type of the modern! emblem of motion and power! pulse of the continent!"[10]

The democratization of politics advanced in tandem with the modernization of daily life. By the 1840s, adult white men could vote in nearly every state, regardless of whether they owned property, which, in the cities, only a minority did. Several midwestern states flush with newcomers from Europe extended the franchise to immigrants who declared their intention to become citizens but had not completed the naturalization process. In many states and localities, elections of some sort were held at least once a year. There were many offices to be filled, from town coroner to president, and many citizens eager to earn a regular salary for serving, or at least vowing to serve, the public good.

The informal, deferential ritual of voting that Jefferson and his Federalist rivals had inherited from colonial days was gradually giving way to a more systematic and democratic one. Instead of gathering in a central square or at a crossroads and announcing one's choices out loud or scrawling them out by hand, most American men began casting ballots printed and distributed by competing parties in a myriad of polling places located near where they worked or lived. When it came to choosing who would occupy the most important office in the land, ordinary men were no longer inclined to give their social superiors the benefit of the doubt. By 1832, every state but one (the planter fiefdom of South Carolina) was choosing presidential electors by popular vote instead of leaving that critical power to the state legislature. When Alexis de Tocqueville took his short but momentous tour of the country in the early 1830s, he marveled, with some exaggeration, that "it is difficult to say what place is taken up in the life of an inhabitant of the United States by his concern for politics. To take a hand in the regulation of society and to discuss it is his biggest concern and, so to speak, the only pleasure an American knows."[11]

## Bucktails Rising

The growth of political enthusiasm helped generate a bevy of operatives eager and able to stoke and channel it. A mass party grew
first, and most robustly, in Van Buren's home state. By 1820, one of
every seven Americans was a New Yorker, a percentage that declined
only gradually for the remainder of the century. No one knows who
began calling New York "the Empire State," but the term nicely captured the burgeoning variety of ethnicities, religious denominations,
and economic pursuits there, as well as its geographic spread from
the Atlantic Ocean north to the Canadian border and westward to
the shores of Lake Erie. Thousands of immigrants were risking their
health clearing land for the Erie Canal while native-born Americans
and foreigners worked side by side setting type and stitching clothes
in the workshops of Manhattan, hub of what was already the nation's
largest city. Many more raised wheat and pigs to feed both their own
families and wage earners all over North America.

The battle for political power in the state mirrored its size and
heterogeneity. The presidencies of Thomas Jefferson and James Madison turned their party into the dominant one in New York, as well
as the nation. But success inevitably bred conflicts among ambitious
Republican individuals and factions. The stakes of competition had
grown from the era just after the War for Independence, when wealthy
gentlemen divvied up the scattering of unpaid offices among themselves. By the early 1820s, New Yorkers elected or appointed some
fifteen thousand officials—more than one for every hundred residents;
debate about how best to advance the public welfare often turned into
a personal matter.

After the War of 1812, Van Buren helped organize a group of
young Republican politicians who challenged the sway of Governor
DeWitt Clinton and his associates, many of whom owned sizable es-
tates and had been groomed to run the affairs of state. The upstarts
called themselves the Bucktails, a term borrowed from the deer-tail
symbol of Tammany Hall in Manhattan. They published their own
newspaper—*The Albany Argus*—and began to organize a faction of
the party dedicated to advancing "the fairly expressed will of the majority" against "Federalists" (real or imagined) whom they accused

of thwarting it. Every Bucktail swore to obey a code of discipline akin to that of a combat unit. "Tell them they are safe if they face the enemy," Silas Wright, a close ally of Van Buren's, wrote to a comrade during one crisis, "but that the first man we see *step to the rear*, we *cut down* . . . they *must* not falter or they perish."[12]

A prime occasion to demonstrate that will and discipline soon presented itself. In 1819, a sharp national recession threw many small farmers and artisans into debt. In a cash-poor economy, repayment was often an arduous task, and a prison cell potentially awaited anyone who could not satisfy his creditors. The fact that most men who owned no property were still ineligible to vote added to their frustration.

In New York, the Bucktails leapt into the breach. A year before, Van Buren had led a successful drive to outlaw incarceration for debtors. Now, against Clinton's wishes, Bucktail members of the state legislature demanded that a convention be held to amend the state constitution, which had undergone few changes since the revolutionary era. At the gathering held in the state assembly during the late summer and fall of 1821, Van Buren backed a proposal to broaden the franchise to any man who paid taxes, labored on the public roads, or had served in the militia. He argued for it in debate with erstwhile Federalists, the most formidable of whom was James Kent, an esteemed legal scholar and the former chief justice of the state supreme court. Kent warned that giving the vote to men without property who were crowding into metropolises like the one 145 miles to the south on the Hudson River would destroy the "plain and simple republics of farmers" who were the moral bedrock of the nation. Voicing a traditional fear of mass democracy, he cautioned that demagogues could use "inflammatory appeals" to whip up "the worst passions of the worst men." But the respected jurist was waging a battle he had no chance to win: by the 1820s, the celebrators of mass democracy far outnumbered its detractors.[13]

Van Buren, whom the legislature had recently elected to the U.S. Senate, countered with a theory of political morality based on labor. It was unjust, he charged, to deny men on whose toil and taxes New York depended a role in choosing its leaders. The propertyless were "the bone, pith, and muscle of the population of the state" and posed no danger to the social order they sustained. Since a clear majority of the delegates sided with the Bucktails, Van Buren easily carried the day. By 1826, the state legislature did away with all restrictions on the suffrage rights of white male citizens. In just five years, the electorate had expanded by almost 300 percent.[14]

However, the Bucktails' warm regard for the working man turned to solid ice at the color line. At the 1821 convention, they voted as a bloc to retain a property qualification for free Black men. James Kent and his allies objected. As erstwhile Federalists, they held true to the anti-racist traditions of their old party; in 1799, a Federalist legislature and governor had initiated the gradual abolition of slavery in the state; in gratitude, the few Black men in New York who enjoyed the limited franchise voted faithfully for the party of Alexander Hamilton and John Adams. But to Van Buren and his flock, African Americans were, by nature, dependent wretches, incapable of thinking or acting for themselves. They would, charged Erastus Root, an ardent Bucktail and a member of the state assembly, always be "following the train of those who ride in their coaches, and whose shoes and boots they had so often Blacked." So the convention extended the franchise only to "men of color" who owned "a freehold estate" worth at least $250, debt-free. At the time, fewer than a hundred Black men could qualify. New York was hardly alone in restricting the vote by race. By the eve of the Civil War, only five New England states allowed African Americans to exercise the franchise.[15]

The outcome of this conflict about race and democracy bore a significance that stretched far beyond the decision reached inside Albany's ornate old capitol. Elsewhere in the nation, politicians were emulating what the Bucktails had done. Every state that joined the union after that date passed a law that effectively barred nearly all Black men from voting.[16]

The creators of what would become the Democratic Party thus made clear that their Democracy would include and seek to represent only "the People" of the majority race. They routinely charged their partisan opponents of being "aristocrats" whose condescension toward white farmers and wage earners was a malign remnant of Old World feudalism. Unlike the Federalists and, later, most Whigs,

Democrats would welcome immigrants from every European nation and religion. They would speed naturalization for Irish fleeing the Great Famine of the 1840s, dispense patronage jobs to poor Catholics and Jews, denounce the king of England and the tsar of Russia and the Ottoman caliph for keeping ethnic minorities in the cage of empire. But they either dismissed the brutal realities of slavery in their own country or argued that Blacks held in bondage by "the lords of the lash" were no worse off than were the factory hands exploited by "the lords of the loom."

Few Bucktails or their like-minded counterparts in other Northern states had an economic stake of their own in preserving slavery. Those who survived until the 1860s did not mourn its demise. New York had passed its gradual emancipation law when Van Buren was seventeen, and the family freed the slaves it owned soon afterward.

However, the idea of liberty for African Americans posed a threat to his ambition of creating a party that could win a majority in every region. The Missouri Compromise of 1820 had temporarily quieted sectional tensions; as they moved west, white Americans could choose to live in a slave state or a free one, prospering as they could. Officeholders who aspired "to interfere with the question of slavery" were thus jeopardizing the peace of the nation—and the future of a party that vowed to defend the common white man against his adversaries.

The Bucktails' triumph at the 1821 convention emboldened them to turn their embryonic faction into an organization that critics quickly blasted with a metaphor that would long endure—a "complicated and corrupt" *machine*. Van Buren traveled down to Washington to begin his term in the Senate. But he departed confident that his associates in Albany were "overflowing with kindly feelings towards myself" and had "full and almost unquestioned possession of the State Government." The politician whom journalists had taken to calling "the Little Magician" (although, at five foot six, he was just a little shorter than average height) had begun a process that would lead, within a decade, to the election of Andrew Jackson, the first president not raised in wealth and comfort.[17]

With Van Buren's guidance, his allies, now dubbed the Albany

Regency, came up with a strategy for holding power in the Empire State for years to come. They established offshoots in most of New York's fifty-odd counties. They took care to dispense patronage jobs to men who understood the politics of their local communities. They appointed only strict loyalists to every judiciary post from the state supreme court to humble justices of the peace.

Naturally, the machine's opponents charged it with scheming to eliminate all competition. Regency men countered, in their speeches and the pages of *The Albany Argus*, that modern parties were actually "among the firmest bulwarks of civil liberty" because they encouraged lively debate about the issues of the day and mobilized citizens to vote for candidates who shared their views. Internal discipline sharpened those debates, ensuring that once a position was taken, it would be followed. Partisan competition so enthralled them that they wagered large sums of money at election time to test their expertise, as well as to fatten their wallets. "Bet on Kentucky, Indiana, and Illinois, jointly if you can, or any two of them; don't forget to bet all you can," Van Buren wrote in 1828 to Alexander Hamilton, Jr., who, despite his paternity, was an ally.[18]

In one of the great ironies of political history, the Little Magician was conjuring up a party of a new type that vowed to restore the principles of a deceased one. The "old Republicans," led by Jefferson and Madison, adhered to the doctrine of states' rights and strict limits on federal power, as stipulated in the U.S. Constitution. Its leaders believed that a society of self-reliant yeoman farmers was morally superior to an urban one crowded with impoverished factory hands below and haughty financiers above. They feared a strong national state would always serve the interests of the rich and the well-connected; corruption would be ingrained in its bones.

Van Buren and his Regency comrades aimed to emulate their revolutionary forebears. Like Jefferson, they opposed a national government that chartered national banks, printed paper money, raised tariffs on industrial products, and used the federal budget to build turnpikes and canals instead of leaving that task to individual states. In retirement, Van Buren reflected that the Democratic Party he did so much to create was simply Jefferson's party reborn. It had, he claimed, "undergone no change, either in its organization, its principles, or the general political dispositions of the individuals of which it has been composed." Of course, the mass party the Democrats became had evolved, in both ideas and constituencies, far beyond the modest clique that emerged from the conflict within George Washington's cabinet in the late 1790s. Without the votes of urban wage earners, it would rarely have won elections in booming states like New York and Ohio. But their faith in the wisdom of Jefferson had a logic and power of its own. As the novelist James Fenimore Cooper reflected, in America, "the democrat is the conservative and, thank God, he has something worth preserving."[19]

In 1824, Van Buren, then New York's junior senator, made a pilgrimage to Monticello, where the eighty-year-old Jefferson was overseeing the completion of his beloved University of Virginia. "I derived the highest gratification," recalled Van Buren in his memoir, "from observing that his devotion to the public interest . . . was as ardent as it had been in his palmiest days . . . He seemed never to tire in his review of the past and in explanations of the grounds of his apprehensions for the future." The proto-party Jefferson led had appealed to whites in both the North and the South and destroyed the Federalists as a national force. For Van Buren, that was another excellent reason to champion its ideals.[20]

During the early 1820s, the U.S. Senate adjourned for more than half of each year, which gave Van Buren ample time to forge ties with fellow admirers of the "old republic." Garbed now in suits of darker colors that befitted an established politician, he met with such stalwart Jeffersonians from Virginia as Spencer Roane and Thomas Ritchie, who were seeking to form an organization in their state akin to the Albany Regency. He was aware of other embryonic parties growing in Nashville, led by John Overton, and in Concord, New Hampshire, where Isaac Hill was the primary organizer. In social origins, the leaders of these enterprises had nothing in common. Ritchie hailed from landed gentry and was known as an elegant dancer, while Overton was, according to one historian, "considered the wealthiest man in Tennessee."[21] Van Buren had a modest, if stable, upbringing, but Hill escaped a family driven into poverty by his father's insanity. Lame due to a childhood mishap, he had to educate himself and gained prosperity only by starting a local newspaper (the *New-Hampshire Patriot and State Gazette*), a print shop, and a bookstore.

But differences of status did not prevent Van Buren and his associates from pursuing a common mission. To revive the "old republic," they would employ tools their mentors had mistrusted or not even considered: an explicitly partisan press, a disciplined organization, and emotional, divisive appeals to a swelling electorate of ordinary men. The goal of electing Andrew Jackson president gave them the opportunity to put these methods to work in the nation as a whole.

## Organizing the Jackson Party

What became known as "the Jackson party" emerged from an angry controversy that grew out of the 1824 contest for the White House. Every serious candidate for the presidency that year was nominally a Democratic-Republican—the organization Jefferson had founded nearly three decades earlier. Since the Federalists no longer ran candidates for federal office and President James Monroe was not running for a third term, one's party affiliation did not matter.

What ensued was a furious competition among four veteran politicians, each of whom hailed from a different state. Van Buren and his Regency backed William Crawford, the austere, fiscally cautious secretary of the treasury from Georgia, who they believed could unite "old Republicans" from both North and South. But, this time, the Little Magician's touch betrayed him. The other three contenders— Kentucky's Henry Clay, the Speaker of the House; Massachusetts's John Quincy Adams, the secretary of state; and Andrew Jackson, the former general who was a senator from Tennessee—all won more popular votes than Crawford, who suffered a stroke midway through the campaign. Just 350,000 Americans cast ballots, barely a quarter of those eligible. About 150,000 chose Jackson, giving him a clear plurality and a decent claim to the office.

However, since none of the candidates received a majority of the electoral votes, the House of Representatives had to choose a winner—the second and, so far, last time that has occurred. According to the Twelfth Amendment, each state delegation would cast a single vote for one of the three candidates with the highest counts. That provision eliminated Clay, who came in fourth but with an electoral tally large enough either to put Jackson over the top or to nudge Adams close to victory. One evening in early January, the Kentucky lawmaker visited the son of the second president and arranged a deal: Clay would urge his supporters in the House to vote for Adams, if the latter would make the Kentuckian his successor at the State Department, the most prestigious post in the cabinet. A month later, after much vote shifting and haggling, Adams was elected president with the votes of thirteen out of the twenty-four states.

Jackson's followers quickly blamed the result on "a corrupt bargain," a term that textbooks still repeat. At the time, their invective was more alarmist. The defeated candidate's young ward and key aide, Andrew Jackson Donelson, bitterly condemned the pro-Adams congressmen "who betrayed the constitution" and now waited for the new president to reward them for their "iniquity." The retired general himself snapped that if Americans accepted the crooked result, "they may bid farewell to their freedom." The "rights of the people," Jackson fulminated, "have been bartered for promises of office."[22]

The cause did not match the temper of the outrage. Clay's bargain with Adams struck no crippling blow at the heart of the republic. The two men had actually forged a rather natural political alliance. Both advocated a central government that could finance roads and other "internal improvements," a higher tariff to protect domestic manufacturers, and keeping the Bank of the United States in business—all of which Jackson vehemently opposed. Moreover, when added together, their popular vote had surpassed Jackson's by 2,727 ballots. Their pact was thus hardly "the theft of the presidency," a charge flung against Adams by Jackson's contemporary admirers and echoed, as late as the 1980s, by Old Hickory's most respected biographer.[23] However, the perception that corruption infected the highest office in the land did provide an excellent opportunity to organize a movement against the new administration in the name of "the people"—as well as to install Jackson in the White House, where he allegedly belonged.

In Old Hickory, then in his late fifties, the nascent movement had rallied behind a candidate who splendidly embodied the qualities of a multitalented American man on the make. He had a background more humble than Van Buren's—but enthralled his followers with a brutal charisma the New Yorker could never match. As a teenager, Jackson fought in the War for Independence and was captured by the British. In the first of several famous battles with authorities he considered illegitimate, the boy earned a scar on his forehead when he angrily refused to clean the boots of a red-coated officer of the Crown. After reading law, Jackson moved to the frontier, where he fought Native Americans and began his political career. In the 1790s, he got elected to the House of Representatives and then to the U.S. Senate before returning to Tennessee to make his fortune. Jackson speculated on plots of land, selling some at a healthy profit and growing cotton on the others. Naturally, he purchased Black men and women to do most of the actual labor and never seemed to regard them as anything other than hardworking commodities. In 1804, Jackson wrote that one of his business partners "made at least one trip to the downriver slave markets, looking to 'carry on negroes in exchange for groceries.'"[24]

All this occurred before Jackson vaulted to national renown as the commander of a volunteer army that defeated British regulars at the Battle of New Orleans, the final confrontation in the War of 1812. He had already earned a reputation for tenacity and decisiveness as a major general in the Tennessee state militia—for which his troops gave him the nickname "Old Hickory." While epic, the 1815 battle at the mouth of the Mississippi was also unnecessary. The combatants were unaware that in far-off Ghent, Belgium, the two warring countries had already signed a peace treaty—whose lead American negotiator, as it happens, was John Quincy Adams. But millions of Americans longed for a military hero, and after the victory at New Orleans, Jackson fit the bill.

Soon after the election of 1824, Van Buren grasped the value of becoming a Jackson man and got busy knitting together a partnership of fellow anti-Adams politicians. They accused the president of being a closet Federalist, of squandering federal funds, even of pimping for Tsar Alexander I in his earlier post as U.S. envoy to

Russia. Most seriously, they blasted Adams for harboring abolitionist sympathies. The latter charge helped secure Jackson the support of John C. Calhoun, although the South Carolinian was then serving as Adams's vice president. Isaac Hill in New Hampshire and Thomas Ritchie in Virginia also rallied to Old Hickory, while the Little Magician persuaded Amos Kendall and Francis Blair from Kentucky, James Buchanan from Pennsylvania, and Thomas Hart Benton from Missouri to join the movement as well.

A number of states and counties took the novel decision to hold conventions calling for the erstwhile military hero to be nominated in 1828. In another show of enthusiasm, Jackson clubs sprang up in hundreds of localities; members sang ditties about the Battle of New Orleans, munched on barbeque, and mounted street parades. In the dawning age of mass politics, "party" was functioning both as a noun and an intransitive verb.

Meanwhile, John Quincy Adams was proving quite capable of damaging his own cause. In his first annual address, given in December 1825, the president asked Congress to approve an ambitious set of policies, including a large system of roads and canals and a national university, without worrying about whether any of them were popular with voters. Do not be "palsied by the will of our constituents," Adams advised the lawmakers, seemingly unaware he had just given a priceless gift to his political adversaries.[25]

By the time the next presidential campaign began in earnest, the "Jackson party" already seemed on the road to victory. In the midterm elections of 1826 and 1827, its adherents won narrow majorities in both the House and the Senate. Adams backers—now calling themselves National Republicans to emphasize their desire for a more potent federal government—had endured a schism in several of their Northern bastions; evangelical Protestants in upstate New York and New England were flocking to the Anti-Masonic Party, which accused the elite fraternity of conspiring to murder former members who divulged its secrets. Early in 1827, Van Buren secured Ritchie's agreement to cooperate in building a permanent organization that would "draw anew the old Party lines" and relax sectional tensions by uniting "the planters of the South and the plain Republicans of the north." That fall, he assured Jackson he would carry New York, where most of the "fifty Republican Presses" in the state had "already come out in your favour." Do not bother responding to the "calumny" and "vituperation" hurled against you by your enemies, Van Buren counseled the candidate, who, he knew, longed to lash back. Rely on our organization to carry the day.[26]

The result of the 1828 race proved the wisdom of Van Buren's strategy. In voting that began in Pennsylvania on October 31 and ended in Tennessee two weeks later, Jackson easily defeated Adams in the first genuinely two-party election in the nation's history. The victor took the electoral vote of every state outside New England except for tiny Delaware, and Maryland, which divided its electors about equally between the two men. Most impressively, Jackson won 56 percent of a popular vote that was more than three times greater than that recorded for *all* the contenders in 1824. The increase was due to mass enthusiasm as much as to the gradual dismantling of property qualifications for white men. More than half of all eligible voters cast ballots, roughly *twice* the percentage from the previous quadrennial contest. Turnout in presidential elections has ebbed and flowed since then, but it has rarely dropped below 50 percent.[27]

Partisans and scholars have explained Jackson's sweeping victory in starkly different ways. In the mid-twentieth century, progressive historians like Arthur Schlesinger, Jr., argued that hard-pressed farmers and urban wage earners viewed Old Hickory as a fierce battler for their economic interests. Later, social historians who correlated precinct and census records contended that Adams drew most heavily from pietistic evangelicals who favored his objections to slavery and hard drinking, among other moral issues, while Lutherans and Catholics who wanted the government to leave them alone tended to favor Jackson. But the big planter from Tennessee scored his most lopsided margins among his fellow white Southerners. He won some 81 percent of the popular vote in his home region, whose development depended on the labor of enslaved men and women. The candidate who initiated an era of "Jacksonian democracy" thus drew his strongest backing from the most blatantly unequal region in the land.

## Jacksonians in Power

Yet many Americans did view the capture of the presidency by a self-made, blunt-speaking fighter from the hinterland as a sea change in their politics. Midway through the twentieth century, Richard Hofstadter noted that "Jackson's election was more a result than a cause of the rise of democracy." Few contemporary observers of any persuasion made that distinction. "The scepter was about to be wrested from the hands" of the hereditary elite, wrote James Parton, a popular biographer. "We find . . . nearly all the silver-forked civilization of the country . . . united in opposition to General Jackson, who represented the country's untutored instincts." Neither Jackson nor his most avid followers hankered for an equality of conditions for white Americans; only early socialists espoused such a "utopian" notion. But the cause of equal access to wealth and property, which they did embrace, had a powerful appeal to what the New York editor William Leggett called "the producers of the middling and lower classes" who burned with resentment against "the consumers, the rich, the proud" and "the privileged."[28]

Such mass emotions gave Jackson and his party the opportunity to build a coalition that would dominate national politics for most of the next three decades. The men whose shrewd labors had done so much to put Jackson in the White House had tutored themselves well in the art of campaigning, and most quickly turned their attention to consolidating their victory. The Bucktail experience in New York provided a method to emulate on a grander scale. Exploiting the power of patronage and establishing a network of newspapers that stretched across the land did much to help the Jackson party mature into an organization equipped for durable supremacy.

In 1832, Henry Clay, one of Jackson's most skillful foes and soon his opponent in that fall's election, made an eloquent speech on the floor of the U.S. Senate in opposition to a number of executive nominations, including that of Van Buren to be minister to Great Britain. In order to defend "the honor and character of the Government" the Kentucky lawmaker declared it was necessary to expose "the pernicious system of party politics adopted by the present administration."

New York senator William L. Marcy, a stalwart of the Albany Regency, responded with a martial metaphor that soon became notorious: "To the victor belong the spoils of the enemy."[29] Enough embarrassed lawmakers from Van Buren's own party voted against him to doom his nomination.

Marcy's remark temporarily stalled the career of the very person he meant to defend, but it succinctly evoked how the budding Democracy went about filling the ranks of the small but growing federal bureaucracy. When Jackson took office, roughly ten thousand Americans worked part- or full-time for the U.S. government. Nearly three-quarters were employed by the Post Office Department. In 1841, when Van Buren stepped down from the presidency, the federal workforce had almost doubled; postal "officers" then made up nearly 80 percent of the total.

For Americans who neither belonged to the military nor lived in the District of Columbia, the postal service was the only arm of the national state they routinely encountered. The local postmaster had an unmatched opportunity to affect how his local community understood and interacted with whichever party held power. Using the same "franking privilege" available to members of Congress, he could send out mail for free and echo partisan messages. As one Jacksonian loyalist admitted, "A village postmaster with the franking privilege and only ten dollars per annum income has more influence than a city postmaster with $5000." These ubiquitous figures, like most other Democratic officeholders, were assessed a portion of their salary to fill the party's coffers for future campaigns.[30]

Right after taking office, Jackson gave key leaders of his party the freedom to fire postmasters who had sided with Adams or were suspected of disagreeing with the "old Republican" doctrine of the new administration. In anticipation of the openings created by the firings, hundreds of former campaign workers joined the Inauguration Day mob that infamously crashed into the White House, muddying the carpets, smashing the china, and drinking up all the liquor they could grab. During the next year, the administration fired more than four hundred postmasters and appointed Jackson loyalists in their places. When Old Hickory stepped down from the presidency in 1837, some 13 percent of all local postal officials had been dismissed and replaced. Most of the turnover occurred in the small towns of New England and the middle Atlantic states, where Jackson's support was shakier than in the big cities and the South.

Such blatant awarding of the spoils of office violated the Founding Fathers' ideal of politics as a public-spirited endeavor. It was also ironic that politicians who favored a less powerful federal government persistently employed the power of the state to reward their friends and sack their enemies. But however deplorable partisan patronage might be, it helped establish the Jackson party as an institution with roots in nearly every corner of the nation. Most voters seemed unconcerned that a postmaster might not share their politics. And patronage soon became a bipartisan malady. When the Whigs captured the White House in 1840, they demonstrated how lightly they regarded the same principle they had condemned their opponents for betraying: under Presidents Harrison and Tyler, a higher percentage of postmasters got dismissed than under their Democratic predecessors.[31]

The postal system exercised another function just as vital to politics as were the men who staffed its offices: it charged newspapers and magazines a rate of only a penny or less per copy. The discount predated the era of mass parties and stemmed from a desire to ensure that these "easy vehicles of knowledge," as George Washington had called them, would "stimulate the industry and meliorate the morals of an enlightened and free People." By 1830, post offices were distributing more newspapers—sixteen million—than letters. A decade later, their circulation by mail had more than doubled.[32]

These periodicals had little in common with the irregular broadsheets of Washington's day, which did not go through the mail and were mostly consumed by a tiny, educated elite. By the 1830s, most papers appeared every weekday, except holidays, and were often sponsored and subsidized by a political party. Naturally, their editors advanced the partisan cause in both news and opinion—and Jackson loyalists published more papers than did their adversaries. Some, like *The Albany Argus* and the *Washington Globe*, were semiofficial organs of the party. Others, like the "penny papers" in New York City edited by James Gordon Bennett, a Democrat, and Horace Greeley, a Whig, appealed to plebeian readers with graphic accounts of crime as well as reports on public affairs. From 1790 to the year of Jackson's first election as president, the number of newspapers in the United States increased by nearly tenfold, to 861. Few left any doubt about who they wanted their readers to vote for and which policies they ought to be supporting. In return, Jackson named fifty-nine editors to jobs in his administration. As one antebellum chronicler aptly put it, "Newspapers are to political parties in this country what working tools are to the operative mechanic."[33]

The only Jacksonian organ with a sizable national audience was the *Washington Globe*. Its editor, Francis Blair, a land speculator and journalist from Kentucky, had lost nearly his entire fortune during the financial slump of 1819. This turned him into a lifelong hater of big banks and a proponent of debt relief. In 1828, he joined the Jackson party, partly because Adams backers (like his old friend Henry Clay) were opposed to aiding debtors. Prone to hero worship, Blair quickly became enamored of Old Hickory's "rugged masculinity" and "lofty principles" and eagerly took up the president's request that he launch a pro-administration paper in the capital city.[34]

The *Globe*'s circulation grew modestly until 1831, when it acquired a large building and printing equipment of its own. For the next decade it thrived, thanks to what Blair called "the generous devotion of the friends of the president." Daily readership climbed to more than seventeen thousand (about half of D.C.'s population), and some four hundred local papers around the country routinely reprinted its copy. Blair's paper was a prime asset for his party and his president. But he did exceedingly well for himself, too. Printing contracts from many cabinet departments netted Blair and his partner, John C. Rives, about $365,000 during that same period—close to $10 million in today's money. Blair used some of the cash to purchase nearly a thousand acres of land in nearby Maryland on which he built an estate he named Silver Spring.[35]

His *Globe* practiced a style of partisan journalism whose basic elements changed little from the Age of Jackson to the years of Trump. It employed gentle sarcasm: a column from June 1831, titled "Daily Misrepresentations of the Opposition Press," countered the notion that Van Buren was "corruptly maneuvering" to become vice president and then get "Gen. Jackson" to resign with the "Answer:

Every body knows who knows both the men, that this is such stuff as dreams are made of." It amplified the populist wisdom of the party faithful: in the spring of 1832, Blair attended a meeting in New Orleans of the Democratic Citizens of Louisiana at which one speaker passionately declared that "General Jackson had always been the favorite of the PEOPLE, while he had been feared, hated, and opposed by the aristocracy of the country" and also managed to put in a good word for Van Buren—"a poor boy who without the aid of friends or fortune rose early to distinction."

*Globe* editors were fond of contrasting the principled character of their own side with the allegedly mean and petty disposition of their adversaries. During the campaign of 1832, the paper reprinted an editorial from the *Kentucky Republican*, a brother periodical, that belittled the backers of Henry Clay: "They support their candidate for the Presidency by slandering General Jackson—we shall endeavor to support ours by convincing the public of his virtues and qualifications, and the strong claims he has upon his country." Every good Democrat in Congress and the cabinet was expected to read the *Globe* and echo it in their speeches and policy papers.[36]

No issue during Jackson's administration shaped his party with more force or duration than his decision to oppose a recharter of the Second Bank of the United States. The combative president engaged in other big controversies, of course. The forced removal of thousands of Cherokees from their homeland in Georgia, begun under Jackson and completed during Van Buren's term, underlined in blood and starvation the Democrats' exclusive commitment to advancing the fortunes of white people. And by compelling South Carolina to rescind its vow to nullify tariffs Congress had passed, the president made clear the supremacy of federal power in general, and his power in particular.

But the battle over the "Monster Bank" in the early 1830s was an epic struggle to counter the sway of high finance and determine what elected officials could and should do to promote or restrain it. For

Jacksonians, it was and, for later Democrats, long remained a decisive contest to fence capitalism within moral boundaries. Van Buren used his position as vice president during Old Hickory's second term to navigate how both his leader and his party battled a foe that, for them, represented an aristocracy of wealth that conspired to throttle the chance for ordinary white men to improve their lot within a fast-growing economy. The Bank of the United States, agrees one scholar, "was a concentration of political and economic power able to tyrannize over people's lives and to control the will of their elected representatives."[37]

Chartered in 1816, the bank spurred development by expanding credit in promising locations. But it was acutely vulnerable to populist attack: private investors owned most of its shares, and its directors used tax revenues to grant loans and invest capital where they pleased. Sometimes, they took part in election campaigns to reward a friend or punish a critic. The dollars issued by the bank were also the closest thing to a national currency the country had.

Nicholas Biddle—the bank's urbane, wealthy president—did not try to hide his distaste for what he considered the archaic backwardness of the laissez-faire beliefs espoused by "old Republicans." He worked with Henry Clay to develop a strategy to force Jackson to recharter his bank or use his resistance to it against the president in the 1832 campaign. Biddle and Clay should not have been surprised when Old Hickory, who had fought several duels as a young man, swore to defy them. On the evening of Independence Day in 1832, Van Buren visited an ailing Jackson in the White House. He recalled that the president took his hand and "passing the other thro' his long white locks he said, with the clearest indications of a mind composed, and in a tone entirely devoid of passion or bluster—'the bank, Mr. Van Buren is trying to kill me, but I will kill it!'"[38]

That vow to commit political homicide became a prime exhibit in the rhetoric of a moral economy that harked back to Jefferson's agrarianism and allowed the Democrats to claim they were still the party of the common man, in the city and on the land. Jackson turned his refusal to recharter the Bank of the United States into a grand populist drama, the language of which has been echoed in every subsequent economic crisis. A week after he met with Van Buren, Jackson signed his name to a thundering veto of the bank's recharter: "It is to be regretted that the rich and powerful too often bend the acts of government to their selfish purposes." The president argued it was unjust for a publicly created institution to grant loans and invest capital wherever its well-to-do directors decided it was prudent to do so.[39]

The suspicion his fellow Democrats felt toward financial institutions ran even deeper than that. The very idea that bankers could get rich by investing money they did not earn seemed to violate God's injunction to Adam (and all mankind) to earn his bread "in the sweat of thy face." In 1840, the editor of a party paper in Mississippi asked why a rich man should "be allowed the privilege of drawing interest on three dollars for every one they own." Many a Democrat even opposed the issuing of paper money, then the province of banks, instead of relying on "specie"—coins made of gold or silver. Senator Thomas Hart Benton, Missouri's leading Jacksonian, condemned Biddle's institution as "the Whore of Babylon," charging that it conspired to enrich the Northeast and starve his region's farmers of capital.[40]

The economic logic of their position was shaky at best. It assumed the superior virtues of a preindustrial nation of small farmers that was rapidly receding into memory and myth. It also enraged urban businessmen who relied on easy credit and emboldened Clay and other anti-Jackson politicians to organize the new Whig Party to oppose what they considered the "tyranny" of "King Andrew the First." But the view that carried the day was Van Buren's opinion that his side in the Bank War was defending "the vital principle—the sovereignty of the popular will—which lies at the foundation of free government." Brandishing that message, Jackson was easily reelected in 1832, defeating Clay by a landslide in both the popular vote (which he carried by nearly fifteen percentage points) and the Electoral College.

Following his victory, the president withdrew federal funds from the Monster Bank and transferred them to "pet" state banks run by loyal Jacksonians. Biddle quickly counterattacked; he demanded immediate payment on loans his bank had made to financial institutions around the nation, which shoved the burden onto individual debtors, many of whom could not raise the cash. A sharp recession ensued.

When the Senate, controlled by the president's foes, passed a motion of censure against Jackson, the Democrats intensified their organizing in key states and regained a majority in the upper chamber.

Van Buren later wrote in his memoirs, "Never before were our material interests so severely and wantonly injured as they were by the successive struggles of the second Bank of the United States to obtain a renewal of its charter." No historian would back up that claim. Many of the state banks that were the beneficiaries of Biddle's defeat engaged in reckless speculative investments that did small farmers and artisans no good.

But the great Bank War would not be the last time a successful political strategy ignored or flouted conservative thinking about the economy. Jackson's position on the Second Bank became one of his most significant legacies. It helped inspire later campaigns against the "money power" by figures like William Jennings Bryan, Woodrow Wilson, and Franklin D. Roosevelt that led to the passage of such landmark measures as the Federal Reserve Act, the progressive income tax, and the National Labor Relations Act. Beginning with the Bank War, the Democrats gained an invaluable reputation as "the people's party" and compelled their opponents to wrest the title away from them.[41]


## Containing Multitudes

Politics in antebellum America was an intensely local affair. Both Democrats and their Whig rivals had to craft an organization village by village and state by state. Outside the South, the key to winning a durable majority was to assemble and hold together a coalition as demographically broad as that which had twice won the presidency for Jackson—or the "military chieftain," as the president liked to call himself. Each year on January 8, Democrats commemorated his victory at the Battle of New Orleans with local rallies, resolutions, and odes in party organs. "Friends of Jackson," declared *The Cincinnati Enquirer* in 1844, "while the old man is yet with the living, shall we not proclaim our love for him for the dangers he has braved—the victories he has won over enemies in the field and again in the cabinet!"[42]

But Old Hickory, who died a year later, could not transfer his enormous popular appeal to his last vice president, who was better at creating a party than leading one. Van Buren did capture the White House in 1836, although he won just a bare majority of the popular vote against three Whig opponents. The new president entered the White House with no ambition other than to continue the policies of his predecessor, who could have won a third term if he had chosen to run again. In his inaugural address, Van Buren hailed America's "human prosperity not elsewhere to be found," and he retained most of Jackson's cabinet members. With a majority in Congress and most of the states, Democrats fought off Whig attempts to expand credit and issue paper currency instead of relying primarily on specie.[43]

But Van Buren's political magic soon ran into an opponent he could not finesse with cautious words or subdue with a potent partisan alliance. Two months after he took office, a financial panic spread from English banks to their counterparts in New York City. By the fall of 1837, the nation was suffering from the worst depression in its history; prices of agricultural and factory products plummeted, while business foreclosures soared. True to his principles, Van Buren blamed greedy speculators and too easy credit for this "unusual derangement in the general operation of trade." The president did propose an independent Treasury that would hold the government's funds instead of allowing them to accumulate in risky state banks. But as hard times endured, Congress balked at creating the new institution. Like his heroic predecessor, Van Buren gave banks too much blame for economic woes and the federal government too small a role in healing them. In a speech to lawmakers early in 1840, he reaffirmed his faith that "the less government interferes with private pursuits the better for the general prosperity."[44] No Democratic president in the twentieth or twenty-first century would agree.

Van Buren's popularity never recovered. In 1840, he lost his bid for reelection to William Henry Harrison, a sixty-seven-year-old politician from Ohio who had gained military fame decades before by crushing a major Native American revolt in the Upper Midwest. He was the nominee of an opposition party that flattered the Democrats by employing an enhanced version of the kind of mobilizing techniques Van Buren and his followers had pioneered. The Whigs began as severe critics of "King Andrew" during Jackson's second term in the White House; their name harked back to the English faction that opposed the tyranny of monarchs in the eighteenth century. But they became a true rival party only during Van Buren's administration, when nearly every state turned into a battleground as canny managers whipped up the faithful with a mixture of ideological zeal and inducements to show up at the polls.

The Whigs' 1840 campaign of unprecedented hoopla, and purposeful underplaying of big issues, was partly responsible for that year's unprecedented turnout—of more than 80 percent of eligible voters. The new party won a landslide in the electoral count as well as a majority in Congress.

Such Whig managers as Horace Greeley and Thurlow Weed, brilliantly, if dishonestly, adapted the Democrats' anti-elitist message in ways that both surprised and flustered Van Buren and his associates. Whig imagery featured a log cabin that Harrison never actually inhabited, falsely depicted Van Buren eating off gold plates and guzzling champagne in the White House, and organized massive rallies where the president was mocked as "Van, Van, Van—Van's a Used Up Man." A distiller named E. G. Booz hawked whiskey in bottles shaped like tiny wooden houses. Whig speakers downplayed the economic issues—the tariff and the Second Bank—that had given rise to their party in the first place. Depicting their party as the moral protector of the home, they also invited women to their rallies, breaking an unwritten rule as old as the republic.[45]

In response, the only memorable innovation Democrats could muster was to dub Van Buren "Old Kinderhook," in hopes the nickname would remind voters of the president's bond with Old Hickory. Party activists began shortening the moniker to "O.K.," as in "Down with the Whigs, boys, O.K.," popularizing an idiom that had been recently coined. But in every other way, the Whigs had defeated Van Buren at his own game.[46]

Harrison's victory initiated the enduring practice of ferociously competitive two-party campaigns—although the elderly president succumbed to pneumonia just one month into his term. For the next decade, Whigs and Democrats employed similar tactics for drumming up the morale of their loyalists and making sure they, along with the small but critical minority of independent-minded Americans, made it to the polls.

A letter sent from the Democratic Central Committee of New York to party activists two weeks before the midterm election of 1842 details a strategy that, with minor changes, remains in use today. William L. Marcy and his fellow leaders instructed town and district committees to correct their voter lists, "procure speakers to address the people," and check off the names of good Democrats "as they arrive and vote." Activists were urged to bring such voters *"to the polls in the early part of the day,"* knowing Whigs were doing the same. The committee emphasized that, while the prospects for victory were "cheering," vigilance was mandatory. "Let us not, we beseech you, in a contest on which so much depends, be caught napping," it concluded. In Illinois, two years before, a Whig state assemblyman named Abraham Lincoln had written a similarly precise "plan of organization" for his side.[47]

A well-drilled corps of activists was particularly vital in big states where neither party could count on victory. Take New York and Ohio—by 1840, the first and third most populous states. In the five presidential contests held after Jackson left office, the Empire State voted for the winner *every* time; if New York had voted differently, neither Van Buren in 1836, nor James K. Polk in 1844, nor the Whig nominee Zachary Taylor in 1848 would have become president. Ohio voters favored the losing nominee in three of those contests. However, on all but one occasion, a margin of less than 5 percent separated the main contenders in the Buckeye State. Neither party held the governorship or control of the state legislature in either state for more than four years in a row. Instability goaded both parties to heights of mobilization: throughout the 1840s, Ohio and New York posted, at close to 92 percent, the highest turnout of any states in the union.[48]

In such a hypercompetitive environment, debates within the partisan fold took on added significance. In Ohio during the 1840s, "soft" Democrats like Governor Wilson Shannon allied with Whigs to allow state banks to issue paper money. At the same time, Shannon sought to placate the "hards" by backing a bill to make individual stockholders liable for losses to depositors when a financial institution failed. But bitter divisions over how many banks to charter and what services they could offer continued to plague Ohio Democrats for much of the decade. Most small towns were stable bastions of one party or the other, which left local activists little room for error.[49]

Ohio Jacksonians could, however, make common cause on matters of race and slavery. Like their partisan brethren in New York, they successfully opposed giving free Blacks the right to vote or even to testify in court. Most Ohio Democrats resented both Southern slaveholders (for "degrading" the value of labor) and abolitionists (for crusading to free millions of people belonging to "an ignorant and depraved class" who, they feared, would drive down wages and debauch Northern society). In 1836, a white mob in Cincinnati, just across the river from the slave state of Kentucky, twice destroyed the printing presses on which James Birney published *The Philanthropist*, an abolitionist newspaper. Not every rioter was a Democrat, but the columns of party organs refrained from condemning the violence.[50]

In New York, while the Albany Regency kept the party competitive in rural areas and small towns, the upstate machine had little influence on conflicts that divided Democrats in the metropolis on the Hudson. During the 1830s and 1840s, the main conflict in New York City was between Tammany Hall and an Equal Rights insurgency composed largely of white artisans. The sachems of Tammany signed up every legal voter, many of whom were recent immigrants from Ireland or the German states, and some illegal ones; they denounced "monopoly" in the abstract while courting favors from local corporations, even some that favored rechartering Biddle's bank.

Their critics in the Equal Rights movement made their backing for the Democracy contingent on its candidates' taking a hard line against privileges bestowed by the government on established businesses—what its leader William Leggett called "a conspiracy of the rich." Soon after Van Buren's election in 1836, *Democrat*, organ of these self-styled radicals, denounced "Mother Tammany" as the "old harlot eager to embrace any new movement in order to win elections" and warned its readers to "beware . . . the treachery in the leering eyes of the old hag!" Tammany's ability to get such rebels to view the party as a lesser evil was an early test of how it would persuade social movements to put aside their disagreements with the Democratic establishment long enough to vote.[51]

New York City was also home to a magazine that instilled Democrats with a sense of being in the vanguard of global enlightenment. *The United States Democratic Review* began publication in 1837 in the nation's capital with the blessings of President Van Buren and funds he secretly raised. But it began to flourish intellectually only when it moved to an office in downtown Manhattan three years later. Edited by John O'Sullivan, a charismatic Columbia graduate still in his twenties, the *Review* published poetry by Whitman and Whittier and stories by Hawthorne and Poe alongside sharply argued, often lyrical commentaries on current politics and visionary essays on the nation's future.

"The Great Nation of Futurity" was O'Sullivan's hymn to the promise of his multiethnic, self-governing homeland. This "nation of many nations," the editor predicted in 1839, "is destined to manifest to mankind the excellence of divine principles." Comparing the United States to a church, O'Sullivan rhapsodized about "its congregation an Union of many Republics, comprising hundreds of happy millions, calling, owning no man master, but governed by God's natural and moral law of equality, the law of brotherhood—of 'peace and good will amongst men.'" A few years hence, O'Sullivan and his fellow Democrats would use his concept of "manifest destiny" to justify America's bloody conquest of Mexico. But when the young editor coined the phrase, he was rejoicing in the utopian potential of a nation so free it would have no reason to make war at all.[52]

In their multitudinous diversity, the Democrats in America's largest city were a microcosm of the antebellum party in the North. What united wealthy merchants, radical artisans, pragmatic Tammany bosses, and writers smitten by majestic ideals might be little more than a devotion to Andrew Jackson and a fierce antagonism toward bankers. Hatred for the rich and powerful has always been a precious gift to politicians who are adept at exploiting it. Old Hickory's biography and magnetism had given all these men a reason to join the party, and his anti-elitist zeal encouraged them to remain there. As a teenager in 1833, Walt Whitman caught a glimpse of the president, who was making a tour of Brooklyn. After Jackson's death, he praised, in the Democratic organ he edited, his "Hero and Sage": "His weather-beaten face is before us at this moment . . . with his snow-white hair brushed stiffly up from his forehead, and his piercing eyes quite glancing through his spectacles . . . Your great soul never knew a thought of self, in questions which involved your country! Ah, there has lived among us but *one* purer!"⁵³


## Danger Signals

Yet a party that included both Walt Whitman and Jefferson Davis could not ignore its contradictions forever. Beginning with Jackson's triumph in 1828, Democratic leaders had prospered by mobilizing a congeries of voters who shared their repugnance for metropolitan elites and sanctimonious reformers and felt they deserved a chance to rise to economic comfort, if not wealth. At the same time, a notable minority of Democrats owned slaves; their desire not just to protect their human property but to expand the institution westward fit poorly with their talk about "equal rights" and vows to topple "aristocrats" and "monopolists."

As long as most Americans depended more on governments closer to home than the one in Washington City, this conflict remained dormant. With the exception of the Bank of the United States, the tariff, and the postal service, the party in charge of the national government was essentially running a machine for producing symbolic identities—and dispossessing Native Americans. In 1840, Van Buren's final year in office, the entire federal budget totaled $24.3 million—equivalent to just $635 million today. "Love the State and let the nation save itself," a leader, Silas Wright, had advised his comrades as they assembled the Jackson Party in the late 1820s.⁵⁴

Then the slaveholding officials of the Republic of Texas asked to join the union. In 1843, President John Tyler, Harrison's successor, enthusiastically took up their cause. The plantation owner from Virginia had essentially abandoned the Whig Party that had nominated him and hoped to get elected in his own right, as a Democrat. Texas annexation quickly became an issue no politician could safely ignore—and one only the federal government could resolve. For the aging Jackson and his admirers at the *Globe* and the *Democratic Review*, it turned "manifest destiny" from a soaring, consensual abstraction into a rationale for forcing Mexico to give up a huge part of its territory to its larger, aggressive neighbor.

Van Buren, like most Northern Democrats, was torn between his desire for territorial expansion and his fear that admitting another slave state would jeopardize the regional compact that had made his and Jackson's presidencies possible. He also worried that the annexation of Texas could lead to war with Mexico. The decision would probably be made by whoever won the White House in 1844. "For the first time in American history," writes one historian, "conflicts connected to slavery transformed the dynamics of a presidential election."[55]

The Democrats triumphed that fall. But first they denied the nomination to Van Buren, whom most party activists preferred. At the opening of the party's convention in Baltimore, Van Buren had a clear majority of the delegates, but his ambivalence on Texas emboldened his enemies. First among them were John C. Calhoun and his corps of pro-slavery, pro-annexation allies. They persuaded the delegates to revive a rule, not used since the 1832 convention, that required a nominee to secure two-thirds of the vote. It was, in effect, a Southern veto. Despite its critics, the party would stubbornly retain the requirement for a supermajority for almost a century—until Franklin Roosevelt's second nomination in 1936.

In the early balloting, neither Van Buren nor anyone else came close to gaining that margin. Managers for the more prominent contenders huddled in a back room to make a deal. On the ninth ballot, James K. Polk, considered a "dark horse" (though he was a former Speaker of the House and governor of Tennessee) was nominated by acclamation. The Democrats also adopted a platform that called for admitting Texas to the union. From his estate outside Nashville, Andrew Jackson sent his good wishes. Before the convention opened, he had indirectly rebuked Van Buren for waffling on the burning question before the republic: "You might as well . . . attempt to turn the current of the Mississippi, as to turn the democracy from the annexation of Texas," he told his old friend and ally.[56]

That fall, Polk campaigned as "Young Hickory" and narrowly defeated Henry Clay, the Whig nominee, with just under half the popular vote. To no one's surprise, the key prize in the Electoral College was New York, which the Democrat carried by a mere five thousand votes. The state and the presidency almost surely would have gone to Clay if a third-party candidate had not been on the ballot. In one of the great ironies of American political history, that candidate was James Birney, nominee of the anti-slavery and anti-Texas Liberty Party—the same man who had seen his press demolished by a Cincinnati mob full of Democrats eight years before. Abolitionists had much warmer feelings for the Whigs who opposed annexation than they did for Polk's party—although Clay, like Polk, owned slaves. So the nearly sixteen thousand ballots cast for Birney in the Empire State (about a quarter of his national total) essentially handed the presidency to a man who was determined to expand the empire of slavery as soon as he took office.

Actually, Polk did not have to wait that long. Just three days before leaving the White House, John Tyler signed a resolution that Democrats had pushed through Congress inviting Texas to become what would be the largest state in the country. Its formal admission at the end of 1845 began a process of threats and troop movements that, by April of the following year, had hurled the United States into war with the Republic of Mexico.

Less than two months later, Andrew Jackson died, content in the knowledge that Texas statehood had secured "the safety, prosperity, and the greatest interest of the whole Union." Before his death, the general lamented that President Polk preferred to create his own party organ, which led Francis Blair to sell the *Washington Globe*. "You have done your duty to this great party," Jackson told his publicist and old friend. "You have left it united & prosperous, and I pray god it may so continue."[57]

One humid day the following summer, David Wilmot, a thirty-two-year-old first-term Democratic congressman from Pennsylvania, introduced an amendment, or proviso, to a bill appropriating funds to be used once the war with Mexico had ended. It arose from a fear that gripped a growing number of Northern politicians from both major parties: that the "slave power" of the South was using its sway over the federal government to enlarge its territory at the expense of free labor and free lands.

Neither Wilmot nor his allies cared much about the horrors of

human bondage. What worried them was the impact that a broad expansion of slave territory would have on the economic future of "the
free white man of this country," as one New York congressman put
it. Polk had named fellow slaveholders to run the main executive departments as well as to most high offices in the military and the nation's embassies abroad—although the population growth of the free
states was outpacing that of the South. If unchallenged, the war with
Mexico would give the slave power a grand opportunity to enlarge its
empire as well as its influence within the republic. The key clauses of
the Wilmot Proviso read: "As an express and fundamental condition
to the acquisition of any territory from the Republic of Mexico by the
United States . . . neither slavery nor involuntary servitude shall ever
exist in any part of said territory, except for crime, whereof the party
shall first be duly convicted."[58]

With the backing of most Whigs and Northern Democrats, the
Wilmot Proviso twice passed the House, only to be shot down in
the Senate by an equally solid bloc of Southerners and a few of their
sympathizers from above the Mason-Dixon Line. One of Wilmot's
most prestigious allies was Martin Van Buren. The former president
denounced the expansion of slavery as "a heresy so revolting" that it
would flout the wishes of citizens of free states and would not be either "wise or expedient."[59] An ominous crack had begun to widen in
the foundation of the house of Democracy that he, Jackson, and their
ambitious compatriots had built.

# 2

# TO CONSERVE THE WHITE MAN'S REPUBLIC, 1848–1874

*Nothing will do any good which does not take the slavery question out of Congress forever.*
—SENATOR STEPHEN A. DOUGLAS, CHRISTMAS DAY, 1860[1]

*To the light of other days when liberty wore a white face and America wasn't a Negro.*
—TOAST AT A DEMOCRATIC MEETING IN BERGEN COUNTY, NEW JERSEY, 1863[2]

*The Democratic Party has been . . . the only hope and refuge to which the oppressed of Ireland could flee . . . The opposition on the other hand, whether known by that name Federalists, Know Nothings, Free Soil or Republican . . . has distinguished itself by . . . its narrow bigotry . . . and its open hostility for the poor and laboring classes.*
—THE PILOT, BOSTON'S LEADING CATHOLIC NEWSPAPER, 1864[3]

*I love its memories and revere its past.*
—OHIO DEMOCRATIC CONGRESSMAN SAMUEL "SUNSET" COX, ON HIS PARTY, 1872[4]

Amid the upheaval of the Civil War era, no Democrat was able to remain a dominant figure in the national party for decades at a stretch, as had Andrew Jackson and Martin Van Buren. But two men—Illinois senator Stephen A. Douglas and the New York financier August Belmont—played outsized roles in shaping the aims of their organization and its efforts to achieve them. Before and after the war, the Democracy remained stronger in the South than in any other region. But, as leading pro-Union Northerners, Douglas and Belmont struggled to hold the organization together when most of their Southern brethren were intent on tearing it and the Union apart. Only by clinging to Jacksonian principles, they maintained, could the party regain the favor of white Americans in all parts of the nation.

From the start, their Democracy had been a machine for generating rhetoric and policies that raised the hopes and furthered the interests solely of Americans whose roots lay in European soil. The tribunes of "egalitarian whiteness" assured ordinary farmers and wage earners that they could take their racial supremacy for granted. Democratic officials swore, over and over, to protect their "liberty" to improve their lot against threats from wellborn financiers and haughty abolitionists alike. Jackson's victory over the Monster Bank in the 1830s became the master symbol for the party that would not allow capitalists, evangelical crusaders, and their friends in government to throttle opportunities for the many.[5]

As the conflict over slavery rose to a shattering crescendo, prominent Democrats like Douglas and Belmont described themselves routinely as the defenders of white supremacy; most continued to make it their primary "principle" through the next two decades. In the North, class animus often coursed through their arguments. Democrats accused economically comfortable Republicans of wanting to free the slaves and give them jobs and the vote so they could destroy the fragile status and power of plebeian white men and their families.

But the centrality of the battle over Black freedom made any arguments for moral capitalism seem less urgent, if not less relevant. Democrats had always preached a racist creed. Yet in framing every argument, explicitly or subtly, as a way to conserve the white man's republic, they adopted a defensive position that did not serve them well—either morally or electorally.

Douglas is now known mainly for his lengthy debates with Abraham Lincoln during their race for the U.S. Senate in 1858—a race that Douglas won, only to lose the presidency to the Republican standard-bearer two years later. But in the decade preceding the Civil War, he was the only Democrat who had a true national following.

For his part, Belmont chaired the Democratic National Committee through five consecutive election cycles, beginning with Douglas's failed run for the White House in 1860. A wealthy investor, Belmont did what he could to keep the national party endowed with funds, while often opposing measures to aid ordinary white voters whom Democrats needed to regain their status as the majority party. Since Jackson's presidency, the party had leaned on its government employees to finance national campaigns with a small portion of their salaries. But no laws kept wealthy men from donating any sums they desired, and Democrats needed Belmont and his friends to counter the sums that Whig and Republican bankers and industrialists lavished on the nominees of their parties.

The dissimilar backgrounds of Douglas and Belmont suggest the diversity of the Democracy's Northern leadership, even as it waged a furious internal battle over the expansion of slavery. Douglas was a self-made Jacksonian in a hurry. Born in 1813, he left his family's small Vermont farm as a teenager to "see what I could do for myself in the wide world among strangers." That quest took him first to labor in a carpenter's shop, then to study briefly in a private academy, and then to serve a stint reading law. At the age of twenty, Douglas departed for what was then called "the West." He arrived in central Illinois with only $1.25 to his name. Just two years later, in 1835, he captured his first political office—as state's attorney or prosecutor for eight fast-growing counties in the middle of the state. Over the next decade, Douglas became one of the most prominent Democrats in Illinois, whose population had tripled since he moved there. The state legislature elected him to the U.S. Senate when he was still in his early thirties. A husky man of five feet four inches, the aggressive orator and crafty strategist had earned his nickname, "the Little Giant."[6]

Belmont's path to political fame and personal fortune began a continent and a class apart. He was born, also in 1813, as August Schönberg to a prosperous and devout Jewish family in Alzey, a village in the Rhineland that Prussia soon wrested from Napoleonic rule. Belmont began his own apprenticeship at fifteen, serving a far more exalted patron than Douglas had ever known. For several years, August dutifully swept floors and polished desks in the offices of the Frankfurt branch of the Rothschild family. When he reached adulthood, he was promoted as an aide to one of the Rothschild partners, with whom he traveled around Europe, developing a taste for the fine arts. In 1837, Belmont arrived in Manhattan during a stock market panic and soon set up his own Wall Street firm; it became the Rothschilds' exclusive agent in the United States. Less than a decade later, the still-young man was worth an estimated $100,000. He would gradually turn that modest fortune into a much larger one— enough to buy and expand a mansion on lower Fifth Avenue that boasted the first private ballroom in the city and to build two Thoroughbred breeding stables. By the 1870s, the immigrant banker had become one of the richest men in America. The Belmont Stakes, the final leg in horse racing's Triple Crown, is named for him.[7]

It is not entirely clear when Belmont became a Democrat or why—although his wife's uncle John Slidell, a powerful Louisiana congressman, encouraged him to do so. But by the early 1850s, the financier was already donating large sums to the party and boosting the presidential cause of James Buchanan, a former secretary of state from Pennsylvania. In 1860, Belmont became chairman of the Democratic National Committee and converted that post from an honorary sinecure into one that had a major responsibility to steer the party to victory. He became the de facto manager of Douglas's presidential campaign—and continued to head the DNC for another dozen years, longer than any chairman in its history. Belmont was the first leader of a type the Democrats have always needed but that has often damaged its populist reputation: a man of great wealth who generously invested both his time and a portion of his fortune in the party.

The financier had stopped practicing Judaism by 1849, when he married Caroline Slidell Perry, daughter of Commodore Matthew Perry, the leading naval officer in the Mexican War, who would soon achieve lasting fame for opening up Japan to American trade. The couple raised their children as Episcopalians. But Belmont's political adversaries inside and outside his party refused to recognize his apostasy. For them, he would always be a sinister figure who used "Jew gold" to buy elections and further the wicked designs of his "tribe."[8]

The upwardly mobile Little Giant from mid-America and the rich immigrant from Gotham worked together well because they shared a singular goal and a sensibility to match. While ritually intoning the founding ideals of the Jacksonian gospel, both men demonstrated a willingness to do whatever it might take to keep their party whole and restore it to the dominant position it had held during the nearly twenty years from Old Hickory's election to Polk's departure from office. Belmont, in a candid moment, advised delegates to the 1864 national convention, "We must bring to the altar of our country the sacrifice of our prejudices, opinions, and convictions—however dear and long cherished they may be—from the moment they threaten the harmony of action so indispensable to our success." In so doing, added the DNC chairman, the delegates would be expressing their "pure and disinterested patriotism, tempered by moderation and forbearance."[9] In the throes of the greatest crisis the nation had ever undergone, he counseled the Democrats to dedicate themselves to winning elections by any means necessary.

## Coming Apart in the 1850s

The need for pragmatic behavior lay in the internecine battle that consumed the party in the aftermath of the Mexican War. In 1847 and 1848, David Wilmot again introduced his proviso to ban slavery from the territories conquered from America's southern neighbor. Again, his measure passed the House but failed in the Senate, as Southerners from both major parties voted as a bloc to preserve the option of extending their internal empire of bondage.

Northern Democrats faced a time of choosing. To placate slaveholders and their favorite politicians meant alienating a growing number of voters in the free states. If plantation grandees could take their human property anywhere in the nation they pleased, how would white workers and small employers compete? But to stand against the slave power would surely lead to a rift, even a split, in the party whose majority status depended on Southern votes.

At their national convention in 1848, Democrats chose a presidential nominee who floated a proposal on slavery expansion he thought would satisfy both factions. Lewis Cass was an undistinguished career politician from Michigan and a veteran of the War of 1812 who had led the fight in the Senate to defeat the Wilmot Proviso. He announced, "I am in favor of leaving to the people of any territory . . . the right to regulate [slavery] for themselves, under the principles of the Constitution." Cass depicted this policy as a simple application of his party's long-standing belief in states' rights and democratic decision-making. But it would have erased the line between future slave and free states established in 1820 by the Missouri Compromise. Neither Cass nor his supporters seemed to understand that, if adopted, their scheme would ensure a bitter struggle for power, both in the states and nationally, that could easily erupt into mass violence.[10]

For Martin Van Buren, the nomination of Cass on such a platform was a final, insupportable outrage in an intraparty fight that had begun when he lost the party's nod at the convention four years earlier—despite having amassed a majority of delegates. In the intervening years, New York Democrats had dispersed into feuding camps, based on personal rivalries and views about the expansion of slavery. Van Buren's faction, known as the Barnburners, echoed Jackson's hostility toward economic elites for a purpose Old Hickory, the defender of slavery, would have abhorred. They declared, "Free labor and slave labor . . . cannot flourish under the same laws. The wealthy capitalists who own slaves disdain manual labor, and the whites who are compelled to submit to it . . . cannot act on terms of equality with the masters."[11] Their opponents, the Hunkers, were loath to say or do anything that might alienate the South by encouraging talk of limiting, much less abolishing, slavery. They accused the Barnburners of being "fanatics" whose radical views would drag the party down to defeat. At the national convention that May in Baltimore, neither state faction was able to win the credentials fight, so no delegates from New York cast ballots for the presidential nomination. After the party selected Cass, a Hunker favorite, Van Buren and his allies stomped out of the hall. About the only thing the two factions could agree on was establishing the Democratic National Committee, to take charge of the campaign and every subsequent one.

The Little Magician soon made his adversaries pay for repudiating what he saw as the cherished principles of their partisan home. A month after the convention, several hundred Barnburners and a smattering of pro-Wilmot Democrats and Whigs gathered in Utica, New York, to establish the Free Soil Party. They nominated Van Buren for president, an action confirmed later that summer by a larger meeting in Buffalo. In an early sign of the fragility of the existing party system, the Free Soilers nominated Charles Francis Adams for vice president. The Whig newspaper editor from Massachusetts was the son of John Quincy Adams, whose "corrupt bargain" in 1824 gave an unintentional boost to Van Buren's effort to assemble the party that would defeat his father's bid for a second term.

Cass narrowly lost the 1848 election to Zachary Taylor, a military hero of the Mexican War. If the Michigan senator had carried New York, he would have captured the White House. But Van Buren exacted revenge on the party he had done so much to create by taking 26 percent of the vote in his home state. Taylor was the second Whig elected president and the last; like William Henry Harrison, he owed his nomination almost entirely to his exploits on the battlefield. Also like his predecessor, he died of illness early in his term.

The 1848 contest was Van Buren's final electoral hurrah. He retired to Lindenwald, an estate outside Kinderhook, which he designed to resemble an Italian villa. It featured one of the first indoor toilets in the country. He left a gaggle of Democrats to navigate through or around the issue of slavery in order to return the party to what they all felt was its natural place in command of the American state.[12]

Douglas dedicated himself to that task from the end of the Mexican War until his death in 1861. If he succeeded, a grateful party would surely nominate him for president. His approach was quite simple, although implementing it required frequent alterations of tactics and alliances: resolve the controversy over the expansion of slavery in a way that would not only unite Democrats north and south but also reduce abolitionists to a brigade of impotent radicals. Douglas believed, in the words of his biographer, that as "the only remaining national party," the Democratic Party's "mission . . . was now the mission of the Union, for without the party there would be no Union."[13]

As chairman of the Senate's Committee on Territories, Douglas had the power to further his ambition. He managed to get a number of measures passed individually that, in total, became known as the Compromise of 1850. The admission of California as a free state pleased the North; passage of an act that required legal authorities everywhere in the United States to arrest escaped slaves and return them to their owners gratified the South.

Douglas understood that the Fugitive Slave Act would meet resistance in the North and that it contradicted his party's long-standing principle of local and state control. But he insisted the measure would "never be repealed" and that Northern states would faithfully execute it. When abolitionists in Boston and elsewhere stopped local police from apprehending fugitives, they only increased Douglas's resentment of them as religious zealots whose unlawful behavior could make sectional peace impossible. In 1852, he wrote to the editor of a Democratic organ, "I have determined never to make another speech upon the slavery question; and I will now add the hope that the necessity for it will never exist."[14]

That year, Americans did elect a Democrat to the White House and swelled the party's majorities in both houses of Congress. The Little Giant had sought the nomination for himself, but he spoke loyally and tirelessly for the ticket led by Franklin Pierce, a former New Hampshire senator. Nathaniel Hawthorne penned a fawning campaign biography of Pierce that echoed Douglas's belief that to agitate for an end of slavery would mean "tearing to pieces the constitution, breaking the pledges which it sanctions, and severing into distracted fragments that common country which Providence brought into one nation." The Democratic nominee gained a landslide in the electoral vote, carrying all but four states. At the beginning of 1854, seeking to capitalize on the renewal of Democratic hegemony, Douglas introduced a bill in Congress that ended up playing a big part in destroying it.[15]

His Kansas-Nebraska Act seemed to offer both a clever and, to his mind, democratic solution to the controversy over whether to allow slavery to exist in any of the Western territories that would soon have a large enough population to become states. Refining Cass's idea from the 1848 campaign, Douglas proposed to give voters—who were, of course, all white and male—the absolute power to decide on the matter. Brandishing the slogan "Let the People Rule," he claimed the measure was true to the founding ideals of the republic itself. The Kansas-Nebraska Act, Douglas declared before packed Senate galleries, applied "that great fundamental principle of Democracy and free institutions which lie at the basis of our creed, and gives every political community the right to govern itself in obedience to the Constitution of the country."[16]

But to enact that "principle" meant repealing the Missouri Compromise. That prospect understandably cheered politicians from the slave states who were eager to expand their "peculiar institution" north of the line Congress had drawn in 1820. In fact, a quartet of senators from Dixie who lived and dined together at a boarding house on F Street near the Capitol had persuaded Douglas to include a repeal clause in the legislation. But that move was too much even for many of the Northern Democrats who had damned the Free Soil revolt and had no love for abolitionism. "The whole work was done by the Southern plotters," charged Francis Blair, Old Hickory's close friend and erstwhile editor of the *Washington Globe*, "operating through their automaton whom they pull with a string." Manipulating its diminutive puppet from Illinois, the "slave power" aimed to tighten its grip on the federal state in perpetuity.[17]

After four months of furious debate and with the backing of President Pierce, the Democratic Congress passed the Kansas-Nebraska Act. Its enactment drove a sharp, regional wedge into the majority party—the very opposite of the result Douglas had planned. On the Boston Common, the Little Giant was hung in effigy. In September, a huge audience in Chicago, the metropolis of his own state, greeted Douglas with "an uproar of shouts, groans, and hisses" and an occasional "missile." After a frustrating two hours, Douglas gave up the stage and returned to his hotel, trailed by members of the jeering crowd.[18]

In the midterm election of 1854, enraged voters turned on Democratic nominees in nearly every state and district outside the South. The party lost a remarkable seventy-four seats in the House—and majority control—to a loose coalition of "anti-Nebraska" candidates who had abandoned their old parties in protest at what Douglas and his allies had done. Over 80 percent of the Democrats who had supported his bill were hurled out of office. Soon the party's embrace of "Let the People Rule" would touch off a miniature civil war in the territory of Kansas, where pro- and anti-slavery settlers battled with guns, swords, and fire.

Then in 1856, the Democrats got lucky. James Buchanan, a sixty-five-year-old career politician from Pennsylvania, ran for president against a divided opposition of two new parties that had supplanted the Whigs, who'd torn themselves apart on sectional lines over the issue of slavery and then dissolved. There was the American Party, or "Know-Nothings"—who railed against recent immigrants, particularly Catholic ones—and the Republicans, who vowed to fight for "Free Soil, Free Labor, and Free Men." The party that ran on that slogan would soon gain the votes of the mass of white Northerners who feared the expansion of slavery would pose a deadly threat to the interests of ordinary white farmers and craftsmen. But in 1856, with less than half the popular vote, Buchanan triumphed by taking every slave state and just four free ones, including his own. His party also narrowly regained control of Congress.

The glow of victory faded quickly. In March, just two days after Buchanan's inauguration, the Supreme Court issued a 7–2 decision in the case of *Dred Scott v. Sandford* that shredded any hope that Douglas's idea of "popular sovereignty" might offer a permanent truce in the widening sectional conflict. In his majority opinion, Chief Justice Roger Taney, appointed two decades earlier by his good friend Andrew Jackson, asserted that enslaved people were, in effect, simply items of property. Even free Blacks could never become citizens. Congress could no more prohibit a white citizen from settling in a territory with his slaves than it could bar him from bringing along a horse or a plow. Buchanan, who had secretly lobbied two justices to join Taney's opinion, sternly urged all Americans to "yield obedience" to the high court. In their rush to placate slaveholders, both the chief justice and the president had betrayed their party's vaunted reverence for local rights without a word of explanation or apology.[19]

A number of prominent Democrats had already abandoned the party in protest against the Kansas-Nebraska Act; in 1856, David

Wilmot actually chaired the Republican platform committee. But during Buchanan's administration, the trickle of Northern deserters became a flood. At least fifteen erstwhile Democrats were elected as Republicans to either the Senate or a governorship. Half the members of Abraham Lincoln's first cabinet in 1861 had once been stalwart Jacksonians. Some of these "Democratic Republicans" aimed the same charge at Buchanan they had earlier trained on the Whigs who defended the Bank of the United States: the president was, wrote Francis Blair, "the tool" of a "Black oligarchy"—this time not of financiers but of the "Slave Power." A series of scandals that revealed how administration officials had bribed judges, diverted tax revenues to campaigns, and lined their pockets with public funds also sped the exodus from Buchanan's party.[20]

The *Dred Scott* ruling appeared to be a decisive victory for the South, but Douglas, desperate in his opportunism, greeted it as a confirmation of his own views. He agreed with Taney that the signers of the Declaration of Independence had not meant to include Black people in their sweeping faith that "all men are created equal." After all, "negroes were [then] regarded as an inferior race," a judgment he saw no reason to alter. Moreover, the court's ruling, Douglas insisted, would not stop citizens in a given territory from rejecting slavery. The right to possess human property in any jurisdiction, he argued, was "worthless . . . unless sustained, protected and enforced by appropriate police regulations and local legislation." Douglas was straining to uphold the crumbling status quo he had forged in Congress and to retain the allegiance of Northern voters he feared were drifting away from the Democracy. It was a futile ploy. "If he persuaded himself that the decision and popular sovereignty were not incompatible, . . . he convinced few others," observes his biographer.[21]

As men with passionate and uncompromising convictions increasingly dominated politics both North and South, Douglas had become a national politician without a dependable national base. Republicans decried him as a man who cared for nothing but keeping his party united and his presidential hopes alive, although the price of both was the perpetuation of human bondage. In one of their 1858 debates, Lincoln charged that Douglas "carefully excludes the thought that there is anything wrong with slavery . . . [He] can't logically say that he don't care whether a wrong is voted up or down." Meanwhile, the Illinois senator became something of a pariah among Southern Democrats when he broke with the president who favored allowing the empire of slavery to grow. As a true believer in popular sovereignty, Douglas had condemned Buchanan for recognizing a government in the new state of Kansas that had legalized slavery, despite a preponderance of settlers there who vehemently opposed it. In the Senate, Jefferson Davis of Mississippi and other administration allies got Douglas ousted from the chairmanship of the Committee on Territories. "The people of the Southern States constitute, for all practical purposes, the Democratic Party," Dixie partisans gathering in Charleston, South Carolina, claimed early in 1860. "No constitutional right or principal [sic] which they unite in demanding can be ignored or refused." Many thought that should include repealing the ban on the importation of enslaved human beings from other nations, which Congress had enacted in 1807. As the race for the presidency in 1860 began, Douglas's adversaries inside the party as well as outside it appeared to be as strong and numerous as his friends. He could, however, count on August Belmont's backing and, if he secured the nomination, his financial largesse. But first he had to win the prize.[22]

The bitter differences among Democrats produced a vicious struggle for the nomination that presaged the real combat which began just a year later. In April, the party assembled in Charleston for its quadrennial convention. Buchanan, knowing how unpopular he had become, declined to run again. But the Democratic National Committee was still in the hands of his loyalists; they chose the site knowing its residents were hostile to Douglas. Indeed, the galleries bristled with pro-slavery zealots.

For six hot days, delegates battled over whether the platform would endorse popular sovereignty or the administration's vow to enable slavery in all the territories. Finally, Douglas's position eked out a majority, which triggered a walkout by delegates from seven Dixie states. "We say go your way and we will go ours," declared one enraged Mississippian. But enough Southerners, and a smattering of their Northern supporters, remained in the sweltering hall to keep the Little Giant from gaining the two-thirds margin he needed.

After fifty-seven inconclusive ballots, the delegates adjourned. They agreed to try again in the middle of June, this time in Baltimore, where slavery was legal but not so fiercely defended.[23]

The fresh venue failed to prevent the party from flying apart. Douglas wrote to Belmont about how to keep his enemies from disrupting the gathering in Baltimore. The Illinois senator waxed bizarrely optimistic. He reported "the most cheering news from the South . . . I have just rec'vd [sic] a letter from a delegate in N.C. who says that the State will be all right." But Douglas was no better judge of the stalemate in his party than he had been of the North's embrace of popular sovereignty.[24]

In Baltimore, the Democrats again descended into chaos as the participants accused one another of treachery to the venerable principles of their party. Again, a majority of Southerners stormed out of the hall. This time, however, with Belmont serving as chairman, enough delegates stood their ground to award Douglas the nomination he had hungered for since entering politics in his early twenties. But across town, a pro-Southern rump was passing its own platform and nominating its own candidate for the White House: John C. Breckinridge, the incumbent vice president from Kentucky, who had to be convinced to accept an honor he feared would ensure the election of Abraham Lincoln. Both Democratic conventions, seeking to disprove their sectional loyalties, nominated a candidate for the second spot who came from an opposing side of the Mason-Dixon Line: Herschel Vespasian Johnson, a former governor of Georgia, ran on the ticket with Douglas; the Oregon senator Joseph Lane teamed up with Breckinridge.

Nobody was fooled. As *The New York Times*, then a Republican paper, wrote gleefully, each ticket "will aim specially and primarily to defeat of the other." A new Constitutional Union Party also entered the fray. Its nominees called plaintively for all citizens to pledge their allegiance to the nation and not to their own sections, hoping an abstract patriotism would transcend the bitter conflict over slavery. But they appealed mainly to former Whig voters in such border states as Virginia and Kentucky who refused to take a side in the impending conflict; it was nowhere close to a national majority.[25]

Aware he now had little chance of winning the election, Douglas took a daring step no previous candidate for president had attempted—and that his rivals all shunned. He traveled around the country during most of the summer and fall, giving campaign speeches. Douglas's swing through the nation violated the dictum, rooted in the tradition of republican virtue and the example of George Washington, that "the office should seek the man," not the other way around.

But the Little Giant yearned to show he was sincere in his determination to keep the Union intact; he also hoped to rally local Democrats to his side by greeting them in the flesh. From New England to the Deep South, Douglas lambasted Buchanan for backing the Breckinridge ticket and declared, yet again, that popular sovereignty was "as old as free government itself" and "the principle upon which every battle of the revolution was fought." But the senator's reception in Dixie ranged from tolerant to hostile, and he cut that leg of his journey short. Toward the end of it, a leading daily in Alabama sneered that he "did well to turn his course Northward. There are some portions of the South where the utterance of such sentiments might have led to the hoisting of that coat tail of his that hangs so near to the ground to the limb of a tree, preceded by a short neck with grapevine attachment."[26]

August Belmont paid for a portion of Douglas's tour and sought to raise additional campaign funds from other wealthy men in finance, commerce, and industry—particularly his friends from New York City. "If we could only demonstrate to all these lukewarm and selfish moneybags that we could carry the state," he wrote to Douglas in July, the gold would flow. But fear of losing Southern customers kept their cashboxes closed. The sole "moneybags" who did contribute to Douglas was Samuel Colt of Connecticut, who, portentously, had made his fortune producing firearms. Democrat operatives in key states who pleaded to Belmont for financial assistance were regretfully turned away.[27]

The result in November was predictable—and soon proved catastrophic. Capturing all the free states, Lincoln won a clear majority of the electoral vote. But his name did not even appear on the ballot in most of the South, and he won just under 40 percent of the popular tally overall. Douglas took 30 percent of the votes, but his support was spread too thin. He won a plurality only in Missouri. By the time

Lincoln was inaugurated in March 1861, the legislatures of seven states, all of which Breckinridge carried, had seceded. The slavery question was indeed "out of Congress," as Douglas hoped it would be. But by April it had caused a war in which more than 700,000 men would die from the fields of southern Pennsylvania to the foothills of New Mexico.

The breakup of the Democratic Party made the bloodiest conflict in American history possible, even likely. A party united behind Douglas may have defeated Lincoln; if Breckinridge had been the sole nominee, the Republican would undoubtedly have swept the North by even greater margins than he did. But if the Little Giant had been the only Democrat in the field, he may have picked up enough states in the South to offset losses in the North, much as Buchanan had four years earlier. Although the voter turnout of 81 percent was the highest in American history, it was noticeably lower in Illinois and Indiana, where an untold number of Democrats, perhaps discouraged by the split in their party, did not show up at the polls.

Douglas lived just long enough to see the ultimate ruin of the strategy he believed would keep his party on top and his nation together. A heavy drinker who suffered from chronic rheumatism, he took sick early in May 1861 and died a month later at the age of just forty-eight. In the post-election speeches he had managed to deliver, Douglas called on his fellow Democrats to support Lincoln's new government: "There are only two sides to the question," he told a large Chicago crowd that now cheered him. "There can be no neutrals in this war, only patriots or traitors." But his stubborn adherence to a middle ground between halting slavery and expanding it had stoked the fires that made neutrality utterly impossible.[28]

## Cold to "Fanatics," Warm to Hibernians

Amid their momentous crackup, Northern Democrats shared one impulse that did much to define their party through the Civil War and the early years of Reconstruction. They despised a variety of ideological zealots who they branded as "fanatics." In 1844, that ardent Jacksonian Nathaniel Hawthorne published a brief satirical tale that expressed this worldview with eerie details typical of his short stories. Out on a Western prairie gather a "vast assemblage" of "reformers" who cast an assortment of once-cherished items into a massive bonfire. Into the flames go military medals, barrels of liquor, Bibles, Shakespeare's plays, love letters, and more. All "that nonsense is done away," exults a "rude figure" who scorns a defender of tradition for "lording it over his fellows." As the dismayed narrator watches this "Earth's Holocaust," he reflects that true believers will never achieve the perfect order they seek. Evil resides not in bad ideas but in "the heart . . . wherein existed the original wrong of which the crime and misery of this outward world were merely types." The tale appeared in the pages of *The Democratic Review*, the party's unofficial literary organ.[29]

Abolition was, for Hawthorne and his fellow partisans, the most alarming of all radical causes. To crusade for the equality of the races, Democrats agreed, was to upset the balance of nature as well as the foundation of the republic, which, Douglas maintained in 1858, "was made . . . by white men for the benefit of white men and their posterity forever."[30]

But Democrats believed anti-slavery zealots were merely a symptom of a larger disease infecting the body politic. When Lewis Cass declared, in 1852, that he was "opposed to all the isms of the day," he was referring to the variety of reform enthusiasms that had sprouted in the wake of the Second Great Awakening—the evangelical upsurge that spawned thousands of new Protestant churches while convincing a growing number of Americans that, in their righteousness, they could speed the coming of the Kingdom of God. Temperance, diet and dress reform, women's rights: Democrats viewed each of these causes as species of "fanaticism" or "Puritanism"—advanced by men and women like those in Hawthorne's story whose attempts to perfect the world risked destroying the very order that gave them the freedom to spout their foolish creeds. There was a "madness which fanaticism always arouses in the human heart," declared one Democrat from Massachusetts, a hotbed of reform activism. The only way its adherents could succeed would be by grabbing control of the federal state and vastly enlarging its coercive powers, aims that Democrats had always resisted.[31]

This was an unmistakably conservative worldview, but it was not an elitist one. Democrats caricatured abolitionists and their ilk as officious figures backed by moneyed families who wanted to foist their "isms" on ordinary white people. Some claimed that Republican opponents of slavery who attacked that "domestic institution" might next attempt "to meddle with family arrangements in their own states—to force their . . . creed down the throats of other men." It was not an irrational fear. After all, many of the same people who wanted to liberate the slaves also wanted women to enjoy equal rights in marriage and politics and everywhere else. As Hawthorne suggested in his dystopic tale, those who wanted to destroy one institution that had served Americans well enough in the past probably yearned to burn all of them down.[32]

Ironically, this logic was a main reason why Irish Catholics, themselves beset by ethnic and religious bigotry, became a stalwart base of the Democratic Party. The same "fanatic" reformers who crusaded for abolition and women's rights tended to despise the Hibernian throng who fled the Potato Famine that devastated their island in the 1840s and '50s. The Irish had composed more than a third of the immigrants arriving in the United States since early in the nineteenth century. But those who settled from the mid-1840s on sparked a nativist panic unlike anything the nation had experienced before. They often came malnourished and owning nothing but the clothes they wore; many were illiterate. By 1850, more than 40 percent of all immigrants hailed from that unfortunate land.

Unlike many earlier migrants from Ireland, those of the famine generation were firmly devoted to their church and its clergy. Under British rule, no other institution had rooted itself among the peasants, sympathized with their plight, and given them a reason for pride in an identity that was as much national as spiritual. Hoping to become prosperous farmers, other groups of Europeans tended to disperse to the countryside soon after their ships arrived in urban ports. Germans often settled in cities, too, but most were literate and had mechanical skills that enhanced their market power.

But, despite their agrarian origins, most Irish Catholics who emigrated during the famine years lacked the resources, and perhaps the confidence, to set out on a journey to the hinterlands, where priests were scarce and few parishes yet existed. They quickly found work erecting buildings and bridges, driving goods and people through the cities, and cleaning other people's homes and caring for their children. By 1855, almost nine out of ten unskilled laborers in New York City were Irish immigrants. A small but growing minority owned small businesses, from taverns to construction firms. But to most other white Americans, Irish Catholics seemed an unruly, unwashed mass of people who drank too much, fought too easily, and clung to a faith that was anathema to American ideals of liberty and self-rule.[33]

It was the latter charge, or fear, that fueled the nativist wave that began in the mid-1840s and crested a decade later. Vowing to combat "Papist" dominance, middle- and working-class Protestants joined such organizations as the Order of the Star Spangled Banner and the Order of United Americans, whose very names signified an offensive against the alien peril. In the North, such groups attracted thousands of conservative Whigs searching for a new political home as their own was crumbling. In 1854, the anti-immigrant, anti-Catholic forces came together in a new political body, officially named the American Party. Because members pledged to feign ignorance when asked about the organization, it soon got dubbed the Know-Nothings. The party quickly enrolled a million members in lodges across the country. By 1856, Know-Nothing voters had elected seven governors, eight U.S. senators, and more than a hundred congressmen—and controlled seven state legislatures, all in the North.[34]

For Democrats, the rise of the new party was both a threat and an opportunity. On the one hand, the Know-Nothings appealed to middle-class Protestants in cities from Chicago to Boston who had usually favored the Democracy since Jackson sat in the White House. Their invective against the Irish and their Church clearly struck a chord among Northerners who mistrusted Democrats for catering to the slave power. Evangelical Protestants sought to counter all manner of immoralities they blamed on Catholics in general and the Irish in particular. In Massachusetts, the Know-Nothing legislature passed a bill that imposed a six-month sentence on anyone who sold as little as a single glass of beer and began an investigation of alleged sexual outrages in Catholic convents. In 1854, St. Louis nativists rampaged through a poor Hibernian neighborhood known as Kerry Patch. "There will be a lot of blood spilt before the Irish find out which stall they belong in," vowed one Protestant merchant.[35]

Yet such fervent, well-organized bigotry also left its targets no political alternative but the only party that welcomed them, defended their culture, and was willing to offer them government jobs. Since Jefferson's era, Democrats had always championed religious toleration. Now they turned it to their political advantage. In New Hampshire, Franklin Pierce worked to repeal a religious test for state offices that excluded non-Protestants. As president, he appointed a Catholic from Philadelphia, James Campbell, to run the post office department, from which the lion's share of federal patronage positions flowed. As native-born Protestants shunned urban branches of the Democracy, Irish Catholics began to take their places.

The logic of the rhetorical barrage turned many Irish Democrats into apologists for slavery. If the radical abolitionist and Unitarian divine Theodore Parker felt free to blast Irish Catholics as "a wretched race of people for us to import and breed from in America" who became "vassals of the slaveholders," then why shouldn't a diocesan newspaper counter that anti-slavery fanatics planned "to take off from the Negro his manacles and put them on the hands and feet of Catholics"?[36]

The scorn had a class-conscious edge: the Irish workers who organized early trade unions in Northeastern cities and on the canals feared potential competition from freed slaves. The firebrand Mike Walsh, born in County Cork, became the idol of "shirtless" New York City Democrats in the 1840s by denouncing "the slavery of wages" as well as the "fanatical hypocritical set of imbecile humbugs" who advanced temperance laws. Plebeian voters elected Walsh to the state legislature and then to Congress. By the mid-1850s, the hard-drinking politician who wielded a silver-tipped cane had become as pro-Southern as any Northern man in his party. The condition of Blacks in bondage, Walsh announced, was no worse than that of white factory hands. After all, Blacks had simply inherited a master; the wage-slave was forced "to beg for the privilege" of having one.[37]

Thus, in the crucible of the sectional crisis, Irish Catholics and

Democrats had forged a resilient bond. Through the remainder of the nineteenth century, Republican politicians often surrendered to the impulse to attack a large and visible ethnic group that their own base of rural evangelicals deplored as criminals and saloonkeepers. "The strength of the Democratic party for years," asserted Republican senator John Sherman in 1870, "has been the pest houses of the cities where vice breeds." Predictably, the voters he insulted returned the invective and stayed faithful to the party that, whatever its faults, had kept its faith with them.[38]

## Democrats at War

During any major war, the opposition party faces an excruciating dilemma. If it rallies behind the administration in power, it risks submerging its own identity in the embrace of the nation's cause. But if it criticizes how the government is conducting the war, it will be accused of letting down the troops or, worse, of committing treason. The opponents grow stronger only when the military fights to a stalemate or suffers defeat. But winning the debate might mean losing the war. And losing the Civil War would have been a catastrophic defeat for democracy, by any rational definition of the term.

Democrats understood the quandary the Civil War forced on them, but they could not agree how to respond to it. Some fretted about alienating their former brethren who had deserted to the Confederacy, where, in a nostalgic attempt to emulate the spirit of the early republic, party affiliations were banned. But in the Union Army, it was not uncommon for Democratic-voting officers to lead troops who shared their partisan preference into battle against men who had been Democrats before the war and, if they survived, would return to the party again, with a vengeance, after Robert E. Lee's surrender. Democrats in the loyal states clashed over the basic question of whether to forge a temporary alliance with Lincoln's government or to treat it as a political adversary. The stakes were high for the party—and even higher for the country.

At the onset of the conflict, thanks to the departure of Southerners elected in 1860, Republicans held large majorities in both houses of Congress and governed most of the loyal states, too. Yet Democrats had kept their organizations and their partisan press intact. Most of the men who had been leading figures in the Northern party before the war continued to hold office. They could seek to obstruct the designs of Lincoln and other Republican leaders, while mobilizing for elections to come. America's experiment in self-government might be in peril, but the partisan furies would not keep still.

Nearly all Democratic politicians took one of two positions—which contemporaries labeled simply as favoring either "war" or "peace." The first group, which included August Belmont and most of Stephen Douglas's erstwhile admirers, insisted that defeating the Confederacy was paramount, both to ensure the survival of the Union and to assure voters that the party was true to the cause. Belmont himself recruited and supplied a German-American regiment in the Union Army and traveled across the Atlantic to urge the British and French governments to grant loans to the Union and not to recognize Jefferson Davis's would-be nation. "War" Democrats criticized Lincoln vigorously when he suspended habeas corpus and jailed several of his harshest critics. But they were careful not to advocate stopping the war short of victory.

In contrast, "Peace" Democrats refused to downplay their discontents with the president and his party. "To suspend the Constitution in order to preserve the Government," thundered Ohio representative George Pendleton late in 1861, "would be to stop the current of blood in the veins in order to preserve the life." The faction he helped lead accused Republicans of undermining the founding principles of the nation in a myriad of ways—from initiating conscription to issuing paper money. Faithful, in their minds, to Jacksonian traditions, they viewed the governing party as a band of sectionalist usurpers whose fanaticism had largely brought on the war and whose "tyrannical" rule had to be checked and defeated. One historian of the Peace Democrats writes, "Their rhetoric . . . was quite similar to the language the Patriots used during the American Revolution." But Republicans condemned Pendleton and his allies as "Copperheads," and the poisonous reptilian metaphor has endured.[39]

Few Copperheads actually rooted for the Union to lose. Pendleton consistently voted to appropriate funds the military needed, as did nearly all his fellow Democrats in Congress. But they did argue for an early end to hostilities so that the country might have a chance to return to what they rhapsodized as the political comity of ante-bellum days. In his successful campaign for governor in 1862, New York's Horatio Seymour coined a pithy slogan to express this yearning: "The Union as it was, and the Constitution as it is."[40]

That conservative motto inevitably led to a rejection of every major step the Republican administration and Congress took to transform the South and empower African Americans. Both War and Peace Democrats spoke out strongly against acts that authorized the confiscation of property belonging to Confederate officials, including freeing their slaves. They blasted both the Emancipation Proclamation and the draft initiated in 1863 as blatant violations of the Constitution. And when the army began to sign up Black men that same year, Democratic papers did not restrain their loathing. To arm slaves, fumed the *Chicago Times* (which Stephen Douglas had helped found) was "disgraceful to the civilization of the age, and disgraceful to ourselves. The slaves are practically barbarians. Their instincts are those of savages."[41]

To govern the nation again, Democrats would have to persuade the Peace and War factions to unite, at least during election campaigns. As in the past, this meant engaging in a round of difficult struggles in the individual states where power brokers had different calculations of what positions would benefit their party and their own careers.

Ohio was a bastion of Copperheads. Democrats there seethed at the high profile of financiers and factory owners in Lincoln's party. White workers who feared competition from freed slaves—and burned the homes of Black residents in Toledo and Cincinnati in the summer of 1862—shared their class hostilities. In addition, fervent Jacksonians viewed the 1863 National Banking Act—which reduced the number of banks that could issue currency and regulated those that qualified—as a reversal of Old Hickory's victory over Nicholas Biddle and his genteel ilk. Demographic factors mattered, too: most of the white people who settled in the southern half of the state were either migrants from Dixie (known as "Butternuts") or Catholics from Ireland or Germany for whom the Republicans were just

Know-Nothings by a different name. They applauded Pendleton, the dapper congressman who represented Cincinnati and its environs, and considered his attacks on Lincoln's "tyranny" to be the height of patriotism. They cheered Clement Vallandigham, a congressman from Dayton, who claimed the president's high-handed acts deserved impeachment. Abolition, he charged, would pose a dire threat to the jobs and status of white workers. "The constitution as it is, the Union as it was, and Niggers where they are," declared one of his cruder Dayton disciples.[42]

Less oppositional voices had a following in the state as well. Samuel Cox, who represented the state capital of Columbus, had been a Douglas protégé; like his mentor, he refused to support any notion that the war could be settled short of victory. Cox's convictions and rhetorical skill helped make him his party's candidate for Speaker of the House, a race that, given the Republican majority, he inevitably lost.

However, on the question of slavery, Cox essentially agreed with the Copperheads, although he stated his opinion in more decorous prose. He accused all abolitionists of fraud because a few of the well-born in their ranks had avoided the draft by paying substitutes to serve in their place. Cox added, "Thou shalt not degrade the white race by such intermixtures as emancipation will bring." The biblical language derived from its source: an updated version of the Ten Commandments that Cox released on the eve of Lincoln's signing of the great Proclamation. Even a prominent War Democrat was willing to bestow on racial supremacy the status of holy writ. Like others in his faction, Cox kept his hostility to abolition separate from his allegiance to the Union. In the foreword to a collection of the speeches he gave in Congress during the war, he wrote, "In the perusal of these pages, no one will find any aid, by speech or vote, given to those who raised the standard of revolt." Cox realized his party would never regain power if it were permanently branded as a network of traitors.[43]

In contrast, Vallandigham, the most notorious Peace Democrat, refused to give any quarter to an administration he believed was as much a danger to a free and orderly society as the regime soldiers clad in blue were fighting to destroy. "I am for suppressing all rebellions," he declared during his campaign for re-election in 1862. "There are two—the Secessionist Rebellion South, and the Abolition Rebellion, North and West. I am . . . for putting down both." Vallandigham lost to a Republican war hero, aided by a gerrymandered district, even as many War Democrats were winning theirs. But he did not stop assailing a slew of administration measures, including the draft, as blatant violations of the Constitution.[44]

The Ohio Copperhead's defiance provoked an equally rash reaction from the Union commander in his state. In April 1863, General Ambrose Burnside issued an order clearly directed at Vallandigham: "Treason, expressed or implied, will not be tolerated in this department." When Burnside's target kept up his verbal broadsides, more than a hundred soldiers arrived at his house in the middle of the night, broke down his door, and arrested him. The next day, an angry crowd of Democrats set the offices of Dayton's Republican paper ablaze; Burnside responded by placing the entire county under martial law. Then a military court tried Vallandigham and sentenced him to prison for the duration of the war.[45]

These official acts turned the intemperate politician into something of a martyr to his fellow Democrats. They denounced what seemed a clear violation of both the First Amendment and the right of due process. Across the North, Democratic officeholders and ordinary partisans alike rallied to support the Ohio firebrand. New York governor Horatio Seymour wondered "what kind of government it is for which we are asked to pour out our blood and our treasures." Abraham Lincoln defended the actions of his officers. But he did release the now-famous dissenter from jail—only to order him sent south to Confederate lines, where the ironic gesture was promptly rejected. Vallandigham ended up an exile in Canada, where he dispatched messages predicting that liberty-loving Americans would soon topple the tyrant in the White House.[46]

That fall, the Ohio Democratic convention nominated the arch Copperhead for governor, although pro-war members of the party protested the decision. Vallandigham portrayed himself as the candidate of hardworking men forced to fight "for the few who had money and wanted to use the government to increase and protect it." But stuck in Canada, he could not take to the stump and won less than

40 percent of the vote. Union soldiers rejected his class-conscious appeal and overwhelmingly cast their ballots for his opponent, who ran on a fusionist ticket of Republicans and War Democrats. Even troopers who usually voted Democratic turned against Vallandigham and his supporters, whom one called "demagougs [sic] who are appealing to the lo[w]est prejudice and passion of our people." When he learned the result, Abraham Lincoln wired the victor, "Glory to God in the Highest. Ohio has saved the Nation." The state's voters, in or out of uniform, were not about to hand the most powerful office in their state to a politician who implied that the thousands of young men who had fallen in combat had died for nothing.[47]

In New York, most Democratic leaders refused to echo the Copperhead's bitter message. Vallandigham stood up for his principles, as abhorrent as they were. But back East, his fellow partisans knew that to fall on that disloyal sword would ruin their chances of governing their own state and, given its huge electoral vote, make it almost impossible for Democrats to regain the presidency. In 1860, Lincoln had won a landslide in the state, everywhere outside New York City. Thanks to Catholic voters and the organizational prowess of Tammany Hall, Democrats could still count on sturdy majorities in Gotham. But they would have to avoid the taint of treason if they hoped to triumph again north and west of the Hudson River. So while New York Democrats condemned Lincoln's "radical" acts of emancipating the slaves and initiating a draft, they insisted their motive was to keep the nation united so as to speed an end to the war.

August Belmont was the chief choreographer of this balancing act. He rallied Democratic bankers and merchants in Gotham to support the war effort and advised both Lincoln and his secretary of state how to keep European governments on their side. He denounced the bizarre idea floated by the city's Copperhead mayor, Fernando Wood, to declare New York City an independent republic that could prosper by trading freely with the Confederacy and every other nation. Belmont contributed part of his fortune to turn the *New York World* into the leading voice of pro-war Democrats, befriending its young editor, Manton Marble, and sponsoring his membership in the exclusive Century Club. In 1862, he worked successfully to elect Horatio Seymour governor of New York. Finally, the head of the DNC persuaded George McClellan, whom Lincoln had sacked as commander of the Union Army for lacking aggressiveness, to be his party's next nominee for president.[48]

But New York Democrats were a tempestuous bunch, and Belmont could not control the actions of plebeian city dwellers. The atrocious riot that took place in Manhattan in the middle of the summer of 1863 demonstrated the limits of the influence wielded by the local party's mercantile and political elite. On July 13, federal provost marshals were preparing to hold a draft lottery in the big city; some labor unions called for a general strike of protest, but that peaceful tactic was quickly overwhelmed by men bent on violent, racist fury. Roving mobs of white working-class New Yorkers prevented the lottery from taking place and wreaked vengeance on residents they blamed for a sectional conflict that had, to their dismay, turned into a war to free the slaves.

Rioters targeted the authorities: they stripped and beat up police, smashed and looted the houses of rich Republicans, and set on fire the office of the abolitionist *Tribune*, edited by Horace Greeley. But they committed their most savage acts against the most vulnerable group of New Yorkers. They burned down the Colored Orphan Asylum and murdered more than a hundred Black people, some of whose bodies were mutilated before or after death. Not all the rioters were of Irish stock, but a majority certainly were, and they were not shy about declaring their partisan sympathies. "Whites could avoid humiliation, beating and robbery," according to the historian Timothy Meagher, "by claiming, 'I am a Democratic Catholic.'"[49]

Party leaders responded to the mayhem as one might have expected from cautious, craven politicians: they condemned the violence but sympathized with the perpetrators. On the second day of the riot, Governor Seymour, with the chieftains of Tammany standing alongside him, began a short talk to a crowd of angry white boys and men outside city hall by addressing them as "my friends." He then promised to get the draft lottery postponed or canceled if they "refrained from further riotous acts." That same day, the leading editorial in *The World* bemoaned the killings and damage to property but blasted the draft as unconstitutional. It posed rhetorical questions: "Does any man wonder that poor men refuse to be forced into

a war . . . perverted almost into partisanship. Did the President and
his cabinet imagine that their lawlessness could conquer, or their
folly seduce a free people?" The riot ended only after New York militiamen rushed back from the Battle of Gettysburg to aid the local
police. Their victory against Lee's forces and several subsequent
ones helped Republicans carry most state elections that fall.[50]

The next year's presidential race would test whether Northern
voters shared the Democrats' discontent with Lincoln's policies—
and if the party could heal its internal divisions long enough to give
its nominees a chance to win. In 1862, they had taken thirty-eight
House seats away from the Republicans and, despite the setbacks of
the following year, were sanguine about regaining federal power.

Early in 1863, August Belmont began to groom McClellan to run
for president. The general was young (just thirty-eight) and handsome, and most of his troops had adored him. Of vital importance,
McClellan, despite his firing by Lincoln, was a firm War Democrat
and thus could help defuse Republican charges that his party was
infested with Copperheads. That he had never run for office and was
an indifferent speaker mattered little. McClellan would run on the
image Belmont and his allies designed for him. Thus, *The World* flattered the general with several glowing features, and Belmont convinced War Democrats in Congress that a man who had led brave
soldiers into battle could appeal to voters wary and weary of veteran
politicians like themselves.

Early in 1864, at his mansion on Fifth Avenue, the financier convened the first meeting of the DNC since the war began. Members
decided to hold the party's nominating convention as late as possible that summer to take advantage of what they expected would be
mounting discontent with the unending war and the draft and taxes
imposed by Lincoln and Congress. Belmont predicted that, as president, McClellan would bring about "the salvation of the republic,
the restoration of the Union, and the restoration of the Constitution
and its laws." The general would also return his party to what Democrats believed was their rightful place at the head of the national
state, where they could bind together a populace ripped apart by fanatics both North and South.[51]

But to achieve that goal compelled Belmont and his allies to placate partisan stalwarts who were not about to mute their hatred of Lincoln and all his works. At the 1864 convention—which met in Chicago near the end of August, later than any such gathering before or since—the War Democrats got their presidential nominee but allowed their Peace brethren to choose his running mate and draft the platform. Joining the ticket with McClellan was George Pendleton, the prominent Copperhead congressman from Cincinnati. The platform, just 506 words long, curtly offered "sympathy" to the soldiers and sailors of the Union after detailing a massive, unconstitutional abuse of power by their civilian and military commanders. In its most provocative section, it condemned Lincoln's "four years of failure to restore the Union" and called for an immediate end to the fighting. It also welcomed the slave South to rejoin the Union with, evidently, no hard feelings. The brief document said nothing at all about such economic issues as banking, the tariff, and the rights of workingmen on which the Democracy had once staked its claim to represent a majority of voters.[52]

Political platforms carried great weight in the nineteenth century; parties and their newspapers distributed them widely, and candidates swore, if elected, to implement them. But after Union troops, under the command of William Tecumseh Sherman, captured Atlanta in early September, the 1864 platform was perilous to run on, and McClellan, who knew how much Union soldiers detested it, did not even try. A week after the convention adjourned, he formally accepted the nomination with a letter that effectively repudiated the idea that the bloodshed should cease before the North had won. Peace Democrats railed at his betrayal. Some even demanded a new convention. Breaking with party tradition, a leading Copperhead paper in Ohio dropped McClellan's name from its masthead.

Republicans delighted at the rift while continuing to describe all their adversaries as incipient traitors. *The Chicago Tribune*, the leading pro-Lincoln paper in the Midwest, did not shirk from hurling false charges daubed in anti-Semitism: "Will we have a dishonorable peace, in order to enrich Belmont, the Rothschilds, and the whole tribe of Jews, who have been buying up Confederate bonds, or an honorable peace won by Grant or Sherman at the cannon's mouth?"[53]

Still, Belmont and other leading Democrats thought victory was

possible, even likely. Most Copperheads endorsed the ticket, however grudgingly. And both Peace and War factions believed voters
were tired of the prolonged slaughter and would reward them for
denouncing Lincoln's decision to free millions of Black people who
could move North and endanger the racial and sexual order by mat-
ing with whites. Belmont backed up his own confidence with cash:
he put $4,000 down on McClellan in a bet with a fellow financier,
N. E. Thalmann, and dared other rich Republicans to make similar
wagers.

But the DNC chairman ignored, or refused to account for, signs
that his ticket was doomed. The capture of Atlanta turned Union
victory from a distant hope into an impending reality. The Democrats failed to get courts to rule that soldiers were ineligible to vote
in the field, and Republicans won almost every state election held in
October. At the end of the campaign, Belmont asked McClellan to
embark on a short speaking tour, similar to the long and exhausting
one Douglas had made four years earlier. But the general declined,
perhaps fearful of drawing bad reviews for his oratory. He did reassure the DNC chairman that "all the indications coming within my
personal observation . . . are favorable in the extreme." McClellan
worried only about "the power of the Republicans to develop some
unthought plan of rascality."[54]

Abraham Lincoln needed no dirty tricks to retain the White
House. Aided by the capture of Atlanta and a platform that vowed to
seek unconditional surrender, he took 55 percent of the popular tally
and electoral vote majorities everywhere but in the border states of
Kentucky and Delaware and McClellan's home state of New Jersey.
The Democrats also lost thirty-four seats in the House, wiping out
their gains from 1862.

In retrospect, their showing was not as dismal as it seemed at
the time. Democrats came within a few thousand ballots of taking
New York and Pennsylvania, the two most populous states, and ran
competitively in many others. In races for governor, they averaged
more than 46 percent of the vote. Against a president who was on
the verge of winning a war for the survival of the Union, they had
demonstrated an ability to unite, if not prosper. After the results
came in, Horatio Seymour, who narrowly lost his own bid for reelec-

tion, struck an optimistic note. He was "entirely satisfied with the result . . . It shows that a majority of the people are with us when they act freely."[55]

Yet the free citizens who actually cast ballots that year had effectively voted to end the most egregious form of white supremacy. On January 31, 1865, the House of Representatives passed the Thirteenth Amendment, which abolished slavery; the Senate had approved it nine months before. Just seventeen Democratic congressmen voted in the affirmative. The bloodiest war in U.S. history did not end until April 1865, but the battle to define whom the new republic should serve had already begun.

## Revival Against Reconstruction

For Democrats, the next presidential election became a test of what, if anything, they had learned from their uncomfortable, unprecedented near decade in the minority. On Independence Day 1868, they gathered in Manhattan to choose a presidential ticket and adopt a statement of convictions to guide them through the postwar world. The convention met in Tammany Hall on East Fourteenth Street, where the party's strongest urban contingent, led by the New York boss William Magear Tweed, went about assembling, precinct by precinct, the apparatus that selected and then elected the men who ran the big city and would be essential to winning an Electoral College majority that fall. The building itself testified to the resources the Tammany machine could muster: completed earlier that year, it included "a library, concert room, club room, committee rooms, a restaurant," and a massive gallery large enough to seat 3,500 people. Even the Republican *New York Times* was impressed: "The great hall . . . appeared with the festooned coats-of-arms, the blue satin, fringed with gold, the great chandelier of a pattern of unique beauty, and the draped flags." Huge photos of the party's "heroes, philosophers and martyrs"—from Jefferson to McClellan—lined the walls.[56]

August Belmont had persuaded the members of the DNC to stage the convention in his home city, disappointing those politicians, particularly from the Midwest, who favored a location not associated with high finance and a corrupt urban machine. The chairman signaled his triumph by giving the opening address to the quadrennial gathering. Belmont urged Democrats to wage the fall campaign on a promise to return to their antebellum glory, with Black people deprived of every right save that of no longer being commodities in flesh. He predicted voters would remember that "under successive Democratic administrations," the nation "rose to a prosperity and greatness unsurpassed in the annals of history," including the conquest of Mexico and "our golden empire on the Pacific." He insisted that Americans would reject "the ruthless tyranny" of radical Republicans in Congress who had instituted a "military dictatorship" and "raised into power" a "debased and ignorant race, just emerged from servitude." He abhorred the process of Reconstruction that Congress had wrested from President Andrew Johnson the year before and was convinced a majority of white voters did, too. *The World*, unofficial organ of the New York party, advised platform makers to focus on attacking "an irresponsible oligarchy upheld by a standing army and negro [*sic*] votes."[57]

Yet a sizable number of Democrats, particularly in the Midwest, were not content to wage the 1868 campaign solely on a call to repudiate the efforts by Congress and the military to protect the rights and lives of recently freed women and men. Having turned class resentments to their advantage before and during the war, they now pounced on a new issue that might enable them to do so again. Led by Ohio's George Pendleton, the party's last candidate for vice president, they proposed inflating the money supply to boost the economic prospects of wage earners and small farmers.

Driving their demand was the federal government's decision to contract the currency after the Union victory. In 1866, Hugh McCulloch, secretary of the treasury, had begun to withdraw from circulation the millions of "greenback" dollars issued during the war so that the currency would be based, once again, solely on gold or silver—or specie. But such a "hard money" policy was a boon to bankers, who could charge high interest rates, and to big bondholders, who could demand repayment of loans in specie, which was scarcer, and hence more valuable, than greenbacks. A sharp, if short, recession in 1867 spurred Democrats west of the Alleghenies to call for relief from a cycle of debt—much as the New York Regency, under Van Buren, had demanded back in the 1820s. The newly founded National Labor Union, the first organization that attempted to represent wage earners in every part of the country, threw its support behind the greenback cause as well. Ohio partisans blasted both Eastern financiers and "New England Radical manufacturers" for opposing a remedy they claimed would help ordinary citizens struggling to make a living with their hands as well as their wits.[58]

Here was a splendid way for Democrats to move beyond their losing battle against emancipation and become again the party that had ridden into power with Jackson by denouncing "a conspiracy of the rich." But it was also drenched in irony: Jackson and Van Buren had been firm opponents of paper money, and, during the war, Pendleton and most of his fellow partisans had voted *against* the law creating the greenbacks they now wanted to preserve. But the political stakes were clear. Referring to the Republicans who had led the war against the slave power and were now the party of Black voters everywhere, the leading Democratic newspaper in Ohio candidly explained, "The nigger has been the trump card of the Federalists for the last ten years, and with it they have beaten us in every encounter. But this is a very different question, and one they could not so easily handle. Seize hold, then of this measure . . . and victory will, as sure as the earth revolves, perch upon our banners."[59]

Pendleton and his supporters planned to turn the greenback issue into the lever that would lift the former Copperhead from Cincinnati to the nomination and place him in the White House. As the convention was gaveled to order inside the big hall on Fourteenth Street, the politician known as "Gentleman George" because of his well-groomed looks and suave manner appeared to have nearly a majority of delegates in his pocket.

But the Ohioan and his soft-money idea posed a direct challenge to the incomes and beliefs of Belmont and other wealthy Eastern Democrats, and they moved deftly to counter both the man and his plan. First, they defeated an effort by Midwestern delegates to repeal the two-thirds rule. Then they cajoled Horatio Seymour into running for the nomination, although he had recently confessed, with apparent sincerity, that the presidency was "a place far above his merits and beyond his aspirations." Because, as wartime governor of New York, Seymour had opposed the draft and warmly defended Vallandigham's right to speak, he was acceptable to erstwhile Peace Democrats. On the twenty-second ballot, Ohio delegates, with Pendleton's grudging approval, shifted all their votes to Seymour, and the deed was done. They did, however, force onto the platform an unmistakable demand for softer money, stated in a ringingly moral phrase: "One currency for the government and the people, the laborer and the office-holder, the pensioner and the soldier, the producer and the bond-holder."[60]

The dispute over the greenback plank proved to be the opening shot in a conflict about economic winners and losers that would roil the party repeatedly during the rest of the nineteenth century and beyond. But, aside from distributing a campaign poster showing a farmer and a craftsman at work, Democrats played down class identities that fall. Running against Ulysses S. Grant, they posed instead as the defenders of a white America under siege by Republicans and their dark-skinned lackeys. Party journals in every region sounded the alarm against racial "amalgamation" and what one Louisville paper called "the monstrous . . . negro equality doctrine." In the Deep South, bands of Democrats intimidated Black voters, whom Congress had enfranchised the year before. One terror group in Louisiana dubbed itself the Seymour Knights; the nominee himself blamed the opposition party for stirring up the violence. The appalling tactic worked, to a degree. In Georgia, Grant received not a single vote in eleven counties where most residents were Black. The Democrats carried that state and Louisiana, too.[61]

It was far from enough to steal the entire election. In the most competitive states that lay in the East and Midwest, turnout was close to 90 percent, and Republicans took them all, save Seymour's New York—which his party had not carried since 1852. Still, having gained more than 47 percent of the vote against the general who had saved the Union, Democrats could now believe the politics of war were safely behind them. They also gained twenty-four seats in the House of Representatives, a rare occurrence for a losing party in a presidential election. A majority of white men probably voted Democratic that fall. It was certainly something to build on.

Planning for that brighter future, party leaders in the North began to move away from the candid appeal to racism and resistance to the federal authority on which they had waged the 1868 campaign. The next year, every Democrat in Congress voted against the Fifteenth Amendment, which mandated that the right to vote could not be "denied or abridged" on the basis of race or "previous condition of servitude." In 1866, no Democrat in either house had backed the Fourteenth Amendment, which gave anyone born in the United States the rights of citizenship and "equal protection" of its laws. But after the Fifteenth Amendment passed, most Democrats accepted the result and began to adopt a gentler tone toward the Reconstruction process they continued to loathe. "Let there be no dissension about minor matters, no time lost in the discussion of dead issues," congressional Democrats told voters several months before the midterm election.

After picking up thirty-one House seats in 1870, they made this "New Departure" more explicit. The Reconstruction amendments were, declared one prominent Ohio Democrat, "the natural and legitimate results of the war . . . a settlement in fact of all the issues of the war." That Democrat was Clement Vallandigham, which suggests how much the party's electoral calculations had changed. The notorious former Copperhead still burned to reverse the federal "usurpation" of states' rights and to reestablish white supremacy throughout the land. But he and his fellow Northern Democrats knew they would not succeed if they kept rerunning their wartime campaigns. In 1871, August Belmont wrote confidently to the party's gubernatorial nominee in Ohio, "The game of charging us with disloyalty and Copperheadism is played out."[62]

That did not prevent Democratic politicians in the South from playing a duplicitous game. Officially, they acquiesced to Black suffrage and began lambasting Republicans for raising taxes to pay for governments, both state and federal, that were rife with corruption. At the same time, they made no protest when the Ku Klux Klan and other vigilante groups filled with former Confederate soldiers attacked African American voters and the officeholders, Black and white, they had elected. As Republicans increasingly feared to campaign and clashed about how to respond, Democrats, some of whom belonged to the KKK, began taking control in county after county and state after state. By 1872, empowered by acts of Congress, the army had suppressed the Klan. But the political damage had been done and would endure. Democrats gradually returned to dominance in Dixie with the invaluable assistance of armed men who made truly democratic elections impossible.

For the next presidential contest, Democrats effectively rewarded their Southern wing with a gift soaked in irony. They gave their nomination to Horace Greeley—the former abolitionist and long-time editor of the *New-York Tribune*, which had stood by Lincoln's government throughout the Civil War. But in 1872, the journalist whose snowy neck-hair beard resembled the mane of an elderly lion abandoned the Republican Party to protest multiple scandals that engulfed members of Grant's cabinet. Greeley helped form a new organization, the Liberal Republicans, which duly nominated him to challenge the incumbent. Southern Democrats warmed to Greeley because he vowed to stop "interfering" in the politics of their region. By dividing the majority party, he might actually defeat the man who had vanquished the Confederacy.

But Southerners failed to persuade many of their fellow partisans in the North who could never forgive Greeley's past "fanaticism" and fierce attacks on their principles and patriotism. After the Democratic convention endorsed Greeley, a disgruntled activist from Wisconsin compared his party "to a good shepherd dog, which receives the lash from his master and curls down at his feet and after the whipping licks the hand that administered the blows." August Belmont grudgingly declared his support for Greeley, although two decades before, the editor had slurred him as a Jew with "dual allegiances" for trying to buy the presidency for Franklin Pierce with the Rothschilds' lucre. But the banker also shocked the convention by resigning as chairman of the DNC; he then declined to campaign for his party's ticket that fall. Belmont, a veteran strategist, could guess what was coming. Greeley won less than 44 percent of the popular vote, the worst showing by a Democratic nominee since the debacle of 1860. As if in penance, the political chameleon dropped dead less than a month after the election.[63]

Democrats finally recaptured a share of federal power by taking advantage of the type of event that has always buoyed the opposition party in America: economic catastrophe. One Friday in mid-September 1873, Jay Cooke & Company, a major railroad investment firm, declared bankruptcy, setting off the greatest financial collapse to that point in the nation's history. The following Monday, to avoid its own collapse, the New York Stock Exchange shut down for the first time in *its* history. Soon, dozens of railroads, the pivotal industry in Gilded Age America, defaulted on their debts, causing a noxious ripple of business failures all over the land. Farm prices plummeted, and thousands of unemployed wage earners trudged through the cities in search of a handout. Major strikes by coal miners and railroad workers further shook the confidence of businessmen and consumers. The Grant administration was no more prepared than its predecessors to take steps to alleviate the suffering or calm the anxieties of its working-class citizens. According to the dogma of economic liberalism adhered to by both major parties, depressions were cleansing events that exposed inefficient or immoral operators. Capitalism would surely rebound; it always had.

In the campaign of 1874, that conventional wisdom did not stop Democrats from casting their opponents as a band of heartless, corrupt, and inept administrators doing the bidding of plutocrats on Wall Street. Many in the South and West called on Congress to print more money and regulate the railroads—a tentative, if meaningful, step away from the laissez-faire gospel the party had preached since its founding. Grant's veto of a bill to print more greenbacks played into their hands. It proved, according to the Democratic organ in Cincinnati, that the president was the tool of "a privileged class located mainly at one little portion of the Union."[64]

Democrats also assailed the continuing occupation of the South. But many Northern Republicans had grown frustrated with the costs of Reconstruction too and were ready to leave Black people to the mercies of their former masters. So Democrats aimed most of their fire at the failure of Grant and his party to nudge the economy back to health.

It was a wildly successful strategy, if a rather obvious one. That fall, for the first time, every congressional election was held on the same day in November, which tended to diminish the import of local issues. Voters swept the Democracy into power in twenty-three of the thirty-five states, losing only in their rivals' citadels of northern New England and the Upper Midwest, where evangelical Protestants predominated. Democrats stormed into nearly a two-thirds majority in the House of Representatives, taking close to a hundred seats away from the Republicans. They also gained eight Senate seats, narrowing their deficit substantially in the upper chamber. "Republican Party Struck by Lightening [sic]," headlined a Buffalo paper. "It is but the first battle in a long campaign which has just been won," editorialized the *New York World*, adding, "We have yet to fight and win its Waterloo."[65]

The party that a decade before had been shunned by many Americans as a haven for traitors was now poised to regain the White House and, with it, to reclaim its status as the majority party. Democrats governed fast-growing cities from New York to St. Louis, as well as states across the East and Midwest. They still enjoyed the loyalty of Catholic and most immigrant voters and could count on overwhelming support from white Southerners. A Nashville paper crowed, "The whole scheme of Reconstruction stands before the country today a naked, confessed, stupendous failure." Redemption for defenders of the white republic seemed at hand, made possible by the unity of Democrats, the bad luck of their adversaries, and a modest revival of moral capitalism—for whites only. Old Hickory and Old Kinderhook would have been pleased.[66]

# 3

## BOSSES NORTH AND SOUTH,
## 1874–1894

*Try to drive Tammany Hall out of this community? Why,*
*you might as well try to drive out the government.*
—JOHN KELLY, DEMOCRATIC BOSS OF NEW YORK CITY, 1877[1]

*Existing conditions more vitally affect the workingman than*
*the capitalist, because the latter can protect himself, while*
*the former is rendered powerless.*
—*THE TAMMANY TIMES*, 1893[2]

*Can we afford to leave [South Carolina] . . . in the*
*hands of those who, wedded to ante-bellum ideas, but possessing*
*little of ante-bellum patriotism and honor, are running it*
*in the interest of a few families and for the benefit of a*
*selfish ring of politicians?*
—"THE SHELL MANIFESTO," GHOST-WRITTEN BY BENJAMIN
TILLMAN, 1890[3]

*When the Democrats of the New South mouthed phrases*
*about real democracy, they were lying.*
—EDWARD L. AYERS, HISTORIAN[4]

It is fitting that journalists and self-styled reformers routinely began
to describe local and state political parties as "machines" run by
"bosses" only in the final three decades of the nineteenth century.
During the Gilded Age (the name lifted from an 1873 novel coauthored by Mark Twain), Americans transformed a society of farms

and villages into an industrial dynamo that generated the rapid growth of cities and factory towns all over the nation. For the first time, earning an hourly wage by toiling for a single boss became a common experience. An increasing number of those jobs required workers to build, fix, or tend a powerful, efficient machine or keep up with the rapid pace it set. Without the countervailing power of either strong unions or a regulatory state, industrial bosses usually took more care to maintain their equipment than to protect the health and boost the living standards of their employees.

The writers and activists who applied these machine metaphors to organizations whose business was to win votes and run governments seldom did so approvingly. They longed for officeholders whose sole motivation would be to serve the public good, not to grab wealth and treat voters as cogs in their apparatus of power. Still, the ubiquity of such negative terms conveyed a certain respect for the ways in which professional politicians had been able to create institutions that dominated public life in some of the nation's largest cities from New York to California—and in certain Southern states without whose votes the Democrats could never hope to win a national election. As long as "the educated and honest people . . . show a curious incapacity for fulfilling their public duties," scolded a young patrician in 1886, machine politicians who "are able to become perfectly familiar with all its workings" would remain in charge. In writing those words, Theodore Roosevelt announced his determination to repudiate the apathy that afflicted his upper-class peers.[5]

Bosses and machines thrived in both major parties during the Gilded Age, but Democrats needed them more than did their rivals, and they acted accordingly. To take the presidency and have a hope of controlling Congress, they had to carry some big states in the North as well as hold the Solid South. While Democrats governed most large cities in the Northeast and Midwest, rural voters in those regions still preferred the party that had "won" the Civil War. Donations from wealthy industrialists like Andrew Carnegie, John D. Rockefeller, and Gustavus Swift flowed almost exclusively to Republicans, compelling their opponents to find other sources to fuel their campaigns—while praising themselves for being the party of the ordinary white man instead of nefarious "special interests."

Despite such disadvantages, Democrats managed to hold a share of national power for two decades after their sweeping victory in the midterm contest of 1874. They controlled the House of Representatives for all but four years in that span but the Senate for *only* four. Their presidential nominees took a plurality of the popular vote in every election save that of 1880 and carried nearly all the largest cities. Yet because the United States was still a rural nation, Democrats twice suffered narrow losses in the Electoral College.

The absence of a majority party turned American politics into a nastier and more explicitly partisan business than ever before. When they deemed it necessary, both parties engaged in such venal tactics as vote buying, ballot stuffing, and even closing down precincts that favored their rivals. Secret ballots were not introduced until the 1890s and took a decade or more to be adopted in many places. But only the Democrats gained power by terrorizing one race of people before enacting new state constitutions in the 1890s that disenfranchised most African Americans altogether. Republican attempts to institute federal oversight of congressional elections failed to overcome Southern filibusters and divisions within the GOP itself. Out West, Democratic stalwarts and labor unionists campaigned to exclude Chinese immigrants from the land, a cause that triumphed in part when Congress excluded laborers from the declining Asian empire in 1882.[6]

Republicans did unite behind a nonviolent way to decisively tilt both the Senate and Electoral College their way. From the 1860s until the end of the century, Congresses they controlled established ten new states in the sparsely populated trans-Mississippi West. Six were admitted to the union in a rush from the fall of 1889 to the summer of 1890. Naturally, all these states began as GOP strongholds. For years, many had fewer residents than the nation's average congressional district.[7]

Still, Democratic bosses and their machines kept the party competitive in national elections throughout the last quarter of the nineteenth century—when they helped produce the highest turnouts of eligible voters in U.S. history. There was a stark regional difference in the methods bosses employed to produce majorities: in the former Confederacy, party chieftains used illegal and legal means to prevent most Black men from exercising the franchise. In Northern cities, their brethren worked just as hard to persuade adult male residents to vote, including countless European immigrants they rushed to naturalize. Facing harsh discrimination in work and housing, most of these newcomers welcomed the Democrats' advances—just as Irish Catholics had before the Civil War. In its strongholds, the Gilded Age party thus represented an often cynical blend of racial supremacy and class and ethnic uplift.

Both breeds of machine men did have one impulse in common: they promised and, in quite limited ways, delivered benefits to millions of white small farmers and wage earners, awash alike in the currents of an economic sea change that threatened to pull them under. In both North and South, bosses had to confront social movements from the left—labor in one region, populism in the other—that set forth a more thoroughgoing vision of moral capitalism, one that promised economic security and political power to that same plebeian majority. To defeat or co-opt those challengers, party leaders began to move away, in deed if not in rhetoric, from the Jacksonian doctrine that the government that worked best for ordinary men was a government that governed least. They articulated the vision of a moral economy even as, like Old Hickory, many acted to repress or exclude working people of different races whose plight was worse than theirs.

## How the Tiger Roared

If Tammany Hall conjures up any images today, they are likely to be the cartoons Thomas Nast drew back in the early 1870s that depicted the Democratic boss William Tweed and several of his partners in crime, whose names are familiar only to historians of Gotham. Tweed with a bulging moneybag in place of a head, Tweed pressing his giant thumb down on the helpless metropolis, Tweed as a vulture grown obese on the flesh of the city treasury: such scorching illustrations Nast made for *Harper's Weekly* boosted the prosecution's case against the sleazy Manhattan Democrat and his "Ring." They remain, 150 years later, among the most devastating portrayals of urban corruption ever created.

But absent historical context, images can deceive. Compared to the Tammany chieftains who ran the local party and much of the city government in the 1840s and '50s, Tweed's rule was actually rather brief: he and his allies consolidated their power in New York only in 1868, when they hosted the Democratic Convention in Tammany's ornate headquarters near Union Square. They lost it entirely less than four years later, after the boss was arrested and then sacked from his post as leader of the Hall.

Even during his short heyday, Tweed never lacked for potent challengers from within his own party. As the former chairmaker amassed a fortune of more than $2 million (the equivalent of almost $40 million today) in bogus legal fees and kickbacks from contractors, he was breeding the hostility of such rich and well-connected New York Democrats as August Belmont and Samuel Tilden, a distinguished attorney and chairman of the state party. Their faction was dubbed the Swallowtails, after the long dress coats worn by men of their class. *The New York World*, still edited by Belmont's protégé Manton Marble, routinely fumed about the Tweed Ring's "faithless and inefficient discharge of public duties . . . their extravagant expenditures of the public moneys."[8]

So when Tweed stumbled, his intraparty adversaries were ready and able to pounce. Tilden gathered solid evidence of the boss's venality, while he and his allies backed Democrats for office who represented what the state chairman called "a union of honest men against a combination of plunderers." In 1873, Tweed was packed off to the city jail, where, following an escape to Europe and recapture, he died five years later. Nast's deathless cartoons, the work of an ardent Republican, thus helped the party he loathed rid itself of a fleshy evildoer who made every Democrat look bad.[9]

Tweed's downfall gave those who replaced him at the helm of the local Democracy a chance not just to redeem the machine but to reinvent it. Tammany Hall did so quite effectively under two bosses whose organizational and political skills far exceeded those of their disgraced predecessor. First came "Honest" John Kelly, a devout Irish Catholic, who reigned as leader of the New York Democracy from 1872 until a year before his death in 1886. Kelly bequeathed his post to Richard Croker, whose Irish Protestant parents had brought him across the ocean as a toddler during the Great Famine. Croker presided over a larger and more inclusive party that seldom lost a local election for the rest of the century. Despite Kelly's moniker, neither he nor Croker were shy about taking advantage of the financial opportunities that came their way. Each accumulated a fortune primarily through "honest graft"—the term coined by a veteran Tammany lieutenant to describe speculation in real estate based on inside tips from city hall insiders about where parks and other municipal projects would be built.[10]

But neither Kelly nor Croker let the pursuit of wealth hamper their ability to control a metropolis critical to their party's national ambitions. The Civil War had changed many things in American politics. But New York remained the largest swing state, and any presidential hopeful who could carry its electoral votes (about 10 percent of the total) was still likely to be elected. That was a major reason why a resident of the big city chaired the Democratic National Committee until late in the 1870s. The two Gilded Age bosses turned the Tammany tiger, an image Nast had concocted to attack the machine's ruthlessness, into a symbol of self-confidence and authority. It kept roaring as a powerful institution until the 1930s, long enough to become a model for successful machines in San Francisco, Chicago, Albany, and Pittsburgh—and a metaphor of rule by urban bosses everywhere.[11]

John Kelly was the epitome of a self-made entrepreneur who rose to the top of what was one of industrializing America's most competitive enterprises. He devoted himself to the political game only after gaining respect and a large following in one of Manhattan's toughest neighborhoods, the Fourteenth Ward on the Lower East Side. Kelly was born in 1822 to impoverished immigrants from County Tyrone, in the north of Ireland. His father, who owned a small grocery store, died when Kelly was just eight years old, and the boy embarked on a series of jobs that enmeshed him in the complex, often violent world of the plebeian city. Kelly worked by turns as a paper boy, an office boy, and an apprentice stonecutter, before plying the latter craft at his own shop. In his spare time, he battled blazes with a volunteer fire company, organized a target-shooting club, and fought other young men in amateur bouts and street battles against rival neighborhood gangs. At six feet tall and two hundred pounds, he intimidated most opponents before they could take a swing at him. "He sought no quarrels but retreated from none," recalled *The New York Times*.[12]

But command of a street gang hardly prepared one to steer a political party. When he reached adulthood, Kelly distanced himself from his thuggish youth. He read Shakespeare and took leading roles in several nonprofessional stagings of the Bard's plays. He trained himself to be a smooth speaker, if not a memorable one. A faithful Catholic, Kelly regularly attended Mass at St. Patrick's Basilica, on the Lower East Side. By the time he turned thirty, the formidable young man, who, with his trim beard, resembled a square-headed Ulysses S. Grant, had gained considerable clout in the Fourteenth Ward.[13]

Kelly brought the same pugnacious ambition to the citywide partisan fray. He joined Tammany Hall in the winter of 1853 and, just nine months later, was elected alderman from his ward in a landslide. The following year, impatient to rise, Kelly ran for Congress against a flamboyant incumbent from his own party: Mike Walsh, notorious for blasting wage slavery and claiming that Blacks in the South had an easier life than his white working-class constituents. In a four-way race, Kelly scratched out victory by a mere eighteen votes.

Walsh charged that his young rival had stolen just enough ballots to win. Kelly quickly parried the incumbent's blow with a devastating counterpunch. It turned out, he told the press, that Walsh, who had emigrated from Ireland as a child, had never bothered to become an American citizen. When the Thirty-fourth Congress convened late the following year with a sizable contingent of Know-Nothings in the chamber, John Kelly was its sole Catholic member. He denounced the bigoted statements that some of his new colleagues hurled at his Church but took no active part in the crisis over slavery that was cleaving the nation in two.

By 1858, Kelly was back in New York, resuming his climb to the top of the local party as well as helping himself to a modest fortune. As the sheriff of New York County, a post Kelly won twice, he was entitled to pocket all fees collected for services rendered. These ranged from moving criminals from one jail to another to empaneling jurors, at about thirty cents a head. Once Kelly charged the county almost $1,000 to carry out a hanging. The sheriff also took

care neither to incur Boss Tweed's enmity nor to become dependent
on his favors. In 1872, with a reputation for fair dealing that was
not entirely deserved, Honest John was a logical choice to succeed
the corpulent felon-in-waiting. When he moved into his big office
inside Tammany's massive headquarters, Kelly enjoyed the support
of the Swallowtails and other local businessmen who hoped to profit
from an efficient and relatively uncorrupt partisan body. An effective
machine was also a coalition. As one historian reflects, "A successful
boss had to show himself a pretty honest broker, trusted to give every
important interest a hearing."[14]

The new boss quickly put together an organization designed
to accomplish that end. He named a leader for each of the city's
twenty-four assembly districts. These men became miniature bosses
within their own bailiwicks: they hired "captains and sub-captains"
to attend to the needs of specific wards and precincts. As motivation, Kelly based the allotment of patronage jobs on the number of
votes each district tallied for the machine's nominees. He and his
aides also assumed the power to decide who received these plum
appointments—a switch from the previous system, in which elected
officials had that authority. When Tammany ran the city, it had more
than fifteen thousand jobs to dispense. For the first time in the Hall's
history, the boss was thus truly a boss; every alderman, sheriff, or
assemblyman who owed his victory to Tammany essentially worked
for him.[15]

To be successful, a district leader had to devote his life to his
work. A Tammany man could run for city or state office, but the
fate of his career depended on how well he served the machine. To
a degree, this also meant serving the needs of the inhabitants of his
district. At the turn of the century, the longtime chairman of the Fifteenth Assembly District, graced with the patriotic name of George
Washington Plunkitt, gave a series of candid interviews to William
L. Riordon, a journalist for the *New York Post*, who turned them into
a book. Plunkitt, a second-generation Irishman first appointed to his
post by Boss Kelly, freely and often wittily shared his opinions about
the virtues of partisanship and the naïveté of upper-class reformers,
whom he dubbed "mornin' glories" because they "withered up in a
short time, while the regular machines went on flourishin' forever,

like fine old oaks." Most famously or infamously, Plunkitt also defended the fortune he had made by practicing "honest graft."[16]

But the most revealing feature of Riordon's book was an appendix that detailed a typical day in the district boss's "strenuous life." It began at two in the morning when Plunkitt was awakened to post bail for a saloonkeeper arrested for not paying his excise tax and ended near midnight at a Jewish wedding reception. Plunkitt spent the intervening hours helping victims of a fire at a tenement house, fixing problems of constituents at their workplaces or finding them jobs, convening a meeting of his district captains to identify every likely voter, and attending a church fair where he "kissed the little ones, flattered their mothers and took their fathers out for something down at the corner." Urban reformers justly castigated Plunkitt and his men for enriching themselves through corrupt means available only to top Tammany officials. The machine, as an Irish American paper put it, was a coalition of "the ten thousand dollar politicians" and "the ninety cents laborers." But in return for Plunkitt's assistance and good cheer, all he asked of the male citizens of the Fifteenth District was that they turn up on Election Day to vote for Tammany's nominees.[17]

Under Kelly's leadership, the men of the machine worked in a variety of ways to establish their reputation as a dependable friend to working-class New Yorkers. Plunkitt's daily rounds were essential but hardly sufficient to that end. Tammany paid loyalists to canvass precincts and work at polling stations for $7.50 a day—triple the wage earned by a journeyman carpenter. Rhetorical sympathy for their plight flowed routinely, too. Kelly established two newspapers—the *Star* and the *Evening Express*—that could be counted on to bash any foe of Tammany as "the friend of monopolists and the corporations . . . in their aggression on the public interests and the rights and welfare of the people." In the pit of the depression of the mid-1870s, Kelly urged wealthy New Yorkers to "relieve the laboring classes of this city" from hunger and cold, hinting they should create jobs for the unemployed. But the boss rebuffed demands by unions and radicals that the city institute a public works program, lest higher taxes alienate rich Democrats like August Belmont.[18]

Tammany also engaged in numerous acts of ethnic and religious solidarity. Irish immigrants and their children comprised some 40 percent of the city's population during the Gilded Age; most belonged to the Catholic Church. They knew not only that John Kelly was one of them but also that a large number of his district leaders, like Plunkitt, were, too. In 1880, Tammany's first Irish boss also worked to elect New York's first Irish (and first Catholic) mayor—the wealthy shipowner William R. Grace. At the same time, Kelly kept faith with his plebeian brethren by warmly endorsing the Irish Land League, a large and growing movement on both sides of the Atlantic that campaigned to stop evictions of tenant farmers and cursed the rich families that owned most plots of land in the British colony. Tammany also helped fund Church orphanages and mental asylums. In November 1876, the boss cemented his emotional ties to Hibernian Catholics as well as to many of their co-religionists when he married Anna Teresa Mullen, niece of John McCloskey, the Archbishop of New York. The year before, the pope had named McCloskey the first American cardinal. The prelate performed the wedding himself, resplendent in a deep red cassock, bejeweled miter, and a huge gold cross.[19]

But class and ethno-religious empathy did not guarantee a string of election victories or ward off competitors in the New York Democracy. By the time of his marriage, Kelly had severed his ties with Samuel Tilden and most of his Swallowtail compatriots; among the prominent ones, just August Belmont remained on Tammany's side. After Tilden had been elected governor in 1874, he rebuffed Kelly's choice for a key state patronage job and then refused to campaign for his picks in the next municipal election. The governor also encouraged his Manhattan allies to organize a new organization, the Irving Hall Democracy, to run against Tammany's nominees. When Kelly's men won most city offices anyway, the boss resolved to thwart Tilden's run for the presidential nomination. That effort failed, too.

Boss Kelly sensibly put his anger aside long enough to urge New Yorkers to rally to Tilden's cause. The ongoing depression, coupled with the waning of white support for protecting Black rights in the South, gave Democrats a good chance of capturing the White House for the first time since James Buchanan had sullied their name. If Tammany did not turn out the vote for Tilden, the party faithful elsewhere would not be forgiving. So five days before the election, Kelly, who always loved a parade, put on one of the largest in the city's history. A procession of some forty thousand men, wearing new tricolor uniforms, marched with torchlights from Washington Square to Tammany's garish hall a mile away; more than two hundred thousand New Yorkers came out to watch them, as well as to gaze at floats carrying ships and steam engines and to listen to dozens of brass bands.[20]

Tilden carried New York by a healthy thirty-two thousand votes; Gotham supplied enough ballots to offset the Republican margin in rural areas upstate. The Democrat won a slim majority of the popular vote in the nation as well. But he lost the presidency to Rutherford B. Hayes, after a famously long and bitter dispute over which candidate had won the electoral votes of three states in the Deep South that went unresolved until two days before the inauguration. But John Kelly had done his partisan duty. He could also take satisfaction in the results he really cared about: Tammany won control of all three branches of the city government, and Democrats allied with the Hall took many state offices, too.

Then, just weeks after the 1876 results came in, the machine faced a challenge that struck at the heart of its working-class base. As governor, Samuel Tilden had appointed a dozen influential members of the city's wellborn elite from both major parties to a special commission charged with coming up with ideas about how to break the grip of urban corruption. Its report, issued in the late winter of 1877, argued that universal male suffrage was at the root of the problem. If "the excesses of democracy" could "be corrected," then responsible, disinterested men would be able to keep spending low and budgets balanced. The commission proposed an amendment to the state constitution that would create a special board to handle the financial affairs of every town and city in New York State. In local elections, only men who owned property worth at least $500 or who rented high-priced homes would be eligible to elect these new guardians of each resident's economic future. The law would have excluded as many as two-thirds of the male adults in Manhattan. The Republican majority in the state legislature passed the amendment, cheered on by most businessmen and upper-class foes of Tammany Hall.

Although he no longer sat in the governor's chair, Tilden backed it as a way to dethrone the machine. But it could only become law if the next legislature enacted it again.[21]

This gave Kelly and his lieutenants a grand opportunity to do what they did best: motivate their base to turn out and vote. The *Evening Express* shouted that "Men, Not Money" should decide how cities should be governed. Tammany orators damned the "oligarchy of wealth" that had drafted the amendment, while the local Hibernian press reminded readers that, fifty years before, the British Empire had stripped the franchise from Irish peasants too poor to meet a property requirement. Unionists who had scorned Tammany for cozying up to the Swallowtails now sounded the same alarm: "The elective franchise," vowed labor editor and veteran Democrat George McNeill, "is a privilege and power that must be retained by the wage labor class even at the cost of bloody revolution."[22]

A rush to the barricades with arms in hand would not be necessary. In the election of 1877, Tammany nominees won all but five of the city's twenty-one seats in the state assembly; Kelly derided the elite reformers who thought they could "drive Tammany Hall out of this community." When the legislature, still run by Republicans, convened in Albany the next spring, it declined to re-pass the controversial amendment. Under Kelly, the machine often had to run against candidates from smaller and newer Democratic groups like those of Irving Hall, and Tammany lost its share of battles. But no one would dare try to rip the vote away from its constituents again.[23]

By the time Honest John died on June 1, 1886, after a long illness, leadership of Tammany had already begun to pass to a younger generation of men whose careers bore few, if any, scars from the party's travails in the Civil War era. First among them was Richard Croker—a Kelly protégé who combined an aggressive nature and a love of riches with a strategic cunning that exceeded that of his mentor.

Croker also made his way upward with his fists as well as his mind. He'd spent his youth in an East Side neighborhood where gangs ruled the streets. After dropping out of school at thirteen, he got a job as a railroad machinist. But it was as a chief enforcer in the Fourth Avenue Tunnel Gang that he came to the notice of Tammany Hall leaders. At a picnic ground favored by the Hall, Croker beat up one of the East Side's most renowned fighters. Machine men encouraged the young tough and the other members of his crew to become "repeaters"—to cast multiple ballots not just in Manhattan but in Brooklyn and Philadelphia, too. They rewarded Croker for services rendered by getting him elected to a seat on the board of aldermen at the age of twenty-five and then to the office of coroner by his thirtieth birthday. A year later, Kelly helped him win acquittal on a dubious charge of being an accomplice to the murder of a Tammany rival. Clearly, Honest John was grooming Croker—whom one critic described, against type, as a "mild-mannered, soft-voiced, green-eyed chunk of a man"—to keep the machine humming for years to come.[24]

In 1886, the very year Croker took over as boss, Tammany faced an even more serious threat to its hold on the city's white wage-earning voters. This time, the challenge emerged from within the working class itself. A few years earlier, unhappy with the Democrats' reluctance to antagonize local employers, a group of union officials had formed the United Labor Party. Their initial forays into independent politics yielded less than 10 percent of the vote. But to improve its prospects, the ULP sponsored its own newspaper and organized a network of neighborhood clubs where its supporters could discuss how to break the manacles of wage slavery or, at least, mitigate their pain.

In 1886, the ULP convinced Henry George, one of the most famous men in America, to run for mayor on its ticket. George, a former Democrat, was the author of a bestselling economics tract, *Progress and Poverty*, and had also written knowingly and passionately about the plight of land-poor Irish tenants. While he was visiting with Land Leaguers in Ireland in 1882, the authorities arrested him "as a suspicious stranger." George also enjoyed the warm support of some local priests who saw him as an ally in their efforts to secure better housing and wages for their parishioners.

That October, at a mass rally, he bristled with scorn for the Tammany men who controlled the city of more than two million: "This government of New York City—our whole political system—is rotten to the core." Officeholders enriched themselves on privileges and bribes, he charged, while "we have hordes of citizens living in want and in vice borne of want, existing under conditions that would appall a heathen." The ULP renamed its clubs after George and greatly expanded their membership. If elected, the radical author could have posed a more profound danger to Tammany's dominion than either the Swallowtails or the suffrage scolds had mustered. He vowed to drive all corrupt officials out of government and replace them with stalwart members of the labor party.[25]

The machine's candidate—Abram Hewitt, an iron manufacturer and former congressman—did triumph at the polls, and the labor party soon fragmented into quarreling factions. Henry George returned to the Democratic fold. But even in losing, the ULP cut deeply into the sinew of Tammany's constituency. George won a plurality in districts heavy with second-generation Irish Americans, including Plunkitt's Fourteenth, as well as in ones filled with German and Jewish workers and their families. On the other hand, most newer and poorer immigrants stayed loyal to the machine on whose constant care and occasional cash they depended.[26]

Croker and his lieutenants understood that the forces of discontent that had fueled the rise of George and the ULP would continue to persist in a metropolis of stark inequalities, so they moved rapidly to address and co-opt them. Tammany turned away from wealthy candidates like Grace and Hewitt who, once elected, tended to resist its patronage demands anyway. They began to run owners of neighborhood businesses whose self-making, like that of the boss himself, appealed to voters mired in daily misfortunes. Increasingly, its nominees for alderman and the state legislature bore German or Jewish names. "By suggesting that the proprietors of grog shops had as much claim [to office] as men of wealth and standing," writes one scholar, "the machine implicitly attacked the values of the existing social order."[27]

Tammany leaders also borrowed an organizational idea from the George campaign and turned it into a resource that would anchor the party in the big city for years to come. They opened clubhouses in every Assembly district—and not only to give partisans a place to talk politics and pick candidates. In these neighborhood institutions, local residents from every white ethnic group came to get help with the law or inquire about a job or attend a party—refreshments gratis. Under Tweed and Kelly, machine men had usually gathered in or next door to saloons; its rival factions and parties had, too. But such venues excluded respectable women, as well as teetotaling men, and the owners had to make a profit. Clubhouses also enabled the chieftains of Tammany to separate the faithful from dilettantes. "Patronage rewards," observe two New York historians, "were now reserved for those who labored long and hard in clubhouse vineyards."[28]

Gradually, the clubhouses also nurtured something the machine had never possessed before—a culture that mixed politics with wholesome pleasures. They held picnics in city parks, fishing trips on the Hudson River, and athletic meets with events tailored to different ages and both genders. "The boys of Senator Roesch's district, the Seventh will have an outing on the seventh of September, to Witzel's Point View Island" announced a column in *The Tammany Times*. "There will be a monster parade in the morning and another in the evening . . . The entire route of the night parade will be ablaze with a magnificent display of fireworks." One club set up a bowling alley for men and a card room for women. The weekly paper, which began publication in 1893, demonstrated the organization's willingness to show itself off to the public while sprinkling a bit of esteem on its foot soldiers, dozens of whose names appeared in every issue.[29]

By 1892, this strategy had done much to restore Tammany's control over the party and a tiger's share of the city's bureaucratic posts. Rival Democratic groups that had once defied the Hall no longer existed. The machine also lifted a financial burden from its own nominees. During the Kelly era, a man who wanted Tammany's blessing—or that of a competing organization—had to furnish an "assessment" appropriate to the office he sought. Candidates for judgeships paid as much as $20,000; to run for the state senate cost a man at least $30,000. But Croker was able to raise ample funds from businesses, big and small, whose owners knew they would be repaid in contracts, favorable legislation, or both. It was still a corrupt bargain, but at least those elected to serve the public did not have to spend so much time reimbursing themselves.[30]

The boss himself accrued enough kickbacks and other forms of graft, "honest" and otherwise, to bask in an affluence equal to his power. Croker owned seven homes, including an estate in Palm Beach to which he traveled in his own railway car, and a stable of Thoroughbreds. His misbegotten wealth horrified elite reformers, but most Gotham voters didn't seem to mind. When Croker embarked on vacations in Europe, thousands flocked to the pier to see him off.

In 1892, Croker also found time to pen a short article for a popular literary magazine boasting about the organization he ruled. He likened it to a battalion in the field. "A well-organized political club is made for the purpose of aggressive warfare," the boss declared. "It must move, and it must always move forward against its enemies. If it makes mistakes, it leaves them behind and goes ahead."[31]

Prior to the Gilded Age, urban Democrats had always claimed to be for "the people." Yet in the heyday of August Belmont and Horatio Seymour, few party leaders actually came from below or had a grasp of the needs and desires of those who did. Under Kelly and Croker, Tammany commanded a white working-class army of modest size that helped itself to the spoils of the city and passed some along to the civilians who harbored them. The machine operated as a welfare state in embryo, albeit one dependent on the protean political calculations of its leaders and the men they lifted into office and limited to efforts that aided individuals one by one instead of a class in need. An ethnically inclusive and durable state that enacted compassionate policies instead of caring gestures would require the commitment of a national party. When that kind of Democratic Party came along in the 1930s, it placed Tammany Hall on a path toward oblivion.

## Making a Solid South Carolina

Democratic bosses in the agrarian states of the former Confederacy were spurred by the same motivation as their counterparts in the urban North: a desire to take and hold power in an intensely competitive era. Given the poverty of the region and the divide between its small number of city dwellers and its rural majority, machine-

makers in Dixie had less money to raise and spend, and fewer opportunities to dispense the kinds of quotidian assistance Tammany's
constituents took for granted. Yet they still had to strike a convincing
pose as the allies and benefactors of voters who, as always, wanted a
party—and a government—that both sided with them and humbled
their adversaries. Of course, the great fear of most Gilded Age Democrats in the South was the potential that their fellow Black citizens
might freely exercise their constitutional rights—and any group or
individual who helped them do so was a sworn enemy. Not until that
peril was soundly defeated would the Solid South be born.

Although white supremacists agreed about the end, they disagreed furiously about the means. The main division was between
racists who took a paternalistic approach and those who insisted on
terrorizing Blacks into submitting to white rule. Often, men of the
first type had grown to adulthood during slavery and yearned to
return to an order they wrapped in myths about kind masters and
happy "darkies." Their opponents tended to be a younger and more
bellicose sort, men who shared Richard Croker's definition of politics as a kind of warfare. For these new men of power in the South,
however, war was not simply a metaphor; violence was an essential
method for winning elections and warning African Americans to remain forever in their inferior place—in public life, in the economy,
and in relations between the sexes.

In South Carolina, the clash between the two styles of bossism
took on a particular intensity. Black people made up roughly three-
fifths of the state's population throughout the Gilded Age. Every
Democrat had to demonstrate that he had an effective strategy to
prevent the majority and its few white allies from holding state power,
as they had for several years during Reconstruction.

Race was not the only cause of fierce conflict in the Palmetto
State: the same animus between big planters and small farmers, both
owners and tenants, that existed elsewhere in the Deep South divided Democrats into two irreconcilable factions. Looming on the
fringe of this internal fight was a growing third-party movement
that demanded relief from constant debt and neglect by politicians
who did little to back up their rhetoric of being the farmer's friend.
Paternalists frowned on helping people who, they believed, should

be helping themselves. Their white militant opponents sympathized with the agrarian revolt. But any man who hoped to succeed in state politics had to make clear how he would keep Black people down.

During the first decade following Reconstruction, the acknowledged leader of the South Carolina party was a landed aristocrat in his sixties with the lineage-soaked name of Wade Hampton III. Given his reputation as a man of breeding and honor, it is unlikely anyone called Hampton a "boss"—although his political dominance in the state certainly warranted the title. Born in 1818, Hampton belonged to one of the oldest and wealthiest families in South Carolina. In addition to a large estate outside Columbia, the state capital, his family owned a 12,000-acre cotton plantation in the rich, alluvial soil of the Mississippi Delta. Wade, the eldest son and patriarch-to-be, managed the tract and the more than three thousand slaves whose labor made them rich. His family also purchased a 2,300-acre expanse in the mountains of North Carolina—which they dubbed High Hampton—where he could indulge his passion for hunting deer and bear. During the 1850s, Wade also dabbled in politics, serving two terms as a Democratic member of the state legislature. But his sole ambition was, it seemed, to continue a pleasant life as a man of wealth in the last state to retain a property qualification for voting.

While the Civil War dashed that hope, it also opened up a bloody new and politically advantageous career. Hampton quickly rose through the officer corps of the Confederate Army to become a lieutenant general and commander of the cavalry in Robert E. Lee's Army of Northern Virginia. Although Hampton had no prior military training, his lofty rank was a tribute to his managerial abilities, his air of charismatic authority, and his fearlessness in combat. But the fact that he could afford to purchase weapons for soldiers in a unit called Hampton's Legion certainly smoothed the way.

His men won most of their battles, and, aided by an adoring home-state press, their commander emerged as South Carolina's foremost military hero. An 1863 portrait of Hampton with a high forehead, curly hair, a full beard, and a stern but calm expression soon became nearly as familiar in the state as images of Robert E. Lee or Jefferson Davis. He enhanced his stature by refusing for weeks after the surrender at Appomattox, in April 1865, to accept that the war had actually ended. Hampton dashed off a frantic note to Davis, who had fled to Texas: "No suffering which can be inflicted by the passage over our country of the Yankee armies can equal what would fall on us if we return to the Union." Only the desperate plea of his wife, Mary, not to leave her and their children without protection from the blue-clad soldiers swarming into their town persuaded him to give up the fight.[32]

Hampton quickly set to work to restore as much of the antebellum order as possible. He continued to believe in rule by landed gentlemen over poor whites as well as freed Blacks. But as a shrewd conservative, he understood that for things to return to a semblance of the status quo ante, some things would have to change. He urged Southerners to rally behind President Andrew Johnson's excessively lenient Reconstruction policy in order to defeat the "radical" one the Republican Congress wanted to foist upon them. He acquiesced in the Thirteenth Amendment, hoping that Black voters, with few economic resources, would defer to governance by their former masters. He also hired ex-slaves to toil on his vast, now partly ruined, lands under contracts that prohibited them from leaving to work for anyone else. Meanwhile, he led a group of former Confederate officers who revived the Democratic organization in the state. In 1868, he was elected as a delegate to the party's national convention, where he dutifully voted to nominate Horatio Seymour for president.

On his return from Manhattan, Hampton addressed a huge crowd in Charleston that greeted him, according to The New York Times, as a "conquering hero." He used the occasion to state his determination never to abandon the Lost Cause or to accept a biracial order. The "principles" of the Confederacy were still valid, Hampton assured his admirers, and he hailed the fact that Democrats in all regions were united against their "radical" opponents. "I am thoroughly convinced," he told them, "that the great heart of the Democracy . . . beats in profound sympathy with the suffering South . . . and that it is unalterably fixed in its purpose . . . to bring back the Southern states to their place in the Union, with all their rights, dignity and equality unimpaired." He then dispensed some stern advice about how to prevent Black men, whom Congress had recently enfranchised, from taking over the state government. "Agree among yourselves and act firmly on this agreement, that *you will not employ anyone who votes the Radical ticket.*" The *Times* bluntly subtitled that section of his speech, "NEGROES MUST VOTE THE DEMOCRATIC TICKET OR STARVE."[33]

Black South Carolinians were equally determined to vote for whomever they chose. That same year, a convention with an African American majority drafted a new state constitution that mandated a public education for all children and terminated both imprisonment for debt and a property qualification for voting. Free elections, under the supervision of federal troops, inevitably produced a new legislature controlled by Black officials and their white compatriots. Unable to defeat this coalition at the ballot box, thousands of Democrats joined the new Ku Klux Klan and other terrorist groups. When called before Congress in 1871 to testify about the violence, Hampton accused Republicans of inflating the "Ku Klux" problem to hide their own failure to fulfill Lincoln's promise of charity toward their defeated foes. But he never stopped preparing, with a group of trusted partisans, for the time when they could retake power from what they considered to be an illegitimate regime dependent on the votes of an ignorant, inferior people.[34]

In 1876, they took a giant step toward that goal. Hampton ran for governor against Daniel Henry Chamberlain, the Republican incumbent. Democrats, surging with confidence since their midterm victories two years before, were willing to use any means to end a government run by a Republican coalition of former slaves and their white allies.

Hampton traded on his wartime heroism and a sense of noblesse oblige. Alongside partisan campaigners dressed in red shirts, he traveled throughout the state on horseback, speaking to massive, friendly crowds. He pledged, if elected, to respect the rights of African American citizens and even read an affectionate letter from an ex-slave turned minister who vowed he would "vote for you and will get all the Black men I can to do the same."[35]

Yet Hampton was quite aware that thousands of other Democrats were not relying on harmonious rhetoric to secure his election. Rifle clubs of white partisans, some dressed in red shirts, busted up Republican meetings and drove freedmen away from the polls with whips and clubs and guns. "The way things are going is not right," one Black South Carolinian pleaded to Governor Chamberlain. "They have killed col'd men in every precinct." But, with only a small number of federal troops remaining in the state, the incumbent could do little to stop the aggressors besides reporting their crimes. On Election Day, Hampton won a narrow victory, by just over a thousand votes. Justifiably protesting that the Democrats had terrorized their way to victory, Chamberlain refused to accept defeat until the following spring. When he finally gave up, the man who replaced him proclaimed a statewide day of thanksgiving. God, declared Hampton, had lifted "the radical yoke" from the necks of the (white) people he loved.[36]

But the Almighty did not bestow on the new governor and his party the power to run South Carolina as they saw fit. For that, they needed a machine, albeit one that had to operate in thirty-three mainly rural counties, most of which had fewer residents than an average ward in New York City. The critical driver was a network of clubs, organized by precinct. Any Democrat who hoped to make his way in politics had to join his local club, as was true in the district clubs Tammany assembled several years later. But few, if any, of the clubs in South Carolina sponsored family picnics or excursions. They were weapons designed to wage electoral combat and ensure the fidelity of community leaders to the party that had "redeemed" the state. Local newspapers routinely printed the names of club members, who were expected to meet regularly during campaign season. Anyone who is "not with us, with the Democratic Party," Hampton declared, "is a traitor to his state."[37]

For the next decade, the aging hero led the South Carolina party while also helping Dixie Democrats regain their powerful status in the nation at large. In 1879, the state legislature elected him to the U.S. Senate, while Hampton loyalists succeeded him as governor and in other executive offices. Most white voters remained indebted to the general both for his service to the Confederate cause and for vanquishing the scourge of "Negro rule." Some younger Democrats bridled at his studied paternalism and envied his status; they labeled him a "Bourbon" who, like France's last royal dynasty, had allegedly "learned nothing and forgotten nothing." But that was a misnomer:

Hampton had certainly learned how to rise to power and maintain it at a time when his state and the South as a whole were grappling with the most wrenching changes in their history.

After 1876, Hamptonian Democrats found ways to repress Black voters without beating or killing them, a strategy that managed to quiet most of their white critics in the North. They shuttered polling stations in many Republican precincts and printed tissue-thin tickets for their own nominees that, when bundled together, made it easy to vote multiple times by pressing down firmly on the top ballot. The legislature packed as many Black voters as possible into just one of the state's seven congressional districts and allowed a Republican to win it. The governing party's most imaginative scheme, enacted in 1882, was the "eight-box law," which required voters to deposit ballots in separate containers for various offices. This baffled illiterate voters and confused even many literate ones. Poll managers, most of whom were Democrats, had no obligation to come to their aid. Like other shrewd bosses, Hampton also doled out patronage to men who could be counted on to promote his career and his policies. In several counties with Black majorities, he scattered a few low-level jobs to African Americans.[38]

Hampton and fellow members of the conservative elite believed the redemption their tactics had secured would keep them in power as long as they desired. But by the mid-1880s, away from the big plantations, the commercial hub of Charleston, and the state capital in Columbia, economic discontent was beginning to grow among white farmers. And the kind of men who had first used rifles and clubs to elect Hampton and his ilk were now aching to replace them.

The unrivaled leader of the rising faction was Benjamin Ryan Tillman, as skillful and vicious a boss as the white Democracy ever produced. He was born in 1847 to a family with a small plantation in hilly Edgefield County, which had a reputation for savage feuds among whites and cruelty toward local slaves, who composed a majority of the population. The teenage Tillman longed to fight for the Confederacy, but a cranial tumor in 1864 destroyed his left eye, and it took him two years to recuperate. For the rest of his life, the missing eye gave him a menacing look that emboldened his followers and intimidated his adversaries.[39]

By Hampton's 1876 campaign to topple the state's Reconstruction government, Tillman was fully capable of doing his part. He created a rifle club, Tillman's Hussars, that warned Republicans to stay away from the polls and shot to death a Black state senator who protested. On Election Day, he managed a polling station for the Democrats in Edgefield that reported just two votes for the opposition party. A Black Republican named Robert Chandler reported that a group of white men wielding pistols had scared his people away. "Benny Tillman said they had been the rulers of Carolina and they intended to rule it," Chandler testified.[40]

A decade later, the ambitious brute from Edgefield County found a potent new cause he combined with the old one to ascend to leadership of his party and his state. Across the rural South, crop prices were falling, while furnishing merchants and commodity brokers held a whip hand over the fortunes of small landholders and tenant farmers alike. Tillman himself had amassed two thousand acres of farmland, on which he employed gangs of laborers he liked to supervise on horseback, "driving the slovenly negroes to their work," as his son later put it. But the plantation boss appreciated the discontent of far less prosperous whites and moved shrewdly to address it.

In the mid-1880s, Tillman began giving speeches that brilliantly blended an attack on the monied class and its allies in the state party with a promise to keep throttling the Black majority. Merchants and bankers "make money whether it rains or not," he charged. But hardworking "real Democrats and white men" were fast losing the ability to compete with big landowners, an increasing number of them foreigners, and the Black sharecroppers who tilled many of their acres. That Tillman was a major landowner himself did not seem to strike most of his listeners as hypocritical. "I had rather a thousand times go down with my brother farmers than fatten at their expense," he asserted. As Andrew Jackson had demonstrated half a century before, adroitly spoken empathy with the plight of ordinary men could trump vast differences in wealth. Tillman's admirers began calling him their "agricultural Moses." Playing the role of Pharaoh in this biblical metaphor, of course, was Wade Hampton, hero of the Lost Cause, his mustache grown white and his tight gray tunic having been exchanged for a roomy three-piece suit.[41]

In 1886, to take on Wade Hampton and his fellow conservatives, Tillman organized a new group, the Farmers' Association, to be his all-white, intraparty battering ram. Its members quickly took over most Democratic clubs in the state. Then, in 1890, the agricultural Moses launched a campaign for governor. He ghost-wrote a widely circulated manifesto that attacked the governing elite as a cabal of "aristocrats" who used their money and servile newspapers to prevent any true "champion of the people" from defying their power. He appeared at one rally in Columbia where Hampton also spoke and mocked the senator's outrage at being called an "aristocrat." "The grand mogul here who ruled supremely and grandly cannot terrify me," Tillman snarled just a few feet from the shocked Hampton. "I do not come from any such blood as that." That summer, Tillman's faithful club members wrested control from other delegates to the Democratic convention and picked him to run South Carolina. The general election in November was just a formality. For good measure, the state legislature, most of whose members were Confederate veterans, refused to renominate Hampton, then seventy-two, to another Senate term and named a Tillman protégé in his place.[42]

In his inaugural address, the new governor, dressed like "a plain farmer trying to look respectable," bragged that he had not merely replaced the old boss with a new one but had made a popular "revolution." He distilled a potent brew of racist and populist phrases: "Democracy, the rule of the people, has won a victory unparalleled in its magnitude and importance . . . The triumph of democracy and white supremacy over mongrelism and anarchy, of civilization over barbarism, has been most complete."[43]

Tillman moved quickly to install a new order intended to reassure white farmers that he could back up his rhetoric with action. A challenge to his brand of racial agrarianism was growing across the South and the Great Plains. By 1890, a new organization called the National Farmers' Alliance and Industrial Union had signed up more than a million members in the South and Midwest with an ambitious program that included public ownership of railroads, a more flexible currency, support for labor unions, and government warehouses ("subtreasuries") where farmers could store such staple crops as wheat and cotton until their prices rose to a more pleasing level.

Alliances were also running independent tickets that had the potential to woo hard-pressed farmers away from their long-established competitors. They boasted more than twenty thousand members in South Carolina alone, close to 10 percent of the state's adult white population. In 1892, leaders of the insurgency from all over the nation met in Omaha, Nebraska, to form the People's Party—the Populists.

As Tammany bosses had found ways to lure third-party labor voters to return to the fold, so Tillman worked hard to woo Farmers' Alliance supporters back to the Democracy. He endorsed their national platform while arguing that easier loans from state banks would be a more feasible and less radical idea than the subtreasury. He strongly backed the coinage of silver as well as gold, which resonated with small landholders who blamed rich bankers in New York and London for tight money and high interest rates. And he called for the establishment of agricultural colleges to train young men in techniques for modernizing the farm economy, a task the elite state university in Columbia had largely neglected. Tillman also appealed to evangelical Protestantism, the faith of most South Carolinians, by restricting the sale of liquor to state dispensaries and sending police to raid homes that sold black-market spirits. The local Women's Christian Temperance Union, whose national leader had endorsed the People's Party, advocated outright prohibition. But those female reformers were pleased that Tillman was taking a moral stand that all previous governors of South Carolina had shirked. As a side benefit, the state stores gave him a fresh set of patronage jobs to dispense.

Most important, Tillman reminded whites in stark terms what a split in the Democratic vote would mean for the fate of the racial order. "You cannot divide without bringing ruin," he told them. To gain an edge, a third party would have to campaign for Black votes, and Democrats would be forced to do the same. Down that path lay ruin: It "means in the long run political debauchery & corruption with a final division of offices between the races & a return to the evils of the reconstruction era."[44]

In 1892, Tillman took one loathsome step further in his unstinting defense of white domination. He vowed to lead any mob that lynched any Black man accused of raping a white woman. The brazen statement reversed his earlier censure of mob justice, and Tillman did not repeat it for fear it would dissuade Northern investors from doing business in the state. But he was glad to accept a hand-made banner—given to him by admirers at an upcountry campaign stop—that acclaimed him the "Champion of White Men's Rule and Woman's Virtue." In the 1892 presidential election, the People's Party received just over 3 percent of the vote in South Carolina—the lowest total it recorded in any former Confederate state. In a primary election that summer, Tillman had easily defeated a former governor and ally of Hampton for a nomination that effectively guaranteed his reelection. Through methods fair and foul, Boss Tillman had employed populist rhetoric to make the Populist party an irrelevancy in South Carolina.

Throughout his career, frank, often crude language, tinged with venom, was perhaps Tillman's greatest asset. He proudly described himself as "a plain, blunt man, who tells his thoughts and views straight at the mark." That kind of rhetoric convinced poor white farmers, who had fought for a failed cause led by grandees like Hampton, that he despised rich whites above and "ignorant" Blacks below as much as they did. His fellow bosses up north in Gotham did more to improve the lives of their followers—and rarely spewed racial bile while doing so. But both traded on an authentic identification with "their" people to shape a Democratic Party they could command.[45]

## The President Who Hated Bosses

It is perhaps ironic that the man Democrats nominated three straight times for the highest office in the land and who won it twice detested both Tammany and Tillman, a sentiment they vigorously reciprocated. Contemporary historians tend to dismiss Grover Cleveland as a "hardworking plodder" with little imagination and no charisma, a president who declined to aid ordinary citizens struggling to survive during the depression of the mid-1890s. In a culture that reveres the fit and thin, the obesity of a leader his own nephews called "Uncle Jumbo" diminishes his retrospective standing, too. But from his election as president in 1884 until economic calamity struck a decade later, Cleveland's popularity surpassed that of any other politician in either party. He remains the only Democratic nominee besides Andrew Jackson and Franklin D. Roosevelt to win a plurality of the popular vote on three consecutive occasions. Clearly, millions of Americans saw something in the man worthy of their esteem and their ballots.[46]

That Cleveland hated the influence of bosses and machines was perhaps the most significant reason he made it to the White House. Those men and their institutions won many an election—and certainly knew how to build local parties that would endure. But outside their bailiwicks, they were easy to malign as corrupt and unprincipled. Cleveland's presidencies were undistinguished at best; he spent a good deal of time finding men of "character" to appoint to patronage jobs and haggling over Civil War pensions. He left most policy decisions to Democrats in Congress and rarely spoke to the press. But he was rigorously honest and incorruptible, and these traits won him a measure of acclaim in an era when most politicians were neither.

Cleveland was born in New Jersey in 1837, the son of a Presbyterian minister. At the age of eighteen, he moved to Buffalo to study law, then entered local Democratic politics in what was a Republican stronghold. Elected mayor in 1881, Cleveland vetoed attempts by local aldermen to dole out lucrative contracts to businesses that would award them in turn. Party elders like Samuel Tilden hailed him for defying the Buffalo "ring." Less than a year later, they convinced him to run for governor. That fall, he won in a landslide. During the campaign, Cleveland declared that all politicians should be "trustees of the people"; his managers turned that phrase into a pithy motto that underlined his loathing of graft: "A public office is a public trust."[47]

Cleveland quickly gave Boss Kelly sound reasons to mistrust him, profoundly. The new governor vetoed a measure proposed by Tammany's men and passed by the state legislature that would have cut the fare on the elevated railroad in New York City to five cents per ride. Cleveland also vetoed a bill that would have limited the workday for conductors on those lines to twelve hours a day. For good measure, the governor also opposed the renomination of Thomas Grady, the state senator who had sponsored the fare bill. Grady, a Tammany stalwart and splendid orator, was notorious for his "open patronage of the worst saloons and bawdy houses" in Albany, according to Allan Nevins, Cleveland's admiring biographer. "When up-State Democrats thought of Tammany," adds Nevins, "they thought of the draft riots, the Tweed Ring, the political gangsterism of an ignorant, venal Irish element that was deeply repugnant to their Anglo-Saxon traditions."[48]

But Cleveland's vetoes were motivated more by ideology than ethnic prejudice. Cleveland firmly believed he should take no action that would give one group public aid or an economic advantage over another. Only when the government maintained a rigorous neutrality toward all interest groups could the capitalist economy remain, at least in theory, open to all. Four years later, as president, Cleveland vetoed a seemingly innocuous bill that would have let the Agriculture Department donate seeds to counties in Texas whose farmers were suffering through an intense drought. "Though the people support the Government," he declared, "the Government should not support the people." By the same logic, Cleveland opposed the high tariffs dear to Republicans from industrial states. They gave a massive subsidy to "aggregated capital," which raised costs urban workers had to pay for basic commodities. He also railed against the typical corporate apologist "who proposes that the government shall protect the rich and that they in turn will care for the laboring poor."[49]

In an era of rampant corruption, many of those struggling wage earners may have agreed with Cleveland's suspicion of an active government. As one historian puts it, "The men who cheated and lied their way into office were the last ones who should be trusted with broader authority."[50]

But the bosses of Tammany Hall knew that a hands-off state benefited mainly the interests of the few who had already become wealthy on the labors of the many. As practical men, they also realized that a party that sided with Cleveland was likely to treat them as a burden rather than an asset.

That assumption proved true in 1884 when the Democrats met in Chicago to nominate a presidential ticket. John Kelly sent two of Tammany's best orators to convince the delegates that, as governor, Cleveland had shown by his vetoes that he was hostile to the needs of workingmen and their families. With such a record, they claimed, he could not carry New York State. Edward S. Bragg, a former Union general from Wisconsin, rose to rebut the Manhattan naysayers and drew a huge ovation with one angry line: the young men of his state loved Cleveland, said Bragg, "not only for himself, for his character, for his integrity and judgment and iron will, but they love him most for the enemies he has made." His candidate won nomination on the second ballot. For the next cover of *Harper's Weekly*, Thomas Nast drew a remarkably lean Grover Cleveland backed by a cheering crowd as John Kelly sulks behind him, a long knife dangling impotently from his hand.[51]

That fall, Cleveland finally broke his party's string of presidential defeats stretching back to Lincoln's victory in 1860. He got help from a small but influential group of Republicans, nicknamed the Mugwumps, who recoiled from the GOP nominee, James G. Blaine, who had a history of shady dealings with railroad lobbyists. The apostasy of famous, elite figures like Henry Ward Beecher, Carl Schurz, and Charles Francis Adams, Jr., swayed few votes directly. But newspapers routinely printed their opinions, and Nast helped their cause by drawing Blaine in the buff, tattooed with the names of numerous scandals he could not erase. Such unaccustomed support helped Cleveland win the most popular votes nationwide as well as the swing states of Connecticut and New Jersey.[52]

However, if he had not carried his own state, he would have lost in the Electoral College. Tammany ended up giving Cleveland its formal endorsement, but the machine stayed idle for most of the campaign. For his slim thousand-ballot victory in New York State, Cleveland could thank a third-party candidate—the prohibitionist John St. John, most of whose seventeen thousand voters normally voted Republican. An evangelical minister, Samuel D. Burchard, did commit a memorable gaffe near the end of the campaign that may have convinced more Catholics to vote for Cleveland. In Blaine's presence, the incautious reverend sneered that the Democrats were the party "of Rum, Romanism, and Rebellion." But the decision by a critical number of Burchard's fellow Protestants to vote for the marginal party that crusaded to abolish the "liquor trust" was enough to doom Blaine's chances in the Empire State.

As president, Cleveland behaved much as he had as governor—which pleased those who loved him for his character but did little to address the problems of a fast-growing industrial nation. When railroad workers mounted a strike against Jay Gould's Southwest line in 1886, he counseled the two sides to submit the dispute to arbitration, advice that both quickly rejected. He strongly opposed the growing demand by Democrats like Tillman to inflate the money supply by monetizing silver as well as gold. Cleveland shut African Americans out of postmaster jobs in the South but refrained from making racist comments. The president gave his most passionate attention to reducing the protective tariff: "The simple and plain duty which we owe the people is to reduce the taxation to the necessary expenses of an economical operation of the government," he argued toward the end of his term. It was the kind of statement any antebellum Democratic president could have made. But the recitation of the Jacksonian gospel did nothing to aid wage earners toiling long hours for little pay, often in dangerous conditions.[53]

Railing against high tariffs was not enough to win Cleveland reelection in 1888. In yet another of the extremely close contests that were the Gilded Age norm, he lost to Benjamin Harrison (grandson of the first Whig president, who had defeated Van Buren), although he did manage to edge out the Republican in the popular vote. Of course, the GOP would probably have won a plurality of ballots cast if Black men had been able to vote as freely as white ones.

Once again, the result pivoted on New York. This time, Tammany, now under Boss Croker, urged district leaders to drum up the vote for the party's nominee. But a feud between the president and the Democratic nominee for governor, David Hill, cut into Cleveland's support in upstate precincts, and Harrison carried New York by about thirteen thousand votes. The loser had no regrets: "We were defeated, it is true," Cleveland wrote to a friend, "but the principles of tariff reform will surely win in the end."[54]

When he staged a rematch four years later, the plague of internal division struck the dour incumbent instead. James Weaver, nominee of the new left-wing People's Party, took several Western states that usually voted Republican and cut into Harrison's support in others. The Democrats also drew votes from an untold number of industrial workers after the Republican governor of Pennsylvania dispatched the state militia to crush a bitter strike against the Republican owners of the world's largest steel mill in the town of Homestead, seven miles down the Monongahela River from Pittsburgh. This time, Cleveland had the full support of Tammany Hall and carried his own state by forty-five thousand votes. The working-class Bowery went for the Democrat by the astounding margin of 388 to 4; the district captain there assured Boss Croker, "Harrison got one more vote than I expected, but I'll find that fellow." Cleveland won almost twice as many electoral votes as Harrison, and Democrats regained control of both houses of Congress.[55]

Yet just as Cleveland was moving back into the White House, he faced a far more urgent matter than lowering the tariff. In February, one of the biggest railroads in the nation went bankrupt, triggering a sell-off on Wall Street. In early May, the country's leading rope maker failed, too, and stockbrokers panicked. Hundreds of banks closed their doors, and scores of railroads went into receivership. Tens of thousands of jobless men tramped along the highways and begged for handouts; farmers had to slash their prices, yet they still had trouble finding wholesalers to buy their crops. The growing depression put Cleveland, armed with his laissez-faire convictions, to a severe test.

He utterly failed. The president refused to listen to pleas that he ask Congress to spend money to create jobs fixing the nation's roads. In 1894, he backed up the decision by his attorney general Richard Olney, a railroad lawyer and friend, to send federal troops to arrest union men who were staging a nationwide train boycott against an employer who exploited his workers. The sole remedy to reverse the downturn that Cleveland did endorse was one demanded by industrialists and financiers that would split his party in two: a defense of the gold standard.

Since the beginning of the depression, anxious depositors had been depleting the nation's reserves of gold, for which Americans could redeem their paper dollars. Cleveland, adhering to the dubious wisdom of conservative economists, believed that, to restore confidence, Congress had to repeal a bill passed in 1890 that required the government to buy a certain amount of silver each month. The president claimed that silver, which was far more plentiful than gold, spurred inflation and thus discouraged businessmen from investing. "Our unfortunate financial plight," he told federal lawmakers that August, was "principally chargeable" to the "use of a currency greatly depreciated according to the standard of the commercial world." We must, he insisted, "provide for the use of the people the best and safest money."[56]

As with Jackson's Bank War sixty years earlier, the ensuing conflict stirred up assumptions and fears whose emotional power transcended the dry details of monetary policy. Cleveland and his supporters in both major parties, most from the urbanizing East, clung to the gold standard as the basis of "sound money" and, by extension, a stable economy. Their critics, who were dominant in the rural West and South, scorned it as a virtual conspiracy by stockbrokers and creditors everywhere to keep interest rates high and small businesses and their employees perpetually in debt. After a three-month-long filibuster by his backers in the Senate, the president got his way, and the Silver Purchase Act was repealed. Then, in 1894, he further inflamed his adversaries by asking J. P. Morgan and August Belmont, Jr., two of the nation's wealthiest bankers, to exchange some of their gold for $50 million in U.S. bonds.

In South Carolina, Ben Tillman saw an opportunity to thrust himself forward as a leader of the forces arrayed against the "money power." He decided to run for the Senate in 1894, a contest he was sure to win, and came up with an attack on the president of his own party that was both remarkably belligerent and instantly memorable. "When Judas betrayed Christ," Tillman told a crowd gathered in the upcountry town of Winnsboro, "his heart was not Blacker than this scoundrel, Cleveland, in deceiving the Democracy." He then employed an agrarian metaphor he knew would delight his followers: "He is an old bag of beef and I am going to Washington with a pitchfork and prod him in his old fat ribs."[57]

In that fall's election, Democratic candidates who agreed with "Pitchfork" Ben urged Americans to distinguish them from the portly president they considered a Wall Street lackey. But, as in the throes of every economic calamity, voters took out their anger on the party in power. In New York City, a reform ticket defeated Tammany's nominees. The Democrats lost an extraordinary 125 seats in the House, more than half their caucus, and also relinquished control of the Senate. Only in the Deep South did they remain the majority party; even the former slave states of Kentucky and Maryland elected as many Republicans to the House as Democrats. "It was the greatest slaughter of innocents since the days of King Herod," quipped Champ Clark, a congressman from Missouri who also went down to defeat. Populists increased their total votes, but the Republican tide swept most of their candidates away, too. No other American party has ever enjoyed a more crushing midterm triumph.

The debacle had one salutary consequence for the battered Democracy. Grover Cleveland and his followers who clung to the Jacksonian notion that federal power would always benefit the rich and privileged were exposed for doing just that instead of aiding the unemployed and the indebted. By the 1890s, bosses both North and South had become rather consistent voices for at least the white victims of Gilded Age capital. Now they and the growing number of Democrats who took their side would have to back up their rhetoric with deeds. The most consequential rebuilding of the party since its creation was at hand.

# 4

## THE PROGRESSIVE TURN,
## 1894–1920

*While I do not want to array one class against another,
I am willing to array all the people who suffer from the
operation of the trusts against the few people
who operate the trusts.*
—WILLIAM JENNINGS BRYAN, 1896[1]

*The Democratic Party favors the full exercise of the
powers of the Government for the protection of
the rights of the people.*
—WILLIAM JENNINGS BRYAN, 1908[2]

*The Republican party is just the party that* cannot *meet
the new conditions of a new age.*
—WOODROW WILSON, 1916[3]

On Labor Day in 1896, William Jennings Bryan traveled to Chicago
to tell a crowd of fifteen thousand people why he was running for
president. After flattering the wage earners for producing the goods
on which all Americans depended, and quoting both Abraham Lincoln and King Solomon in praise of labor, the Democratic nominee
made a little joke. On a recent swing through Iowa, he had learned
"an idea" from a group of pigs he had seen "rooting in a field and
tearing up the ground." On the downstate Illinois farm where he
had been raised, Bryan recalled, "we put rings in the noses of hogs"
to prevent them from wreaking that kind of damage. "And then it

occurred to me," he said, "that one of the most important duties of government is to put rings in the noses of hogs." That meant passing laws "which will prevent any citizen from destroying more than he is worth," and which would prevent "others . . . from injuring us."[4]

It was a signal moment in a campaign that would do much to define the Democratic creed for decades to come. With his porcine metaphor, Bryan was implicitly rejecting the skepticism about government intervention in the economy held by each of his party's standard-bearers from Andrew Jackson to Grover Cleveland. Of course, the 1896 nominee did not spurn the memory of Old Hickory himself—that would have been akin to a Republican defiling Lincoln's grave. Bryan dutifully cited the Democratic icon as a kindred spirit: "Andrew Jackson said there were no necessary evils in government; that its evils existed only in its abuses." But he put that statement to a use that the seventh president—who believed anyone favoring a strong federal hand in business or the workplace had to be acting for "selfish purposes"—would not have welcomed. Bryan boldly demanded that the government undertake the aggressive and permanent regulation of private wealth, particularly the profits amassed and wielded by industrial corporations. In the same speech, he also warmly endorsed labor unions and concluded with a plea to the workers in the crowd not to allow their employers to "coerce" them to vote for William McKinley, his GOP opponent.

These positions, articulated in bracing prose, made Bryan the first Democratic nominee ever to win support from nearly every prominent white radical in the land. The Populists endorsed him, although many in their Southern contingent balked at fusing with the same party they had left in anger just a few years before. So did Henry George and Edward Bellamy, whose books condemning the economic and moral sins of corporate capitalism had been read by millions. After his release from prison for leading a national railroad strike and boycott in 1894, Eugene V. Debs declared himself to be a socialist. But two years later, the union leader who had been prosecuted by Cleveland's Justice Department wrote to Bryan, "You are at this hour the hope of the Republic—the central figure of the civilized world." A Republican editor from Kansas later recalled about the campaign, "It was the first time in my life and in the life of a generation in which any man large enough to lead a national party had boldly and unashamedly made his cause that of the poor and the oppressed."[5]

Still, Bryan lost and rather decisively. He drew just under 47 percent of the popular vote and did not carry a single state in the Northeast or Upper Midwest, the most populous and wealthiest sections of the country. Yet he so embodied the new spirit of his party that the Democrats nominated him again four years later and then once more in 1908. On each occasion, the Nebraskan went down by a greater margin than in the contest that had preceded it.

Chatting with journalists a day after his final defeat, Bryan compared himself to a drunk who kept trying to enter an indoor dance somewhere in Texas. The first time the fellow was "gently" escorted from the hall. The second time, he got "pushed somewhat vigorously" away. Finally, the organizers of the event booted him down the stairs. The inebriate dusted himself off and remarked, "I know what is the matter with those people up there. They can't fool me. They don't want me in there." Bryan, a lifelong teetotaler, may have intended the yarn to soften the despair of his admirers who had just learned that he would never run for president again.[6]

As long as Bryan served as their titular leader, Democrats remained a minority in Congress. In the 1896 contest, they recovered thirty-one House seats they had lost in the depression-fueled debacle of two years before. Yet not until 1910 did they regain a majority in the lower chamber, which the party had controlled through most of the Gilded Age. It took Woodrow Wilson's victory two years later— against a bitterly divided opposition—for them to wrest back a majority in the Senate as well.

Yet in running and losing more times than any other nominee in his party's history, Bryan changed the Democracy in ways that would help many of its future candidates win. Like Jackson and the nineteenth-century Democrats who emulated him, he sought to curb the power and influence of finance capital. But unlike Old Hickory, he hailed the growth of organized labor. In 1908, the man his followers dubbed the Great Commoner received the first endorsement that the American Federation of Labor, the largest working-class institution in the land, had ever given to a presidential candidate.

Bryan's early support for such progressive measures as the direct election of senators, a graduated income tax, public ownership of the railroads, federal insurance for bank deposits, and a more flexible monetary system enabled Democrats to shift their image from a party that gazed backward toward its antebellum glories to one that allied with many of the reform movements that matured in the early twentieth century—and sought to turn their wishes into law.

Woodrow Wilson would erect his New Freedom, Franklin D. Roosevelt his New Deal, and Harry Truman his Fair Deal on the foundation of alliances and policies Bryan had laid. For a half century after the 1896 race, Democrats waged nearly every national election as the party that promised to build a government that would grow, as necessary, to serve the interests of wage earners and small farmers and be a countervailing power to corporate America. "Shall the People Rule?" Bryan's campaign asked in 1908. Democrats since Jackson had essentially been asking that same question. But no longer would they cast doubt on the need for a stronger federal state to answer it affirmatively.

At the same time, under Bryan's leadership, Democrats stubbornly upheld certain key elements of the Jacksonian legacy. They either kept silent about or actively abetted the white South's construction of as cruel and rigid an order of racial supremacy as existed in most European colonies. They continued to welcome immigrants from anywhere but East Asia (epileptics and anarchists excepted). And they still viewed a government job as a reward for partisan services rendered or anticipated rather than merit and usually looked the other way when a well-placed Democrat used his public office for personal gain. Bryan rarely voiced a qualm or second thought about any of these matters. He was, after all, the loving son of Silas Bryan, a judge from southern Illinois who had idolized Stephen Douglas and once blasted "the black Republican press."[7]

On the rare occasions when Bryan did depart from racist orthodoxy, he kept it private. In 1906, when party notables from the South resisted his call to nationalize the railroads for fear that would lead to integrated passenger cars, Bryan told the press, "I have spoken for myself and for myself only." Later, with no reporters present, he scolded a group of Dixie Democrats that their "personal objections to riding with Negroes" were standing in the way of "a great national reform."[8] In 1908, W.E.B. DuBois, repulsed by President Theodore Roosevelt's unjust discharge of Black troops at a post in Texas, announced he would vote for Bryan. But the Democratic nominee ignored the overture that might have gained him several thousand Black votes while losing him many more white ones.

Bryan's style of campaigning did represent a sharp break from a tradition of stuffy restraint adhered to by both major parties. Before the 1896 race, presidential nominees were expected to deliver a formal speech of acceptance, weeks after the convention had chosen them, and then stay home, occasionally venturing out to give another stilted address or two. To embark on a speaking tour around the nation was considered an unseemly form of self-advertising that betrayed a candidate's desperation and a lack of faith in the party's foot soldiers to whip up constituent fervor themselves. In 1860, Stephen Douglas had broken the mold but only because he was anxious to show he could appeal to Democrats in every region; his humiliating reception in the South that year made his decision easy to ridicule. Horace Greeley had sped his death by taking to the road while in ill health during the 1872 campaign. And in 1884, the Republican James G. Blaine made his own futile tour to rally voters, while Grover Cleveland remained in Albany, tending serenely to the business of his state.

But Bryan was to political speechmaking what Babe Ruth was to hitting home runs. He had the oratorical skill of a magnetic preacher—and a messianic certainty, driven by his devotion to Christ and the literal truth of the Bible, as well as to populist economics. It was, after all, Bryan's bravura "Cross of Gold" speech given at the Democratic convention that summer that had lifted him from darkhorse status to his party's nomination.

So he joyfully campaigned for three straight months in 1896, resting only on the Sabbath. Reporters chronicled that Bryan traveled more than eighteen thousand miles, nearly all by rail, and gave 250 planned speeches, as well as countless impromptu ones— including one in the early morning from a railroad car with shaving cream wreathing his face. The thirty-six-year-old candidate made the unprecedented tour to offset the mighty financial advantage his Republican opponent enjoyed: McKinley had nearly ten times more money to spend, much of it donated by industrial titans like John D. Rockefeller. But Bryan might have conducted his campaign the same way even if his resources had equaled those of the GOP. He loved addressing huge audiences and knew that most of the people who came to hear him thrilled at the experience.[9]

Bryan was thus the chief forerunner of a style of politics inextricably bound up with personality that we now take entirely for granted. He received as many as a quarter million letters during the 1896 campaign, most brimming with an admiration that often spilled over into reverence. "God has brought you forth and ordaind [*sic*] you, to lead the people out of this state of oppression and despondency into the Canaan of peace and prosperity," gushed a furniture salesman from Pittsburgh. That Bryan was the youngest major-party nominee in history, with an energy that matched his age, made him all the more compelling. Despite his loss, he seemed to be gesturing toward a future in which politicians would tame capitalism instead of capitalists bridling them.

## An Ambitious Minority

Yet that future would not arrive while Bryan remained the most prominent Democrat in the land. The reasons why reveal both the political shortcomings of the image he crafted and the burdens left by the men who preceded him at the helm of the party. The Great Commoner was essentially a protest candidate. In railing against "the great fortunes which are accumulated in cities" and the rich man "who wants the Government to destroy the people," he built a base as loyal as that of any Democrat since Old Hickory. But Republicans branded him a dangerous "Popocrat," and the pejorative label stuck, even after the Populist Party itself faded away. His fierce opposition in the 1900 campaign to the bloody conquest of the Philippines drew on the cherished principle of self-government and struck a chord even with some elite Republicans and prominent intellectuals like William James, who told a friend he had "fallen in love with" Bryan "so, for his character," that he was "willing to forget his following."[10]

But the United States had become an industrial powerhouse with an overseas empire in the six decades since Jackson's rule—and it was difficult for any politician to question the merit of those galvanic changes. The giant firms, often emblazoned with the names of such moguls as Carnegie and Swift, produced a cornucopia of goods and plenty of jobs, most at low wages, that millions of native-born Americans and European immigrants abandoned their farms and villages to take. Manufacturing and machine-driven agriculture were the engines of the nation's growth, and both depended on loans from financiers like J.P. Morgan and, increasingly, on the gyrations of the stock and commodities markets. These loci of power were mainly in the Northeast and Upper Midwest, where, nearly everywhere, Republicans called the shots.

Condemnation of the imperialist war Americans were waging on the other side of the globe might have been an electoral boon for Democrats in 1900 if the Philippine independence forces had gained the upper hand. But the brutal efficiency of the U.S. Army and divisions among their poorly equipped Filipino adversaries made its victory seem inevitable and thus McKinley's seem probable.

So the same Bryan whom his adoring followers regarded as a savior appeared to his opponents in the other party and to some in his own as either a dangerous radical or merely a strident voice repeating the same grievances to diminishing effect. His support in both 1896 and 1900 from the Populists, whose platform called for government ownership of the railroads and telegraph, gained him the votes of leftists angry at the power of "the big money" while confirming the threat he posed to anyone who gained from or at least identified with the existing order. As the historian Richard Hofstadter observed about an earlier insurgent hero, "He was an agitator by profession, and the agitator is always vulnerable."[11]

Still, under Bryan, most Democrats had something they had lacked during Cleveland's years of narrow triumph followed by the devastating reverse in 1894: a common ideological purpose. Fusion with the Populists had been more than an electoral strategy; the third party's voters shared the grievances Bryan voiced and agreed with the solutions he offered, although many favored a larger federal role in aiding labor and small farmers. Stuck in minority status as a "party of outsiders," Democrats also nursed the same grand ambition to topple the reign of big capital, with its headquarters on Wall Street and corporate offices in metropoles from Boston to Chicago. The difficulty in realizing it lay in turning the culturally dissimilar and regionally separate centers of Democratic strength in the white South, the Irish-led machines in the urban North, and erstwhile Populists in the mountain West into first an electoral majority and then a governing one. Republicans had a somewhat narrower base, composed largely of evangelical Protestants (then the largest religious cluster in the land). But, backed by the money and influence of the chieftains of industry, this made them the respectable choice and turned their social homogeneity into a virtue.

Of course, the sole region where Democrats wielded power uncontested was also the place where party leaders made quite sure most citizens of another race could not take part in politics at all. By the end of the nineteenth century, nearly every Southern state had completed the disenfranchisement of Black people begun in the waning years of Reconstruction. To do so, most shelved such shifty tactics as South Carolina's eight-box rule, which were subject to fraud and vulnerable to legal challenges. "If we disfranchise the great body of Negroes, let us do it openly and above board," a Richmond paper declared in 1898, "and let there be an end to all sorts of jugglery."[12]

Southern leaders thus amended their constitutions to bar nearly all African Americans from exercising the franchise but did so without violating the letter of the Fifteenth Amendment. Inevitably, this required some new kinds of "jugglery." The document South Carolina enacted in 1895, dictated by Ben Tillman, compelled every prospective voter to pay his taxes six months before an election, own property assessed at $300 or more, and be able to read and write any section of the state's new constitution to the satisfaction of a county registrar. The few African American delegates at the convention protested what a local white paper admitted was "the blatant overthrow of Negro suffrage." In response, Robert Smalls, a Black Union hero of the Civil War, offered a provocative measure he hoped would expose the hypocrisy of the white majority: prohibit interracial sex but require any child that resulted from the transgressive act to take his father's name and inherit a portion of his wealth. It was swiftly voted down.[13]

The new restrictions based on owning property and being debt-free did threaten to undermine Tillman's image as the "Moses" of ordinary white farmers. Equivalent to about $8,000 today, $300 may not have been a huge sum for a piece of property. Still, if rigorously enforced, that part of the new constitution would have disenfranchised many of the state's white men, too. Poll taxes added to the burden on the cash-poor.

However, the elimination of any plausible revival of "Negro rule" in a state with a Black majority gave many plebeian whites an excuse to withdraw from electoral politics altogether. By the election of 1908, only sixty-five thousand South Carolinians voted—fifteen thousand fewer than in the presidential contest thirty years before, although the state's population had grown by 20 percent over that span. During the first decade of the new century, fewer than half of white men and less than a tenth of Black ones cast ballots in the states that had once joined the Confederacy. "The Negroes, who are almost all Republicans, feel it is useless to vote," commented a Louisiana reporter in 1902, "while the whites, who are almost all Democrats, feel that it is unnecessary." Turnout did sometimes increase for competitive Democratic primaries in which only whites could participate.[14]

Despite having drastically narrowed the franchise, most Southern politicians embraced the economic gospel of equality for whites only that Bryan was preaching. They did away with democracy at home while denouncing the exploitation of their white constituents by Northern capital. Thus, Dixie state legislatures forced cuts in railroad rates and reduced working hours for their hard-pressed employees. They endorsed both the direct election of senators and a progressive income tax. They welcomed the growth of unions in the building trades and the railroads—while opposing them in the textile mills that moved down from New England to take advantage of cheaper labor. These steps convinced most Populists to switch back to the Democracy. In truth, their only alternative was utter marginality. Still, the return to "the party of the fathers" did encourage Democratic leaders to turn the South into what the great C. Vann Woodward would call "the most thoroughly 'Bryanized' part of the country."[15]

The most famous re-convert from Populism was Tom Watson, a big landowner and magazine editor from Georgia who had abandoned the Democracy in the 1890s after serving one term in Congress. Actually, in Watson's view, it was Grover Cleveland who had betrayed the ideals of the splendid party that Andrew Jackson had first brought to power. "Oh, for an hour of that stern old warrior," the Georgian mused in 1892, "before whose Militia Rifles the veterans of Waterloo melted away, and before whose fiery wrath the combined money-kings bit the dust!"[16]

In 1896, delegates to the Populist convention vainly asked Bryan to make the eloquent Watson, leader of the third party in Georgia, his running mate. But the Democratic standard-bearer refused to dump Arthur Sewall, the Maine businessman his party had already chosen to run for the second spot. A pro-silverite, the New England shipbuilder brought regional balance to the ticket and, it was hoped, some urgently needed funds. Watson sulked about the snub for several years, then ran two races for president on the moribund Populist line. In 1908, he received a mere twenty-nine thousand votes nationwide. Finally, Watson acknowledged that it was "impossible to do anything in the South outside of the Democratic Party." He vowed, "I am going to devote the balance of my life to driving . . . deserters and do-nothings" out of the party.[17]

Over the next decade, Watson gained a new set of followers and national attention by hurling volleys of animus at both the wealthy elite above and racial and religious minorities below. He warned that "the bloodiest struggle between the rich and poor that ever drenched a continent with human blood" would break out if the rule of "big money" were not ended. He loudly backed the anti-corporate measures that fellow Democrats proposed in the state and nation, while helping elect like-minded partisans in Georgia.

At the same time, in the pages of his magazine, *The Jeffersonian*, he curdled into as virulent a race-baiter as Ben Tillman had ever been. In 1909, still resentful at Bryan for not running with him in 1896, he accused the popular Democrat of "flirting" with Black leaders during his final campaign for president and, horror of horrors, having "cordially met and hospitably entertained" with "negro delegations." Watson combined his hostility toward Black people with the paranoid accusation that Catholics and Jews were engaging in separate "conspiracies" to debauch the citizenry. In 1915, his fiery editorials inspired a gang of anti-Semites to drag Leo Frank—a Jewish factory manager in Atlanta falsely convicted of rape and murder—from jail, drive him across the state, and strangle him to death at the end of a rope.[18]

Out in the Rocky Mountains, Popocrats could practice a form of Bryanism less corrupted by the poison of white Anglo-Saxon Protestant supremacism that infected Watson and his followers in Dixie. The People's Party that blossomed in that sparsely settled region drew its numbers and energy not from farmers but from coal and silver miners, a sizable chunk of whom were European immigrants from Catholic and Orthodox lands across the Atlantic. Since the 1880s, they had waged bitter, often violent strikes to force their employers, Republicans to a man, to pay them a living wage, provide them with livable quarters, and recognize their unions.

In the Gilded Age Congress, the GOP majority had carved the region that stretched from the Canadian border south to Colorado into seven individual states. Their combined population of fewer than two million elected almost one-seventh of the U.S. Senate, and their clout in the Electoral College roughly equaled that of Ohio, which had more than twice as many people. Voters in the new states rewarded their partisan benefactor with legislative majorities and gave not a single electoral vote to any Democratic nominee for president.

In 1892, the People's Party disrupted this tidy arrangement, and Rocky Mountain politics would never be the same. That year, James Weaver, the Populist nominee, won Colorado, Nevada, and Idaho—and came close to taking Wyoming from the GOP as well. With the support of pro-labor Democrats, the radical third party also swept into power in Colorado, home to nearly half the region's inhabitants. They quickly enacted woman suffrage and an eight-hour day for public employees before the depression battered the state and brought the Republicans back into control. Still, during their brief heyday in the mountain sun, the Populists elected more state and local candidates than in any other region.

Although Bryan was a loyal Democrat, his rise gave disappointed insurgents in the Rockies and their working-class voters a reason to believe their cause might yet triumph, if under a different name. His party's embrace of "free silver" also united the miners who dug the metal out of the earth and the bosses who paid them badly to do it—while winning over small farmers who hoped an increase in the money supply would make it easier for them to borrow money and pay back their debts. In 1896, the Great Commoner took the votes of most ordinary citizens on his way to sweeping every state in the region. He won Colorado with a remarkable 85 percent of the vote.

For the next two decades, voters in the mountain states supported Democratic nominees for president almost as reliably as did white Southerners. Only in 1904, when the national party, in an ill-considered lurch back to Clevelandism, chose Alton Parker, a lackluster judge from New York, did the Republican candidate—President Theodore Roosevelt—break that streak. As Bryan prepared to run again in 1908, the Democratic National Committee tipped its hand by choosing to hold the nominating convention in Denver, one of the few cities outside the South that the Great Commoner had carried in his two previous campaigns. Partisan identity was never as strong in the mountain states as in the flatter regions back East, where the major parties had been developing their organizations and honing their lines of attack since before the Civil War. But, in Colorado and neighboring states, Bryan's argument for a government that would side with labor and help farmers and small businesspeople mitigate the injuries of economic change became gospel for self-described progressives in both parties.[19]

The Democrats' embrace of state-sponsored reform in the nation also compelled a change in the behavior of the men who ran its bastions in the urban North, although they moved, as always, at their own pace and in their own fashion. Tammany Hall had been winning elections and governing Manhattan and, on occasion, New York State for decades without much help from, and sometimes with the active hostility of, whoever happened to be their party's nominee for president. Holding on to local power had always been the Hall's paramount concern and that of its newer counterparts in Albany, Boston, and a sprinkling of other Northeastern metropolises. Moreover, the saloon-owning Irish Catholics who bossed the machines never really warmed up to Bryan, the Bible-thumping, teetotaling orator from Nebraska whose heart clearly lay in the pastures, fields, and peaks of middle America.

Yet the bosses were also shrewd politicians; they knew a stand-pat posture during an age of reform would not keep them in power or loosen the GOP's grip on the federal government. So during the early years of the twentieth century, they began to initiate or endorse measures that nurtured a true, if embryonic, welfare state, instead of the informal, charitable gestures on which the machine had built its renown as the friend of the poor. In 1906, Tammany came out for public ownership of the city's utilities and vowed a battle against "criminal combinations of capital." In 1911, the talented young Tammany-weaned leaders of the state legislature—Alfred E. Smith and Robert F. Wagner—spearheaded passage of a bill creating the Factory Investigating Commission after a horrible fire at the Triangle shirtwaist factory in lower Manhattan had taken the lives of 146 workers, most of them female immigrants.[20]

Neither act was born of simple altruism. The publisher William Randolph Hearst was running for governor with Tammany's backing and had made the demand for municipally owned gas and water central to his campaign. Smith and Wagner wrote their landmark bill only after Socialists had organized a mass funeral on the Lower East Side for the victims of the Triangle disaster that attracted a throng of 120,000 mourners. With the city's labor movement swelling to a quarter of a million members, leaders of the Hall now had to build alliances with the kinds of activists who, after Henry George's defeat in 1886, they had been able to co-opt or silence. When a woman suffrage referendum made it onto the state ballot in 1915, Tammany invited its local activists to hold meetings in its clubhouses and helped them with canvassing, although party leaders did not actually endorse votes for women, knowing how unpopular it was among its male, working-class base. The measure failed at the polls, but the drivers of the machine understood that cooperation in the present could attract a new Democratic constituency in the near future.

The departure did not mean leaving behind the old ways that had brought success—and profits—to the machine throughout the Gilded Age. Charles Murphy became chief of the Hall in 1902 and remained in charge until his death in 1924. Like his predecessors, he had risen from a working-class milieu that admired and frequently rewarded a man who excelled in competitive sports and saloonkeeping—and displayed his devotion to the Catholic Church. Like Kelly and Croker, Murphy let no opportunity to use public jobs to accumulate private wealth pass him by. Soon after ascending to leadership of Tammany, he purchased a fifty-acre estate on Long Island with enough space for a nine-hole golf course.

Murphy also made sure his fellow Hibernians would continue to control the machine and receive the best patronage jobs in the police department and the white-collar bureaucracy. He managed this feat of ethnic persistence even as immigrants who had nothing in common with most Irish Americans except their lowly origins and white skin became a majority in large parts of Manhattan and in Brooklyn, where Boss Hugh McLaughlin reigned in much the same fashion. In the early twentieth century, the many thousands of Jews fleeing the tsarist empire and Southern Italians who moved into tenements in the Lower East Side of Manhattan made that neighborhood among the most crowded in the world. But from 1908 until the early 1930s, every Democratic candidate who sought to represent the district on the board of aldermen and in either house of the state legislature could trace his ancestry back to the Emerald Isle.

At the same time, Tammany leaders on the East Side signed up Jewish associates who worked diligently to keep their ethnic brethren from "wasting" their votes on Socialists. Italians, many of whom returned to the Old Country when they earned enough to buy property there, did not take as active a part in public life and thus posed less of a threat to Irish domination. Through methods both new and traditional, New York's bosses thus reproduced themselves and won most contests, keeping the nation's largest city a Democratic stronghold, even as Republicans governed most of the nation west of the Hudson River.

## Progressives in Power

But midway through the administration of the last Republican who defeated Bryan, the GOP's winning streak came to an end. William Howard Taft never really wanted to be president; in 1906, he had confessed to his wife, "Politics, when I am in it, makes me sick." But Teddy Roosevelt, trusting his secretary of war to continue advocating for his brand of progressivism, had convinced him to run. By 1910, however, Taft was siding with conservatives in his party on a number of critical issues, and his erstwhile, now angry, mentor was considering running against him.[21]

Democrats, who had backed TR's anti-corporate stand more often than had many lawmakers in his own party, saw an opening and dashed through it. In that fall's elections, they swept into control of the House of Representatives for the first time since the debacle of 1894. They basked in a sixty-six-seat majority and did well enough in contests for state legislatures to pick up ten additional seats in the Senate. Voters in several big Northern industrial states elected Democratic governors, too. Among them was Woodrow Wilson in New Jersey. The president of Princeton University had gained a national reputation by writing provocative books about politics and history, but he had never run for office before.

The party that went on to nominate Wilson for president two years later was more confident of realizing its ambitions than it had been since the depression of the 1890s. But it remained essentially the party that Bryan had built. The three-time loser kept his vow not to compete for the 1912 nomination. Still, he deployed his stature and voice to make sure that whoever carried the party's standard that fall would follow his lead.

First, Bryan wrote most of the platform, echoing the one he ran on in 1908. Then he got delegates to pass a resolution to oppose any candidate favored by a trio of wealthy New York financiers—including August Belmont, Jr.—"or any other member of the privilege-seeking and favor-seeking class." Finally, he switched his own vote to Wilson from Champ Clark, the Speaker of the House, which broke a deadlock and was the pivotal act that handed victory to the governor from New Jersey. The last two acts enraged Democrats who thought

Bryan was just stoking turmoil and his own ego. But leading progressives were delighted at what one magazine called his "moral power and patriotic devotion." Walter Rauschenbusch, a leading theologian of the Social Gospel, described his ability "to wrest control of his party at least for a time from evil hands." Woodrow Wilson would thus go into battle with a party committed to the same ideas Bryan had been declaiming consistently since 1896.[22]

The 1912 campaign was one of the more unusual presidential competitions in history. The leading contenders were Wilson and Theodore Roosevelt, nominee of the new Progressive Party, whose slogan, "Let the People Rule," turned Bryan's question from 1908 into a brash affirmative. The two men agreed about one big thing: the federal government should regulate corporate power in order to benefit wage earners and consumers and root out the corrupt bargains politicians made routinely with industrialists and their minions. A third candidate—Eugene V. Debs, proudly running on the Socialist ticket—wanted to abolish private business and the wage system altogether. His 6 percent of the vote was the apex of support any Marxist running for the White House has ever received. Although Taft, the forlorn incumbent, had initiated more anti-trust prosecutions than any president before him, he remained an indifferent campaigner. That all his opponents branded him a passionless reactionary showed how much the rhetoric of moral capitalism had captured both parties. The president who had won easily in 1908 carried just two states and a pitiful 23 percent of the popular vote.

What the narrative of the four-man circus obscures is the rapid ascendancy the Democrats had made from an embattled minority bottled up in disparate regions to a national force prepared to carry out a vigorous, anti-corporate agenda. With a seven-seat margin in the Senate and a two-thirds majority in the House, they could pass almost any legislation they wanted. This remained true even after the 1914 midterm election, when Democrats lost sixty-one seats in the lower chamber. Wilson had inherited the party's agenda more than he shaped it. Before being elected governor of New Jersey, he had disparaged labor unions and faulted big business only for favoring a protective tariff. He had never endorsed Bryan for president. "I do not in the least despair," Wilson wrote to a friend early in 1910, "of seeing the Democratic party drawn back to the definite and conservative principles which it once represented."[23]

However, once the academic-turned-politician began to run for the White House, he began to court both Bryan and his large following in the party. "The masters of the government of the United States are the combined capitalists and manufacturers," Wilson declared in a manifesto written for the 1912 campaign. By the time he took the oath of office, Wilson had committed himself to achieving the most far-reaching changes in federal policy since Reconstruction. While opportunism may have been his original reason to tilt toward the progressives who dominated his party, he soon became a believer. His appointment of Bryan as secretary of state—a post that often went to a party leader—seemed to make the conversion complete, although Wilson never spoke in the messianic populist tone that had made the Great Commoner many friends and even more enemies.[24]

By the end of his first term in office, Wilson and his fellow partisans in Congress had enacted several major pieces of legislation that fulfilled the central planks in their 1912 platform—which had condemned "monopolies" and vowed "to protect the people from injustice at the hands of those who seek to make the government a private asset in business." In the Underwood Tariff Act of 1913, they reduced rates from 40 to 25 percent and instituted an income tax on the richest Americans. With the Clayton Act, passed in 1914, they sought to toughen the existing anti-trust law and set up a new commission to enforce it. The 1916 Adamson Act guaranteed an eight-hour day to railroad workers (the most critical employees in the land). Along with the earlier creation of the Labor Department, whose first secretary was a former top official in the United Mine Workers, it strengthened the bond between the American Federation of Labor and the Democratic Party and elicited howls of "labor tyranny" from Republicans. Finally, the new Federal Reserve System, established in a bill written by Representative Carter Glass, aimed to abolish the "dominion" of "the money trust" over the nation's banks. Bryan often traveled to the Capitol from the State Department to help Democrats resolve disputes about what a law should include and then to whip up support for the final versions.[25]

The main purpose of the expanded national state the Democrats began to build in the years from 1913 through 1916 was to restrain and regulate corporate power, not to redistribute the wealth. Most new government employees were hired to administer new agencies like the Federal Trade Commission, the Federal Reserve, and a bevy of services to farmers provided by the Agriculture Department. The income tax law passed in 1913 had a top rate of just 7 percent— which only the minuscule number of Americans who earned at least $500,000 a year had to pay. Democrats had thus struck some blows for the kind of moral capitalism that Bryan, the People's Party, and their fellow anti-monopolists had long demanded. Yet they did little to raise the living standards of wage earners or to make it easier for small farmers to secure loans at interest rates they could afford, or to break up wealthy firms that hired millions of workers and made popular consumer goods. But then, the legislators who drafted the bills had never intended to achieve those ends. They aimed to put rings in the noses of corporate hogs, not to cut off their limbs and dole the meat out in equal portions to ordinary people.

The Southern Democrats who essentially ran Congress during Wilson's first term naturally played the major role in shaping the key laws that made it to his desk. In 1912, a special subcommittee chaired by Representative Arsène Pujo of Louisiana had held well-publicized hearings that revealed widespread collusion by a trust of large bank and investment houses to manipulate stock prices. The findings made the income tax and a central bank difficult for most members of Congress to oppose.

Every committee chairman in the House who wrote one of the regulatory bills during Wilson's first term hailed from a safe seat in Dixie: Oscar Underwood and Henry Clayton were from Alabama, William Adamson came from a district near Atlanta, and Carter Glass represented one in rural Virginia. Though the president had made his career in the North, he had grown up in Georgia as the son of a Presbyterian minister who supported the Confederacy.

Conservative critics, most of whom were Republicans, blasted the regulatory reforms as "socialistic" and charged that Bryanite radicalism, with its strongest strain in Dixie, had now infected the entire body politic. The New York *Sun* called the Federal Reserve Act a "preposterous offspring of ignorance and unreason" whose "provisions for a Government currency and an official board to exercise absolute control over the most important of banking functions is covered all over with the slime of Bryanism."[26]

But Southern Democrats were careful to avoid taking any step that threatened to weaken the Jim Crow order. They aided workers on the railroad but no one who toiled on someone else's farm or in someone else's home—the only jobs most Black people were able to get. Reducing tariffs and giving a central bank control over monetary policy were boons to agrarian firms and other small proprietors who needed easier access to capital. Five of the twelve new branches of the Federal Reserve just happened to be located in Southern or border cities. Yet only a small number of African Americans owned their own businesses.

At the state level, Southern Democrats accelerated the progressive turn begun in Bryan's heyday. They enacted bans on child labor in textile mills, regulated railroads and food production, and required every young person to go to school. Like their counterparts in Congress, they aimed to construct a system based on a vision of "egalitarian whiteness." Andrew Jackson would likely not have approved of the laws they passed and the new bureaucracies they created, but most progressive Democrats shared the same racial beliefs as their forerunners eight decades before; Bryanism thus kept faith with the party's most ignoble tradition after all.[27]

The Democrats emerged as a party of economic reform at the same time as socialist and labor parties were surging to an influential status in the legislatures and cultures of other industrializing nations across the Atlantic. Americans and Europeans had several important goals in common: implementing progressive taxation, supporting labor unions, creating a shorter workday, and regulating the operations of industrial firms. Bryan took two lengthy tours of Europe in the years after his 1900 campaign and praised the superiority of city-owned public utilities to those back home run by private companies. In Germany, he even also lauded that country's socialist party, the largest in Europe, for having "educated the working classes to a very high standard of political intelligence and to a strong sense of their independence and of their social mission."[28]

But his Democrats were not a party rooted in the proletariat, nor did they share the ultimate goal of replacing capitalism instead of compelling it to benefit the majority of the population. Debs's Socialist Party, which reached a zenith of 118,000 members in 1912, aspired to be as powerful as its comradely counterpart in Germany. But the deep racial and ethnic divisions and inequalities in America turned class consciousness into just one identity among many that wage earners expressed instead of the driving force of their worldview. And given the white South's pivotal role in the Democracy, party leaders would never think of encouraging white workers to ally with Black ones for their mutual benefit.

The clout of the agrarian South did not prevent Democrats from attracting a small but influential new constituency that remains with them still: left-leaning intellectuals from the urban North. Since Jackson's tenure, most serious writers and artists, in or out of academia, had disdained the party as a bastion of drunk Irishmen, violent racists, venal bosses, and irrational hayseeds. Such illustrious writers as Walt Whitman and Nathaniel Hawthorne had contributed to *The Democratic Review* in the 1840s, but after its editor became a passionate defender of slavery and the war with Mexico, many Northern readers abandoned it.

The prominent liberal author and journalist Walter Lippmann recalled that in the prosperous German Jewish enclave of turn-of-the-century Manhattan where he grew up, Grover Cleveland's name "was uttered with monstrous dread" while Bryan was regarded as "an ogre from the West." At its founding in 1914, *The New Republic*, whose editorial policy Lippmann did much to shape, viewed Theodore Roosevelt as the most likely politician to steer the United States toward a sensible middle ground between what the magazine viewed as the equally destructive ideologies of socialism and individualism.[29]

But Woodrow Wilson gradually won over the magazine's editors, most of its contributors, and probably the bulk of its forty thousand readers as well. His intellectual credentials and bearing were part of his appeal. The first president to have earned a PhD and run a major university gave graceful speeches full of soaring ideals, even if, as *New Republic* editor Herbert Croly complained, he did manage to "make even the most concrete things seem like abstractions." Wilson also cultivated prominent liberal thinkers like the philosopher John

Dewey; he invited them to the White House and appointed a few to posts in his administration.[30]

He also impressed the growing number of pro-labor intellectuals with his appointments to the Commission on Industrial Relations— perhaps the most class-conscious federal inquiry in U.S. history. Chaired by Frank P. Walsh, a left-wing Democrat from Kansas City, the Commission's staff was heavy with investigators known for their sympathy with the grievances of wage earners. They interviewed a wide range of unionists and employers and published, in 1915, a majority report that demanded "drastic" action to redistribute wealth and protect the right of workers to organize unions.[31]

In 1916, the president's nomination of Louis Brandeis to the Supreme Court made a strong case to any progressive intellectuals he had not yet persuaded. During the preceding decade, Brandeis had earned a national reputation as the "people's lawyer" by representing wage earners and consumers in court against employers and financiers. He pioneered the use of expert witnesses to establish the social facts undergirding his legal arguments and helped write the Federal Reserve Act. His 1914 book, with the provocative title *Other People's Money and How the Bankers Use It*, used the revelations of the Pujo Committee to advocate strict curbs on big financial firms like that of J. P. Morgan, which funneled money to large corporations that crushed small businesses. As the first Jewish nominee to the court, Brandeis predictably became the target of every anti-Semite in the land, including the president of Harvard University. In private, William Howard Taft voiced the outrage of conservatives who felt the legal system they cherished was under attack. Brandeis, seethed the former president, was "a muckraker, an emotionalist . . . , a socialist . . . a man of infinite cunning . . . of great tenacity of purpose, and, in my judgment, of much power for evil." For the editor of *The New Republic* and his fellow liberal intellectuals, the battle to confirm Brandeis became a symbolic struggle between rational, public-spirited reformers and bigoted reactionaries. If both the future justice and the president who chose him were Democrats, how could they themselves not be Democrats as well?[32]

The persistence of that partisan identity for more than a century is also rooted in the new powers Wilson and his party created for the administrative state. In modern societies, most intellectuals view themselves as altruists and view working in the state apparatus, particularly at a high level, as a fine way to put that impulse into practice. In so doing, most are, of course, also feeding their own egos. But it is hard to resist the opportunity to apply one's ideas about what policies to adopt and what kind of rhetoric will advance them. Beginning with the Wilson era, Democrats have consistently been the national party identified with expanding the public sphere, and the one that welcomed men—and soon women—who made a career of studying and then advancing the ends government might serve.

The Brandeis appointment, and his confirmation by the Senate that June, had a more proximate significance as well: it was the opening shot in Woodrow Wilson's reelection campaign. Democrats had good reasons to be anxious about his chances. Republicans were unified again, and they had a nominee, Charles Evans Hughes, who, as governor of New York a few years earlier, had earned a progressive reputation by signing such measures as a forty-eight-hour workweek for child laborers and limits on corporate donations to campaigns. No Democratic president but Andrew Jackson had ever won consecutive terms, and none since Franklin Pierce had gained a majority of the popular vote. And the big losses the party had suffered in the 1914 midterms did not augur well for the contest two years later.

Out of both necessity and conviction, Wilson and his advisers resolved to run on his image as an anti-corporate reformer, even if his record did not always back that up. They calculated that if the incumbent could combine wins in most Western states with the reliably solid South, he could offset Republican strength in the Northeast and industrial Midwest. This strategy required the Democrats to win over voters who had backed Roosevelt's Progressive candidacy in 1912 and regretted that the Bull Moose had now returned to his ancestral political home. In July, a leading Colorado Democrat wrote to the president's physician and friend, "The appointment of Brandeis has had a greater effect upon the Progressives here than anything else." To bolster their appeal to such voters, as well as to their own base, Democrats included in their national platform promises to abolish child labor, enact an eight-hour day and a "living wage" for all government employees, create a safety bureau to curb industrial accidents, construct public highways, and expand federal loans to farmers. For the first time, the party officially declared its support for woman suffrage, albeit by individual states instead of a constitutional amendment—as the Republicans were demanding. The document contained no mention of either Black Americans or immigrants. To do so would have risked dividing a party united in its desire to ensure that "special privilege" and "commercial interests" could no longer use the government "for their selfish ends."[33]

Democrats combined an appeal to reform with a pledge to keep the nation out of the Great War, which, since the summer of 1914, had claimed millions of lives in Europe and the Middle East. Although Congress, at Wilson's request, had doubled the size of the army earlier in 1916 and authorized a draft for future conflicts, neither the president nor most in his party favored the massive military buildup or employed the kind of bellicose, anti-German rhetoric that Theodore Roosevelt and most other prominent Republicans used.

For a party committed to a new age of peace and reform, Democratic leaders designed an innovative campaign that used techniques borrowed from specialists in the new professions of public relations and advertising. The DNC had opened its first headquarters in the capital city in 1913. But it essentially marked time until beginning to plan the party's next national convention. Vance McCormick—the new chairman elected in 1916—was a newspaper publisher and erstwhile politician who put both of those experiences to good use. He quickly set up an apparatus that featured a publicity bureau staffed by crack journalists. They fashioned sophisticated appeals to women, labor, and other groups and every ten days sent out print-ready articles and cartoons to more than four thousand daily papers. They also produced a film showing Wilson at work and two lambasting Hughes that were screened in an untold number of theaters around the country. The PR campaign employed a style, pioneered by muckraking journalists, meant for citizens who needed to be more aroused than educated. "The average man wants material served up to him in a direct way . . . He expects directness, the dramatic. He is trained to short sentences," the progressive activist Frederic C. Howe wrote to a Wilson adviser.[34]

These techniques were a marked departure from the classically elegant, if long-winded, style of rhetoric that Bryan and Wilson had mastered. They helped offset the large financial advantage the Republicans had enjoyed for the past two decades. Hughes's decision to run primarily on a vow to reinstate the protective tariff made him seem a relic of the Gilded Age, even as Teddy Roosevelt and other dynamic speakers traveled the country to inspire the GOP faithful.

The election result was as close as observers in both parties had predicted. Wilson won by just twenty-three electoral votes, with 49 percent of the popular tally. As expected, Hughes carried nearly every state in the Northeastern quadrant of the nation, with the exception of New Hampshire and Ohio—the latter of which Republicans could usually take for granted. But he did not concede until two weeks after the election because many ballots in close states were in doubt. In the end, if Wilson had not carried California (which he won by just 3,773 votes), he would have lost the election.

The Democrats' winning coalition looked a lot like the one that had rallied to Bryan's losing cause two decades before. Both Wilson and Bryan swept the South and the Mountain West and retained the loyalty of Irish Catholics in the cities. Unions affiliated with the American Federation of Labor, however, had far more members in 1916 than in 1896, and most endorsed and worked to reelect the incumbent. They were a particularly strong force in Northern California; Wilson would have lost the election without them. The number of immigrants from Southern and Eastern Europe had also swelled since 1896. Yet, whether naturalized or not, most were not yet accustomed to voting; those who did make it to the polls sided no more with one major party than the other.

The close election failed to solidify the Democrats' hold on Congress. They retained an eleven-seat majority in the Senate but won six fewer House seats than the Republicans and retained control only because the handful of representatives from minor parties voted with Wilson's when it came time to select the Speaker and the chairmen of all the committees.

Bryan played a critical part in keeping the Democratic president in power. Although he had resigned as secretary of state the year before in protest over Wilson's hostility toward Germany, the specter of a Republican in the White House roused him to partisan action once again. From the middle of September until Election Day, Bryan took to the road, spending most of his time in swing states west of the Mississippi, where he drew crowds as large and enthusiastic as in any of his own campaigns. The election, writes one historian, "was a referendum on four years of far-reaching progressive legislation and on the progressive Democratic party that had evolved since 1896." That was one kind of evolution that Bryan, the biblical literalist, believed in.[35]


## Winning a War and Losing the Voters

A month after Wilson was inaugurated for a second term, the United States went to war and his triumphant coalition gradually began to splinter. Most Democrats in and out of Congress had been opposed to sending Americans to participate in the carnage that, by the spring of 1917, had claimed the lives of millions of combatants and civilians. After all, their president had won reelection, if narrowly, by running on the slogan "He Kept Us Out of War." When Wilson asked Congress for a declaration of war in early April, only fourteen Democrats in the House and just three in the Senate defied him. But most voted aye more to show resolve in the face of renewed German U-boat attacks on American merchant ships than to express enthusiasm for the president's mission of creating a world "made safe for democracy."[36]

One of the congressmen from Wilson's party who voted against going to war was North Carolina's Claude Kitchin, who held the powerful posts of majority leader and chairman of the Ways and Means Committee, which was responsible for initiating every revenue bill in Congress. Kitchin lamented that "the long night of a world-wide war" would "extinguish . . . the only remaining star of hope for Christendom"; he predicted that "all the demons of humanity will be let loose for a rampage throughout the world." Despite opposing the president of his own party, Kitchin retained both his high positions for the duration of the war. So did the anti-militarist chairman of the Senate Foreign Relations Committee, William Stone of

Missouri, who voted against war because he feared that "if we go into it, we will never have the same old Republic."[37]

The unified spirit of patriotic zeal, which erupts at the onset of any armed conflict, cooled rather quickly in the nation at large. By the fall of 1917, the closely matched contingents of Democrats and Republicans in Congress were heatedly debating whether to levy an excess profits tax on corporations that churned out supplies for the army, which firms should get large military contracts, and whether to ban the manufacture and sale of alcoholic beverages in order to conserve grain and, perhaps, moralize the populace. That November, Morris Hillquit, a socialist lawyer running for mayor of New York City on an anti-war platform, drew 22 percent of the ballots in a four-man race; the incumbent, the sole candidate who gave his unqualified endorsement to Wilson's leadership, failed to win even a quarter of the vote. Resistance to the new conscription law was widespread; more than 3 million men never bothered to register, as required, and nearly 350,000 who did register either failed to show up for induction or deserted once in uniform. William Jennings Bryan stopped giving anti-war speeches after Congress made its fateful decision in April. But he then devoted most of his energy to promoting the twin causes of woman suffrage and prohibition. Bryan knew that millions of rank-and-file Democrats were ambivalent, at best, about enlisting young Americans in a crusade to end all wars by waging the bloodiest one in history.

The conflict did improve "the health of the state," as the critic Randolph Bourne famously put it, and the expansion of federal authority boosted the power of some Democratic constituencies while alienating others. Samuel Gompers and his fellow labor leaders were thrilled at the doubling of union membership, which the administration's tacit support made possible. In November 1917, Woodrow Wilson became the first president to address a convention of the American Federation of Labor, founded three decades earlier. The nationalization of interstate railroads, for the duration of the war at least, fulfilled a long-held dream of the left and spurred demands for public ownership of the energy industry as well. Seven months after the war ended, Congress passed the Nineteenth Amendment, whose subsequent ratification by the states on August 18, 1920, finally gave women everywhere in the nation the right to vote.

But a flood of indictments of dissenters who ran afoul of the harsh Espionage Act of 1917 and the Sedition Act of 1918 infuriated many of the same progressive intellectuals and journalists who had persuaded themselves that Wilson was one of their own. In 1918, even *The New York World*, the high-circulation Democratic daily that had been a virtual administration organ, accused the president of "undertak[ing] the Prussianization of American public opinion." From Georgia, Tom Watson vented his own outrage at both the repression and the draft as moves "to prepare the country for a change of government . . . from a Republic to a military despotism."[38]

That fall's midterm elections, held just six days before the Great War ended in Europe, demonstrated the consequences of distressing one's core activists and publicists. Republicans, claiming that the president was behaving as an "autocrat," won control, narrowly, of both Houses of Congress for the first time in a decade.

In what was left of Wilson's time in the White House, that defeat became the overture of a Democratic debacle in the making. The eighteen months after the armistice saw multiple intersecting conflicts that the party's leaders either failed to resolve or made a good deal worse. The administration stood by as employers and police defeated a massive strike by steelworkers who demanded the "industrial democracy" they'd been promised would be their reward for producing the commodities of war. Then, Attorney General A. Mitchell Palmer ordered a series of raids on the homes and offices of thousands of radicals, jailing some and deporting others. These acts alienated civil libertarians who had clung to a hope that the wartime crackdown on dissidents would disappear once the guns fell silent on the Western Front. In Chicago and several other cities, white residents launched homicidal attacks on Black migrants who had moved North for work, and some of the newcomers responded with deadly blows of their own. Given their Southern base, Democrats refrained from casting blame where it belonged. Finally, back in Washington, Woodrow Wilson's cherished dream that the United States would lead the world in erecting a diplomatic order that would avoid future wars crashed to earth in the fall of 1919 when the Republican-led

Senate refused to ratify the peace treaty he had signed in Paris. Having suffered a massive stroke that summer, the president could only hope he might recover "to bring this country to a sense of its great opportunity and greater responsibility."[39]

In 1920, the electoral consequence of all these failures and setbacks was the most statistically abysmal outcome in the long history of the Democratic Party. Its presidential nominee won just 34 percent of the popular tally and not a single electoral vote outside the South. No Democrat won a Senate seat in any other region, and the party's candidates took only a tenth of the House districts outside Dixie to end up with less than a third of all seats in the lower chamber.

It did not matter that the Republican presidential nominee was a one-term senator from Ohio, Warren G. Harding, who was virtually unknown outside his own state and had no legislation or big ideas to his name. The Democrats, besides an inability to run on their recent record, had to keep faith with Woodrow Wilson by defending the peace treaty, which had no chance of being ratified. At their convention in San Francisco, they also fought over the merits of Prohibition, which had become the law of the land just a few months before. As evangelical Protestants, most Southerners hailed it, but urban machines and their voters, voicing the objections of their immigrant and Catholic constituents, derided it as an assault both on tradition and "personal liberty." It took the delegates forty-four ballots to nominate James M. Cox, largely in the hope that, as the sitting governor of Ohio, he could carry his home state, one that had been critical to Wilson's victory in 1916. Because the platform did not mention Prohibition at all, Bryan, for the first time in his adult life, refused to campaign for the party's ticket.

A quarter-century after his first run for president, the Democrats had given up all the electoral terrain the Great Commoner and his progressive allies had fought to occupy and alienated the new constituencies they had diligently worked to persuade. Republicans were once again the majority party in the West and throughout the industrial North, with the exception of New York City and a few other urban beachheads. Samuel Gompers, still president of the AFL, endorsed Cox, but nearly forty leaders of unions affiliated with the federation signed a statement denouncing the incumbent administra-

tion for various misdeeds and praised Harding for "favoring unionism and collective bargaining." In 1920, the Democrats even lost the
votes of many Hibernian Catholics bitter at Wilson's reluctance to
pressure the British to grant independence to Ireland. If it had not
been for the states of the former Confederacy, the two-party system
would have been moribund.[40]

Yet, despite the dismal result, the Democrats did not turn entirely
away from their commitment to a form of moral capitalism, advanced
by the state, that Bryan had championed as their leader. In 1922,
the three-time loser refreshed his progressive gospel, proclaiming,
"The power of the government to protect the people is as complete
in time of peace as in time of war. The only question to be decided
is whether it is necessary to exercise that power." That he meant this
as an argument for Prohibition as well as for measures to aid working people and rein in corporate power did not lessen its validity for
many party activists. In 1920, the Democrats had nominated for vice
president a vigorous and eloquent thirty-eight-year-old assistant secretary of the navy with a famous name whose distinguished, if brief,
record of reform in the New York legislature suggested he might one
day be able to carry on the tradition Bryan had begun. Franklin Del-
ano Roosevelt was certainly eager to try.[41]

# 5

## IT'S UP TO THE WOMEN,
## 1920–1933

*The only way to get things in this country is from the
inside of the political parties.*
—CARRIE CHAPMAN CATT, LEADER OF THE WOMAN
SUFFRAGE MOVEMENT, 1920[1]

*Men who work hard in party politics are always recognized, or
taken care of in one way or another. Women, most of whom are
voluntary workers and not at all self-seeking, are generally
expected to find in their labor its own reward.*
—ELEANOR ROOSEVELT, APRIL 1928[2]

*Now the test has come, as never before, since we had
the suffrage—the test of the power and loyalty of
women voters. Governor Alfred Smith . . . has listened
with sympathy, with knowledge and understanding to the
aspirations of working women for leisure, for fair wages,
for a good life. Will the women of this country recognize
the service this man has rendered them, and the help he
has given to the weak and the oppressed?*
—FRANCES PERKINS, LABOR ADVOCATE AND DEMOCRAT,
OCTOBER 1928[3]

The 1920s was a wretched decade to be a Democrat. In three straight
presidential elections, just one of the party's nominees managed to
draw as much as 40 percent of the popular vote. That candidate,
Alfred E. Smith in 1928, was the sole member of the hapless trio to

capture any state outside the South, and he won just two of them. By the middle of the decade, the party was too poor even to afford a headquarters for its national committee. Republicans also enjoyed majorities in both houses of Congress throughout the period, although Democrats did make gains in each midterm election. But the GOP's dominance overall enabled its lawmakers to roll back many of the tax and regulatory policies Woodrow Wilson had signed into law.

Democrats fared somewhat better in gubernatorial contests. They kept their grip on statehouses throughout the South and managed to elect governors rather consistently in New York, New Jersey, and Ohio, as well as in a handful of small states west of the Rockies. Yet not since the 1860s had the Democrats been shut out of national power so decisively and for so long.[4]

Six decades after the war that tore both the nation and the party asunder, another intense, albeit nonviolent, internal conflict kept the Democrats mired in minority status. Faithful partisans from the South and West, most of whom were white evangelical Protestants who strongly backed Prohibition, bridled at the largely Catholic "wets" from New York and other big Eastern cities who believed the growing, increasingly polyglot urban population represented the political as well as the demographic future. In "the tribal Twenties," ethnocultural tastes and affinities overshadowed the agreement among Democrats that the "reactionaries" of the GOP had to be stopped from restoring the power of the wealthy and big corporations that Wilson and a Democratic Congress had begun to diminish. William Jennings Bryan, as ardent a foe of "the liquor traffic" as he had always been of Wall Street, fanned the flames of disunity with a series of bellicose statements. "If the wets expect to obtain control of the Democratic Party and make it the mouthpiece of the underworld," he threatened in 1923, "they must prepare for such a struggle as they never had before."[5]

Yet during the same decade a largely unheralded band of white female Democrats blazed a path to future victories by advocating reforms to improve the lives of working-class people. Some of these activist women had husbands and children and the resources to afford domestic labor; others shared their intimate lives with a female partner, taking care not to publicize that relationship in a society decades away from viewing it as legitimate. All tested the limits of the new freedoms that suffrage and the greater opening of professions to women made possible.

They differed on the merits of Prohibition, but that didn't prevent them from embracing a common agenda and building an organization—the Women's National Democratic Club—to press their views on male leaders and the nation beyond. The group included erstwhile social workers like Frances Perkins and Belle Moscowitz, trade unionists such as Rose Schneiderman and Mary Dreier, popular journalists like Emily Newell Blair, the tiny number of Democratic women who held public office, and one future first lady. They operated somewhat autonomously from the party's male chieftains and yet were ultimately dependent on their power and goodwill. Unsurprisingly, the women could not stop those leaders from behaving in self-destructive ways and refusing to apologize for the damage they caused.

But the members of the female Democracy did soon turn into prophets without much honor. They spoke out, reliably and vigorously, for such policies as protection for labor organizers and the creation of a minimum wage and maximum hours that, a decade later, ended up becoming hallmarks of the New Deal. In so doing, they emulated what Bryan had achieved in his three losing campaigns for the presidency. Like him, they helped expand what most Democrats believed the federal government could and should do to benefit ordinary Americans and restrain those with extraordinary wealth. Ironically, Bryan's own crusade for Prohibition was consistent with that faith in a larger, altruistic state.

Similarly, leading figures in the Democratic women's network in the 1920s espoused the broad vision of a welfare society their fellow male partisans would embrace when the calamity of the Great Depression made it both more popular and more urgent to do so. In contrast with female activists in the increasingly conservative GOP, they articulated a species of class-aware liberalism that sought to humble the power of big business.

Their vision did depart in one signal way from that which Bryan had championed in his multiple swings across the continent. His eloquence had always been trained primarily on the metropolitan malefactors of great wealth for polluting the market for small proprietors and driving many out of business. Bryan's call to attach rings to the snouts of corporate hogs revealed his agrarian origin and sympathies, although he welcomed the AFL's endorsement in his 1908 race against Taft. But most prominent Democratic women hailed from big cities and urged their party to take a more aggressive, more explicitly pro-union stand. They burned to do away with the exploitation of the women, men, and children who toiled in factories, in mines, and on the docks.

Sadly, like Bryan, few did anything to challenge the racial order male Democrats had erected and were determined to preserve. Like most white Americans, the women regarded that order as immutable, if somewhat regrettable. As a result, a full century after the founding of the "Jackson Party," the common welfare they envisioned remained limited almost entirely to members of their own race.

"We women in the home . . . have allowed certain practices which are wrong to grow up among the business men of the country," wrote Eleanor Roosevelt just after she and her husband moved into the White House in 1933. "Had we always insisted that the men take into account the human element that entered into business there would not be the fight there is to-day over what is the fair standard of living for every one in this country." She gave her book the sanguine title *It's Up to the Women*. Roosevelt based that challenge on the example of the female activists she had worked with inside the Democratic Party during the previous decade. Echoing the appeal for suffrage, they believed women, long praised and patronized as *the* moral force in society, should be in the forefront of transforming American capitalism into a system that would provide a decent life to those who produced its bounty yet received a grossly unequal share of it. Now wielding the vote, feminists attempted to bend the party to their will and desires. Not until the 1970s would they do so with such unity and purpose again.[6]

## A Gathering of Forces

What spurred these energetic, self-confident women to cast their lot with a party whose prospects for governing the nation seemed so dim? Given the Democrats' history on issues most female activists had cared deeply about, it was hardly a natural choice. After all, the party had opposed the abolition of slavery, its urban bosses had loathed the temperance movement and greedily pursued "honest graft," and most Democrats were slower to endorse woman suffrage than their Republican counterparts. As president, Woodrow Wilson supported what became the Nineteenth Amendment only when it was about to sail through Congress anyway.

Indeed, some of the leading members of the Democrats' female network had first engaged in electoral politics within a different partisan home: Theodore Roosevelt's Progressive Party in 1912. For Belle Moscowitz, who had lived and worked at a settlement house in Manhattan, TR was the sole presidential candidate that year who understood the value of "our social workers" who dedicated themselves to combating the poverty and powerlessness that plagued immigrant neighborhoods. Jane Addams, the celebrated founder of Hull House in Chicago, agreed and gave a secondary speech for Roosevelt's nomination. The Progressives also appealed to female reformers like Moscowitz because, unlike the GOP and the Democrats, they took an uncompromising stand for universal suffrage. Joining Moscowitz as delegates to the third party's 1912 state convention were the president of the local Women's Trade Union League, the woman president of the New York Consumers League, and a number of other leading activists of both genders who belonged to the intersecting worlds of settlement houses and progressive academia and journalism.[7]

By the early 1920s, however, both Teddy Roosevelt and the Progressives had expired, and most of these same women flocked to the party TR had always detested. By then, Democrats were the only major political force that sought to represent, however imperfectly, the interests of native-born and white immigrant women who toiled for wages in factories or at home and who believed in forcing the wealthiest Americans to pay higher taxes to promote the public welfare. The Republicans of the Jazz Age had become, in contrast, staunch defenders of the liberty of corporations to operate pretty much as they wished. The GOP was also home to most of the white Protestant nativists who pushed through Congress the bills that effectively

banned new immigrants from the Catholic, Jewish, and Eastern Orthodox regions of Europe and excluded East Asians entirely.

As a Jew, Belle Moscowitz inevitably recoiled from the GOP's
harsh nativist turn, but it was the Democrats' new willingness to
aid labor's cause in New York City and State that convinced her and
other social workers to join the party. The ghastly fire that consumed
the Triangle Waist Company in Greenwich Village in March 1911
kindled a set of events that did much to turn women like Moscowitz
from skeptics into fierce partisans.

Frances Perkins, scion of a family of New England Congrega-
tionalists, was then a young settlement house worker and avid suf-
fragist. She happened to witness the horror of the inferno from a
house nearby. "People who had their clothes afire would jump," she
recalled. "Even when [the firemen] got the nets up, the nets didn't
hold in a jump from that height . . . There was no place to go. The
fire was between them and any means of exit . . . They had gone to
the window for air and they jumped." Some of the 146 workers who
perished in the flames could be identified only by the names on the
pay envelopes they clutched in their hands.[8]

Before moving to the Village in 1909, Perkins had worked in settlement houses in Chicago and Philadelphia and had become an ardent socialist. A member of Manhattan's bohemian left, she declared
"I am a revolutionist" at a public meeting and so entranced the novelist Sinclair Lewis that he proposed marriage from a sidewalk outside her apartment building one balmy summer evening. Flattered
but unsmitten, she turned him down.[9]

But the Triangle tragedy started both Perkins and Moscowitz
on a path to redefine the moral core of Democratic politics. Perkins
got hired as one of the post-fire investigators empowered to enforce
stricter safety regulations in state factories. In that position, she grew
to know and respect Al Smith and Robert Wagner, the two young
Tammany stalwarts who had pushed the law through the New York
legislature. Belle Moscowitz attended angry protest meetings after
the Triangle fire. She then landed a job gathering and judging grievances from employees and employers in the local garment industry.
But the bosses got her fired for siding more often with workers and
their unions than with employers.

Like nearly all other women who became active Democrats in the 1920s, Perkins and Moscowitz regarded themselves as feminists; they believed ratification of the Nineteenth Amendment should be merely the start of winning greater influence for their gender in every sphere of American life.

But first they felt it necessary to wage a prolonged debate with sister feminists from the National Women's Party. Members of the party (which did not actually run candidates for office) had made their reputation in 1916 and 1917 with aggressive picketing of the White House that led to their arrests. After suffrage was won, they began a campaign to persuade Congress to pass an equal rights amendment. But most Democrats of both genders feared an ERA would do away with laws and court rulings that limited the hours, set a floor under the wages, and guarded the health and safety of women who toiled in factories like Triangle.

Unionists had endorsed these reforms as steps toward winning similar protections for *all* workers; they and their middle-class allies also defended them for recognizing, as Eleanor Roosevelt put it, that "women *are* different from men." An ERA would, they feared, imperil the real, if still fragile, gains won by and for millions of women who led difficult lives at work. In return, they would get nothing but an abstract statement of equality that pro-business judges and politicians could easily exploit. Pauline Newman, a leader of the International Ladies' Garment Workers Union, scornfully evoked what women's jobs were like before protective laws were passed: "We were 'free' and 'equal' to work long hours for starvation wages, or free to leave the job and starve!"[10]

Meanwhile, away from the sweatshops of Manhattan, another breed of feminists found the Democrats useful to furthering both their policies and their personal ambitions. Women who ran for office in the 1920s had to struggle against the condescension of male leaders and voters who recoiled at the idea of their sisters or mothers taking part in the bruising competition for victory and its spoils. Until late in the decade, they also had to overcome the fact that fewer women than men were making their way to the polls. Not until 1928 did that gender gap narrow to single digits in a national election. Still, a number of women in both major parties ran for Congress and governor, and a few were elected. Twelve women—four of whom were Democrats—served in the House of Representatives during the 1920s. Most of that dozen succeeded a husband who had either retired or died.[11]

Like their counterparts in New York City, the more prominent Democratic female politicians pushed hard for programs that would benefit women and children. Nellie Tayloe Ross was elected governor of Wyoming in 1924, just a month after her husband, the incumbent, died suddenly of a burst appendix. She spent much of her two-year term trying, in vain, to convince the Republican legislature to ban child labor and devote a third of the royalties the state earned from oil and mining claims to fund the public schools. That same year, Mary T. Norton got elected to Congress from Jersey City after she had campaigned to establish public nurseries—childcare centers—for working mothers in her town. Four years later, Ruth Bryan Owen, the eldest daughter of William Jennings Bryan, captured a seat in the House of Representatives from a Florida district that stretched from the Keys all the way up to Jacksonville. Like nearly all her counterparts, Owen had spent many years volunteering for progressive, feminist causes. While living in Miami, she had been president of the local Consumers League, the local Woman's Club, and the local PTA. Soon after she took her seat, Owen proposed that Congress create a new cabinet department devoted to the welfare of Home and Child.

Ross and Owen were confirmed "drys," while Norton, a Catholic who owed her victory to Jersey City's Democratic machine, believed just as strongly that the state had no right to stop Americans from selling and buying beverages they enjoyed. But neither they nor any of the other prominent Democratic women in the land seemed to care enough about the issue to jump into the internal battle over Prohibition being waged by the male leaders of their party.

Their reluctance was due, in part, to the subordinate place they occupied. Beginning in 1920, both Democrats and Republicans took steps to demonstrate, at least publicly, that they no longer catered to or were led solely by men. Both parties organized women's divisions, named an equal number of female members to their national committees, and chose women to be delegates or alternates to their national conventions. But rarely did a woman who had not gained the sponsorship of one or more powerful men rise to an official post— even after, with words and signals, she had assured them that she had no thought of challenging their sway. "A woman on her own had as much chance" to amass political influence, quipped Emily Newell Blair, a popular magazine writer from Missouri who became vice chair of the Democratic Party, "as a Du Pont to sit in President [Franklin] Roosevelt's cabinet." When she lobbied the New York legislature, the thirty-three-year-old Frances Perkins dressed in what her biographer describes as a "somber Black dress" with "pearls" and a "matronly demeanor," to make sure that politicians would not write her off as frivolous or ogle her as an object of desire. Perkins kept a private file of her interactions with Albany insiders, which she labeled "Notes on the Male Mind."[12]

## New Servants of Democracy

The need to placate powerful men did not prevent Perkins and her sister Democrats from organizing a formidable network of women inside the party. They began by adapting an institution that had been a seedbed for several of the key reform campaigns of the Progressive Era: women's clubs. In 1910, at least a million women were regularly attending a local gathering where they could hear a lecture, read up on current affairs, and participate in civic improvement efforts that went under the name of "municipal housekeeping." Most clubs tried to avoid any hint of partisanship, even in states where women already had the vote. Some even avoided the topic of suffrage itself, lest it turn a consensual setting into a combative one.

In the aftermath of the electoral debacle of 1920, Emily Newell Blair started thinking about how to turn more women into Democrats. The daughter of a genteel family from the mining town of Joplin, Missouri, she had left her job as a schoolteacher to become one of the more popular magazine writers in America. Blair, like most other feminists who attached themselves to the party, had only recently chosen a side, although her attorney husband was a longtime Democrat.

Suffrage was her first political passion. In 1916, Blair led a silent, six-hour protest of women—a "golden lane"—at the Democratic convention in St. Louis that refused to support the constitutional amendment pending before Congress. But she had always favored "a centralized government" that could push through reforms such as the abolition of child labor and had "argued the Bryan side as to trusts and railroads and the money question." Blair was also thankful to the Great Commoner for having silenced a throng of miners in Joplin who tried to stop her from giving a brief argument for suffrage before one of his speeches there in 1914: "Imagine, if you can, my feelings as Mr. Bryan comes to my side, lifts his big hand, and his big voice booms out above their chant: 'You will hear the lady first!'"[13]

The female vote in 1920 tilted heavily to the GOP. Named vice chair of the National Committee the following year, Blair knew few women would join the party if it meant attending a steady round of meetings run by and dominated by men. So in 1922, with the aid of Marion Banister, sister of a powerful senator from Virginia, Carter Glass, she encouraged female Democrats to form clubs of their own and traveled around the country to help them do it. "It was," Blair wrote, "a technique of organization that women understood."[14]

With several dozen like-minded allies, Blair established an umbrella group, the Women's National Democratic Club, to promote the cause and began publishing its *Bulletin* to tout their progress. In ten states, they also created Schools of Democracy, where women spent up to a week imbibing party doctrine and learning how to give a speech and stage a meeting. DNC chairman Cordell Hull, a former congressman from Tennessee who would go on to serve as Franklin Roosevelt's secretary of state, encouraged the new initiative, although Blair had to remind him to include her in meetings of his otherwise all-male committee. The DNC could certainly use her help. In 1922, its underpaid staff had to squeeze into "four crowded, small rooms" in downtown Washington.[15]

Blair and her allies made an impressive contribution to building a grassroots party while also keeping the national one in business. During 1922 alone, they oversaw the founding of more than a thousand local clubs, while their training schools graduated an untold number of women prepared to spread the Democratic gospel and bring in the vote. The local clubs also raised money for the cash-poor party. Early in 1924, with funds contributed largely by Florence "Daisy" Harriman, wife of a New York financier, the WNDC purchased for its headquarters a small but handsome building just north of the White House. For several years in the mid-1920s, the site also functioned as the office of the penurious DNC, which kept its desks and archives there. Blair dubbed the partisan clubs "new servants of democracy." Her reference to domestic labor was telling, if ironic. Until male Democrats put together a well-organized and amply funded campaign in 1928, they depended on "their" women to provide the party apparatus with any home at all.[16]

From their D.C. "clubhouse," the women promoted a version of the party they hoped workingwomen would rush to join. *The Bulletin*, printed in a union shop, boasted that Democrats stood for an eight-hour day, a ban on child labor, "equal pay for equal work," and a progressive income tax. In 1923, it reprinted a long, two-part feature from *The New Republic* about a Polish immigrant who began toiling in the beet fields of Michigan when he was just six; an errant knife sliced off parts of his fingers. "Wlad," lamented the author, was "a stoop-shouldered miniature man who does not know how to play." When *The Bulletin* attacked the protective tariff, a stand that united Democrats more than any other, it usually did so with an awareness of how it affected women of modest or little means. One article in 1923 mentioned that Republican lawmakers had imposed a 30 percent levy on washing machines. Another, titled "The Tariff in the Wardrobe," lambasted the high price of wool caused by the import tax on that commodity.[17]

As the 1924 campaign season began, the women's network was growing in size and confidence. Every issue of *The Bulletin* celebrated the opening of new local clubs; by early 1926, there were some 2,500 of them, representing nearly every state and all the most populous counties. That June, at the party's national convention in Manhattan, 17 percent of the delegates and alternates were women, including the chair of the credentials committee, Lena Jones Springs, from Lancaster, South Carolina—a textile town reputed to be the birthplace of Andrew Jackson. While far from parity, the total was twice as large as that in 1920 and outpaced the number of women who took part in the GOP's gathering. Most of the female delegates had stumped for suffrage or worked in other reform movements; nearly all had professional experience as journalists, attorneys, or local officials. They were clearly ready and able to play a larger role in shaping the future of their party.[18]

Then came the fiasco of the Democratic convention—held in the old Madison Square Garden, a huge red-brick building demolished two years later. The leading contenders for the nomination spoke for quite different regions of the country and a fervent group of followers who reviled the other. Al Smith, then serving his second term as governor of New York, made no secret of his disgust for Prohibition and the Ku Klux Klan—which trained its hatred on Catholics like him as much as on African Americans. William Gibbs McAdoo, son-in-law of Woodrow Wilson and his erstwhile treasury secretary, did his best to revive the coalition of white evangelicals from the South and West that had thrice made William Jennings Bryan the darling of his party. In 1924, this meant acquiescing to the sectarian populism of the KKK while blasting Gotham as "the seat of that invisible power represented by the allied forces of finance and industry." McAdoo's admirers dismissed his background as a wealthy attorney and former railroad president who, though raised in the South, had lived in Manhattan, off and on, for nearly three decades. He shared their resentments and could also trade on his connection to the last Democratic president, who had died that February.[19]

The rivals and most delegates did agree about strengthening and extending the kind of moral capitalism both Bryan and Wilson had advocated. The 1924 platform endorsed "strict public control and conservation of all the nation's natural resources," aggressive anti-trust prosecution, federal aid to education, a more progressive income tax, and a curb on "excessive private contributions" to federal election campaigns. Some of these planks harked back to the Progressive Era; others would not be implemented until the 1960s, if then. But cultural antagonisms, not economic promises, roared through the humid Garden, muting all talk of common purpose.[20]

For two sweltering weeks, the managers for Smith and McAdoo struggled to find some argument or concoct some deal that would persuade enough undecided delegates to lift their man above the two-thirds threshold still required for nomination. The galleries, packed with the Tammany faithful, howled with scorn when Bryan, who favored McAdoo, spoke from the floor against a proposal to condemn the KKK by name. His plea to change the subject from religious bigotry to the "gigantic combinations of capital" that exploited farmers and workers made few, if any, converts.[21]

Although McAdoo could claim some high-profile supporters who were either Catholic or Jewish, everyone knew his chance to win depended on pro-Klan delegates from the South. The first radio audience in the history of conventions listened to the stalemate with dismay or amusement. Finally, on the 103rd ballot, delegates rallied behind a compromise figure—John W. Davis, a respected but colorless former solicitor general and Wall Street lawyer who had avoided taking a strong stand either on alcohol or the Klan.

To her surprise, Lena Springs received forty-two votes for the vice-presidential nomination, making her the first woman to contend for either spot on a major party ticket. It was a purely symbolic move. She lost by a wide margin to Charles W. Bryan, younger brother of the Great Commoner and the progressive governor of Nebraska. Pairing him with Davis, it was hoped, would help counter the third-party challenge of Wisconsin senator Robert La Follette, who had mounted a vigorous anti-corporate, pro-labor campaign designed to appeal to populist Midwesterners.

The ensuing Davis campaign was not merely a failure; it was an embarrassment. The Democratic nominee had no gift for public speaking; on the trail, he delivered formal addresses, free of emotion and full of ambiguous phrases that, as Emily Blair recalled, "left private citizens cold." The ambiguity, at least, had a purpose. Davis was straining to bridge the unbridgeable rift in his party, which forced him to make statements that satisfied no one. As H. L. Mencken described him:

> A lawyer on leave from the ante-room of J. P. Morgan, with a brief waiting for him against the day he is beaten, he has to posture before the populace as a Liberal . . . A candidate dependent upon the votes of Southern Methodists and

Northern Catholics, he has to be against the Ku Klux Klan
without being against it, and to whoop for liberty without
scaring the Anti-Saloon League.[22]

That fall, Mencken, the renowned columnist for the *Baltimore
Sun*, heard a speech in Chicago by the Democratic nominee and,
with his pen dipped in acidic glee, reported, "At the exact moment
when [Davis] began to hymn liberty in words that would have moved
a lieutenant of cossacks or even a Federal judge, the gallery began to
yell 'Give us beer!' The eminent speaker . . . was eloquent but that
gallery was still more eloquent. It said more in three austere, pathetic
words than he had been saying in a thousand."[23]

The new DNC chairman, Clement L. Shaver, a coal-mine owner
from West Virginia, made matters worse by counseling Davis to
attack La Follette as a dangerous radical while offering only slight
criticisms of Calvin Coolidge, the incumbent. This probably helped
alienate many a progressive-minded voter who might have been seeking an alternative to a Republican Party that had shifted hard to the
right since Teddy Roosevelt's death in 1919.

Back in Washington, leaders of the Women's National Democratic
Club did what they could to sell this unattractive message to voters
they hoped would be willing, if not eager, to accept it. Incredibly,
*The Bulletin* portrayed the debacle in Madison Square Garden as "a
memorable fight for principles and power" in which "Miss Democracy simply bided her time and waited" until Davis was chosen. The
editors then played up the nominee's mildly pro-labor record—in
contrast to Coolidge's background as a union buster. The WNDC
also sent local clubs an innovative pamphlet titled "Arguments For
Husbands Who Do Not Want Wives To Vote." Yet the prospect it
raised of a one-day strike by "all of the women holding business positions" in offices, department stores, and restaurants was unlikely to
sway its target male audience. If nothing else, the national club's efforts during the 1924 campaign proved its partisan loyalty, essential
to increasing women's influence in the future.[24]

The result of the election was even worse than most Democrats
had feared. In the three-way race, Davis won just under 29 percent of
the popular vote. He finished behind La Follette in every state bor-

dering the Pacific as well as in the traditionally Republican strongholds of Iowa, Minnesota, and Wisconsin. Although no one tallied
preferences by gender, observers agreed that women voted even more
decisively for the GOP than did men. Democratic candidates for the
House did better in both regions, losing only twenty-one seats overall and just two in the Senate. But the election left the DNC deep in
debt and the party without a clear or effective direction. Who would
lead the rebuilding?

## Enlisting with the Happy Warrior

To most members of the women's network, the answer was obvious.
Since his days in the state assembly, Al Smith had demonstrated
both a keen understanding of the problems of white working-class
New Yorkers and a sincere desire to come up with solutions for them.
He welcomed and came to depend on the aid and advice of Belle
Moscowitz, Frances Perkins, and several other members of their cohort; while Smith was no feminist, that stance made him far superior
to the typical male pol in either party who coveted women's votes but
did as little as possible to earn them. During the chaotic 1924 convention, Franklin Roosevelt had placed Smith's name in nomination
with a bravura address that concluded, "He has a personality that
carries to every hearer not only the sincerity but the righteousness of
what he says. He is the 'Happy Warrior' of the political battlefield."
The most influential and experienced women in his party were eager
to serve in his electoral army.

What's more, Smith was a proven winner, at least in a state whose
electoral votes any Democrat who hoped to be president would have
to carry. As the nominee in 1924, he would certainly have ensured
the defeat of a party that was barely on speaking terms with itself.
But he could hardly have performed worse than the stiff, unappeal-
ing attorney whom the exhausted delegates chose at the end of their
painfully long convention. That fall, Smith eked out reelection as
governor by 3 percent of the vote, as Calvin Coolidge was burying
Davis in the Empire State by a margin of almost two to one. The
straitlaced Republican president who had recently signed the most

exclusionary immigration law in U.S. history even carried every bor-
ough of New York City, more than a third of whose population had
been born in another land.

Smith's unusual political image appealed to female reformers,
too. He combined the practical persona of an Irish Catholic boss
with the grand ambitions of a dedicated progressive. Born in 1873,
the teamster's son grew up in the Bowery, where he quickly mastered
the skills of a Tammany ward heeler while declining to stuff his pockets with money made from graft, honest or otherwise. Campaigning
for the state assembly, Smith treated men in his district to beer and
their kids to sodas; in Albany, he invited dozens of fellow pols to
weekly corned beef and cabbage dinners at a local hotel. As one of his
first biographers wrote, there was "nothing to put Smith apart from
the men in the street, except his brains and his industry."[25]

His speeches articulated rousing egalitarian promises in a language ordinary voters could enjoy. He employed, marveled Frances
Perkins, "pungent, racy talk in the language of the people . . . that
would make people remember things and would also make them
laugh at the same time."[26]

Soon after Smith's first election as governor in 1918, he offered to
appoint Perkins to the state industrial commission, the most prominent and best paid government position any woman had ever held
in New York—or anywhere else in the country. But she postponed
making a decision, fearing she would have to parrot the views of her
benefactor and disappoint her fellow labor reformers. Her mentor,
Florence Kelley, a former socialist and founder of the National Consumers League, tearfully urged Perkins to take the job. Then Smith
needled her to recognize that the uses of government trumped the
comforts of independence: "If you girls are going to get what you
want through legislation," he told Perkins, "there better not be any
separation between social workers and the government." She agreed
to the appointment, and her new boss persuaded the state legislature
to approve it.[27]

A few months later, Smith asked his new commissioner to meet
him in his suite at the Biltmore Hotel in Manhattan. "Somebody
told me youse wasn't a Democrat," he began. Flustered, Perkins responded that since New York women had voted in 1918 for the first

time, she had not yet registered with a party. However, she did allow "that when the Democrats are in power [in Albany] all the bills that I'm interested in get passed, or at least put forward a little bit." But when the Republicans have control, "they all get sat right on and nothing that I'm interested in gets through." Smith then made a robust case, rooted in the Tammany creed, that only those who belong to a "good, well-organized party" can ever accomplish much in politics. When Democrats "know . . . that they can rely on you to vote with them . . . and speak up for them," he told Perkins, they will help you advance the issues you care about. Perkins promised she would enroll in the party right away. "It was a clear, practical, politician's explanation to a naïve, inexperienced person," she recalled. The experienced reformer was being too modest. Perkins was hardly unsophisticated in the ways of the partisan world. But Al Smith had persuaded her to yield to the exigencies of power.[28]

During their eight joint years in office, Perkins gradually rose to become the commission's most influential member—and the nation's leading authority on job safety. She ran the state's program for workmen's compensation, schooling factory owners about the need to reduce or ban the use of dangerous materials that injured their employees. Often, the governor and his wife invited her over to a casual dinner, after which the first lady of the state played piano and Smith sang an Irish song or two. Perkins worked on each of his gubernatorial campaigns, and he often turned to her for advice on political matters unrelated to her work on the commission.

But no aide of either gender mattered as much to Smith's career as did Belle Moscowitz. The daughter of a prosperous and pious watchmaker grew up in East Harlem, then home to an enclave of German Jews. She began her activist life in the first decade of the century with a campaign to regulate dance halls and amusement parks where male predators tried to seduce young working-class women. Moscowitz viewed this as a feminist issue, but her attempt to ban "tough" dances like the Bunny Hug and the Grizzly Bear, in which couples pressed close together, alienated the very women it was designed to save.

By the time Smith began running for governor, Moscowitz had abandoned that failed effort at social control and was devoting herself to improving working conditions in the garment trades and fighting for suffrage in New York State. She also became a charter member of the Women's City Club, whose elite roster included such celebrated figures as Frances Perkins, the muckraking journalist Ida Tarbell, and Mary Dreier, a leading organizer of unions for female workers. In 1918, Moscowitz took charge of the effort to convince women voters to cast their first votes for Al Smith.

It was the beginning of a close working relationship between the uptown Jewish mother of three and the Irish pol from the Lower East Side that furthered both their ends. Moscowitz leaned on Smith to deepen his commitment to laboring New Yorkers; he responded by proposing an eight-hour day for women and child workers and a minimum wage for all. On her suggestion, he also backed humanitarian measures to reform conditions in the state's prisons and mental asylums. In return, Moscowitz gave him critical, well-researched advice on whom to appoint to key posts and how to run his campaigns.

Smith also depended on her to craft what a later generation of journalists would call his "messaging." Moscowitz had honed her promotional skills in her early crusades to police dance halls and enact suffrage. For Smith, she deployed them to explain in enticing ways why citizens should back the governor's policies and elect or reelect him to office in order to pursue them. In 1921, she put together an innovative campaign to convince the state legislature to establish the Port Authority, in which officials from both New York and New Jersey would cooperate to finance electric trains that would ship goods more quickly and efficiently between the neighboring states. To sell the idea, Moscowitz produced a film that narrated the harrowing, ninety-one-hour journey of a humble "Mr. Potato" from a New Jersey farm to market in downtown Manhattan. "I've been in this train twenty-six hours. It is terrible!" exclaimed the little spud, whose ordeal left it damaged and shriveled.[29]

Moscowitz never gave interviews to the press, lest she raise male fears about "petticoat government." Still, as Frances Perkins put it, she "ran" Al Smith's public affairs "in [a] subtle way." When she attended regular meetings of the governor's team of advisers, Moscowitz sat apart from the others. Appearing intent on her knitting, she spoke only when spoken to.[30]

Journalists were not fooled. In the middle of Smith's successful

1926 campaign for reelection, *The New Yorker* ran a profile of Moscowitz that described her as indispensable to shaping the governor's image and to nearly everything he sought to accomplish in office. She made the governor "respectable" enough to be a front-runner for the next presidential race, although Smith still sported a brown derby, chewed on cigars, and retained "his habit of talking out of the side of his mouth." Most of her days, the reporter learned, were spent managing the work of government committees, creating copy for upstate newspapers, and "mapping out a new way for Al Smith to hold the public fancy."[31]

That Moscowitz was the governor's right-hand woman did not prevent her from continuing to nurture the network of feminist Democrats she had helped to form. In 1923, she wrote a curriculum for one of the Schools of Democracy that the WNDC organized in New York City. She continued to be active in the Women's City Club, many of whose members sought to emulate her political clout by working through their unions, volunteer groups, and connections to male Democrats. Drawing on her early experience in nonpartisan reform causes, she also organized independent groups of professionals to boost Smith's campaigns. According to Moscowitz's biographer (who was also her granddaughter), "she could mobilize a phalanx of women determined to carry on relentless organizational work [and] . . . her relationship to the phalanx was not one-sided: just as she relied on them, they used her to represent their interests to the party's central powers."[32]

One member of that group had a natural advantage in pursuing their mutual ends and yet took some time before deciding to deploy it. Eleanor Roosevelt led an entirely private life until after her husband was elected to the New York senate in 1910. For nearly a decade, she then essentially did what was expected of a politician's wife. First in Albany and then in Washington, D.C. (where FDR served as Wilson's assistant navy secretary), she arranged dinners at her home for notable men, visited their wives, raised her five children, and mostly kept her name out of the newspapers. Believing "that men were superior creatures" who "knew more about politics than women," she did not even favor suffrage until her husband did. As the niece of Theodore Roosevelt, she was also reluctant to come out as a partisan Democrat.[33]

By 1920, however, Eleanor Roosevelt had become a rising force in the network of social feminists. She joined the League of Women Voters, where she learned to give vivid, elegant speeches and write cogent articles on political issues. Soon she was lobbying Congress to enact the league's farseeing agenda, which included a ban on child labor, a minimum wage, funding for maternity care, and membership in the League of Nations. At the Women's City Club, she made friends and valuable connections. Eleanor was neither given nor did she seek any role in FDR's run for vice president in 1920, save that of dutiful (if frustrated) wife. But she did work hard for Al Smith's gubernatorial campaigns. In 1924, Eleanor teamed up with Belle Moscowitz to register and turn out women voters.

That year, she also found time to concoct a delicious, if rather "dirty," trick to attack Smith's GOP opponent, Theodore Roosevelt, Jr., her thirty-seven-year-old cousin. To alert voters to Junior's quite tangential involvement in the Teapot Dome scandal, which had landed several Harding administration officials in jail, Eleanor had a large working teapot fitted to the top of a Ford sedan. She and other Smith women drove the vehicle around to the Republican hopeful's campaign stops, emitting clouds of steam visible to everyone who gathered to hear him.

Despite her growing visibility in party circles, Eleanor Roosevelt was unwilling to stay silent about the subordinate place such women as Belle Moscowitz and Frances Perkins had accepted in order to advance the policies they cherished. Her articles in popular magazines won her a large following separate from her husband's. In the spring of 1928, she wrote for the popular magazine *Redbook* a scornful critique of how party leaders treated women "of both camps." Male politicians didn't invite women to routine meetings, rarely considered nominating them for office, and "kept [them] in ignorance of noteworthy plans and affairs." She mocked "our statesmen and legislators" for acting like "early warriors gathering around the campfire plotting the next day's attack." They courted women voters but did all they could to keep women activists unheard and out of their way.[34]

At the end of the article, Roosevelt offered a bold way to shake up this infuriating state of affairs. We need, she asserted, "to elect, accept and back women political bosses." Knowing many readers would recoil from that advice, she explained that male bosses no longer lived down to the pattern set by the corrupt denizens of the Gilded Age. For her, the term "boss" referred to anyone who could build a "machine" of and for women voters and turn it into a powerful instrument that could deal with men "as equals" and "choose leaders to act for them and to whom they will be loyal." This strategy, Roosevelt acknowledged, would require women to shed their inclination to volunteer for good causes they seldom were able to see through to victory.[35]

She mentioned just one male politician as an exception to the intolerable rule: the governor of New York, groomed by the Tammany machine. And that year, Al Smith was running for president again, this time with no serious rival for the Democratic nomination.

The 1928 race has gone down in history as the final chapter in "the politics of provincialism" that doomed Smith's chance to win the White House. During the campaign, the governor certainly made no effort to obscure who he was and what he believed. He refused, if elected, to commit to enforcing Prohibition or to deny that he enjoyed an evening cocktail. He attended Mass regularly and displayed an autographed photo of Pope Pius XI on the wall of his office. As Smith's publicity director, Belle Moscowitz churned out daily press releases that highlighted the candidate's loving family and his efforts to help the ordinary citizens of New York State but said almost nothing about the low crop prices that worried staple farmers in the Midwest or the high tariffs that made it hard for many small businessmen to make a profit.[36]

On the radio, which by the late 1920s had become a truly national medium, Smith could not help sounding like a grown-up working-class kid from the Bowery. His rendering of words like "horspital" and "raddio" may not have jarred the ears of big-city listeners, but they certainly came off as alien, if not uncouth, to many a rural voter. While the Republican nominee, Herbert Hoover, was hardly an enthralling speaker, his careful, standard diction irritated no one. "Radio broadcasting has made pronunciation a factor in a presidential campaign for the first time in history," intoned the president of CBS.[37]

What this damning portrait neglects is how Smith's failed run presaged more successful Democratic campaigns to come. Some of the key policies Belle Moscowitz and her fellow partisans promoted were ones FDR and his fellow liberals would later stress as well: the public development and ownership of water power, a minimum wage and maximum hours for wage earners, and higher taxes on the wealthiest Americans, whose rates Republican Congresses had slashed. Late in the campaign, Hoover blasted his Democratic opponent for wanting to take "a long step toward the abandonment of our American system," a "turn to State socialism." Smith scoffed at the charge. Conservatives, he reminded a crowd in Boston, had long condemned what he'd done in New York "to protect the health . . . and the well-being of women and children" with the same inaccurate slur.[38]

Smith also pledged to amend the Johnson-Reed Act of 1924, whose discriminatory quotas essentially banned the relatives and friends of millions of city dwellers from Eastern and Southern Europe from immigrating to the United States. His criticism of the law was milder than his rhetorical assault on the Eighteenth Amendment. But it heartened the white ethnic voters who would soon become the backbone of the New Deal coalition.[39]

Several of the women who had cheered Smith's record as governor traveled around the country to sell his progressive message. Frances Perkins campaigned across New England and the South, heralding Smith as a "great humanitarian" who had boosted "the equality of women, and the protection of the weak." Emily Blair gave numerous speeches back home in Missouri, although she knew Smith's religion and wetness would probably cost him the state. Still, she was so pleased by his positions on "the utility problem, child labor, and other things" that she persevered. Nellie Tayloe Ross, then a vice chair of the Democratic National Committee, gave so many speeches for the ticket that she collapsed of exhaustion and pleaded to have her schedule cut back to just one talk per day. Although she and Blair had been avid prohibitionists, Smith's commitment to advance the common welfare through state action clearly mattered more. "What to me was most important," wrote Blair, "was the direction our economic system was taking."[40]

However, that same passion for change did not extend to the lives of Black Americans. At the Houston convention, where Smith was nominated on the first ballot, a cage made of chicken wire infamously separated the few Black alternates and spectators from the mass of white participants. "[The barrier] makes me feel it is almost impossible to ask a Negro to vote the Democratic ticket this year," a wealthy Democrat from Georgia confided to Franklin Roosevelt. Smith did denounce the KKK's religious bigotry but was silent about its attacks on Black people. Campaigning in Virginia, Frances Perkins reminded white voters who were dubious about backing a Catholic son of Tammany Hall that since their beloved Robert E. Lee had been a loyal Democrat, they had better stick with the party, too. The most virulent racists in public office also echoed the partisan faith, albeit sometimes in cruder tones. "I would swallow the Pope and the whole dern Vatican than vote for Herbert Hoover and negro supremacy in the South," barked Senator Theodore Bilbo of Mississippi.[41]

Neither his labor-friendly progressivism nor his tolerance of racism brought Smith close to victory. He won just eighty-seven electoral votes, as majorities in five Southern states punished the "party of the fathers" for nominating a "papal Governor of New York" who defied the Constitution and had a strange way of talking. Not since the end of Reconstruction had the GOP broken through the Democrats' wall of Dixie. Spurred by the sharp differences between the major candidates, total turnout was 8 percent higher than in 1924.

Without a third-party progressive to challenge him from the left, Smith received nearly twice as many popular votes as had Davis in 1924. But Hoover bested him in his own state by more than a hundred thousand ballots, even as Franklin Roosevelt narrowly won the race for governor of New York. Smith had implored FDR to run for the office, knowing that to carry the state he would need the help of the younger man from a rural county graced with a famous surname and a Protestant identity. Meanwhile, Democrats also lost ground in both the House and Senate. If the Happy Warrior and his zealously reformist followers couldn't lift the Democrats out of the rut of minority status, what ever would?[42]

One could identify key elements of an answer in the returns from industrial towns and cities outside the South, all filled with working-class European immigrants and their native-born offspring. Many of these places had voted for Republican nominees since the Depression of the 1890s. That partisan leaning was due in part to the GOP's advocacy of a high tariff, which protected manufacturing jobs. But in 1928, the total vote in the twelve biggest cities favored Al Smith. White Protestant urbanites stood by the GOP, but Jews and Catholics rallied to the candidate who was loathed by the KKK and the Anti-Saloon League and who vowed to extend to the nation the kind of welfare measures he had enacted in the Empire State. Millions of these ethnic voters were casting ballots for the first time. Most would not get around to registering as Democrats until the 1930s, but the choice they made in 1928 soon hardened into a partisan preference that, for them and their children, would endure until President Lyndon Johnson's downfall four decades later.[43]

Female campaigners played a vital role in nurturing this momentous change in American politics. In Cleveland, Bernice Secrest Pyke, a middle-class white Methodist, rose from leadership of her large and active Democratic women's club to become second-in-command of the local party machine. Pitching the Democratic cause in dozens of neighborhood meetings, she earned respect as what one Polish ward heeler awkwardly called "a good speaker . . . a pepperbox . . . a real he-man." In 1928, Pyke mobilized a regiment of Catholic laywomen and parish priests to register their co-religionists and make sure they made it to the polls. Four years earlier, John W. Davis had eked out less than 10 percent of the vote in the Cleveland metropolitan area, as La Follette drew the lion's share of progressive voters. But in 1928, Smith finished less than seven percentage points behind Herbert Hoover, whose overwhelming margins in the rural counties earned him a 2–1 landslide in the state as a whole.[44]

Other women for Smith made better use of the new electronic medium than the nominee himself. In New Jersey, Congresswoman Mary T. Norton gave radio speeches touting what Smith had done to cut working hours for women and expand funding for public health. Frances Perkins made similar broadcasts on Boston stations that reached the struggling textile towns of New England.

The stark reality of a third straight national drubbing thus contained the elements of a comeback. "The future of the Democracy lies in following the furrow plowed by Al," H. L. Mencken wrote a week after the election. It may have been the most optimistic as well as the wisest prediction the sardonic "Sage of Baltimore" would ever make.[45]


## Toward the New Deal

Al Smith never recovered from the shock of his landslide defeat. Yet soon after, he passed along some sound advice to help Democrats avoid another one. We need, he told fellow party leaders, to create a permanent body to win voters over to Democratic ideas "rather than [to] sit by . . . with the hope of profiting solely by the mistakes and failures of the opposition." John J. Raskob, whom Smith had picked after the 1928 convention to chair the DNC, quickly recruited an executive committee and hired a full-time publicity director to carry out this mission. For the first time in their century-long history, the Democrats now had a national organization that did business all year long instead of coming to life before each campaign and going dormant once voters had their say. The decision was both necessary and tardy: Republicans had launched a similar operation before the 1920 election and had profited from it ever since.[46]

Internal controversy swirled around Smith's choice of Raskob. Placing a self-made millionaire who had been a top executive at Du-Pont and General Motors at the helm of the party apparatus rankled both inveterate Bryanites and urban progressives. But Raskob did help parry the charge that the Democrats were riddled with "socialistic" notions. More important, he managed to turn an organization that had little money and no headquarters into one whose financial worth nearly rivaled that of the corporate-friendly opposition. Like August Belmont decades before him, the erstwhile executive lavishly drew on his own fortune—donating as much as $30,000 a month—to enhance the fortunes of the "party of the people." He also leaned on a group of wealthy New Yorkers to agree to underwrite a million-dollar bank loan to the campaign; alas, after the stock market crashed in the fall of 1929, quite a few refused to pay their share.

Most of the women who had toiled prominently in Al Smith's

campaign now turned, with the same energy, to the dual tasks of winning the next election and gaining more influence in running their party. Appointed by Raskob as the salaried head of the DNC Women's Division, Nellie Tayloe Ross hired two skillful and nearly tireless female assistants. By the midterm contest of 1930, they had organized groups of Democratic women in close to 90 percent of the nation's counties. Some continued the work of the clubs created by Emily Blair, Ross's predecessor in the DNC post. But the new network was designed to expand all over the electoral map the kind of local canvassing Bernice Pyke had pioneered in Cleveland. They were platoons for persuasion rather than Schools of Democracy.

A year after Al Smith's defeat, his party's prospects also began to brighten considerably through no action of its own. The Wall Street crash and the ensuing depression, which gradually merited the term "Great" as hundreds of thousands of businesses closed down and millions of workers lost their jobs, seemed to prove the case that Democrats since Bryan had been making against the corporate moguls who bankrolled the GOP. In 1930, the party won a majority, albeit by a single seat, in the House of Representatives for the first time since midway through Woodrow Wilson's time in office.

At the end of 1928, a disgruntled Belle Moscowitz told a reporter that the "reactionaries are in the saddle" and revealed that she was "almost a Bolshevik in some ways" who did not care if capitalism survived. Four years later, when Franklin D. Roosevelt swept into the presidency and a quarter of the American workforce lacked a job, her statement did not seem quite so radical.[47]

One negative consequence of the Democratic revival was a decline in the salience of feminist issues. To take advantage of the economic crisis and the debacle of Hooverism, leading women in the party boosted ideas like relief for the unemployed and a bill to curb court injunctions against unions while muting demands to protect workingwomen and fund child and maternal care. In 1931, Emily Newell Blair complained in a speech to the National Education Association, a group packed with female teachers, that "women exercise very little influence in politics today." She continued: "You may take my word for it, from one of the women who tried to be an influence in politics and stopped trying." At the same time, Nellie Tayloe

Ross, her successor at the DNC, was writing that her party's chances of gaining national power depended on making a "ceaseless effort" to win over the "millions of women voters, in many of whom political consciousness is yet unawakened." But both women endorsed FDR for the nomination months before the party's convention and then gladly toured the country to speak on his behalf.[48]

FDR's personal charm and his wife's powerful role in his career and in the life of the party were only part of the reason why most female Democrats rallied to his cause. On becoming governor of New York, he had named Frances Perkins to run a new industrial commission with close to two thousand employees; as president, he appointed her secretary of labor; she was the first woman to serve in a cabinet. In her memoir, Perkins praised her boss for taking time, in the early 1920s when he had temporarily withdrawn from public life to struggle with his paralysis, to meet with leaders of the Women's Trade Union League and absorb their wisdom about the necessity for a strong labor movement. Then as governor, he spent considerable time with the heads of both male and female unions and let them know how sympathetic he was to their work. One told Perkins, "You'd almost think he had participated in some strike or organizing campaign the way he knew and felt about it."[49]

In *It's Up to the Women*, Eleanor Roosevelt argued against the notion that Americans of her gender thought about politics in the same ways as the men who wielded state power. She looked forward to "a social order built by the ability and brains of our men" that would "also represent the understanding heart of the women." That distinction was rooted, as she well knew, in a long tradition of those who did not have the vote wielding influence by voicing moral claims and performing the difficult, repetitive labors that compelled powerful men to act on at least some of them. In the 1920s, women finally armed with the suffrage had nudged the leaders of their party to see the wisdom of their hearts and their brains, if not to give them an equal part in shaping its policies. Never again would Democrats debate how to advance the common welfare while ignoring that knowledge and experience. Yet it would be another half century before male leaders echoed the key demands of the women whose unheralded labor made the party apparatus run at all.[50]

# 6

## AN AMERICAN LABOR PARTY?
### 1933–1948

*Our fight is going to be to stop this move to gigantic
Socialism . . . [It] is Bryanism under new words and methods.*
—HERBERT HOOVER ON THE NEW DEAL, 1933[1]

*We are at the beginning of a new chapter in the history of the labor
movement as well as of campaign finance, when an organization of
miners is the largest contributor to a major political party.*
—LOUISE OVERACKER, POLITICAL SCIENTIST, 1939[2]

*If they load down the Chicago platform with repeal of
Poll Tax, Anti-Lynching and endeavoring to erase the Jim
Crowe [sic]—that will certainly be something for us to think
about . . . We may have to be for Roosevelt whether we
like it or not, but I would hate to think it wise to
be placed in that position.*
—ED CRUMP, DEMOCRATIC BOSS OF MEMPHIS, TENNESSEE, 1944[3]

## Top of the World

On November 3, 1936, Democrats won the most complete victory in
the history of partisan presidential elections. Franklin D. Roosevelt
defeated his Republican rival—Alfred Landon, the governor of
Kansas—by the extraordinary margin of 24 percent of the popular
vote. The incumbent captured every state save the longtime GOP
strongholds of Maine and Vermont.[4]

It was not solely a personal triumph. Roosevelt's empathetic eloquence, on the radio and in person, and the relief and jobs programs he signed into law during the throes of the Great Depression, made him a hero to millions of Americans who, contrary to his famous line, had a good deal more to fear than fear itself. "He used to talk to me about my government," people told Eleanor Roosevelt after her husband's death.[5]

But FDR's party soared along with him. Democrats gained a majority of nearly 250 seats in the House of Representatives and almost 60 in the Senate. The GOP emerged from the battering to hold governorships in a mere seven states. Neither Andrew Jackson and his fledgling party in the 1830s nor the Republicans in the 1920s had achieved such electoral domination or swept such a lion's share of federal and state offices.

The coalition that delivered this conquest was remarkably broad, its fault lines obscured behind a common desire to see the New Deal endure and prosper. The party convention that year had abolished the two-thirds rule, but the loss of the South's traditional veto over nominees did not prevent that region's voters from giving FDR majorities even more lopsided than in the heyday of Ben Tillman and Woodrow Wilson. Landon won less than 2 percent of the tally in South Carolina and less than 3 percent in Mississippi. For the first time in history, most African Americans in the North voted for the same party as did nearly all whites in Dixie, where few Black people could cast a ballot at all. In 1936, Arthur Wergs Mitchell, the first Black Democrat ever elected to Congress, also became the first person of his race to address the party's convention when he seconded the nomination of FDR. A poll taken later that decade found that close to 90 percent of Black respondents approved of the president's "economic objectives."

Democrats also picked up the support of those Republicans who saw in Franklin Roosevelt the same kind of progressive energy and fondness for bold ideas they'd seen in his strenuous late cousin and former president with the same surname. In 1933, Fiorello La Guardia was elected mayor of New York City on the GOP line. Taking office on his coattails were an Irish Catholic comptroller and a Jewish president of the board of aldermen. It was the first ethnically "balanced ticket" in Gotham history. The colorful mayor soon became closer to FDR than did the leaders of Tammany Hall, whose Hibernian chieftains had never regained their political footing after Boss Charles Murphy passed away in 1924.

In the manufacturing heartland, the lever that flipped every state into the Democratic column for the first time ever was a political force New Deal policy makers had helped nurture: the growing movement of industrial wage earners. A massive strike wave in 1934—including city-wide general strikes in San Francisco and Minneapolis—had galvanized several heads of older unions to demand that the American Federation of Labor devote its resources to organizing the men and women who toiled at meager wages for the biggest corporations in the land. But the craft-bound chieftains of the old federation refused, claiming that factory hands made unreliable unionists who neither stuck to nor identified with their jobs. In the fall of 1935, the exasperated dissidents, led by John L. Lewis of the United Mine Workers and Sidney Hillman of the Amalgamated Clothing Workers, determined to prove them wrong. They broke from the leadership of the AFL to form a separate organization, soon to be named the CIO—the Congress of Industrial Organizations.

Earlier that year, Congress had given their aspirations a vital boost. In June, lawmakers passed a landmark bill, the National Labor Relations Act, which forbade employers from punishing union organizers and put the federal government in charge of holding elections in workplaces where a majority of employees wanted a union to represent them. Emboldened labor organizers quickly fanned out to industrial centers to test their newly won rights. They feared that the Supreme Court, which had struck down other New Deal measures, would soon rule this one unconstitutional as well.

While FDR was ambivalent about letting labor accumulate too much economic power, he recognized how useful their members and resources could be to expanding the Democratic majority. In 1932, his party's platform made no mention of unions at all. Four years later, it hailed the new "right of collective bargaining and self-organization free from the interference of employers." Roosevelt delivered a rousing acceptance speech at the Philadelphia convention, blasting the "economic royalists" who loathed both him and the "organized power of government" that was challenging their "tyranny."

# TWO CENTURIES OF DEMOCRATS

President Franklin D. Roosevelt speaks at the laying of the
cornerstone for the memorial to Thomas Jefferson in Washington, D.C.,
November 1939. FDR declared on that day: "He lived as we live in the
midst of struggle between rule by the self-chosen individual or the
self-appointed few, and rule by the franchise and approval of the many."

*All photographs courtesy of the Library of Congress unless otherwise indicated.*

GENERAL JACKSON SLAYING THE MANY HEADED MONSTER.

President Andrew Jackson slays the hydra of the Second Bank of the United States, 1836. The largest of the heads depicts Nicholas Biddle, the president of the bank and a symbol of the financial elite that Democrats turned into a symbol of immoral capitalism.

A campaign print promoting President Martin Van Buren for reelection in 1840. Van Buren did more than anyone to create the Democratic Party but was not a successful president. On the column to the left, Andrew Jackson holds his defiant 1832 veto of the recharter of the Bank of the United States.

August Belmont, the New York City financier and chairman of the Democratic National Committee from 1860 to 1872. He built the DNC into an organization that, for the first time in its history, played a critical role in funding the party and steering its affairs.

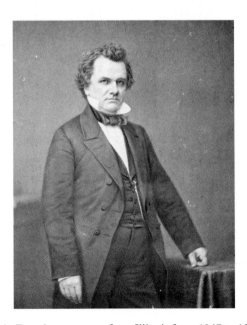

Stephen A. Douglas, a senator from Illinois from 1847 to 1861 and a failed presidential nominee, in 1860. Douglas was the architect of the "popular sovereignty" plan that would have allowed new states to vote for or against allowing slavery within their borders.

New York's Democratic governor Horatio Seymour speaks to a crowd of working-class white men during the bloody draft riots in Manhattan in July 1863. He addressed them as "my friends" and promised to get conscription in the city postponed or canceled if they "refrained from further riotous acts."

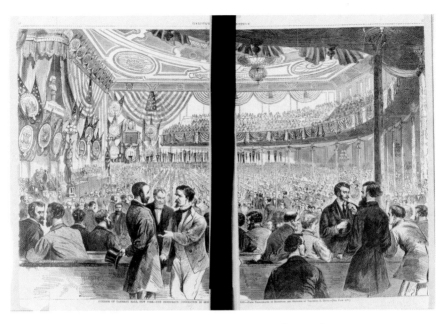

A scene from the 1868 Democratic Convention,
held inside Tammany Hall in Manhattan.

THE TIGER'S PREY.

The Tiger, the symbol of Tammany Hall, about to prey on New York City
in one of many hostile images of the Democratic machine that appeared in
*Puck* magazine during the late nineteenth and early twentieth centuries.

Richard Croker, the Ireland-born boss of Tammany Hall from 1886 to 1902. He wrote: "A well-organized political club is made for the purpose of aggressive warfare. It must move, and it must always move forward against its enemies."

Benjamin Tillman, the fiery racist and populist boss of the South Carolina Democratic Party and the governor and senator from that state in a career stretching from the 1870s to his death in 1918.

William Jennings Bryan in 1896, during the first of his three campaigns as the Democratic nominee for president. Bryan was the leader of progressives in the party until the election of Woodrow Wilson in 1912.

THAT BRANDEIS APPOINTMENT

Chorus of Grief-Stricken Conservatives: Oh, what an associate for such a pure and innocent girl! And we have tried to bring her up so carefully, too!

A 1916 cartoon of new Supreme Court justice Louis Brandeis walking with the female personification of Justice while a "chorus of grief-stricken" members of the economic elite wail in protest. Brandeis, a pillar of legal progressivism, was nominated by Woodrow Wilson. He was the first Jew to sit on the high court.

Frances Perkins: social worker, feminist, advocate for workers, and the first woman cabinet member as secretary of labor during the New Deal.

Eleanor Roosevelt at about the time she became First Lady in 1933: "Had we always insisted that the men take into account the human element that entered into business there would not be the fight there is to-day over what is the fair standard of living for every one in this country."

President Franklin D. Roosevelt preparing to give a radio address in 1936.

Senator Robert Wagner of New York upon hearing the news in 1937 that the Supreme Court had ruled the National Labor Relations Act, which he co-wrote, constitutional.

John F. Kennedy campaigning for president on Labor Day in 1960 before a massive pro-union crowd in Detroit's Cadillac Square. As a signal of organized labor's political power, every Democratic nominee from 1948 to 1964 kicked off his fall campaign in the square.

(*Walter P. Reuther Library, Wayne State University*)

An image of the heyday of the alliance between the civil rights movement and the Democratic Party: vice president–elect Hubert Humphrey shakes hands with Dr. Martin Luther King, Jr., as Coretta Scott King looks on. Both men spoke in December 1964 at a rally in Harlem, the "capital of Black America."

Adam Clayton Powell, Jr., a minister, a congressman from New York City from 1945 to 1971, and a leader of the Black freedom movement.

Chicago mayor Richard J. Daley and his followers in the Illinois delegation cursing a speaker at the Democratic National Convention in that city in August 1968 who had just condemned the "Gestapo tactics" of police against anti-war demonstrators.

A demonstration for gay and lesbian rights at the Democratic National Convention in New York City, July 1976. Four years later, the Democrats became the first major party to ratify a platform plank endorsing gay rights—although only in general terms.

Cesar Chavez, the leader of the United Farm Workers (UFW), nominating California governor Jerry Brown for president at the 1976 Democratic Convention. In supporting the UFW's effort to unionize agricultural labor on the West Coast, Democrats hoped to win the votes of Mexican Americans.

Jesse Jackson, a minister and a leader of the Black freedom movement, who ran for the Democratic presidential nomination in 1984 and 1988 as the tribune of a Rainbow Coalition composed of left-leaning Democrats of all races.

President Bill Clinton and First Lady Hillary Rodham Clinton at the dedication of the memorial to Franklin D. Roosevelt in Washington, D.C., May 1997. As president, Clinton largely pursued centrist policies that some critics argued were a departure from the legacy of the New Deal.

Congresswoman Nancy Pelosi from San Francisco speaks at a hearing of the House Appropriations Committee in 1997. Pelosi went on to become the first female majority leader and the first female Speaker of the House—and an effective fund-raiser and power broker.

Representative Alexandria Ocasio-Cortez and Senator Bernie Sanders after she endorsed him for president at a New York City rally in the fall of 2019. (*Gabriel Hernandez Solano*)

In an explicit nod to labor, he announced, "Liberty requires opportunity to make a living—a living decent according to the standard
of the time, a living which gives man not only enough to live by, but
something to live for."[6]

To back up his rhetoric, CIO leaders mounted the most ambitious electoral intervention in American labor history. They hoped
a Democratic landslide undergirded by unions might give both the
high court and corporations throughout the land a powerful reason
to acquiesce to the fledgling New Deal order. That summer, the CIO
established Labor's Non-Partisan League. Despite its name, the new
organization had a singular and quite partisan mission: mobilize
working-class voters to reelect Roosevelt and expand Democratic
majorities in Congress and the industrial states. Shrewdly, Lewis
and Hillman enlisted the head of an AFL union, George Berry of
the Printing Pressmen, to run the group so that officials in the old
federation would feel comfortable taking part. Under Samuel Gompers, the old AFL had endorsed Bryan once and Wilson twice. But
his federation had donated little money to their campaigns and never
undertook a major effort to convince unionists to vote Democratic.

In contrast, the Non-Partisan League embarked on an ambitious campaign of publicity and fund-raising. The league produced
dozens of radio speeches that framed the election in starkly class-
conscious terms. "It is an issue," declared John L. Lewis in one national broadcast, "of whether the working population of this country
shall have a voice in determining their destiny or whether they shall
serve as indentured servants for a financial and economic dictatorship which would shamelessly exploit our natural resources and
destroy the pride of a free people." The league held thousands of
rallies—including 344 in Ohio alone—and contributed 10 percent of
the funds the Democrats collected during the entire campaign. No
other source donated more. Lewis's own UMW kicked in three-fifths
of that sum by itself.[7]

The time and money were well spent. In 1936, FDR's support
swelled among every group in the population save the wealthy. But
factory towns and the residents of big cities turned in a particularly
large and lopsided vote, fueled by immigrant white wage earners and
their children, many of whom had seldom, if ever, cast a ballot before.

"Mr. Roosevelt is the only man we ever had in the White House who would understand that my boss is a sonofabitch," declared one factory worker.[8]

The Supreme Court evidently followed the election returns as well as the Constitution. In April 1937, by a single vote, it upheld the National Labor Relations Act. The case at issue involved a steel company that had fired ten workers who attempted to organize a union at one of its plants. "Employees have as clear a right to organize and select their representatives for lawful purposes as the respondent has to organize its business and select its own officers and agents," wrote Chief Justice Charles Evans Hughes, the former GOP presidential nominee, for the slim majority. In the two years following FDR's reelection, union membership doubled to eight million.[9]

The Democratic landslide and the high court's acquiescence marked a turning point in the political history of organized labor. Even while endorsing candidates, unions had always guarded their independence from the major parties. Since the movement's birth in the 1820s, many activists had been attracted to radical organizations that championed the rights of labor, despite their poor showing at the polls. But the triumph of a Democratic president who took a clear pro-union stance sounded the death knell of third-party dreams, even if it took a few years for all but hardened left sectarians to get the message. "As it confronted the party system," writes one political scientist, "the CIO faced a decision of whether to betray its benefactor— which was no decision at all."[10]

## Party of a New Type

The rise and political potency of "labor's new millions" quickened a sea change in the Democratic Party that the women's reform network had quietly begun during the previous decade. A critical question when FDR took power in 1933 was whether his party would seek to advocate just one or both main themes of moral capitalism—a breakup of monopoly power and vigorous support for the interests of working-class Americans—while holding on to the White House and Congress and keeping the party united.

The forces behind the 1936 landslide made the decision inexora-
ble: the Democrats would become, for a time, the closest thing the
United States would ever have to a party dependent on the support of
organized labor. "The demands of a large and powerful labor movement," wrote Richard Hofstadter twenty years later, "coupled with
the interests of the unemployed, gave the later New Deal a social-
democratic tinge that had never before been present in American reform movements." The main sin of large corporations would be how
they exploited their workers, not engorgement of their market share.
If they accepted unions as legitimate agents and paid their members
decent wages, the old Democratic animus toward monopoly would
fade, although never disappear entirely.[11]

Despite the tenor of his 1936 acceptance speech and the fears of
Republicans like Herbert Hoover, the scion of Hudson River gentry
was no class warrior. Like his distant cousin Theodore, FDR drew
distinctions between corporations that behaved badly and those
that behaved well; he had no appetite for bashing big business just
for being big—an article of faith for Bryan and his agrarian followers. In a telling speech to an elite San Francisco audience during
the 1932 campaign, FDR had warned "the responsible heads of finance and industry" that "instead of acting each for himself, [they]
must work together to achieve the common end. They must, where
necessary, sacrifice this or that private advantage; and in reciprocal
self-denial must seek a general advantage."[12] The National Recovery Administration—the agency tasked in 1933 with whipping de-
flation by requiring industries to adopt and abide by "codes of fair
competition"—encouraged big firms to abide by this principle until
the Supreme Court ruled it unconstitutional two years later. Still, by
the end of the decade, the Roosevelt administration had abandoned
plans to break up or severely regulate major industrial corporations
and was focused on promoting growth to prevent another depression.

Instead, Democrats began to emphasize the pro-labor strain of
moral capitalism and built a broad new coalition with unions at its
core, along with the Solid South and urban machines. Most party
leaders recognized that, while most wage earners took class divisions
for granted, they longed for a government that, as the historian Lizabeth Cohen puts it, would "police capitalism so that workers really

would get that 'new deal' they deserved." The remarkable growth of the labor movement during Roosevelt's dozen years in office made this alliance desirable for both sides. The number of union members mushroomed from three million in 1933 to fifteen million in 1945—easily the largest spurt of growth in the history of the nation and, perhaps, the world. Membership peaked at just over 35 percent of wage earners by the end of World War II.[13]

The most dramatic gains were made by new organizations founded by the CIO in the mid- and late 1930s—the United Auto Workers, the United Steelworkers, and the United Electrical Workers among them. The AFL kept pace numerically with the group that had split away; by 1945, its affiliates actually had more members than did the CIO, and they, too, backed most Democratic nominees up and down the ballot. Through Roosevelt's dozen years in office, the chairman of the DNC's Labor Division was Daniel J. Tobin, president of the Teamsters Union, one of the largest unions in the AFL.

But the CIO built a reciprocal partnership with the national Democratic Party that the other, looser federation, which included some pro-GOP affiliates, did not try to match. That relationship was a major factor in the transformation of the Democrats into the modern liberal party that won most races for the presidency and dominated Congress during the next three decades. The bond was essential to sustaining the New Deal order—the intersection of the ideology, policies, and powerful coalition that began to build the first welfare state in U.S. history.

Two men hailing from working-class immigrant backgrounds— one a U.S. senator, the other a powerful labor leader—envisioned this party of a new type and labored to shape it in that image. Robert Wagner and Sidney Hillman took quite different paths to their shared ambition. Wagner started his in a Rhineland village, where he was born in 1877, and pursued it first through Tammany Hall and the politics of New York State. His father had owned a small business in the Old Country but made his living as a janitor in the New World, at a salary of about a dollar a day. Discontented with his lot, Reinhard Wagner and his wife sailed back to Germany near the end of the nineteenth century and never returned. But Robert, who immigrated to the United States as a boy, finished high school and then graduated from City College, where he won an award as Class Orator that presaged his future career.

In 1904, he began a rapid rise to prominence in the state legislature, where, with the help of female reformers, he and Al Smith spearheaded programs for labor welfare. Years later, Mary Dreier, erstwhile leader of the Women's Trade Union League, described traveling with Wagner to vegetable farms in upstate New York where young women toiled for as long as nineteen hours a day. The politician, she recalled, "was very astute asking questions about the children," who often accompanied their mothers to the fields.[14]

In 1926, Wagner won a seat in the U.S. Senate by clinging to the coattails of Al Smith, then his state's popular governor. In Washington, he proposed measures to aid the unemployed and use government funds to stabilize the economy. When FDR became president, Wagner seized a unique opportunity to pass bold reforms to markedly improve the lives of working Americans. Leon Keyserling, a twenty-seven-year-old economist on his staff, wrote the National Labor Relations Act, which the press immediately dubbed the Wagner Act, although it was co-sponsored with a congressman from Massachusetts. Later, the senator introduced bills to erect millions of units of public housing and provide every citizen with health insurance. Wagner's reputation as the most prominent and most effective labor liberal in America made him the natural choice to oversee the drafting of the 1936 platform on which FDR ran his bravura campaign for reelection.

Wagner was also one of the very few Democrats in Congress whose empathy for ordinary people did not fade at the color line. In 1934, he proposed a bill to make lynching a federal crime and fought, in vain, to stop Southerners in his own party from filibustering it to death. The New York senator also called for amending the Social Security Act to include domestic workers and farmworkers—the occupations of two-thirds of Black workers in the South. Wagner had come a long way from his start in politics as a protégé of Charlie Murphy. Still, he kept the faith. "Tammany Hall may justly claim the title of the cradle of modern liberalism in America," he told an Independence Day crowd in 1937.[15]

When Sidney Hillman's ship pulled into a Manhattan dock one day in 1907, it seemed unlikely he would ever make common cause with a loyal son of the Democratic machine. Born in a Lithuanian shtetl twenty years before, "Hilkie" had been active in the radical movement that burned to overthrow tsarist rule and establish a republic of workers and peasants in its place. He joined the Menshevik faction of the Russian Social-Democratic Party, whose leader Julius Martov, a fellow secular Jew, opposed Lenin's doctrine that only a cadre of professional revolutionaries could engineer a socialist revolution. In the United States, Hillman earned his keep as an apprentice garment cutter but was more adept at leading strikes than following patterns. In 1914, he was elected president of the new Amalgamated Clothing Workers, whose officials were mostly fellow Jews and members of the Socialist Party of America. "The ultimate aim of the labor movement," declared union secretary Joseph Schlossberg, "is to bring the working class into its own, to transform . . . a Capitalist Society into a free and democratic industrial republic."[16]

By the 1930s, Hillman had embraced a more practical idea of how to get the proletariat more of what it needed, if not all it might deserve. Like Wagner, with whom he struck up a good working relationship, he came to believe the best way to promote the idea of strong unions was to argue that they would boost mass consumption. The low wages most Americans earned made it impossible to pull the nation out of its deep economic slump. As the first section of the Wagner Act explained, "The inequality of bargaining power . . . tends to aggravate recurrent business depressions, by depressing wage rates and the purchasing power of wage earners in industry."[17]

The German-born Protestant and the Lithuanian Jew had personalities that matched their political affinity. Each was as lacking in egotism and a hunger for adoration as any intensely public man could be. One New York journalist who followed Wagner closely described him as "an unassuming man," adding that, "sincere and unaffected, he has neither the desire nor the talent for self-exploitation." The senator, scoffed another reporter, "does not put on a good show." While Hillman was more intellectual and perpetually anxious about fulfilling his goals, he did not seek the media attention other labor leaders craved. By the 1930s, he had abandoned the messianic Marxism of his youth in exchange for the "achievable." "We cannot," he advised his fellow unionists, "wreck the house in which we live."[18]

When Hillman co-founded the CIO, he knew it would flourish only if it secured political support from on high. Organized labor in America had never enjoyed a period of sizable growth unless it had the federal government on its side. So, while never completely abandoning the third-party dream of fellow left-wing unionists, he gave unstinting praise to such influential New Dealers as Frances Perkins and Harold L. Ickes, the secretary of the interior. In the spring of 1936, Hillman warned his fellow Amalgamated officials, "The defeat of the Roosevelt administration means no labor legislation for decades to come." Ickes reciprocated the sentiment. "Hillman," he wrote in his diary, "is one of the ablest and straightest leaders in the whole country." That Ickes did not add "labor" to those adjectives revealed Hillman's significance to building a party buoyed by, but hardly limited to, the ranks of union members.[19]

For the first time in its long history, the Democratic National Committee played a central role in constructing a smooth-running and successful electoral machine. To accomplish that end, the DNC required a novel type of leader, one who understood the party's new demographic diversity and had a sound strategy for mobilizing its parts. James Aloysius Farley, who became chairman in 1932, performed that role through most of FDR's first two terms.

The Irish Catholic from upstate New York made a stark contrast with his immediate predecessor, John J. Raskob, the millionaire tycoon more loyal to his friend Al Smith than to the party. Under Raskob's chairmanship, the DNC had at least been solvent and operated all year long. But Raskob detested unions and federal largesse alike. As early as 1934, the former Republican had grown so hostile to the New Deal that he helped launch the American Liberty League, a group dedicated to saving the republic from FDR and "the communistic elements" he believed were backing him. Al Smith, furious that FDR was occupying the White House instead of him, endorsed the corporate-funded organization, too.[20]

Farley, who never considered being anything but a Democrat, approached the job of chairman much the way an efficient and tireless boss might have managed a big-city party. He immersed himself in the fine details of state politics, tapped longtime Democrats to fill most posts in the DNC, and raised ample funds from individual donors as well as large institutions like the United Mine Workers. No partisan operative in the nation had a greater passion for the quotidian necessities of politics or so astonishing a memory of them. A Democrat from Iowa told the perhaps apocryphal tale of meeting Farley at a campaign stop in his home state and then seeing him three years later in Washington. He bet the chairman would not remember him. Farley gladly accepted the challenge. According to his biographer, Farley "greeted the man by his first name, . . . remembered the hotel where they had eaten lunch, recited the menu, gave an account of who the speakers at the lunch were and what they had said," and then inquired "how his children were, naming each of them in turn."[21]

However, Democrats needed more than a genius for personal politics to form a grand coalition of heterogeneous parts. With Roosevelt's encouragement, Farley established or expanded four separate departments of the DNC, each tasked with wooing a key constituency or keeping it in the fold. He set up a Labor Division, a Youth Division, a Puerto Rican and Spanish Division, and, in a modest break with the party's racist history, a Colored Division.

The Women's Division, the sole one that predated the New Deal, proved to be the most active and best run of them all. Headed by Mary W. "Molly" Dewson, a shrewd veteran of female reform initiatives and good friend of Eleanor Roosevelt, it not only mobilized women voters but also raised funds and pumped out 80 percent of the party literature distributed during the 1936 campaign. Unlike in the 1920s, Dewson and her partisan associates rarely touted measures directed at helping women in particular. After she successfully campaigned to get Frances Perkins named secretary of labor, Dewson told a male aide to FDR, "I am not a feminist. I am a practical politician out to build up the Democratic party where it sorely needs it."

Placing experienced and dedicated women in high positions did not bring new attention to ideas about how to target their unequal status in society. As chair of the House Labor Committee from 1937 through World War II, Representative Mary T. Norton from New

Jersey moved the bill setting maximum hours and a minimum wage for all workers through Congress and then did all she could to block GOP legislation to weaken union rights. But the men who led her party said little about bias against women, and she did not pressure them to change their minds or priorities.[22]

As always, local power remained critical to the Democrats' chances of governing the nation. They still had to run up lopsided margins in cities from the East Coast to the Midwest if they hoped to win control in, or the electoral vote of, any big industrial state. This usually meant relying on and cultivating the Irish Catholic bosses who still held sway—or creating new organizations where none existed. FDR loathed Frank Hague, the autocratic mayor of Jersey City, who got dubbed the "Hudson County Hitler" because he routinely ordered police to rough up left-wing demonstrators. But Hague, who gave Mary Norton her start in politics, corralled enough votes to carry his state for Democrats, so Roosevelt kept his feelings private.[23]

The president could offer urban bosses a valuable enticement unavailable to earlier administrations: thousands of patronage jobs in federal agencies. Chicago mayor Ed Kelly mobilized his polyglot constituents—two-thirds of whom were immigrants or their children—to offset the GOP's advantage in rural downstate Illinois. He made sure that European ethnics of all religions and national backgrounds who voted correctly received the city services they needed. He also doled out aid to African Americans, a group white workers had viciously attacked in the bloody riot of 1919. In return, FDR handed Kelly some thirty thousand jobs to fill with city residents. The boss's coalition included CIO unions, but they were just one of many interest groups that coveted his favor.

Where the GOP had long ruled, the labor movement's numbers gave it more influence in the creation of potent new machines. The last Democratic presidential nominee to carry Pennsylvania had been native son James Buchanan, way back in 1856. Eight decades later, FDR won the state easily, with crushing margins in Philadelphia, Pittsburgh, and the counties surrounding them. In factory towns, union activists often doubled as precinct captains.

While distressed Republicans squabbled among themselves, Democrats maneuvered to build on their triumph. In Pittsburgh,

David Lawrence, a devout Irish Catholic, used an alliance with the nascent United Steelworkers and other local unions to build an organization he would command until his death in 1966. During that span, Democrats never lost a city election. What one historian calls "a workingman's political leader in a workingman's town," the gregarious Lawrence made routine stops at ball games, factories, and Sunday Mass, while keeping his ward chairmen in line. When an underling blamed a rainstorm for his failure to register his assigned quota of Democrats, the boss snapped, "How the hell do you think the weather was on the North Side? Now get the hell out of here and get to work."[24]

Under Lawrence's guidance, the state took a decisive step to the left as well. In 1934, as party chairman, he assembled a ticket that paired George Howard Earle III, a Philadelphia businessman and polo player, for governor with Thomas Kennedy, a top official of the United Mine Workers, as his running mate. They introduced a raft of such pro-labor measures as a ban on child labor and laws to secure a minimum wage and maximum hours and higher taxes on corporations to fund relief programs. This "Little New Deal" promised to free the state from the industrial barons who had blocked economic reform for decades. The state senate, still under Republican control, voted down nearly every item on the wish list. Then in 1936, with FDR's wind at their backs, Democrats gained a majority in both houses and passed a more sweeping package that included a "Little Wagner Act" and tenure for public school teachers. Lawrence hailed it as "the most constructive, liberal and humane" program "in generations."[25]

Along with other prominent Northern Democrats, the state chairman worked diligently to convince African Americans to desert the GOP. In 1934, Lawrence recruited Robert Lee Vann, a Black journalist who would go on to head the DNC's Colored Division, to travel around Pennsylvania, promising patronage jobs to some and relief to all who needed it. Earle, whose Quaker forebears had financed a stop on the underground railroad, hosted a banquet for the Negro Citizens' Democratic Committee a few days before the election. "In less than two years," a journalist reported after Earle took office, Black Pennsylvanians had received more jobs in state government "than the Republicans gave them in forty-two." In 1936,

African American districts in Philadelphia and Pittsburgh that had never backed a Democratic nominee for president before voted for FDR by a landslide of 70 percent. The "party of Lincoln" has rarely been competitive among Black people in the state again.[26]

While local bosses could give African Americans material reasons to abandon the GOP, they lacked the power and, so far, the desire to reject the racist creed that had gripped the national party since its birth. The CIO did not share their reluctance. From the start, the new federation welcomed Black workers into its unions and pressed Democrats to take a strong stand for civil rights. The battle against white supremacy, contended its spokesmen, was a class issue. "Behind every lynching," asserted John Brophy, the CIO's national director and a former Pennsylvania coal miner, "is the figure of the labor exploiter, the man or the corporation who would deny labor its fundamental rights." Such statements of solidarity won the new federation warm endorsements from both the National Association for the Advancement of Colored People and the more radical National Negro Congress. By the end of the 1930s, half a million African Americans belonged to unions, an increase of more than 600 percent from a decade earlier.[27]

For most CIO leaders, interracial organizing was both a practical necessity and an ideological calling. Millions of Black people toiled in the steel mills, auto plants, packinghouses, tobacco factories, and other industries that made up the core of the American economy. To neglect or exclude this growing minority, as most AFL unions had done for decades, invited employers to divide the workforce and recruit Blacks as strikebreakers, as coal operators had done earlier in the century.

What's more, activists from the Communist Party and other radical groups were among the CIO's most dedicated and skillful organizers. They were spark plugs of the pivotal sit-down strike in the winter of 1936–37 at the General Motors complex in Flint, Michigan, and headed both the powerful longshore union on the Pacific Coast and the United Electrical Workers, whose members made appliances for Westinghouse and General Electric. For leftists, the solidarity represented in the slogan "Black and white, unite and fight!" was an indispensable step on the long road to working-class rule. Their utopian vision dovetailed with the goal of CIO leaders to remake the Democrats into a party that could be counted on to serve the interests of labor in a capitalist society. At the founding convention of Labor's Non-Partisan League in 1936, Sidney Hillman predicted, "In the great alignment which will mean liberal forces on one side opposed to the forces of reaction, labor should take its place." It was becoming increasingly difficult to be both an ardent New Dealer, at least in the North, and a vocal defender of Jim Crow.[28]

## The South Rejects, Workers Reelect

To build a durable majority, the Democrats' alliance with the CIO had one striking flaw: while it secured the backing of a large and potent new constituency, it also set the stage for losing an equally sizable and powerful older one. Southern Democrats in and out of Congress enthusiastically backed FDR when he created jobs, subsidized crop prices, and brought electricity—and, later, military bases— to their region, the poorest in the nation. They no longer held a majority of their party's seats in Congress—as they had from the end of Reconstruction through the 1920s. Still, they voted as a bloc on most issues and, thanks to seniority, chaired most committees in both chambers, ensuring their states a steady flow of federal aid.

But industrial unions threatened to strike at the base of their power and their cherished white identity. Not only did CIO unions organize wage earners of all races; they often employed immigrant left-wingers to do it. In the late 1930s, a drive to sign up Southern textile workers ran aground on the shoals of fears, both ethnic and religious. A mill owner's publicist vowed that Hillman might have signed up "foreign born employees" in the North but would "find it different when he tackles the Anglo-Saxons" who operated looms in Dixie. Some evangelical ministers alluding to the presence of godless union organizers told their congregations that the abbreviation "CIO" actually meant "Christ Is Out."[29]

Roosevelt and his aides resisted defining their party as a multiracial one; they feared alienating the white South and could not imagine retaining a durable majority without it. So they agreed to the discrimination against African Americans embodied in the provisions of the National Labor Relations Act, the Social Security Act, and the Fair Labor Standards Act that did not cover workers who labored on farms or in other people's homes. Robert Wagner and his fellow Northern liberals protested these exemptions, rather quietly, lest their colleagues reject the entire bills. In the end, they accepted the compromises that allowed such landmark pieces of legislation to become law.

Dixie Democrats could still sense which way the wind was blowing, and most did not like it at all. In 1937, Senator Josiah Bailey of North Carolina issued a "conservative manifesto" that called for a balanced budget, urged the protection of states' rights, and, in a swipe at aggressive unions, extolled "the American system of private enterprise and initiative." Only a minority of his fellow Southerners signed on to this wholesale repudiation of the New Deal. But Vice President John Nance Garner, the crusty Texan whom FDR had placed on the ticket in 1932 as a reward for his aid in securing the nomination, made himself a lightning rod for Southern protests throughout the second term. Garner called on the president to break the Flint sit-down strike, which he blamed on the Wagner Act. In 1938, the vice president encouraged Representative Martin Dies, Jr., a fellow Texan, to form a Special Committee on Un-American Activities. Dies had already fought to stop the House from passing a color-blind minimum wage standard. "What is prescribed for one race must be prescribed for the others," he explained, "and you cannot prescribe the same wages for the Black man as for the white man." Soon, Chairman Dies and his conservative allies were hauling pro-FDR artists and intellectuals up to the Capitol to grill them about their alleged connections to the Communist Party and other "subversive" groups.[30]

To counter these threats from within, Roosevelt undertook a risky struggle in 1938 to purge his party of congressional opponents of the New Deal. He endorsed liberal challengers against conservative incumbents, most from the South. But a failed attempt to enlarge the Supreme Court, followed by a sharp recession caused by cuts in federal spending and a rise in taxes, had sapped FDR's popularity. In June 1938, a Gallup poll reported that most Americans did not want the administration to move leftward, and all but one of the candidates the president supported (a New Yorker) went down to defeat. That year, a young Texas congressman named Lyndon Baines Johnson watched Maury Maverick—a pro-union firebrand from San Antonio—lose his bid for renomination after he became the only Southern member of Congress to endorse Robert Wagner's proposed law to make lynching a federal crime. "I can go [only] so far in Texas . . . My people won't take it," Johnson complained to a fellow New Dealer. "Maury forgot that and he is not here . . . There's nothing more useless than a dead liberal."[31]

That November, the liberal casualty list stretched far beyond the city of the Alamo. Across the North and West in 1938, the Republicans became a competitive party again. They picked up eighty-one seats in the House and eight in the Senate, and captured governorships in a dozen states—including Michigan, Minnesota, and Ohio, despite the best efforts of unionists there.

Although FDR's party retained a sizable edge in both houses of Congress, the Southerners who ran most of the committees looked forward to bonding with the newly robust GOP minority to defeat or trim back further attempts at spending on public works or other expansions of the welfare state. Florida senator Claude Pepper, one of the few Southern liberals left in the upper chamber, blasted the embryonic coalition on the right for plotting to "give the government of this Nation back to those who have always been the champions of special privilege." William Allen White, a progressive Republican journalist, commented that FDR had shriveled into "a crippled leader of the liberal faction of the Democratic party." He was not referring to the president's paralysis, which the media largely ignored. According to Gallup, a majority of Americans still approved of Roosevelt's performance. Yet since no president had ever run for a third term, it appeared his party could soon be tearing itself apart again in the race to choose a fresh nominee. Well into the summer of 1939, polls that omitted FDR showed John Nance Garner easily outpacing any other Democrat.[32]

Roosevelt defied that precedent and went on to win and serve another full term. By the 1940 election, a second global war had been raging for over a year in Europe and three years in Asia, and many voters worried about putting an untested man in charge of defending the nation. Yet a strong Democratic message of moral capitalism with a well-mobilized labor movement behind it certainly helped keep Wendell Willkie, the corporate mogul turned GOP standard-bearer, from terminating a New Deal order that had only begun to reach maturity.

Wagner and Hillman worked decisively to win that third term. The senator from New York again headed the committee that drafted the party platform. The 1940 version boasted:

> Under Democratic auspices, more has been done . . . to foster the essential freedom, dignity and opportunity of the American worker than in any other administration in the nation's history. In consequence, labor is today taking its rightful place as a partner of management in the common cause of higher earnings, industrial efficiency, national unity and national defense.

That summer, Wagner demonstrated his commitment to racial equality when he proposed a successful amendment to the new Selective Service Act that allowed Black men to enlist in the Army Air Corps and other elite branches of the military. When Jim Farley, who had opposed the intraparty purge, turned against FDR and cozied up to Garner, Wagner got Ed Flynn, Democratic boss of the Bronx, to replace him as chairman of the DNC.[33]

Hillman waged his own struggle within the labor movement itself. He had to beat back a revolt against FDR led by the same man with whom he had created the CIO and who reigned as its charismatic president. By 1940, John L. Lewis had switched from being FDR's champion to his bitter antagonist. The change of heart was based, in part, on principle: Lewis opposed what he took to be Roosevelt's rush to rearm the nation and also thought the incumbent had not been a consistent enough friend to labor. But Lewis also imagined himself a future occupant of the White House and was badly disappointed when FDR chose Henry Wallace, the left-wing secretary of agriculture, to be his running mate. Due to the nonaggression pact between Nazi Germany and the Soviet Union signed in the summer of 1939,

Communists in the unions and those who sympathized with their views cheered Lewis's independent stand. Neither they nor Joseph Stalin favored the defense of Great Britain advocated by FDR.

For Hillman, the reelection of Roosevelt was a cause fundamental to that of labor itself. He spent much of 1940 cajoling and persuading CIO officials and rank-and-filers to spurn Lewis's revolt. In late October, when Lewis gave a national radio address endorsing Willkie, his claim that the utility magnate had "the common touch" fell flat, as did his prediction that a third term might bring "a dictatorship in the land." Industrial unionists continued to be grateful to the UMW kingpin for building a national force that employers and politicians had to respect. But FDR was *their* president, and so the GOP nominee was their enemy. As the CIO council in San Francisco roared, "It takes a wild stretch of the imagination to interpret Wendell Willkie as anything but a reactionary stooge."[34]

The election results that fall demonstrated how vital the Democratic alliance with labor had become—and how necessary to both party and movement. "The New Deal appears to have accomplished what the Socialists, the I.W.W., and the Communists never could approach," wrote the political analyst Samuel Lubell two months after the vote. "[To] draw a class line across the face of American politics." He neglected to mention the strength of the GOP among Protestant workers in rural areas outside the South. Roosevelt also lost much of the support he had received in 1936 from middle-class suburbanites and small business owners—many of them former Republicans who returned to their old party. But crushing majorities among workingmen and workingwomen in the big cities were enough, along with the Solid South, for FDR to score a comfortable victory in the Electoral College. As one newspaper concluded, "Labor was the keystone in the Democratic arch."[35]

## The War Within

World War II gleams in popular memory as a rare time when "patriotism unified a nation." Following the bombing of Pearl Harbor in December 1941, the story goes, Americans put aside their sharp political differences to blast the Axis fascists and militarists back to hell. As a journalist for *The Washington Post* wrote early this century: "Government and industry marched forward together to sell the war effort . . . after a decade of ugly labor strife, [they] impressed upon workers that they were soldiers of production. Duty meant giving nothing less than 100 percent."[36]

While the Second World War certainly had more popular support than any other major conflict in U.S. history, the home front hardly lived up to that image of harmony in pursuit of a transcendent cause. Union officials did pledge to authorize no strikes for the duration of the fighting overseas, and the War Labor Board reciprocated by making it difficult for an employee of a military contractor *not* to join a union if one already existed at his or her workplace. But thousands of wage earners laid down their tools anyway—to protest speedups, wages that did not keep pace with inflation, or, sometimes, having to work alongside a man or woman whose skin was Black.

The shared zeal to win the war did not stop political tempests from continuing to whip through the electorate and Congress. FDR's coattails in 1940 were quite short; Democrats won just seven additional seats in the House and lost a few in the Senate. Then came the 1942 midterms, which showed starkly how little benefit Roosevelt's party reaped from his own popularity, even during wartime. With forty-seven new House members, most elected in the Midwest and the Great Plains, Republicans came within just ten seats of retaking the chamber. They also whittled the Democratic hold over the Senate down to one-third of what it had been after the landslide of 1936. The Republicans actually won a majority of the popular vote in the nation overall—for the first time since 1930. Low turnout was one reason for the outcome: the war and the wartime economy had spurred millions of working-class citizens to move far away from their old homes, and just one-third of those eligible to vote turned up at the polls—the second lowest rate in the modern history of midterm elections.

Republicans and many Southern Democrats read the results as an invitation to defeat attempts to extend the welfare state and reverse liberal programs if they could. We will "win the war from the New Deal," declared a GOP House leader in 1942. The following year, the expanded coalition on the right abolished the Works Progress Administration and Civilian Conservation Corps, which had provided jobs to several million people, and kept Wagner's attempt to provide health insurance to every American bottled up in committee. Roosevelt offered little aid to his embattled supporters in Congress. He devoted his time to the diplomacy of war and making sure the "arsenal of democracy" at home ran smoothly. In 1942, when a right-wing broadcaster accused Hillman of steering contracts to firms organized by his union, the president got the labor loyalist fired from a top post in the government's agency in charge of military production. In the wake of the rebuff, Hillman suffered a massive heart attack and took months to recover.[37]

His movement was also struggling to retain its influence in the political establishment. The growth in union membership, particularly among war workers, alarmed conservatives who feared employers would never again be free to command their employees as they wished. In 1943, public condemnation of a coal strike that John L. Lewis initiated gave labor's opponents an opportunity they had craved since the court let the Wagner Act stand six years before.

That June, two Southern Democrats—Senator Tom Connally of Texas and Representative Howard Worth Smith of Virginia—introduced a bill to prohibit unions from donating to federal election campaigns and also allow the president to seize control of an industry on strike if he deemed it essential "in the prosecution of war." FDR vetoed the law, without lodging a strong protest, and Congress swiftly overrode him. The legislation actually did nothing to stem the growth of union membership. Still, as the historian Alan Brinkley writes, "it demonstrated the degree to which the . . . movement was losing political leverage." Any further erosion could have ominous consequences for America's default party of labor.[38]

Once he regained a semblance of health, Sidney Hillman invented a novel way to prevent that from happening. In the summer of 1943, two weeks after Congress passed the Smith-Connally Act, he persuaded the executive board of the CIO to create a new mechanism to galvanize working-class voters: the political action committee. The CIO-PAC, which Hillman chaired, took a giant step beyond what Labor's Non-Partisan League had sought to accomplish. The league helped steer unionists to Roosevelt's cause in 1936, but it had stayed mostly dormant since then, stymied by the rivalry between the two labor federations that had birthed it. But the PAC would be the exclusive weapon of the CIO, designed as a permanent body that would back pro-labor Democrats in primaries and set forth a visionary program on which they would campaign. Given Hillman's weak heart, he was unlikely to live much longer. But armed with a skillful and durable political apparatus, he believed the industrial labor movement could not just survive but be able to implant itself deep in the heart of the American state and society.

The 1944 campaign became the first and most critical test of his strategy. The Smith-Connally act prohibited unions from donating to general elections. The law said nothing about primaries, however. So the CIO-PAC encouraged labor to pump funds into races where a pro-union candidate was challenging a conservative—and did far better than had Roosevelt's purge six years earlier. In the South, several prominent foes of unions went down to defeat; Martin Dies, the notorious Red hunter from Texas, withdrew from a primary he was sure to lose after the PAC registered hundreds of union members in his district who worked at a big oil refinery. Liberal candidates also got help in eight Southern states from CIO unions that paid poll taxes for some fifty thousand members, most of whom were probably white. CIO-PAC-supported candidates also triumphed in New York, Michigan, and California—states where the labor movement was robust and growing.[39]

Hillman's organization was something less than the "machine" observers called it at the time and yet more than just an unofficial adjunct of FDR's campaign. While the CIO-PAC registered voters, it did not make sure they cast their ballots. Nor did it have patronage jobs to exchange for electoral duties faithfully rendered.

Yet its efforts at political education surpassed anything Tammany or the Pittsburgh machine attempted. In 1944, the CIO-PAC's publicity division generated a stream of vivid brochures and radio broadcasts that gave pro-union citizens good reasons to vote *for* FDR and his fellow liberals instead of merely against their adversaries. In his State of the Union Address that year, Roosevelt had outlined a "second Bill of Rights" that would provide every adult a job, a livable wage, "a good education," and the right to a "decent home" and "adequate medical care." The CIO-PAC fleshed out his proposal with a deftly illustrated "People's Program" that added the demand for a national planning board on which labor, business, and government would be responsible for turning the new Bill of Rights into law. Many of the staff members who designed such materials were sympathetic to communism. But the ideas they expressed were similar to those that British Labour and other social-democratic parties in Europe had long advocated. The wartime alliance between the United States and the Soviet Union encouraged such an ideological popular front. In any case, the publicity division issued nothing that Hillman did not approve.[40]

In June, he also chaired a new group to mobilize liberal sympathizers and tap into their bank accounts. The National Citizens PAC quickly attracted a dazzling selection of renowned Americans, both Black and white: such veteran reformers as Gifford Pinchot and Mary McLeod Bethune, prominent liberal journalists like Dorothy Parker and Max Lerner, such celebrity performers as Orson Welles and Paul Robeson, and even a pro-union industrialist or two. Fifteen percent of its board members were African American. Hillman, according to his biographer, "conceived of the NCPAC . . . as an influence network with lines running straight to the headquarters of allied organizations." The task of its members was to shape public opinion and, by doing so, nudge apathetic voters to elect FDR to a fourth term.[41]

The group's very existence showed that the rise of the CIO and the pro-labor tilt of the New Deal had converted the small but high-profile cohort to which Welles and the others belonged into a key part of the Democratic base. Accelerating a trend begun in the 1930s, the party became the political home of most artists, academics, and policy intellectuals—one that few, except the radicals among them, ever saw a reason to leave. This marked a drastic departure from the Gilded Age, when the party had a lowbrow, disreputable image among the Northern learned elite—then composed, in the main, of white Protestants. It far surpassed the earlier affection for Woodrow Wilson among progressive intellectuals who wrote for *The New Republic* and similar periodicals. By World War II, the Democrats' embrace of ethnic and, to a degree, racial pluralism appealed to a new breed of professors—a swelling number who came from working-class Jewish families—as did its talk of class equality, which appealed to thinkers and artists on the left. Many of these men and women were attracted to socialist ideas, if not necessarily to joining a third party that embodied them.

In 1944, FDR needed each of his party's key constituencies to turn out in large numbers to win what turned into his closest race for the White House. Southerners and big-city bosses considered Vice President Wallace too left-wing on economic policy and too favorable to civil rights. So Roosevelt, whose high blood pressure and chronic fatigue threatened to prevent him from completing another term, quietly agreed to dump him in favor of Harry Truman, a Missouri senator groomed by the Kansas City machine. Republicans used a false rumor that FDR had given Hillman the final say on that critical decision to blast the CIO-PAC chairman as the anti-capitalist wizard behind the presidential throne. They coined the slogan "Clear it with Sidney" and festooned it with all manner of anti-Semitic and red-baiting innuendo. The right-wing Hearst press even ran a limerick contest about the phrase; one winning entry began, "Clear it with Sidney, You Yanks / Then offer Joe Stalin your thanks." The slurs neglected the fact that, in league with other Democratic leaders, Hillman had nudged Henry Wallace off the ticket in part because of his naïve trust in the motives of the Soviet dictator.[42]

Even more than in his previous campaigns, Roosevelt's victory in Northern states depended on rolling up huge margins among working-class urban voters, their numbers swelled by the boom in war industries. Overall turnout, at just 56 percent of eligible voters, decreased from 1940 yet shot up in Detroit and Chicago, where thousands of planes and tanks rolled out of factories, and in the San Francisco Bay Area, home to sprawling naval shipyards. FDR carried California with ease, but he would have fallen short in Michigan and Illinois if union members had not flocked to the polls there. Robert Wagner won his own fourth term in the Senate with help from a little popular front in his state that included New York mayor Fiorello La Guardia, along with the heads of the CIO, the AFL, and the NAACP. Not since its founding in 1909 had the nation's leading civil rights group endorsed a candidate for public office.

Despite the strictures of the Smith-Connally Act, labor managed to raise a substantial sum to back its favored nominees. Members of CIO unions contributed the lion's share of the $2.25 million in donations, nearly all of which went to Democrats. A few weeks after the election, the PAC chairman received a most pleasing letter. "One thing I want to make perfectly clear to you Sidney is my appreciation," wrote Franklin Roosevelt. "It was a great campaign and nobody knows better than I do how much you contributed to its success." FDR added that he was "glad to learn" that the PAC would stay in business for years to come. The president was quite aware that organized labor had provided more funds and precinct walkers than any other interest group in all three of his reelection campaigns. Without its largesse and shoe leather, he might have fallen short in the close Midwestern and Eastern industrial states that did much to decide the elections of 1940 and 1944.[43]

The following April, six weeks after his fourth inauguration, Franklin D. Roosevelt succumbed to a cerebral hemorrhage. He had dominated his party and the public imagination as had no Democrat since Andrew Jackson. But the affection for FDR, unlike that for Old Hickory, was felt by Americans of all races and regions. "Our last president was a member of my family," reflected Orson Welles on a broadcast the day after Roosevelt died, evoking his Fireside Chats. "He lived in our home as I know he lived in yours. My home seems empty now as yours does."[44]

## Saving Truman

That FDR died as the bloodiest war in history was ending in victory surely bolstered both the public's love and grief. Major wars typically disrupt and transform the contours of national politics. But, as the political scientist David Plotke writes, "For the United States the central domestic result of World War II was to cement the Democratic order." No other actor was as essential at binding voters to the party of Roosevelt and the liberal state as the American labor movement.[45]

However, when that movement exercised its muscle at the workplace, it also had the potential to damage Democratic fortunes, at least in the short run. From the fall of 1945 into the late spring of 1946, more than four million union members went out on strike—a larger wave than any other in the nation's history, save that in 1919. Most walked off the job to demand a boost in pay that would enable them to keep up with prices that had shot up by as much as 45 percent during the war. But Walter Reuther, the young leader of the United Auto Workers' strike against General Motors, inflamed corporate executives by demanding something more than a substantial wage increase: an agreement by the company not to raise the prices it charged for its four-wheeled products. GM correctly viewed his gambit as a bold attempt to redistribute the wealth. "You can't talk about this thing without exposing your socialistic desires," a company negotiator snarled at Reuther.[46]

At first, most Americans, thinking as consumers, applauded the novel proposal. But GM executives refused to consider it in any form, and President Harry Truman called on the strikers to return to work while the negotiators wrangled. As the strike dragged on through the winter, public opinion gradually turned against the union, and Reuther had to settle for a modest raise and no say over the price of Cadillacs, Buicks, and Chevrolets. By year's end, inflation had eaten up nearly all the gains autoworkers and their frustrated counterparts in other industries had achieved after months off the job. Union foes in business and government "soon complained of a vicious 'wage-price spiral' that was robbing the public and crippling commerce," according to Reuther's biographer.[47]

With labor on the defensive and a Democrat in the White House who seemed powerless either to stop strikes or keep prices down, the GOP looked ahead to the midterm election with more optimism than at any time since the dawn of the Great Depression. The slogan a GOP publicist concocted for the midterm was brilliant in its simplicity: "Had Enough? Vote Republican." Most voters answered in the affirmative. Winning back dozens of seats in Northern industrial states, the pro-business party took control of both houses of Congress for the first time since the year Herbert Hoover crushed Al Smith—when unions had fewer members than the number of wage earners who walked off the job in 1946. The setback would probably not have surprised the shrewdest political mind in organized labor. But Sidney Hillman did not live to reflect on it or plan his next move. That summer, at the age of fifty-nine, he succumbed to a heart attack.

The new majority quickly pounced on the constituency undergirding the long string of Democratic victories that had now been broken. In the spring of 1947, Republicans teamed up with Southern Democrats—who once again dominated their party's caucus—to pass the Taft-Hartley Act, which promised to "balance" the pro-union tilt of the Wagner Act by recognizing the "legitimate rights" of employers. Robert Taft, the GOP senator from Ohio who crafted the final bill, claimed he meant only to curb the "arbitrary" and "unjust" power of labor leaders over the future of the economy. The son of the former president assured ordinary workers they were still free to choose unions to represent them. The AFL and the CIO vehemently denounced the act, which made sympathy boycotts illegal, encouraged states to pass laws to prohibit union shops, and allowed the president to stop a strike even in peacetime if he deemed it a national emergency. Taft-Hartley "deliberately seeks to create an atmosphere of fear and repression," charged CIO president Philip Murray, and would lead to "a widespread cancellation of civil and political rights."[48]

Truman had a difficult and politically momentous decision to make. Earlier in the year, he had asked Congress to come up with a more limited way to prevent crippling work stoppages. If he vetoed Taft-Hartley, he would appear to confirm the Republican charge that he was captive to the union bosses who had mounted the failed strikes of the year before. Yet if he allowed the bill to become law, as most Americans polled by Gallup preferred, he would lose the confidence of the one group whose aid Democrats would need most if they were to stage a comeback in 1948. Raised by the Kansas City machine to appreciate the value of loyalty, Truman turned down a measure he knew would be enacted and may even have thought was necessary. "The bill is deliberately designed to weaken labor unions," he wrote in his veto message released one Friday in late June. "Because of unions, the living standards of our working people have increased steadily until they are today the highest in the world." By

Monday, a majority of Democrats in the House and nearly half their reduced number in the Senate had joined nearly every Republican to defy the weakened president. The vote revealed that the regional division in Truman's party yawned wider than ever. Only four of the twenty-one Southern Democrats in the upper chamber chose to sustain the veto.[49]

Ill with coronary disease, Robert Wagner was absent when the Senate cast the override vote. A few days later, his son delivered a message from his father to Harry Truman. The New York lawmaker called the passage of Taft-Hartley "one of the bitterest disappointments I have ever experienced. For I was forced to see the work of a lifetime destroyed, while I lay on my back in bed." That May, Wagner had been well enough to condemn the legislation in unusually dramatic terms: "It is not labor, but the opponents of labor, who have too much power," he charged. The new law would "weaken the workers and organizations [who] have been the strongest and most consistent fighting force for economic progress and human betterment." Wagner remained in office for two more years before his health compelled him to step down. He died in 1953. His heartsick denunciation of Taft-Hartley was the last speech he would deliver on the floor of the chamber where he had labored for more than two decades to reshape liberalism and the nation.[50]

But Wagner's dire prophecy did not come to pass. Union power was indeed limited by the legislation he abhorred, though a major push by the CIO to organize Southern wage earners had collapsed before Taft had introduced his bill. Still, Truman's veto may have saved his presidency and the New Deal order his party had created.

That November, Clark Clifford, the White House counsel and the president's trusted friend, wrote a lengthy memorandum that detailed the strategy he thought the Democrats should follow in the upcoming campaign. The party needed to keep intact its "unhappy alliance of Southern conservatives, Western progressives, and Big City labor." The heyday of the urban machines was gone, Clifford wrote. They were "supplanted in large measure by the pressure groups" who demanded that their economic and/or ideological interests be served. Democrats had to keep progressives and Southerners in the fold. But the party, Clifford stressed, "cannot win without the *active* support of organized labor. It is dangerous to assume that labor now has nowhere else to go in 1948. *Labor can stay home.*"[51]

Democrats were hardly unified in believing that Truman deserved a chance to be elected in his own right. During the spring of 1948, the president trailed every leading Republican contender in the polls—including the eventual nominee, New York governor Thomas Dewey. Truman's approval rating in April was an abysmal 36 percent; ominously, he was no more popular in the South than in the nation at large. Some of the prominent liberals who belonged to Americans for Democratic Action, a successor to the National Citizens PAC, tried to convince Dwight Eisenhower, a hero of World War II, to run as a Democrat. Supreme Court justice William O. Douglas considered challenging the president as well.[52]

But due to Truman's tough stand against Taft-Hartley, officials of the AFL and CIO and the independent railway unions were inclined to support him and that convinced the bulk of progressive activists to do the same. "He has given American liberalism the fighting chance that it seemed to have lost with the death of Roosevelt," editorialized *The Nation* in the wake of his veto message. "Now the fight begins, and it will carry on until the votes are counted in '48."[53]

Truman reinforced that image throughout the campaign. On Labor Day, he warned a throng of at least a quarter million people, mostly union members, who crowded into Detroit's Cadillac Square that a President Thomas Dewey would "hit" them with "a steady barrage of body blows" that could include repeal of both the Wagner Act and Social Security. Then he took off on a thirty-one-thousand-mile campaign by rail that stopped mainly in industrial cities and towns from the Midwest to California. The "whistle-stop tour" emulated those William Jennings Bryan had conducted and generated favorable reports on the radio and even in newspapers that ended up endorsing Dewey.[54]

Still, nearly every experienced observer, whatever his or her politics, doubted that a class-conscious message and the backing of labor would be enough to win. Truman was sure to lose millions of normally Democratic votes to two splinter-party candidates. He competed on the left with Henry Wallace, who carried the standard of the new Progressive Party. The former vice president promised to revive the wartime alliance with the Soviet Union that had been destroyed during Truman's tenure, and he basked in the passionate support of a healthy minority of unions in the CIO either led by Communists or favorable to them. On the right, Truman faced a challenge from Strom Thurmond, the governor of South Carolina, whose States' Rights Party burned to punish the president for allowing a strong civil rights plank to be included in that year's national Democratic platform. Given his appeal among white voters in states that Democrats always counted on winning, Thurmond appeared to be the more serious threat; he hailed from Edgefield County, the same violent corner of the state from which Ben Tillman had sprung, and Thurmond was just as adept at turning race-baiting demagoguery into votes. Boss Ed Crump of Memphis endorsed the States' Rights ticket even though he allowed a small number of African Americans in his own city to vote. For a growing number of Southern Democrats, Harry Truman had crossed a Rubicon when he made Black rights the official position of their party. His defeat, they hoped, would bring a welcome return to the old racist orthodoxy.

"Labor did it," Truman told an "intimate friend" who asked him how he defied both the polls and pundits to win in 1948. Of course, the upset victory was not due solely to the 70 percent of union members who voted to keep him in the White House. Democratic managers drove many liberals away from Henry Wallace by tarring him for "following the Kremlin line slavishly," a line echoed by anti-Communists in the labor movement who helped Truman eke out the narrow victories he needed in the union bastions of Ohio, California, and Illinois. In the end, the Progressive candidate drew barely more than a million ballots, enough to flip just one state, New York, into Dewey's column. The prosperous agricultural economy and fear that the GOP might abolish crop subsidies also helped Truman win a number of Midwestern farm states the GOP had carried four years earlier. The president also held on in most of Dixie, although Thurmond captured four states, including his own. The Solid South died that year and would never be reborn—at least until former Democrats like Thurmond converted it into a bastion of the Republican right during the presidency of Ronald Reagan.[55]

While neither third party was successful at denying victory to

Truman, both, in different ways, augured crises in Democratic fortunes. Any presidential nominee who struggled to win the South
would have to offset losses there with gains in populous regions like
the Midwest and Middle Atlantic, where, before the Great Depression, the GOP had dominated. And while the Progressives, battered
by the Red Scare, would never again mount a serious campaign, future left-wing insurgents learned from their failure. Unlike Wallace,
Eugene McCarthy, George McGovern, Jesse Jackson, and even the
formally independent Bernie Sanders all remained inside the party,
where they and their allies challenged the establishment to adopt
their demands or risk alienating their followers. The ideological battle did, at times, nudge Democrats to refresh the New Deal legacy
of reforming capitalism. But it could also leave them divided and
dispirited in the contest with a more united and aggressive GOP.

The chief lesson of Truman's victory in 1948 at the time was that
the Democrats had become a party that, outside the South, depended
on support from city dwellers of all religions and races. The sole institution that could bridge the sharp divisions between inhabitants of
those cities was organized labor. In Illinois, pro-union candidates for
the U.S. Senate and governor polled far better than Truman; their
"reverse coattails" enabled him to win that crucial state by less than
1 percent of the vote. A unified, energetic, and well-funded campaign by labor in Northern states also recaptured Congress for the
Democrats, making the 1946 election seem like a curious anomaly
rather than the harbinger of a new conservative era. Working-class
voters gave almost twice as much support to Truman as did their
middle-class counterparts—a gap that narrowed and then vanished
in later years. The unions certainly did not do it alone, but the Democratic victory would never have occurred without them.[56]

The bond between labor and party remained strong for another two
decades, undergirding the further growth of the liberal state. It could
be glimpsed in symbolic ways: every Democratic nominee for president from Truman in 1948 to Lyndon Johnson in 1964 kicked off

his fall campaign with a Labor Day speech to a big union crowd gathered in Cadillac Square. It yielded substantive results: no major piece of domestic legislation that Democrats enacted from the New Deal through the 1960s succeeded without the backing of labor officialdom. To retain that status, union leaders, like those of any other interest group, had to keep demonstrating their power at the polls. As the journalist A. H. Raskin wrote about FDR, "Labor found him helpful when its political artillery was loaded and well-aimed, but merely friendly when it seemed outgunned in the battle for votes." Hillman's successors understood that the labor movement was fated to be the dependent partner in the relationship with the Democratic establishment. Unless the unions enjoyed at least the friendly neutrality of the federal government, they would always be dangerously vulnerable to their enemies in big business and among conservative politicians in both major parties.[57]

In post–World War II America, the price of that support would be a tacit agreement not to mount a concerted protest against the domination of the economy by big businesses—as long as those firms were willing to recognize and sign contracts with unions. Liberal activists in and outside the labor movement did not stop resenting the sway of GM, U.S. Steel, and their ilk in the marketplace as well as on the factory floor. But the last mass insurgency against monopoly power had expired soon after World War I, and few Democratic candidates or policy intellectuals believed a revival was possible. The resistance of giant firms to a fully social-democratic welfare state also ensured that Congress would scuttle most items in "the People's Program" before most Americans even knew they existed. Social Security, the minimum wage, and Keynesian remedies for economic slumps did, however, become hallmarks of federal policy. The social movement that compelled Democrats to define the right to a union as a linchpin of moral capitalism thus had an ironic consequence. Without intending to, labor helped make corporate capitalism seem as imperishable as the two-party system itself.

# 7

## FREEDOM AND FRAGMENTATION, 1948–1968

*The time has arrived for the Democratic party to get out of the*
*shadow of states' rights and walk forthrightly into the bright*
*sunshine of human rights.*
—HUBERT HUMPHREY, MAYOR OF MINNEAPOLIS, 1948[1]

*The legislative branch . . . must immediately change its childish,*
*immature, compromising, 19th century attitude and not just*
*become a part of the 20th century world*
*but a leader.*
—REPRESENTATIVE ADAM CLAYTON POWELL, JR., 1955[2]

*I cheered when Humphrey was chosen*
*My faith in the system restored*
*I'm glad the commies were thrown out*
*Of the A.F.L.-C.I.O. board*
*I love Puerto Ricans and Negroes*
*As long as they don't move next door*
*So love me, love me, love me, I'm a liberal*
—PHIL OCHS, PROTEST SINGER, 1965[3]

*They've called us rednecks . . . Well we're going to show*
*Mr. Nixon and Mr. Humphrey that there sure are a lot*
*of rednecks in this country!*
—GEORGE C. WALLACE, INDEPENDENT CANDIDATE FOR PRESIDENT
AND FORMER AND FUTURE DEMOCRAT, 1968[4]

## The Issue of the Twentieth Century

The most consequential words spoken at the 1948 Democratic National Convention were uttered by a politician whose name and voice few inside the hall in Philadelphia had ever heard. President Harry Truman delivered a combative but unremarkable acceptance speech, and Senator Alben Barkley gave a rousing keynote address that included the classic jab "What is a bureaucrat? A bureaucrat is a Democrat who holds an office that some Republican wants." The speech helped the Kentucky lawmaker win the nomination for vice president. But when Hubert Horatio Humphrey, the thirty-seven-year-old mayor of Minneapolis, took the podium to demand that Democrats call on Congress to enact a strong civil rights program, he aimed to sever the party from its long heritage as the defender of human bondage and then of Jim Crow.[5]

"My friends, to those who say that we are rushing this issue of civil rights, I say to them we are 172 years late," Humphrey declared in a tone both exultant and defiant. "People—human beings—this is the issue of the 20th century." He went on to assure the audience in the sweltering hall, the sixty million who listened on the radio, and the ten million who watched on television (it was the first convention to be broadcast live) that granting real freedom to Black people would also benefit the United States in the Cold War. "As a leader in the free world," the nation confronted "the world of slavery"— that is, the Soviet empire. "For us to play our part, effectively," he stressed, "we must be in a morally sound position." Humphrey and his fellow liberals would make that defensive theme a central part of their rhetorical arsenal until Congress finally passed the landmark civil rights bills of the 1960s.[6]

As with many a celebrated oration, the timing of the speech, which lasted just nine minutes, mattered more than did the words themselves. Humphrey was asking the delegates to adopt a minority plank guaranteeing every citizen the right to vote and an equal opportunity in the job market and the military. Even those party leaders who shared his views, including the president himself, resisted placing them in the platform because they knew it would infuriate the Southerners who had nearly always been essential to Democrats winning national elections. The Senate minority leader, Scott Lucas, who hailed from Illinois, snapped that Humphrey was a "pipsqueak" whose plank would "split the party wide open."[7]

But the speech and the ebullient, and quite spontaneous, floor demonstration that followed helped convince a majority of delegates— and President Truman, reluctantly—to include the civil rights pledge in the platform. The small number of Southern delegates who stomped out in protest and then mounted a third-party challenge that fall included several prominent figures from the region. One was Eugene "Bull" Connor, a former sportscaster who wielded authority over both the police and fire departments in Birmingham, the largest city in Alabama. But they could not stop Truman from edging Dewey or his party from regaining control of Congress that fall—or Hubert Humphrey from winning a seat in the U.S. Senate.

So instead of being shunned, the young politician from Minnesota became an instant spokesman for a fledgling alliance of Black and white Democrats who were determined to fulfill the New Deal's promise to secure political and economic freedom to Americans— this time of every race. "All we knew," Humphrey later recalled, "was that we, a group of young liberals, had beaten the leadership of the party and led them close to where they ought to have been."[8]

In fact, their triumph was merely a symbolic one. Humphrey and his fellow insurgents hailed their achievement as a new "Emancipation Proclamation." But it had taken the bloodiest war in American history to abolish slavery. And it would be nearly another two decades before Congress turned all the promises made in the 1948 platform into law. For Democrats, the demand for Black empowerment was a "time bomb" with a long fuse planted by left-wing New Dealers and their union allies during the 1940s. When it detonated in the mid-1960s, it fragmented the party and did much to bring an end to the New Deal order that labor, the white South, urban machines, and liberal activists had built together.[9]

The party's internal conflict developed slowly during the long period of postwar prosperity from the late 1940s to the early 1970s, whose fruits were more widely shared than ever before. For the latter achievement, citizens of the world's dominant capitalist nation could thank Democratic presidents and Congresses that built on the legacy of the New Deal. During this "Great Compression," real wages in the United States doubled; manufacturing workers represented by strong unions gained even more. For the first time in modern history, a majority of Americans owned the homes in which they lived. In 1962, a group of social scientists who had completed a study of falling inequality and rising incomes marveled, "The elimination of poverty is well within the means of federal, state, and local governments." At the onset of the long boom, the United States had become the mightiest nation on earth—the leader of a "free world" united by a resistance to communism, if not by a shared practice of democratic rule—as such authoritarian allies as Spain's Francisco Franco and the theocrats of Saudi Arabia made clear.[10]

In much of Western and Central Europe, democracy proved entirely compatible with policies that socialists had long advocated. Under center-left governments, their citizens enjoyed universal health insurance, abundant and affordable public housing, and a free college education. It was the triumph of what one historian has dubbed "social capitalism."[11]

But in the United States, conservatives in both parties blasted such programs as steps down a slope to tyranny and stymied attempts by liberal Democrats to push even a semblance of them through Congress. Thus, the same Cold War that Humphrey claimed the nation would win only if Americans embraced civil rights also chilled the prospect for advancing the Economic Bill of Rights, the wish list for a fully realized welfare state Franklin Roosevelt had championed during the final years of his life.

In some ways, the long conflict with the Soviet Union and its allies around the world was a boon to the party's fortunes. It kept most Americans as friendly to government programs and the progressive income taxes that paid for them as they had been during the New Deal and the Second World War. Public officials and pundits alike held that a well-educated citizenry was essential to containing the threat of communism. As it happened, the millions of young people who attended the new state university campuses and colleges that had been created, with federal aid, across the country during the 1950s and '60s took humanities and social science classes from professors who had decidedly more liberal views and came from a far greater variety of ethnic and religious backgrounds than had their predecessors. One result was that most intellectuals and the urban neighborhoods and college towns where many lived became reliably Democratic and have remained so, although college-educated Americans, as members of the solid middle or upper class, tended to vote Republican through the remainder of the twentieth century.

Yet the fears the Cold War stirred up also forced Democrats with big political ambitions to keep proving they despised the enemy and its ideology and would back whatever policies were needed to combat them. After the debacle of Henry Wallace's 1948 campaign, anyone who could be credibly accused of being "soft on communism" had essentially no electoral future. Humphrey himself took pains to show he could be as unbending in his belligerence as any right-wing Republican. In 1954, he sponsored a nasty piece of legislation that outlawed membership in the Communist Party (though it was never enforced or tested in court). That same year, he denounced the State Department for giving away "half of Vietnam" to the Communists after Ho Chi Minh's forces defeated the French.

When liberals did advocate new domestic programs, most shelved the populist rhetoric that had animated the party's proposals for moral capitalism in the past. Prosperity that was more widely shared than ever before in U.S. history made the old talk of the rich against the poor, of monopolies against "the little man," seem both archaic and unnecessary. "We no longer struggle among ourselves for a larger share of limited abundance," President Lyndon Johnson told the throng in Cadillac Square on Labor Day in 1964. "We labor, instead, to increase the total abundance of all."[12]

That union leaders rarely took issue with such celebratory statements indicated both how far their movement had come—and how ill prepared they were to resist its decline. By the 1950s, mainstream journalists routinely mingled respect for "Big Labor" with a sense of relief that the era of militant strikes and mass organizing drives had passed. When the AFL and CIO merged in 1955, close to 35 percent of American wage earners belonged to unions, a historic high.

But a lopsided number of them worked in large factories making automobiles, televisions, airplanes, and other industrial marvels for such corporations as General Motors, Westinghouse, and Boeing—or drove trucks that delivered such products around the nation. Most unionists lived in a narrow band of states from the Northeast to the Great Lakes or those bordering the Pacific. Outside these regions, labor was vulnerable to attacks by businesses and their conservative friends in both parties, and the swelling population of Sunbelt states with "right-to-work" laws in place would only strengthen future resistance to collective bargaining. Congressional hearings in the late 1950s that exposed corruption in the Teamsters Union also damaged the image of the movement as a whole, even though most unions were honestly run. As the eminent political scientist V. O. Key wrote as early as 1953, labor might be "a numerically great force" but it lacked "proportionate durable political power as a class." The national union leaders who enjoyed the perks of big salaries and media renown did not seem to mind. "We do not seek to recast American society in any particular doctrinaire or ideological images," stated George Meany when he became the first president of the AFL-CIO. "We seek an ever rising standard of living."[13]

For Democrats, the decline of class-conscious antipathy, at least among men quoted regularly in the media, like Meany, had a serious consequence for how Americans viewed the reform initiatives they were able to enact in the 1960s. With a few exceptions—such as Medicare and the Clean Air Act—the party's key initiatives increasingly got perceived as efforts to attack historic injuries based on race instead of those faced by all working men and women. They thus had the potential to divide white and Black Democrats from one another instead of uniting them in a common assault against the corporate and financial elite. Throughout the party's long history, such class-aware rhetoric had denied or kept silent about the cruel persistence of white supremacy. But beginning in the early years of the Great Depression, it had also played a critical role in winning the White House five times in a row and dominating Congress for all but a single term.

Democrats were able to remain the majority party in postwar America as long as they could keep their broad, multiracial coalition together. More voters appreciated what "the party of government" had done for them since the 1930s than shared the Republican fear that the entitlement programs enacted by Democrats would propel

America toward socialism, as Ronald Reagan warned in 1961 about the proposal that became Medicare four years later. Yet as the demand for racial equality that aimed to redress centuries of injustice became more urgent, it also presented Democrats with a dilemma from which there was no clear way out: embrace the demands of the Black freedom movement and alienate white Southerners—and their sympathizers anywhere in the country—or hew to white supremacy and abandon the Democrats' moral claim to be the party of all the people.

## Mr. Civil Rights

The results of the 1948 election came as a relief to Democrats who assumed throughout the campaign that Truman would lose. Victory did little, however, to relax tensions among the leaders of the constituencies most critical to the party's fortunes. African American voters, their numbers swelled by wartime migrants to Northern cities, had greater influence than ever before. There had been only seventeen Black delegates at the Philadelphia convention. Yet if those Black people able to vote had cast a large number of their ballots for Henry Wallace or had stayed home, Thomas Dewey would have slipped into the White House. Still, the Democrats' leaders in Congress, most of whom were Southerners, offered them no legislative gratitude. African Americans would have to engage in disruptive talk and actions against the likes of Bull Connor if they hoped to win their constitutional rights and more.

To put his fellow Democrats—and the nation—on notice for neglecting the needs of Black people was the political calling of Adam Clayton Powell, Jr. The debonair, charismatic, light-skinned minister of what was then the largest Protestant church in America—established by his father—won a seat on the New York City Council in 1941; three years later, voters in Harlem, "the capital of Black America," swept him into Congress, unopposed. Powell was the first person of his race ever elected to that body from the Empire State. He joined the only other Black member of Congress—William Dawson, a loyal lieutenant of Chicago's Democratic machine.

In the years to come, Powell and Humphrey would represent two aspects of the racial liberalism that gradually came to define their party. As the son of a small-town druggist, the white politician from Minnesota grew up in more humble circumstances than did the son of New York's premier Black pastor. But due to racism, only Humphrey could seriously pursue a dream to become president. Still, both men sought, in different ways, to turn the Democrats' pledge on civil rights into strong, enforceable laws. By the late 1960s, both would also become emblems of the party's failure to sustain the New Deal coalition, amid internal clashes that mirrored the battles Americans were fighting over race, class, and war—including the question of whether the dominant order was worth preserving at all.

In the middle of the twentieth century, freedom activists were beginning a surge that would remake American politics and give Powell the opportunity to become the most powerful Black official in the nation. During World War II, the NAACP had boosted its membership by a stunning 1,000 percent. In Black colleges experiencing the same postwar boom as heavily white ones, students demonstrated against conditions on and off campus, defying administrators fearful of losing funding from Jim Crow legislatures. In tiny wooden churches on the edge of cotton fields as well as impressive structures like Powell's Abyssinian Baptist Church, a Gothic marvel with soaring stained-glass windows, preachers compared African Americans to the Jews liberated from Pharaoh and often urged them to engage in protests. "What can happen when you play your part?" the Harlem congressman asked in a 1953 sermon. "Moses played his part" when he beseeched God to forgive the Israelites for worshipping the golden calf. "And God relented . . . 'for thou has found grace in my sight, and I know thee by name.'"[14]

Never content to be a partisan foot soldier, Powell conducted himself as if he were speaking for *every* Black citizen inside the most august hall of power in the nation. "They were the disenfranchised, the ostracized, the exploited," he recalled about the African Americans who wrote to him from every region to share their opinions and solicit his aid. The congressman held his seat for more than a quarter century, eventually rising to the chairmanship of a key House committee. Yet Powell also earned a reputation as a party maverick by stirring up resistance to Democrats who moved too slowly, or not at all, even as he pushed to enact bills to secure freedom for his people. "Defy law of man when in conflict with law of God," he wrote in 1963, after protests against segregation rocked the streets of Birmingham, Alabama.[15]

Unfortunately, the man known as "Mr. Civil Rights" could not resist making big trouble for himself in ways that sullied his reputation. Powell carried on a series of quite public adulterous affairs, had to defend himself in court for evading taxes and allegedly libeling a Black constituent, and hired one of his wives to a well-paid job for which she did no work. Inevitably, his enemies used all of it against him. "He demanded his right as an individual," write two of his biographers, "to indulge himself the same as any other man . . . the right to be as bad as the worst white man."[16]

Yet Powell also played both the inside and outside games of politics with skill, honing a militant image while simultaneously using his status as the nation's most influential Black elected official to nudge racial progress forward. He first rose to prominence as a "race man" and a friend of the Marxist left. In 1940, Powell refused to join a committee to celebrate FDR's birthday to protest the president's frequent visits to a rehabilitation center in Georgia that refused to treat Black people. He also led a bus boycott in New York that compelled the city to hire more African American drivers. For several years in the middle of the 1940s, Powell published a lively weekly, *The People's Voice*, that competed with more established Black periodicals. His staff included a number of journalists who belonged to or were close to the Communist Party; during World War II, the paper took such a benevolent stance toward the USSR that Powell himself joked it was the "Lenox Avenue edition of *The Daily Worker*." Yet after the Cold War began, he turned against the Reds and closed the paper down.[17]

In Congress, Powell found a shrewd way to press the cause of equality as well as to boost his own renown. In 1946, he proposed the first of a sequence of "Powell amendments." Each aimed to withhold federal money from any state that practiced segregation. With the aid of lobbyists from the NAACP, he sought to attach a rider to a bill funding the school lunch program, then repeated the tactic over the next decade to restrict appropriations for military bases and schools.

Whether out of conviction or guilt, most Northern Democrats and some Republicans voted aye, while Southern Democrats predictably voted nay. The amendments sometimes passed the House but died in the Senate.

Yet their significance transcended a mere tally of wins and losses. The Powell amendments "entered the national lexicon" and proved that one lone Democrat had the will and power to compel nearly all-white Congresses to decide whether to keep dodging the moral imperative of their time. In the 1950s, as the Black freedom movement began to grow around the nation, Adam Clayton Powell, Jr., was preaching and practicing the kind of forceful strategy that would eventually make legal racism a thing of the past.[18]

## The New Deal Coalition Under Strain

For that to occur, the three constituencies that, together, had created Democratic victories during the 1930s and '40s would have to either agree about or splinter over the issue of civil rights. As the response to Humphrey's speech at the 1948 convention showed, most labor leaders and liberal activists shared a rhetorical commitment to Black freedom. But when it came to making it a priority for all Democrats, they often hedged and demurred. They were well aware that Southern Democrats, the third leg of the partisan stool, were perpetually on guard against any erosion of white rule in their region and, if possible, in the country at large.

During the 1930s, organized labor had quite effectively performed its own version of the inside-outside political dance that Powell would make his own. Striking for union recognition while electioneering for Democrats had resulted in the movement's greatest membership gains in history. In the wake of Truman's victory in 1948, leaders of both the AFL and the CIO felt confident about retaining their high density in the largest industrial corporations in the land. Collective bargaining with such giant firms as General Motors, Westinghouse, and U.S. Steel resulted in long-term contracts. Corporate profits and union wages tended to rise together as memories of sit-down strikes against "economic royalists" gave way to convictions that America had finally become an "affluent society."[19]

Inside the Democratic Party, labor's influence seemed secure as well. Few unionists thought Truman would fulfill his promise to get the Taft-Hartley Act repealed; even with his party back in control of Congress, the alliance between Republicans and Dixie Democrats was too strong to make that happen. But unions and their members were essential to the party's dominance in Northern metropolises from New York to San Francisco and along the thick industrial belt by the Great Lakes. "Truman Democrats could not win elections or control their own party without support from organized labor," observes one historian. Neither could unions "exert influence in the national state or hope to expand the welfare state except by working within and through the Democratic party."[20]

To put that influence at the service of Black freedom, however, proved a difficult task. Nearly every progressive union official supported the cause. At the 1948 convention, Andrew Biemiller, a former socialist and union organizer, played a critical role in writing the civil rights plank and urging delegates to endorse it. Walter Reuther, president of the million-strong United Auto Workers, then the nation's largest union, backed it strongly too; by a nine-to-one margin, his members pulled the lever for Truman that fall.

But the UAW chief soon learned that many of the same white unionists who preferred a Democrat in the White House chose differently when asked to support one who threatened their racial privileges at home. In the 1949 race for mayor of Detroit, thanks to precincts full of autoworkers and their families, the conservative Republican Albert Cobo defeated the liberal Democrat and former UAW activist George Edwards by a two-to-one margin. A wealthy real estate investor, Cobo claimed that his opponent's support for building public housing around the city would lead to "Negro invasions" of white neighborhoods. In response, the UAW and other CIO affiliates blanketed the city with literature in several European languages that depicted Cobo as a slumlord in cahoots with fellow Republicans from affluent suburbs. But it made no difference. White workers believed they had as valid a "right" to keep Black people from moving next door and threatening the value of their recently purchased homes as they did to receive Social Security payments and enjoy the protection of a powerful union.[21]

That kind of Northern sentiment undoubtedly helped reassure Southern Democrats after their setback at the Philadelphia convention. Although they realized they would no longer be able to dictate their racial views to the party as a whole, as long as they resisted the urge to bolt, they still had a good chance of keeping irritants like Humphrey and Powell at bay. The Democrats' recapture of Congress, after all, meant that long-serving representatives from the nearly one-party South would again chair most of the committees. "They are in a position to force the administration to go far more than half way to meet them in any compromise that is made," wrote Richard Hofstadter in 1949. "The Democratic party thus finds itself in the anomalous position of being a party of 'liberalism,' whose achievements are subject to veto by a reactionary faction."[22]

Truman and his supporters in Congress pushed for a "Fair Deal" that included bills that would have established a national health insurance plan and a commission on fair employment practices banning discrimination against job applicants because of their race. Humphrey spearheaded the civil rights push, but he could not convince his colleagues to amend the filibuster rule that effectively gave Southerners the power to stop any bill they disliked from coming to a vote. As the next presidential race drew near, he and Truman essentially gave up the fight.

Back home in Dixie, white voters helped police the boundaries. A stark example came from the Second District in rural South Carolina. In the 1948 Democratic primary, Hugo S. Sims, Jr., a highly decorated commander of paratroopers during World War II, took on John J. Riley, the incumbent congressman who often voted with the GOP. The veteran had the backing of the local CIO textile union but won the nomination with such banal slogans as "The man who gets elected will be the one who knows and is liked by the most people." Once Sims got to Congress, he supported every significant measure Truman proposed. The young pol insisted he could "work out a liberal program a Southerner can run on and get elected." But he neglected the growing hostility of his white constituents toward the Fair Deal, particularly Truman's integration of the armed forces.

"We call it the Raw Deal down here," snapped one white farmer. Riley took on Sims again in the 1950 primary; this time, he crushed his rival by twenty points.[23]

Some Southern Democrats did retain the antagonism toward big business that had animated the region's fervor for Bryan and FDR. James "Big Jim" Folsom got elected governor of Alabama in 1946 and again eight years later with frequent salvos against the "Big Mules" who reigned over industrial Birmingham. Folsom was also a passionate supporter of organized labor and the Tennessee Valley Authority, the government-run utility that brought electricity to much of the lower South. Wright Patman, a veteran congressman from northeast Texas, kept beating the anti-monopoly drum. He proposed a tax on chain stores and a measure to stop the Federal Reserve from using high interest rates to smother small businesses.

Moreover, every Southern lawmaker understood the need to improve the fortunes of his or her voters, most of whom remained among the poorest white people in the country. Pols who railed consistently against federal attempts to violate the racial "customs" of their states still fought to win defense bases for their districts, even though Jim Crow laws were difficult to enforce on such installations after Harry Truman ordered the military to desegregate. Mendel Rivers, a House member from Charleston, South Carolina, backed Strom Thurmond's "States' Rights" candidacy in 1948. But as he rose to the chairmanship of the Armed Services Committee, Rivers secured a naval base, an air force base, and several other major defense facilities for the area he represented for fifteen straight terms. A colleague once joked that if Rivers "put another thing down in his district it was going to sink."[24]

Whatever their differences, Southern politicians like Patman and Rivers agreed there was no greater danger to the unity of the party—and their status within it—than the liberal activists who had muscled the civil rights plank onto the 1948 platform. The architects of that change all belonged to Americans for Democratic Action, founded a year before the Philadelphia convention. Soon after taking his seat in the Senate, Humphrey became ADA's national chairman. The group he headed was never very large: in its first few years, it had fewer than twenty thousand members, concentrated in big cities and college towns. But it did have the guidance of a roster of liberal all-stars. On the ADA council with Humphrey sat two of the most powerful labor leaders in the country—Walter Reuther and David Dubinsky, president of the women's garment workers union and a top official of the AFL. Eleanor Roosevelt had helped found ADA, as had Reinhold Niebuhr, the country's most eminent Protestant theologian. Arthur Schlesinger, Jr., a young Harvard historian who had already won a Pulitzer Prize, wrote a 1949 book, *The Vital Center*, that was a virtual manifesto for ADA's meld of New Deal idealism and determined resistance to Soviet advances abroad.

ADA members tended to belong to a social class of college-trained professionals that was growing as the size of the traditional blue-collar workforce gradually declined. The ranks of these "amateur Democrats" were filled with attorneys and with men and women who earned a salary in journalism, advertising, or another species of "communications." Many ADAers were Jews, mostly of a secular bent; others worked on its staff. Few of the amateur activists were union members or had any affection for urban machines that owed their existence to wage-earning voters.[25]

ADA, as the successor to the groups of high-profile citizens the CIO had organized during the Second World War, worked to rally progressive officeholders and bend the ear of policy makers in the White House and elsewhere in the executive branch. Leon Keyserling, drafter of the Wagner Act, stayed close to the group while he was Truman's chairman of the Council of Economic Advisers and then joined it after leaving office.

But these professional liberals had to pick their fights with care, lest they be accused of weakening the fragile coalition that kept Democrats in power. Often, that meant downplaying support for civil rights legislation to avoid appearing, in Schlesinger's words, like "another Yankee liberal outfit." However glittering the reputations of its leading figures, neither ADA nor its sympathizers in Congress had the numbers to compete with Republicans and Southern Democrats when they united to defeat extensions of the welfare state. That alliance made it impossible to repeal Taft-Hartley or enact national health insurance, and it shrank an ambitious public housing bill into a minor item in the federal budget.[26]

The fact that Humphrey and his ideological comrades were steadfast Cold Warriors did not prevent right-wingers in both parties from painting them in one or another shade of red. One conservative newspaper in Boston lambasted ADA as "a group of left-wingers hitch-hiking along with the national administration," while a prominent minister in Nashville told his parishioners it was "about as Democratic as Stalin." Such attacks intensified in frequency and vitriol after the onset of the Korean War in 1950. Forced to defend themselves against Senator Joseph McCarthy and his ilk, liberals risked sounding more like celebrants of a mythical consensus about the virtues of postwar prosperity than dedicated agitators for labor, civil rights, and other causes that had brought them into politics in the first place.[27]

## The Fatal Charm of an Egghead Nominee

That high-minded self-image does much to explain the allure of Adlai Ewing Stevenson II. By 1952, the Princeton-educated attorney, whose grandfather of the same name had been Grover Cleveland's last vice president, had spent most of the past two decades working in ever more powerful government posts—alternating with stints at a corporate law firm in Chicago. Stevenson served as general counsel for two New Deal agencies, assisted the secretary of the navy during World War II, then worked with Eleanor Roosevelt to establish the United Nations. His elegant manner, careful preparation, and political discretion greatly impressed the former First Lady, whose influence in the party had diminished little since her husband's death. "Some people gain respect and others lose respect when you are working with them," she recalled. Stevenson was definitely one of the gainers, and he cultivated a close friendship with the woman he praised, in his diary, as "one of the few really great people I have known." Roosevelt's fellow liberals in ADA and elsewhere took notice.[28]

In 1948, Stevenson's great friend implored him to run for governor of Illinois, and after securing the support of Jake Arvey's Chicago machine, he agreed. Stevenson delivered a series of finely crafted, idealistic campaign speeches and benefited from scandals swirling around the GOP incumbent. On Election Day, he surprised all the pundits by soaring to victory; his margin, in excess of half a million votes, was more than ten times larger than Truman's narrow one in that traditionally Republican state. In office, the neophyte politician built a reputation as a crusading liberal. Faced with a legislature controlled by the opposition party, Stevenson fought to establish a state fair-employment practices commission. Though that effort failed, he did convince lawmakers to double the budget for education and welfare and vetoed a loyalty oath—during the heyday of the Red Scare. "We must not burn down the house to kill the rats," he quipped; the remark deftly stated his repugnance for communism while also endearing him to civil libertarians. At the beginning of 1952, Stevenson seemed to harbor no higher political ambition than to get reelected, a wish the majority of Illinois voters would almost certainly have granted.[29]

Then, rather suddenly, the biggest job in the country opened up. In March, Harry Truman announced he would not be running for reelection. The war in Korea the president could neither win nor end and a mounting array of corruption scandals in his administration had driven down his poll numbers and sapped his desire to mount what would surely be another uphill campaign. Stevenson's tenure as governor had won him both the admiration of liberals and the respect of those urban bosses, like Chicago's Arvey and Pittsburgh's David Lawrence, who could still bend big state delegations to their will. Even though the governor refused to mount a presidential campaign for himself, he did hint he was open to a draft.

Stevenson had the good fortune to be the only candidate none of the party's major factions abhorred. At the national convention in Chicago that summer, all but the small Black contingent agreed to support a platform that endorsed the goal of civil rights but declined to call on Congress to do anything to further it. In protest, Congressman Powell led a walkout by sixty African American delegates. This time, for the sake of party unity, neither Humphrey nor ADA forced the issue. As governor of the host state, Stevenson opened the proceedings with an eloquent welcoming address and won the nomination on the third ballot. It was the last time the Democrats' choice would be undecided when their convention began.

Stevenson went on to run perhaps the oddest presidential campaign in the modern era—and certainly one of the most self-defeating ones. The nominee viewed his reluctance to support key demands of his party's largest constituencies as a matter of principle. Focused on "telling the truth to the American people," he resisted, on the basis of states' rights, to back a federal fair employment commission. Then he changed his mind and reluctantly endorsed one but seldom mentioned the issue on the campaign trail. On Labor Day in Detroit, Stevenson told the crowd of workers, a smaller one than had greeted Truman four years earlier, that he approved of some provisions in the Taft-Hartley Act; he then scolded them for not being more active in their unions. The nominee also skipped the annual Al Smith dinner in New York City, sponsored by the local archdiocese, which had become a signal event to reach Catholic voters.

The Democrat's speeches, most drafted by a group of young male intellectuals headed by Arthur Schlesinger, Jr., and the economist John Kenneth Galbraith, were festooned with clever and sometimes moving lines. To a graduating class of marines (which included his own son), Stevenson reflected, "The course of human history is a record, in tragic part, of things done which should not have been done, things not done which should have been done." But most of his speeches dwelled on foreign policy and hedged on key domestic issues that, despite the ongoing conflict in Korea, concerned more Americans than the Cold War did.[30]

On the trail, Stevenson came across more like a detached professor than as a politician eager to win over the crowd. His distaste for mingling with ordinary voters so exasperated Eleanor Roosevelt that she publicly chastised him in her newspaper column: "He must find out how to have the people feel that he is talking to them individually and that they must listen or they will miss something that really affects their daily lives." When informed that Eisenhower's campaign was running television ads—something no candidate had done before—Stevenson disdained the whole idea of promoting himself on what was quickly becoming Americans' favorite mass medium. "What do the Republicans think the White House is, a box of cornflakes?" he scoffed. That fall, the journalist brothers Joseph and Stewart Alsop employed the word "egghead" to describe both Stevenson's bald pate and the intellectual self-regard of the candidate and his speechwriters. The term quickly caught on; no one ever mistook it for praise.[31]

Even with a less aloof nominee, the race against Eisenhower would have been difficult to win. The erstwhile commander of the allied forces who invaded France on D-Day was a hero of the most popular war in American history. The Republican also spurned conservatives in his own party who yearned to repeal most New Deal and Fair Deal programs. That Eisenhower could run on the simple, apolitical slogan "I Like Ike" also minimized the fact that, by about 7 percent, more Americans identified with Stevenson's party than his.[32]

For their part, Democrats refrained from voicing the kinds of arguments for moral capitalism that had done so much to lift FDR and Truman to victory. Their 1952 platform, written days before the party chose its nominee, included just one brief, mild criticism of corporate power while trumpeting the news that the long struggle for economic equity had apparently reached a happy end: "The United States is today a land of boundless opportunity. Never before has it offered such a large measure of prosperity, security and hope for all its people." In sync with this rosy judgment, Stevenson muted the platform's pledge to repeal Taft-Hartley and told the press that big business no longer had any reason to be hostile to his party.[33]

Taking credit for a healthy economy, while a natural message for an incumbent party, evaded the fact that the Democrats remained as dependent on the movement of wage earners as they had been during the FDR years. The percentage of workers who belonged to unions reached its historic zenith in the early to mid-1950s, and most of their leaders still strongly favored Democrats over their opponents.

But crowing about the nation's bounty did not speak to the lingering insecurities of wage earners, just over a decade after the end of the Great Depression. According to polls, most voters did not agree that class divisions no longer mattered in politics. That summer, Gallup reported that majorities believed the Democrats were "run by the labor leaders of the country," while the GOP was "run by a few big business men." Stevenson's resistance to saying anything that might have helped him turn this perception to his advantage was one reason he managed to win just 56 percent of the votes from union households in 1952, compared with the 80 percent Truman had received in his upset triumph. Many workers clearly liked Ike as much as their bosses did. But the Democrat's deliberate coolness toward labor and its causes did not help.[34]

If Eisenhower's victory was predictable, its sweeping nature came as something of a surprise. The Republican who had never run for office before gained 55 percent of the popular vote and carried every state outside the South, save a couple of border states where the Mine Workers union was strong. But Eisenhower also won Tennessee, Virginia, and Florida—a signal that many white Southerners had not forgiven their traditional party for taking a bold stand for civil rights. Meanwhile, Stevenson's ineffectual campaign dispirited the urban voters whose big turn to the Democrats had thrust the party into the majority under FDR. He even failed to win Cook County, home to the Chicago machine, and lost his own state by ten points. Ike's electoral landslide generated narrow majorities for the GOP in Congress as well.

With their party having lost the White House, quite decisively, for the first time in two decades, prominent Democrats debated how to stage a comeback. Powell and his fellow Black activists urged a renewed assault on Jim Crow. They argued that African American voters, who stuck with Stevenson, could shift back toward the GOP if the party repeated the timid stand in its platform and the speeches by its nominee. That would make it all but impossible for Democrats to win back the industrial North. But fear that the solidity of the South was cracking mattered more to the top two Democratic leaders in Congress, both of whom were Texans—Sam Rayburn in the House and his protégé Lyndon Johnson in the Senate.

In May 1954, the Supreme Court's unanimous decision in *Brown v. Board of Education* compelled every Democrat who had any hope of leading the party or becoming president to make a choice. If Chief Justice Earl Warren and his colleagues were justified in ruling that segregated schools were "inherently unequal," then one should start enforcing desegregation and, perhaps, follow the same logic to renew attempts to enact a sweeping law guaranteeing the integration of every public institution in America. Hubert Humphrey praised the court for taking "another step in the forward march of democracy." But he failed to persuade Lyndon Johnson to challenge the resistance of his Southern brethren, skillfully led by Georgia's Richard Russell, who nurtured unrealistic White House ambitions of his own.[35]

After offering no comment for ten days following the decision, Stevenson demonstrated once again his talent for putting elegant prose at the service of a political error—and, in this case, a moral wrong. The South "has been invited" by the court "to share the burden of blueprinting the mechanics for solving the new school problems of non-segregation," he wrote. Appreciating that region's "great complexities in race relations," Stevenson urged the "rest of the country" to "extend the hand of fellowship, of patience, understanding, and assistance to the South in sharing that burden." It was the kind of empathetic plea a president might have issued after a major hurricane. Stevenson's biographer calls it "a curious statement from a man widely considered a liberal."[36]

But even white liberals like Humphrey who cheered the *Brown* decision could imagine no path back to victory that did not include keeping Southern whites in the fold. So most avoided denouncing the Declaration of Constitutional Principles—drafted by Russell and signed by nearly every Southern member of Congress in March 1956—which attacked the members of the high court for "a clear abuse of judicial power" that "substituted their personal political and social ideas for the established law of the land."

Cautious as he was on matters of race and labor, Stevenson won strong admirers for his refusal to adhere to partisan dogma. He inspired well-educated white activists in New York, Chicago, and other big cities to challenge the sway of local machines over appointments and patronage. These "amateur Democrats" also cheered when their hero proposed negotiating with the USSR to cease the testing of nuclear weapons in the atmosphere. They certainly favored civil rights, but the Black freedom movement had not yet grown large or potent enough to force that issue into the heart of national politics.

In 1956, the odd alliance of liberal idealists and wily Southern pols lifted Stevenson to a string of primary wins and then to a first-ballot victory at the convention, held once again on his home turf in Chicago. That uneasy partnership ensured that, at the start of what everyone knew would be a difficult campaign against a popular incumbent, the grievances of Black people would be largely dismissed or neglected. On opening night, Senator John F. Kennedy of Massachusetts, a top contender for the vice-presidential nomination, narrated a film about the party's history that was silent about its past racism while praising President Andrew Johnson during Reconstruction for battling the Republican "hot-heads and fanatics" who sought only "vengeance against the South." A short, abstract section on civil rights appeared at the very end of the party's very long platform. It said nothing about what specific "efforts to eradicate discrimination based on race, religion, or national origin" Democrats might enact if they won the presidency. Fearful of losing Southern votes, Hubert Humphrey refused to join Reuther and other ADA stalwarts who mounted a failed attempt to place in the platform a vow to enforce the *Brown* decision.[37]

For the congressman from Harlem, the time had come to mount a protest his party could not ignore. Stevenson opposed the Powell amendments, thought using troops to enforce the *Brown* decision would be an abuse of federal power, and delayed meeting with the Black lawmaker before spurning him altogether. Powell had routinely attacked Eisenhower, accusing him at one point of wanting to bring back the "good old days of segregation" in the military and other parts of the government. But with a month to go in the campaign, the incumbent enjoyed a massive lead in the polls. So, on October 11, Powell spoke for half an hour with the president at the White House and emerged to tell the press he was endorsing him for a second term. The Black lawmaker soon organized Independent Democrats for Eisenhower in order to rally "disillusioned" liberals to the cause. The group was stillborn, but Powell did give GOP-funded speeches to huge audiences in six cities across the North and Far West. Back in New York, his fellow Black officeholders denounced his decision; some predicted it would end his career. But Powell won a seventh term with ease, taking almost 70 percent of the vote.[38]

Stevenson suffered another crushing, if expected, defeat. This time, he carried just seven states, all in the Deep South except for

Missouri, and 42 percent of the popular tally. The avid support of amateur Democrats gained him votes in the Pacific Coast states, and canvassers for the United Auto Workers kept him competitive in Michigan—where he managed to avoid alienating the Labor Day crowd in Cadillac Square. This time, he told union members that too many Americans remained poor "in this richest, most fortunate country in the world." But, nationwide, the Democrat again won just over half the votes of union households. Powell's desertion helped whittle the African American vote for Stevenson down to 61 percent, the smallest margin since Black people had deserted the party of Lincoln to reelect FDR. Every Democratic nominee has bettered it since then.[39]

Remarkably, Eisenhower's landslide did not boost the GOP's strength in Congress at all. Democrats held on to their slim margin of two seats in the Senate and picked up another two in the House. One explanation for this unusual case of split-ticket voting is that the president declined to campaign for his fellow Republicans. Eisenhower feared that, if his party regained control of Congress, the GOP would roll back New Deal programs like Social Security and the Wagner Act that most Americans favored.[40]

Yet a truly competitive presidential race would probably have resulted in a solidly Democratic Congress, one that might even have defied its Southern contingent to enact a strong civil rights bill. The party recently led by men who relished political combat and were very good at it—FDR, Truman, and such aides as James Farley and Clark Clifford—had twice nominated a man about whom his own chief speechwriter, Arthur Schlesinger, Jr., reflected, "The thought of power induces in Stevenson doubt, reluctance, even guilt." Campaigning first as a war hero and then as an incumbent during an era of prosperity, Eisenhower probably would have defeated any Democrat who ran against him. But the infatuation of middle-class white liberals with a politician who did so little to appeal to labor or Black voters exposed a weakness in their understanding of the electorate that, if uncorrected, would be fatal to the party's chances of regaining the White House and building a larger, more racially egalitarian welfare state. One egghead nominee was too many.[41]

## The New Liberal Hour

As a secular Jew growing up in an ardently liberal family, I never doubted which party I should favor. My parents and all their friends had adored FDR; even if someone they knew cast a vote for Henry Wallace or even Eisenhower, that renegade quickly returned to what was deemed the only fitting political home for decent, intelligent people. In 1960, on the cusp of my teenage years, I happily did my part. That fall, after hearing John F. Kennedy speak at a rally near my home in northern New Jersey, I bought a campaign button the size of a pot pie that I wore until Election Day. It felt cool to cheer for JFK at the drafty Teaneck Armory and exciting to argue his case at my all-male, all-white private school, where most students supported Richard Nixon because their parents did. Neither I nor anyone I knew had given much thought to backing Hubert Humphrey, who also sought the Democratic nomination that year. Humphrey's liberal bona fides were actually stronger than those of Kennedy—who was the only Senate Democrat not to vote to censure Joe McCarthy in 1954 after the bully of the Red Scare made the mistake of accusing the U.S. Army of harboring Communists. But the diligent Minnesotan's race in 1960 against the Massachusetts charmer was akin to a sturdy plow horse straining to defeat a prize Thoroughbred in the Kentucky Derby.

Thrilled by JFK's election, I paid little attention to how close he had come to losing. The shift of a mere 4,500 votes in Illinois and 23,000 in Texas, where allegations of fraud abounded, would have landed the incumbent vice president in the White House. State by state, Kennedy's win seemed to depend on traditional partisan allegiances. He won by a larger margin in Georgia than in his home state of Massachusetts. But the demographic coalition that delivered Kennedy's narrow win was a portent of the party's future. For only the second time in history, a Democrat won the White House while losing the votes of most white people—the majority of whom were Protestant. Truman in 1948 was the first. But Kennedy's coalition was uniquely diverse: only by running up margins of 70 percent among African Americans as well as 82 percent among Jews and nearly 80 percent among his fellow Catholics did JFK edge out Richard Nixon in such swing states as New Jersey, Michigan, and Missouri—as well as Illinois.

The young president could thus have claimed to be the candidate of a new majority spawned by the great twentieth-century migrations to urban America from Europe, Mexico, and the rural South. JFK was not just the first president born in that century but also the first one who owed his victory to a congeries of religious, racial, and ethnic minorities. The struggle to win equal rights for African Americans, the most oppressed of those groups, would consume much of the attention he gave to domestic affairs as well as that of his successor, Lyndon Johnson, and become critical to the party's fortunes thereafter.

But the liberal Democrats who came to power with JFK and vaulted into a commanding position with LBJ governed from a brittle foundation. While more adept than Stevenson at rallying the party's base, they still lacked a message of economic reform that could appeal across racial lines to a working-class majority. The men closest to Kennedy, drawn from a group educated in the best universities, often seemed averse to doing so. As members of a burgeoning meritocracy, they believed, one wrote later, that they belonged to a "democratic nobility" that would cut through sclerotic, boring bureaucracies and tangled interest groups to improve the quality of Americans' lives, rather than merely enabling them to purchase a bigger house stuffed with more commodities.[42]

In the midterm election of 1958, a sharp recession had helped the Democrats gain forty-nine seats in the House and a remarkable fifteen in the Senate. Many of these gains were due to labor voters who turned out to defeat a slew of anti-union, right-to-work laws in six states from Ohio to California. After the election, Walter Reuther gleefully told his fellow UAW officials, "The people chose to identify themselves with the forces of Labor" in "the most significant . . . election in terms of the basic loyalties that has taken place . . . in many, many years."[43]

Yet the Democratic leaders who vowed to blaze what Kennedy called the New Frontier and then launch what Johnson called the Great Society relied on the clout of union leaders to pass laws that did little to boost their movement or the well-being of wage earners overall. The AFL-CIO and such large, liberal unions as Reuther's UAW lobbied hard and skillfully to enact the Civil Rights and Voting

Rights Acts, the anti-poverty program, aid to education, and the bill that created Medicare and Medicaid. Only the last of these directly benefited the mass of white working-class Americans, at least at the time. Democratic vows to repeal Taft-Hartley had become mere rituals for candidates addressing union audiences, and the idea of a universal job guarantee fell into disuse as soon as the unemployment numbers returned to the healthy levels of the mid-1950s.[44]

Spearheading the offensives of the New Frontier and the Great Society were the kinds of middle-class activists, intellectuals, and politicians from the urban and suburban North who had been demanding meaningful action on civil rights since the party's 1948 convention. In the wake of Stevenson's second defeat, DNC chairman Paul Butler (who hailed from Indiana), the leaders of ADA, and such liberals in Congress as Eugene McCarthy of Minnesota had been demanding that Democrats turn their backs on what Butler scorned as "accommodation or attainability or compromise." They must become, once again, he vowed, "a party of principle." The election of so many like-minded candidates in 1958 emboldened Butler and his ilk to condemn the Southerners in their own party who stood in the way. Now, with a handsome, eloquent liberal in the White House, they hoped the time for redeeming the nation's and their party's founding sin had arrived.[45]

The abolition of legal racism during the next four years was indeed a great, if long overdue, accomplishment. But it did not come quickly or easily. The cause to which liberal idealists outside the administration had given their hearts and minds was one Kennedy himself largely sought to avoid or finesse. Until the last six months of his life, JFK was largely a bystander in the bourgeoning struggle against Jim Crow. He made sure, writes one historian, not "to put civil rights anywhere near the top of his legislative agenda for 1961 and 1962" and was content to make slow, quiet progress through executive actions and federal judges appointed both by Democrats and Dwight Eisenhower. Dixiecrats still had the power to stop legislation from reaching the floor of Congress, and the president was too preoccupied with the Cold War to expend political capital on so explosive a domestic matter—one that could jeopardize his chances of reelection.[46]

Kennedy finally took action when the clash between Black insurgents and their sworn enemies made it impossible for him to turn away. In the spring of 1963, Americans saw on television Bull Connor's all-white police force assaulting young Black demonstrators, led by Martin Luther King, Jr., on the streets of Birmingham, Alabama. Two months later, George C. Wallace, the state's governor, disobeyed a court order to desegregate the state university. On June 11, Kennedy gave a nationally televised address in which he posed some urgent rhetorical questions: "Are we to say to the world—and much more importantly, to each other—that this is the land of the free except for the Negroes, that we have no second-class citizens, except Negroes, that we have no class or caste system, no ghettos, no master race, except with respect to Negroes?" Then he outlined what became the most far-reaching civil rights law in the nation's history. Enacted a year later, after JFK's assassination, it outlawed segregation in all public facilities and forbade racial and gender discrimination in employment and education. Later that summer, after the August 28 March on Washington for Jobs and Freedom had drawn a quarter million people of all races to the Mall, the president welcomed King and other movement leaders to the White House.[47]

This reversal of the Democrats' benighted heritage had been gathering steam, gradually, since the rise of the CIO and of Black support for FDR in the 1930s. As with the Wagner Act, it took an alliance between a burgeoning social movement and a liberal administration to make legislative victory possible. Still, only a slight majority of Americans surveyed in 1963—before Kennedy was murdered that November and Lyndon Johnson succeeded him—favored a strong civil rights law, and most whites consistently disapproved of protests against racism even after passage of the legislation the following summer.[48]

For Hubert Humphrey, a chance to shine in the media spotlight as a vanguard of racial liberalism had come again. Johnson, knowing his connections to civil rights activists remained strong and that his Senate colleagues respected him highly, asked Humphrey to manage the bill in the upper chamber, where its fate would be decided. The president knew he would secure a majority in the House, where party leaders could set a time limit on debate. But he feared that Russell and his bloc of diehard Senate Dixiecrats might be able to stall the bill long enough to water down or kill it. That had been the fate of every other serious proposal for racial justice Congress had debated since the end of Reconstruction. Humphrey reveled in the opportunity to succeed at a task he knew might persuade Johnson to offer him the nomination for vice president later that summer.

Both ambitions were fulfilled. Senate debate began in late March and didn't end until mid-June, when lawmakers finally overcame a filibuster and passed the Civil Rights Act by a vote of 73 to 27. The congressman from Harlem celebrated the fact that Title Six of the act enshrined the principle of the Powell amendments into law. All but one Democrat who represented a state that had been part of the Confederacy voted nay, so Humphrey had to partner with GOP leader Everett Dirksen from Illinois to piece together a bipartisan coalition. Some members of the "party of Lincoln" voted for the bill out of principle; others decided that any hope for future victories in Northern urban states depended on winning votes from African Americans and sympathetic white moderates. The division among Republicans on this critical issue helped bring on the drubbing that Barry Goldwater, the GOP's presidential nominee, suffered that November. The conservative senator from Arizona had voted against the bill.[49]

Humphrey's masterful effort earned him praise from rank-and-file Democrats, but then LBJ gave him another difficult assignment to prove his loyalty and political dexterity. At the party's convention in Atlantic City, the senator was charged with squelching a demand by the biracial Mississippi Freedom Democratic Party, the creation of that state's civil rights movement. MFDP activists had taken the long bus ride up north in hopes of unseating their state's official delegates, all of whom were vehement racists who had opposed the Civil Rights Act. Johnson feared that granting their demand would trigger a Dixiecrat walkout that could end up shifting the entire South into Goldwater's column. MFDP spokeswoman Fannie Lou Hamer, whose courageous work for the movement had gotten her fired from her job on a cotton plantation and beaten up in jail, scolded Humphrey for worrying about his own future instead of the justice she and her comrades so clearly deserved. "I'm going to pray to Jesus for you," she told him. Humphrey abruptly broke off the conversation. Later, at a meeting with Martin Luther King, Jr., and movement strategist Bayard Rustin, he pleaded, "The President will not allow that illiterate woman to speak from the floor of the convention."[50]

Privately, Johnson let it be known that any man he picked for vice president would have to abandon any shred of independence. As he was fond of saying, "I want his pecker to be in my pocket." By the time Humphrey took the oath of office the following January, he had performed that metaphorical excision. But opposing and belittling the demands of a rising grassroots movement whose goals he had long championed enveloped him in a thick cloud of suspicion he would never dispel.[51]

The Democrats' recapture of both elected branches of the federal government in 1960 had given Adam Clayton Powell, Jr., an excellent opportunity to demonstrate how he could help advance the goals of both his party and himself. When Congress opened the following year, his Democratic colleagues elected him to chair the powerful Committee on Education and Labor. No Black politician had run a major committee before. In that post, Powell proved himself adept at advancing essential liberal policies—a higher minimum wage, speedier desegregation of public schools, and the controversial new anti-poverty program. He basked in praise from LBJ and Eleanor Roosevelt. House Speaker John McCormack told him in 1964 that he was "always happy" when a bill came out of Powell's committee because "its chances of passage are excellent, even when it receives the 'blind opposition' of the opposite Party."[52]

Away from Washington, Harlem's representative kept using his fame to pressure white authorities who balked at satisfying the demands of an increasingly aggressive freedom movement. In the spring of 1963, Powell traveled to my hometown of Englewood, New Jersey—just eight miles west of Harlem—to endorse a boycott Black parents had organized to force the elementary schools to integrate across strictly monochrome neighborhood lines. "The white man is afraid," he told delighted protesters. Weeks before, Powell had appeared at a rally in his own district with Malcolm X and referred to the militant minister from the anti-white Nation of Islam as his friend. He "had it in his grasp to be a national figure who happened

to be a Negro and a Negro race leader who happened to be a powerful legislator," two journalists wrote about Powell in 1965. It was
an impressive balancing act, one no Black Democrat had attempted
before. Party leaders tolerated his stance, while worrying about if and
when he might denounce them again.[53]

The results of the 1964 election seemed to prove that Americans
had embraced the liberal agenda Kennedy had initiated and Johnson
inherited as what he called "a martyr's cause." LBJ cruised to victory
with 61 percent of the popular vote, a margin that exceeded FDR's
landslide in 1936. Across the North and West, the Texan carried
middle-class suburbs and rural counties that had voted for no other
Democrat in the twentieth century. He won over 80 percent of voters
in union households, 90 percent of Jews, and 94 percent of African
Americans.

Johnson looked forward to working with a new Congress whose
liberal majorities should enable him to enact just about any bill they
desired. A second New Deal whose far-reaching reforms would be
both popular and effective seemed within reach. The richest nation
in the world might even abolish poverty! Of course, Democratic leaders were not happy that Goldwater's opposition to the civil rights
bill had won him five states in Dixie where Jim Crow laws and the
threat of violence prevented most Black people from voting. But even
if LBJ's fear that the historic act "delivered the South to the Republican Party for your lifetime and mine" came true, the rest of America
was surely moving in the opposite direction. "Mississippi, find yourself another country to be part of," sang Phil Ochs, an entertainer on
the emerging New Left.[54]

## Pulling Apart

Just a year after the Democrats routed their GOP opponents, the coalition that had delivered that victory—and had made the New Deal
order possible—began to unravel. Prominent liberals and young
radicals who flocked to Ochs's concerts blasted Johnson's decision
to send thousands of ground troops to save a corrupt client state in
Vietnam, while most union leaders strongly supported the latest fight

against communism. Democratic mayors accused the anti-poverty program of "fostering class struggle" by creating new federal agencies that challenged how they ruled their cities. In Los Angeles and Newark, thousands of poor African Americans rebelled against brutal police actions in particular and the lack of economic progress in general by looting and burning their own communities.

Although a plurality of white Americans backed the Voting Rights Act, passed in the summer of 1965, they had never thought kindly about the Black movement itself, which they associated with breaking the law, however peacefully. Once African American protest became linked with ghetto riots and angry demands for "Black Power," most whites quickly lost patience for taking additional steps to improve what pollsters demurely called "race relations." Encouraged by conservatives in both parties, they also turned against the anti-poverty program, signed into law in 1964. Although the misery among whites in Appalachia had spurred JFK to propose the idea and LBJ to get it enacted, a large part of its funding went to new "community action agencies" in urban neighborhoods that were mostly Black. With a belief in self-reliance as old as the republic, conservatives in both parties accused Johnson and other progressive Democrats of straining to help people who refused to help themselves. "I Fight Poverty, I Work" bumper stickers showed up on expensive sedans and pickup trucks alike.

In crafting the War on Poverty, Lyndon Johnson had forgotten a primary lesson of the New Deal, the genesis of his own political career. Under FDR, Democrats had enacted measures that established Social Security, the Works Progress Administration, and a federal minimum wage, all of which they could credibly claim served the needs of the great majority. But the best-publicized measures LBJ signed, with the exception of Medicare and aid to education, got viewed as benefits to poor and mostly non-white Americans—and the president and his aides argued that the better-off majority should back them more out of sympathy than solidarity. It was a sincere appeal to the better angels of the nation, but it was not effective politics.

The growing white backlash turned many voters against liberals of both races who insisted that enacting good laws was only the first step toward achieving an egalitarian society. Not until the late spring of 1966 did Johnson's approval rating dip below 50 percent. But that fall, Republicans picked up nearly fifty seats in the House and elected new governors in eight states—including California, where a former actor making his first bid for office campaigned for "law and order" and trumpeted his opposition to open housing. Ronald Reagan unseated the two-time incumbent Pat Brown by a million votes. The results of the 1966 election suggested to every politician in America that the liberal surge might be spent.[55]

Over the next two years, each of the Democrats' key constituencies snarled its discontent, with increasing vehemence, toward one or more of the others. That both the right and left wings of the party turned sharply against the Johnson administration provoked an internal crisis as great as Democrats had endured since their years in the wilderness during the 1920s.

The most predictable rift was between conservative Southern whites and liberals at the helm of the national party. Even veteran Dixiecrats in Congress like Richard Russell who, despite their defeat on civil rights, had stuck with the party in 1964 quickly lost faith that Johnson could defeat the Communist enemy in Vietnam; they also did what they could to scale back his Great Society programs, which they attacked as spendthrift boondoggles that did little to benefit white voters. Down South, stalwart foes of integration were getting elected, as Democrats, to several governorships, while others, like Strom Thurmond, were bolting permanently to the GOP.

In 1964, Governor George Wallace of Alabama had run against LBJ in a handful of primaries. The thousands of votes he drew from blue-collar workers and small farmers in Wisconsin and Indiana showed the power of the backlash, then still in an embryonic stage. As the president's popularity kept falling, Wallace decided to challenge him again. In 1968, he vowed to be the scourge of "genteel" politicians and "pseudo-intellectual" bureaucrats who let the cities burn and couldn't stop the Viet Cong from killing American soldiers. With tough populist rhetoric, the former boxer and truck driver echoed the racial resentments and defended the values of those he praised as God-fearing, patriotic white working people in every region of the country.[56]

Wallace and his followers despised the growing number of liberals who spoke out against the war in Indochina and were spawning a movement to dump Johnson from the next presidential ticket. But the rebellions in both the right and left wings of the party made Democratic leaders look flailing and defensive, undermining their image as experienced politicians who understood what voters wanted.

For the kind of "amateur" Democrats who had flocked first to Stevenson and then to JFK, the escalating war in Vietnam posed an issue whose moral resonance came to equal that of vanquishing racism itself. It destroyed the Cold War consensus that had united Democrats across regional and ideological lines since the years when Harry Truman governed in the White House while Joseph Stalin ruled from the Kremlin. Activists prone to sympathizing with every David against every Goliath increasingly viewed the enemy not as a Soviet or Chinese proxy in the Cold War but as a nation of peasants whom the mightiest military in world history was assaulting with genocidal intent. In April 1967, Martin Luther King, Jr., lent his moral authority by joining the anti-war movement with the crusade for Black freedom. In the pulpit beneath the soaring Gothic tower at Manhattan's Riverside Church, the winner of the Nobel Peace Prize denounced the conflict in Vietnam "as an enemy of the poor" and condemned the U.S. government as "the greatest purveyor of violence in the world."[57]

Liberals who had recently been among the administration's most vigorous champions increasingly echoed King's view, in substance if not tone. Vice President Humphrey tried hard to win the backing of Americans for Democratic Action, the organization he had once led, for the conflict he promised would eventually create "a great society in the great arena of Asia." But by the spring of 1967, ADA's younger members had turned sharply against the war, and such veteran members as Arthur Schlesinger, Jr., and John Kenneth Galbraith were losing patience with their erstwhile compatriot's attempt to sell a noxious policy with sanguine lies. That fall, Allard Lowenstein, a young lawyer who had once worked in Humphrey's Senate office, launched a movement of Democratic activists to dump Johnson from the party's ticket. They convinced Eugene McCarthy, a reliably liberal if rather diffident senator from Minnesota who liked to write poetry, to be their standard-bearer. In speeches, McCarthy described his principled stand against the war as similar to Humphrey's crusade for a civil rights plank twenty years earlier. Before the first primaries in 1968, ADA endorsed him.[58]

McCarthy's chance to wrest the nomination from the embattled incumbent depended on persuading Americans who hated the war to turn their energies away from demonstrating to courting primary voters and local party officials. With young canvassers from a host of New England colleges and ample funds supplied by rich donors, he almost won the New Hampshire primary on March 12. He appeared likely to take the Wisconsin primary in early April as well. Before that could happen, McCarthy's startling rise had produced two stunning decisions: Robert Kennedy, charismatic brother of the slain JFK and a senator from New York, entered the race, and Lyndon Johnson announced he was leaving it. With help from the United Farm Workers, an insurgent union led by Mexican Americans, Kennedy won the California primary but was assassinated minutes after declaring victory.

One group of passionate idealists, however, had already given up hope that the Democrats would either pull out of Vietnam or advance the dream of a truly just society at home. Many of the young people in the latter half of the 1960s who joined or identified with the Black Panther Party, Students for a Democratic Society (SDS), or other radical groups had once admired John Kennedy and cheered the aims of the Great Society. In its 1962 manifesto, the Port Huron Statement, SDS had called for the Democrats to become a resolutely liberal party by expelling their Southern wing. The young insurgents also maintained that a "revitalized labor movement" was essential to moving both the party and the country leftward. The statement itself was drafted at a summer camp named after FDR and owned by the Michigan AFL-CIO. During the 1964 presidential campaign, SDS distributed buttons that signaled its ambivalence toward the Democrats. They read, "Part of the Way with LBJ."[59]

But a liberal administration that was fighting what radicals considered a brutal, unjust war made its sympathy for the plight of Black people seem hollow at best. After Johnson won his landslide in 1964, white radicals began to articulate a critique of "corporate liberalism"— a system that did the bidding of business while mouthing empty rhetoric about justice for the poor. At the end of November 1965, I traveled down to an anti-war march in Washington, D.C., where the SDS president, Carl Oglesby, told the crowd:

> We are dealing now with a colossus that does not want to be changed. It will not change itself. It will not cooperate with those who want to change it. Those allies of ours in the Government—are they really our allies? If they are, then they don't need advice, they need constituencies; they don't need study groups, they need a movement. And if they are not, then all the more reason for building that movement with the most relentless conviction.[60]

Thrilling though such words were to a teenage protester, I was still reluctant to abandon the party that seemed on the virtuous side of every domestic issue (besides being a family tradition). The previous summer, I had interned in the Washington office of ADA and watched happily from the House gallery as one Great Society program after another passed by overwhelming margins. When I entered college in the fall of 1966, I immediately signed up with the campus chapter of the Young Democrats and was soon helping run it.

But the assault on Vietnam broke my liberal heart. The following spring, in a fury about the war, I quit the party of LBJ and joined SDS. By 1968, like most New Leftists, I was ready, even eager, to see the Democrats lose power as a fitting punishment for their sins.

No labor officials shared that view. Since its formation in 1955, the AFL-CIO, led by the dedicated Cold Warrior George Meany, had been actively working to undermine Communist influence in unions around the world. According to Meany and most other powerful union leaders, opponents of the war in Vietnam were simply "a threat to America" and perhaps even agents of "Moscow and Peking." Walter Reuther, who had taken the United Auto Workers out of the federation early in 1967 to protest its failure to finance new organizing drives, did think the war was a terrible mistake. But he would say nothing to rile Lyndon Johnson, whose aid he needed in negotiations with the Big Three auto firms. While some local offi-

cials and rank-and-filers around the nation voiced their disgust at
the war, the only national labor bodies that did so were three small
unions that had been expelled from the CIO twenty years earlier for
their sympathies with the Soviet Union and their closeness to the
American Communist Party.[61]

With such scant backing from organized workers, the peace
movement could be portrayed by the media as the exclusive domain
of middle-class dissenters, well-educated and mostly white. Since it
was relatively easy for young men from such backgrounds to get draft
deferments, that image bred extensive animosity toward the protesters, even among working-class people who were turning against a
war that had a murky rationale and seemed increasingly unwinnable.
Longtime labor members of ADA like Gus Tyler, assistant president
of the International Ladies' Garment Workers Union, blamed trou-
blesome "new people" for the group's contentious endorsement of
Eugene McCarthy. After losing most of its union backers, the once
formidable liberal vanguard never wielded much influence in national politics again.[62]

For Democratic politicians who were Black, Vietnam posed a
dilemma more acute than that faced by white unionists or peace
marchers. They knew most of their people agreed with King's harsh
critique of the conflict; prominent radicals like H. Rap Brown from
the Student Nonviolent Coordinating Committee and Huey Newton
from the Black Panthers went even further, declaring war on an "imperialist" system directed by LBJ and his henchmen.

At the same time, African American Democrats also knew that
bitter divisions on the broad left were a boon to the electoral prospects of right-wingers in both parties who aimed to stop or turn
back the recent victories for legal equality that had barely begun to
improve the lives of most Black people. If the liberal alliance that
had stood behind LBJ fell apart, how would they defend themselves
against their true enemies? Days after King's assassination in April
1968, his former aide Bayard Rustin pleaded with the "Negro-labor-
liberal coalition, whatever differences now exist within and among
its constituent forces," to "unite . . . in order to defeat racism and
reaction at the polls." Otherwise, wrote the onetime pacifist who had
become a critic of the peace movement, "we may find ourselves in

a decade of mean and vindictive conservative domination."[63] But a "Freedom Budget" Rustin drew up in the fall of 1966 that aimed to provide every American adult with a job, health insurance, and other items that appeared on FDR's Economic Bill of Rights made no headway against the gales of Black power and a horrible war.

The most renowned Black Democrat was no longer in a position where he could either advance or heal the turmoil besetting his party. As the debate about Vietnam heated up, Adam Clayton Powell, Jr., was losing personal battles, in and out of court, that had come to define him as much as his reputation as an eloquent fighter for his race. In the fall of 1966, a court ordered him to pay a huge libel judgment to a Harlem resident he had once called, on live TV, a "bag woman"—someone who collected cash for organized crime. A House panel was busy writing a report about the ways Powell had abused his chairmanship of the Education and Labor Committee, ranging from using its funds to buy airline tickets for members of his family to hiring his wife for a no-show job. Soon after Congress convened in January, the party caucus stripped him of the post that had won him clout as an effective insider. That March, by a sizable majority, House members voted to exclude him from the body altogether, but in a special election, defiant Harlem voters sent him back to represent them. Meanwhile, Powell kept preaching that only Black power flexed in the streets would force politicians to enshrine its aims into law. He took that message to more than a hundred venues around the country during the remainder of the decade, unwilling to recognize that his time as one of its most commanding messengers had passed.

The 1968 Democratic National Convention opened on August 26 in a metropolis of more than three million people whose mayor had turned it into an armed camp. Boss of the last powerful big-city machine in America, Richard J. Daley was proud that, under his rule, Chicago had largely escaped the violent confrontations that had rocked cities from Los Angeles to Detroit to Washington, D.C. He was determined to use any means necessary to prevent disruption of the convention in his "great city" by the throng of ten thousand people who had come to protest the "party of death." Daley placed 12,000 police on twelve-hour shifts (some wore "hippie" garb to mix with the anti-war protesters), convinced his state's governor to call up 6,000 National Guardsmen, and had some 7,500 regular army troops flown in to put down any rebellion in the city's Black ghettos.

While the intimidating force kept demonstrators far away from the amphitheater where the convention was held, it also underlined the fact that the Democrats were a party under siege from without as well as within. Humphrey was assured of winning the presidential nomination, although he had gained just 2 percent of all the votes cast in the fifteen primaries, none of which he contested. McCarthy remained in the race, as did South Dakota senator George McGovern, who had inherited most of Robert Kennedy's supporters after RFK's assassination that June. But, according to custom, a bevy of insiders—governors, congressmen, powerful state legislators—chose the lion's share of delegates: 81 percent of them that year. They knew the vice president was the only candidate Lyndon Johnson would accept in his place. Even as an unloved lame duck, LBJ still wielded enough influence in the party to stop McCarthy or any other critic of the war from succeeding him.

But relying on Daley to secure an orderly handoff of leadership to Humphrey blew up in all their partisan faces. The night the convention opened, knots of demonstrators, barred from marching to the arena, smashed the windows of police cars and stores. Two days later, as nominating speeches got underway, thousands of cops and National Guardsmen waded into an anti-war crowd gathered in Grant Park, in front of the Hilton Hotel, headquarters for the leading candidates and most state delegations. In what a national commission later described as "a police riot," they smashed clubs over the heads of unarmed protesters and sprayed Mace in their faces; some of Chicago's finest chanted "Kill, Kill, Kill" as they went about their bloody task.[64]

Inside the amphitheater, the delegates were listening to nominating addresses, a ritual everyone knew would have no impact whatsoever on the balloting later that night. But when critics of the war saw television footage of the violence in Grant Park, they erupted in rage. Connecticut senator Abraham Ribicoff turned his nominating speech for McGovern into a rebuke of the mayor and his brutal police. If the South Dakotan were elected president, he said, "we wouldn't have Gestapo tactics on the streets of Chicago." Daley, whose delegation sat less than ten yards from the podium, appeared to roar back, "Fuck you you Jew son of a bitch you lousy motherfucker go home." No microphone was close enough to pick up the mayor's words; lip-readers later deciphered them.

After midnight, the delegates dutifully nominated Hubert Humphrey by the overwhelming margin everyone expected. At the national convention twenty years before, he had been a young champion for Black rights who defied the cautious leaders of his party and won. Now, as vice president, Humphrey embodied a system millions of Democrats condemned for neglecting oppressed people at home while murdering them in Southeast Asia. As the roll call of the states neared its conclusion, the vice president walked into a room by himself at the Hilton and wept. That evening, Theodore White, the author of bestselling histories of presidential campaigns, watched the police assault from his hotel room. He jotted in his notebook, "The Democrats are finished."[65]

Ironically, the platform Humphrey ran on that fall included some of the grandest promises to reform American capitalism the party had ever made. Officially, Democrats vowed to create a more progressive tax system, declared that health care and housing were the right of every citizen, called for amending the Wagner Act to cover farmworkers, proposed a new federal agency to protect consumers from fraud and unsafe products, and endorsed an extension of the war on poverty. It was as bold as the agenda social democrats in countries like France, Britain, and West Germany were advocating at the time.

But the nominee mentioned none of it in his acceptance speech. Instead, Humphrey sought to mollify and uplift a party that was too divided to embrace any newer deal. He began by quoting a prayer by St. Francis about love, then sprinkled platitudes about securing peace in Vietnam and law and order at home. Straining for optimism, Humphrey slipped in a clichéd tribute to tradition: "It is the special genius of the Democratic party that it welcomes change—not as an enemy but as an ally—not as a force to be suppressed but as an instrument of progress to be encouraged." Of course, the nominee did not mention the fact that every time a major party had blundered through a sharply divided convention like this one, its ticket had gone down to defeat that fall.[66]

Humphrey almost escaped the same fate, although he did little on his own to rescue his campaign from the debacle in Chicago that had left him twelve points behind Richard Nixon in the polls. As a fervent liberal on race, the Democrat knew he had no chance to win more than a few states in the South. In 1968, the real contest in Dixie was between Nixon and George Wallace, the candidate of an American Independent Party, created just for him. Wallace incited populist rage against long-haired college radicals and elites in both parties and mused about filling governor's chairs with brawny factory workers who had "about a tenth-grade education." He was intensely popular in his own region. Humphrey carried but one of the eleven states that had rebelled against the Union: LBJ's beloved Texas. In the Deep South, a slim 10 percent of white voters pulled the Democratic lever. It was the party's worst performance ever in what had long been the only region of the country it could count on winning.[67]

Across the industrial East and Midwest, organized labor, bulwark of the New Deal coalition, gave Humphrey a chance to squeeze out a victory. In September, UAW and AFL-CIO officials reported the alarming news that Wallace's class-laced rhetoric and contempt for both major parties were striking a chord among the white rank-and-file. At his rallies in the North, the independent candidate often invited individual unionists, usually from the building trades, to join him onstage. Labor publicists countered with a torrent of literature that informed their members about Alabama's abysmal public services and a tax structure that favored the rich. More than six hundred staffers from the Auto Workers campaigned full-time against Wallace's "strategy of divide-and-rule." Fearing the media would mention the violence that had torn through Detroit's Black community the previous summer, Humphrey declined to open his campaign in Cadillac Square, as had every Democratic nominee since Harry Truman. Yet labor's ferocious drive did much to keep Michigan as well as Pennsylvania, Minnesota, and New York in the Democratic column, although Humphrey still carried only 56 percent of the votes of union households—the same total Adlai Stevenson had managed in his woeful first campaign.[68]

Wallace's strength in the South did not prevent Nixon from winning the presidency by more than a hundred electoral votes. But the Republican bested Humphrey by less than 1 percent of the popular vote and would have to govern with a Congress still dominated by the opposition party. Democrats lost a mere five seats in the House and the same number in the Senate; downballot, most Southerners remained loyal to "the party of the fathers."

When elected vice president four years earlier, Hubert Humphrey had appeared to be a rare politician who could win praise from every segment of the Democratic coalition, except for whites in Dixie. African American voters knew him as the man who pushed the civil rights bill through the Senate. Labor chieftains of nearly every ideological stripe regarded him as their most dependable ally in Washington. Liberal activists, whether or not they belonged to ADA, knew he had always been one of them and saw no reason why that would ever change. At the inaugural parties in 1965, wrote Arthur Schlesinger, Jr., Humphrey had been "the happiest man in the world," dancing "so filled with gaiety and charm and life that everyone else stopped, formed a circle around him, and clapped."[69]

But even before his diligent spinning of the disastrous war in Vietnam turned that joy into ashes, signs of fragmentation in the party ranks were plain to see. Black activists, while pleased with the legislation Humphrey had secured, increasingly resented white leaders who fretted about alienating racist voters if they "moved too fast." As Mississippi Freedom Democratic Party leader Bob Moses explained at the Atlantic City convention, "We're not here to bring politics to our morality but to bring morality to our politics." White union members who acquiesced to integrated workplaces often balked at racially mixed neighborhoods and public schools. In 1964, Californians rejected an open housing law by a two-to-one margin, even as they were backing the Democratic ticket by a sizable, if smaller, margin. Opposition was greatest among manufacturing workers and residents with a high school education or less.[70]

Meanwhile, young activists on the left fringe of liberalism rapidly moved away from "Part of the Way with LBJ" toward vilifying any Democrat who took Johnson's side. Less than three months after inauguration day, SDS organized the first mass demonstration against the war in Vietnam on the grounds of the Washington Monument. In the fall of 1968, the group led Election Day protests in several cities. In Boston, I marched up to the statehouse with my radical comrades, chanting "Vote with Your Feet, Vote in the Streets."

The battle for the Democratic nomination that year, observes the historian Nelson Lichtenstein, "was the last moment in the twentieth century when the most decisive issues facing the nation would be fought out within the house of American liberalism." For more than three decades, the electoral juggernaut that had rumbled into national power with Franklin Roosevelt had largely succeeded in keeping its internal tensions of class and race, region and ideology at bay. Then an unfinished battle for equal rights at home and a stalemated war of counterinsurgency abroad shattered the prospect for even an anxious unity. Although more Americans still identified with the party of FDR than with that of Richard Nixon, its share of the popular vote for president in 1968 plummeted by more than 18 percent from that which LBJ had received. The size of the plunge was almost identical to the one Republicans had suffered between Herbert Hoover's election in 1928 and his landslide defeat four years later. For the first time since the Great Depression, the question of how to steer the Democrats' battered vehicle back on the road to a governing majority was truly up for grabs.[71]

# 8

## WHOSE PARTY IS IT?
## 1969–1994

*Come Home, America.*
—GEORGE MCGOVERN, DEMOCRATIC PRESIDENTIAL NOMINEE, 1972

*Since Southerners still want to be Democrats, why not*
*give them a chance?*
—CHARLES ROBB, GOVERNOR OF VIRGINIA AND
SON-IN-LAW OF LYNDON JOHNSON, 1985[1]

*We stand at the end of a long dark night of*
*reaction . . . For almost eight years we've been led by*
*those who . . . have been prepared to sacrifice the*
*common good of the many to satisfy the private*
*interests and the wealth of a few.*
—JESSE JACKSON, AT THE 1988 DEMOCRATIC NATIONAL CONVENTION[2]

*It's the economy, stupid.*
—MANTRA OF BILL CLINTON'S 1992 PRESIDENTIAL CAMPAIGN[3]

Since its creation, the Democratic Party has never enjoyed a prolonged period of internal bliss. Drawn from diverse regions and a
variety of classes and ethnic clusters, its partisans have always been
engaged in or at risk of descending into battles that, when left unresolved, help the opposition win elections and set the course of national policy. What else could one expect of an organization whose
prominent stalwarts once included both Walt Whitman and Jefferson

Davis—and, a century later, both George C. Wallace and Adam Clayton Powell, Jr.?

The party's first nadir occurred during the Civil War, when the Copperheads demanded peace with the Confederacy. A second came during the 1920s, when Southern leaders could not abide the rising power of big-city Catholics and Jews. As ferociously divided as Democrats were in 1968, they still controlled both houses of Congress and a majority of state governments. In the aftermath of Humphrey's defeat, they would become the most demographically diverse party in U.S history. The example of the Black freedom movement inspired women, gay men and lesbians, Latinos and Latinas, Native Americans, and African Americans to insist that the party embrace their demands for truly democratic reform. In 1972, the DNC elected its first chairwoman, Jean Westwood from Utah; in 1989, Ron Brown from New York became the first Black person to hold that position. As a party that "looked like America," the Democrats were not doomed to fall back to the status of an embattled minority.

Yet over the next quarter century, any consensus among activists and politicians about how to move forward proved fragile and fleeting. Democrats squabbled over whether to continue fighting the Cold War aggressively or to reduce the size of the military machine and allow Third World revolutions to triumph. They debated whether to extend the welfare state or roll it back to show that Democrats disdained "throwing money at problems." They battled over whether to build a new coalition dominated by the young, people of color, and feminists or to make it a priority to appeal to whites from all regions with modest incomes and conservative social views. Except in 1976, when the lingering stench of the Watergate scandal lifted Jimmy Carter to a narrow victory, Democrats lost every race for the White House—by overwhelming margins.

These conflicts and defeats occurred at a time of economic disruption that bred mass discontent across the nation. Inflation and unemployment rose sharply in the early 1970s, resulting in the most prolonged downturn since the Great Depression. The double blow of foreign competition and production outsourcing destroyed the livelihoods of wage earners throughout the industrial heartland, which, for its pains, soon got renamed the Rust Belt.

In the 1930s, economic turmoil had spurred Democrats to make a vigorous and popular case for moral capitalism. Yet the crisis that unfolded four decades later finished off the era of mass prosperity and shrinking inequality that FDR had initiated and his liberal successors had dominated. Unhappy voters now searched the political landscape for figures who could offer effective remedies, if not permanent solutions.

But no Democratic faction satisfied their demand; stymied by internal conflict, the party as a whole never seriously tried. Instead, most of its leaders, elected and otherwise, either acquiesced to or promoted austere budgeting and market-based solutions, elements of the policy agenda later known as "neoliberalism." As early as 1984, the liberal journalist Thomas Byrne Edsall observed that the Democratic Party had "tied itself into knots just at a time when there had been a revival of intense conflict over the distribution of the costs and benefits of government." It was a contest that Republicans, with their hardened antipathy to an interventionist domestic state, were "singularly well equipped to fight."[4] So the opportunity was lost to forge a new coalition of working- and lower-middle-class people of all races who shared, despite their mutual suspicions, a desire for a more egalitarian economic order. It has yet to be regained.

## Reform Triumphs, and the Reformer Is Routed

In the immediate aftermath of the 1968 election, Democratic leaders concerned themselves with fixing a problem that had nothing to do with the economy. After all, unemployment was less than 4 percent and inflation remained low; there seemed no reason why the postwar boom would not continue. In the winter of 1969, the party established a commission empowered to carry out a sweeping overhaul of how delegates to its national convention were chosen. No longer would state party officials be able to select delegates by themselves, even a year or more before the contest began. No one wanted to risk repeating the fiasco inside the Chicago amphitheater at which the victor had run in no primaries and was anointed by a body composed almost entirely of middle-aged and older white men.[5]

The DNC named Senator George McGovern from South Dakota to run the twenty-six-member Commission on Party Structure and Delegate Selection. Both sides in the previous year's internal battle were comfortable with the choice. As a fierce opponent of the Vietnam war, McGovern had made a late dash for the nomination in 1968. But at the close of the tumultuous convention, McGovern stood smiling next to Humphrey on the podium, although he knew having the vice president at the top of the ticket might endanger his own chances of winning reelection in his conservative state. That same day, the senator held a press conference to declare that his party would have to make fundamental changes "if it is to command the respect and meet the needs of our society." The fiasco in Chicago, he predicted, would "mark the end of the old back-room politics and the first birth pangs" of a "new politics centered on people and principle."[6]

Democrats who wanted to weaken the influence of party bosses had been talking this way since Adlai's Stevenson's campaign in 1952. But nearly two decades later, McGovern was pushing against a door that was both open and splintered. Hardly any powerful machines still existed in the big cities where they had once thrived. Tammany Hall declined rapidly after the bulk of its white ethnic voters decamped for the outer boroughs of New York or the suburbs, while the once-mighty organization David Lawrence had built in Pittsburgh did not survive his death in 1966. Only in Richard J. Daley's Chicago did a machine keep winning consistently and retain the ability to keep the oils of patronage flowing to its loyal voters in the sprawling metropolis. Down south, a new Black electorate enfranchised by the 1965 Voting Rights Act was threatening the grip of the "courthouse rings" that had essentially controlled the process of selecting delegates since the end of Reconstruction. In the country as a whole, fewer than 20 percent of American voters lived in places where a Democratic organization was still strong enough to have its way.[7]

McGovern's commission thus had little difficulty setting forth bold proposals for internal changes that the party quickly adopted in time for the next presidential campaign. These included "affirmative steps" to broaden the pool of delegates to include far more women,

young people, African Americans, and Latinos and Latinas; prohib-
iting the heads of state parties from choosing delegates themselves,
as many had long done; banning the "unit rule" that allowed a state
to award all its slots to a single candidate in a multiperson race; and
making the choice of a delegation transparent at every stage in the
process. For the first time in history, the national party had seized
the power to dictate to its affiliates specific "guidelines" for how they
would participate in the most important decision rank-and-file Democrats had the power to make.[8]

The reforms quickly achieved their main goal: to turn the contest for the presidential nomination into one that lived up, at least
formally, to the Democrats' self-image as the "party of the people."
To meet the new inclusionary rules, officials in most states initiated
primaries or caucuses whose results bound delegates on the first ballot. In addition, they encouraged prospective candidates to choose a
diverse band of followers to represent their cause. At the 1972 convention, nearly 40 percent of the delegates were female, 15 percent
were Black, and almost 25 percent were under thirty. The delegations from Texas and California included far more Mexican Americans than ever before. Remarkably, 80 percent of the participants
had never attended one of the party's quadrennial gatherings before.
Politicians and top officials of the AFL-CIO still had a role to play.
But it was no longer a sizable one, and many of these "regulars"
feared it never would be again.[9]

Gradually, the internal reforms accelerated the weakening of the
apparatus that had undergirded the political order FDR and his fellow partisans thought they had built to last. The modern campaign,
with all its high-priced, high-tech tools of persuasion, had come to
stay. Giving any Democrat who could win votes in primaries and
caucuses a chance to capture the nomination turned every race into
a fight for political market share. As in any competitive industry, a
serious candidate had to put together a well-funded organization and
sell him- or herself to consumers of varied tastes and interests. A
credible sales effort required a corps of well-paid consultants with
specialized knowledge: pollsters, field organizers, and those with expertise in forms of new media from television to direct mail and,
later, the digital realm. Of course, all this cost a great deal of money.

Between 1964 and 1976, the cost of national elections almost tripled, to $540 million; without the legislation enacted after the Watergate scandal to curb a number of specific abuses, it surely would have mushroomed even more.[10]

But candidates still had to do a lot of the work of persuasion themselves, filtered through the unforgiving lenses of television cameras. The calm, handsome John F. Kennedy famously bested a perspiring Richard Nixon in their 1960 debates. That mediated triumph didn't prevent the election from being one of the closest in history. But the internal reforms required presidential hopefuls to become skilled, attractive performers on the tube or risk losing to those who were. A 1977 report by political scientists asked, "What would take the place of parties?" Their worried prediction: "A politics of celebrities, of excessive media influence, or political fad-of-the-month clubs . . . of heightened interest in 'personalities' and lowered interest in policy."[11]

McGovern took full advantage of the new world of campaigning he had helped create. In January 1971, he passed on the chairmanship of the reform committee, whose work was mostly finished, to a liberal congressman from Minnesota and announced he was running for president. No Democrat since Andrew Jackson—in the wake of the "corrupt bargain" a century and a half before—had entered the race for the White House so early. Acknowledging some might consider him too hasty, McGovern explained, in a televised address, that "the kind of campaign I intend to run will rest on candor and reason . . . That kind of campaign takes time." It would also require a lot of cash: as the senator was delivering his speech, his campaign sent out a fund-raising pitch to some 275,000 prospective contributors. To rise from the 5 percent of support he drew in polls that winter, McGovern would have to become *the* anti-war candidate in the race. His TV speech made no mention of the news released that same day that in the prior year the size of the nation's economy had declined for the first time since the recession of the late 1950s.[12]

The background of the first Democratic candidate to campaign under the new rules had little in common with that of the cosmopolitan liberals who had flocked to Adlai Stevenson and JFK and would become McGovern's most prominent backers as well. McGovern grew up in a prairie town tucked inside South Dakota, one of the nation's most rural states; his father was a Methodist minister who built his church with his own hands and forbade his children either to dance or to take in a movie. During World War II, McGovern earned a prestigious medal flying thirty-five missions in the cockpit of a B-24 bomber over Nazi-controlled Europe. Because he refused to boast about that experience, most of the young people who worked for him in 1972 and abhorred all things military were unaware they were campaigning for a war hero.

Yet McGovern also yearned to lead the life of an intellectual. On returning home from combat, he enrolled in divinity school to gratify his father, then switched to a graduate program in U.S. history; his dissertation about a violent Colorado miners' strike in 1914 remains a wise, bracing narrative about a signal episode of class warfare in the West. He briefly considered a career in academia. But inspired by left-wing populists like William Jennings Bryan and Henry Wallace, he devoted himself to reviving the Democratic Party in his state, which every GOP nominee in the twentieth century had captured—save the two FDR buried in the 1930s. McGovern deployed the organization he had built to capture a seat in the House and then one in the Senate. By the mid-1960s, the self-made politician was a rising star in a national party that had always preached the virtues of upward mobility.

Yet McGovern resolved to run for president in 1972 as an insurgent who could rapidly assemble a new coalition to replace the one that had failed to elect Hubert Humphrey. Young people of all races, McGovern thought, would rally to a candidate who posed a stirring, moral alternative to the party leaders who had taken the nation into a terrible war as well as to the Republican president who refused to end it.

For the job of campaign manager, McGovern tapped Gary Hart, a charismatic attorney in his mid-thirties who recruited what he boasted was a "massive volunteer army" of anti-war activists across the country. A twenty-six-year-old former Rhodes Scholar named Bill Clinton headed the organization in Texas. As a long-shot candidate, McGovern was initially snubbed by every established figure in the party. But even before he started winning a string of state contests in April, he had picked up endorsements from such ADA leaders (and veterans of the Kennedy administration) as Arthur Schlesinger, Jr., and John Kenneth Galbraith, as well as from celebrities like the actor Shirley MacLaine and her brother, Warren Beatty; the comedian Dick Gregory; the singer Barbra Streisand; and the folk music trio Peter, Paul and Mary. Several of these figures, whom the campaign staff dubbed the "Mighty McGovern Art Players," traveled with the candidate, opening his rallies and speaking at fundraisers. Like the college-age canvassers who fanned out from coast to coast, they believed in his promise to battle the "empty decaying void" of an "establishment center . . . that commands neither the confidence" of most Americans "nor their love."[13]

But idealism and grassroots energy could not, by themselves, convince a majority of either Democratic politicians or primary voters to rally behind a candidate who appealed most strongly to those who shared his fervent resolve to get out of Vietnam as quickly as possible. "Every Senator in this Chamber is partly responsible for sending 50,000 young Americans to an early grave," McGovern scolded his colleagues in the spring of 1970. "This Chamber reeks of blood." The candidate who had fought with honor in a necessary war was determined to extricate the country from a profoundly dishonorable one. But while more than 60 percent of Americans had come to agree it had been a mistake to send troops to Vietnam in the first place, a majority also abhorred the demonstrators who had been making that case since Lyndon Johnson escalated the conflict in 1965. Images of college kids exempt from the draft carrying Viet Cong flags and burning American ones blotted out those of GIs who had turned against the war, like the hundreds of young veterans who flung their military medals onto the steps of the U.S. Capitol in a dramatic protest in April 1971.[14]

The 1972 primary contest turned into something of a free-for-all among candidates chasing after dissimilar constituencies. Hubert Humphrey's bid depended on winning over white unionists and older African Americans, Edmund Muskie appealed to white Catholics, George Wallace again sought to turn the racial backlash to his advantage in the North as well as the South, and Shirley Chisholm nursed hope that, as a Black feminist, she embodied a cleaner break with "the System" than any of her competitors. McGovern, with an

army of volunteers mustered by the largest and best-funded organization in the field, managed to win contests in twenty-one states,
enough to gain a slim majority of delegates at the convention in Miami Beach that July. But having drawn only a quarter of all the combined votes cast in the primaries and caucuses, he would have no
easier time uniting the party than had Humphrey in 1968.

It should not have come as a surprise that the new rules for selecting a more diverse set of delegates had yielded a result that reflected
the profound divisions in the party. "The only logical explanation of
the Democratic Presidential campaign," wrote the *New York Times*
columnist James Reston during the heat of the battle that spring, "is
that it must have been planned by Republicans."[15]

While the party avoided a rerun of the debacle in Chicago four
years earlier, Democrats emerged from the Miami Beach Convention
Center no more unified than they had entered it. Credential fights
broke out between slates of McGovern delegates and those loyal to
party veterans like Mayor Richard Daley. Speakers advocating gay
rights and abortion rights drew cheers and boos in almost equal
decibels. At McGovern's request, delegates voted against including
these controversial demands in the platform. Shirley MacLaine's
argument against the pro-choice plank earned her an angry rebuke
from Bella Abzug, an outspoken feminist congresswoman from New
York City: "A sister never goes against a sister." MacLaine shot back,
"Sisters have a right to have pragmatic politics as well as personal
principles."[16]

The discord itself was telling. The kind of left-wing organizers
who four years earlier had railed against the party and refused to
support its nominee were now an integral, if not always a happy, part
of McGovern's coalition. Most would remain faithful Democrats, albeit chafing at having to make compromises with their principles.
In time, the solid backing of feminists and the LGBT community
would enable the party to present itself as a tolerant, postmaterialist
force that appealed to young Americans in particular. But in 1972,
more voters undoubtedly saw the left-wingers as threats to their traditional beliefs rather than as visionaries of personal freedom.

To have any chance of winning in the fall, McGovern needed
the support of the AFL-CIO, whose campaign arm remained the

Democrats' most potent weapon in the big industrial and urban states that decided most modern presidential contests. In the Senate, he had voted as faithfully for bills labor favored as had Humphrey; what's more, he was the first presidential candidate to endorse collective bargaining for government workers. But the intraparty reforms McGovern helped establish had stripped from George Meany and his allies the power to select pro-union delegates loyal to them.

As men who sprang from blue-collar and often religious backgrounds, the labor chieftains also viewed the young, college-educated activists with countercultural tastes as creatures from a country they had no desire to be part of. In September, Meany (a high school dropout) grumbled to an audience of steelworkers about the Democratic convention, "We listened to . . . the people who want to legalize marriage between boys and boys and . . . between girls and girls . . . We heard from the abortionists, and we heard from the people who look like Jacks, acted like Jills, and had the odor of johns about them." The AFL-CIO Executive Council soon voted, by a huge margin, to remain neutral in the presidential race. It was the first time since the 1920s that a body representing most union members failed to endorse the Democratic nominee.[17]

As he pivoted to the race against Richard Nixon, McGovern did make an effort to win over working-class voters. He made multiple appearances in union halls where he attacked the incumbent's plan to freeze wages to combat inflation and touted his own solid support for labor's agenda. He advocated higher taxes on inheritances and capital gains. He sought to parry the hostility of white wage earners to recipients of welfare (who they wrongly assumed were mostly Black) by promising that, as president, he would guarantee jobs for all. On his behalf, Senator Ted Kennedy spoke around the country to ordinary white Catholics who had revered his slain brothers. And McGovern softened the blow of Meany's rejection by winning the endorsement of thirty-three individual unions—including such large, politically active ones as the United Auto Workers and the International Association of Machinists and Aerospace Workers.

The Democratic nominee also counted on winning broad support from a largely working-class constituency that neither party had seriously organized as such before: Latinos and Latinas. Until the

1960s, most Americans with Spanish-speaking roots had identified primarily by country of origin: Mexican, Puerto Rican, and so on. But emulating the Black freedom movement, politicians and organizers energetically promoted the vision of a people, "La Raza," bonded together by language, traditions, and a common history of Anglo conquest and oppression. In 1972, Democratic officials, led by Representative Edward Roybal from Los Angeles, founded the Latino Caucus to press for influence within the party. McGovern and his advisers welcomed the group and readily agreed that the platform would endorse bilingual education and support for the United Farm Workers, led by the charismatic Cesar Chavez. For the first time, the party officially paid tribute to "the magnificence of the diversity" of the U.S. population. Thus a staple of Democratic and liberal rhetoric was born.[18]

At the same time, McGovern struggled to articulate a more unifying appeal. He made clear that his slogan, "Come Home, America," referred to more than simply ending a horrible war in Southeast Asia. It meant "the end of a system of economic controls in which labor is depressed, but prices and corporate profit run sky-high" and enacting "a system of national health insurance so that a worker can afford decent health care for himself and his family."[19]

But McGovern never emphasized such calls for bottom-up economic reform, and it is doubtful it would have made much of a difference to his electoral fate if he had. After the convention, the mass media settled on an image of his campaign that became impossible to shake. As Jean Westwood, the DNC chair, lamented to the candidate at the end of August, "Resistance to the ticket is not based on our being radical but on our identification with 'them'—with the educated liberals." Party strategists wrote off their chances in the South, although some retained hope that Mexican Americans would deliver a narrow win in Texas, which Humphrey had carried in 1968. But, notwithstanding the avid support he received from Black leaders like Coretta Scott King and Jesse Jackson, the candidate who hailed from one of the whitest states in the union had no experience wooing voters in the inner cities. As polls showed Nixon leading by a large and increasing margin, McGovern's aides lost hope that a big African American turnout would save them.[20]

The consequence of all these flaws, self-inflicted and otherwise, was one of the most crushing defeats suffered by any Democratic nominee in history. McGovern won just 38 percent of the popular vote and carried only a single state, the Kennedy-loving bastion of Massachusetts, and the District of Columbia, with its Black majority. Latinos and Latinas gave Nixon a larger minority of their vote than he had received in 1968. On Election Day, I was volunteering for the Democratic ticket in Portland, Oregon. The unambiguous verdict from states back East came down so early that I stopped house-to-house canvassing a little after 5:00 p.m. Pacific time; one neighbor after another had told me I was wasting my time.

Alarmingly, the nominee of what had long been the political home of most wage earners and their families did far better among residents of well-to-do enclaves like Beverly Hills and the Upper East Side of Manhattan than in the white working-class neighborhoods of Queens and South Gate, an industrial suburb in Los Angeles County. "I live in a rather special world," Pauline Kael, *The New Yorker*'s movie critic, said after the election. "I only know one person who voted for Nixon." Most who did so in places like Queens and South Gate probably did not oppose McGovern's position on the war in Vietnam; they objected instead to what they perceived to be his stance on the emerging conflict in American culture. Ironically, the evangelical minister's son who grew up to pilot a bomber in a popular war and then worked his way up to the political heights had landed on the wrong side of the class divide that had once made his party the default power in the land.[21]

Democrats could console themselves in the knowledge that Nixon's big victory was a triumph of person, not party. In 1972, Republicans actually lost two seats in the Senate and gained a mere dozen in the lower chamber. The president's huge margins in the South, where he won nearly 90 percent of the white vote, yielded the GOP just eight additional members from that region in the House of Representatives. That result was due partly to Nixon's reluctance to alienate conservative and moderate voters who disliked McGovern but continued to identify with the party of FDR and JFK. The pull of tradition and the benefits of seniority still mattered to millions who were able to look past the unfortunate prairie reformer at the top of the ticket. Despite the result, a clear majority of Americans still identified themselves as Democrats.[22]

## Recovery and Relapse

The Nixon landslide only intensified the battle to define what forces should lead the party and which policies they should fight for. The white Southerners who still held two-fifths of the Democrats' majority in the House—close to their average number since the 1930s—could keep Northern liberals from passing any legislation they disliked, although most Dixie congresspeople stopped short of doing anything that would make them pariahs in the party as a whole.

Yet in the wake of McGovern's drubbing, organized internal factions grew like lilies after a rainstorm. Some spoke for the needs of specific demographic constituencies, such as the Congressional Black Caucus, the Latino Caucus, and the National Women's Political Caucus. Others, like the Coalition for a Democratic Majority, aimed to return the party to an aggressive posture in the Cold War or, like Democratic Agenda, led by the pragmatic socialist Michael Harrington, sought to invigorate the commitment to full employment and progressive taxation McGovern had failed to emphasize. In 1973, the election of African American mayors in Detroit, Atlanta, and Los Angeles demonstrated both the power of the alliance between Black and liberal voters in those cities and the alienation of white working-class ones, most of whom backed their white opponents. Nixon's withdrawal of U.S. troops from South Vietnam early that same year removed a major cause of intraparty conflict, but profound ones of identity and ideology remained.

Robert Strauss, a wily Texas moderate who, a month after the election, was narrowly picked to chair the DNC, created the Democratic Advisory Council of Elected Officials to work out compromises on issues that might otherwise lead disparate sets of partisans to rush back to their barricades. But, though he was successful at raising money in telethons and from wealthy donors, Strauss could not speak favorably about one group's priorities without stirring up protests from its rivals. Strauss joked that being chairman was "a little like making love to a gorilla. You don't stop when you're tired. You stop when the gorilla's tired." If Democrats kept showing affection only to their ideological bedmates, their chances of regaining control of the presidency and the national agenda were slim.[23]

Salvation arrived, as it often does in politics, in the form of a massive blunder by the opposition. The Watergate affair began with a sloppy break-in at DNC headquarters by a team of pro-Nixon operatives in June 1972. It gradually mushroomed into a scandal that, two years later, engulfed the administration and compelled the president to resign before Congress would have thrown him out of office. A sharp recession that started in the fall of 1973, marked by an unusual combination of high unemployment and soaring inflation, weakened Nixon and his party even further. The consequence was a midterm election in 1974 that awarded Democrats with a veto-proof majority in the House and more than sixty seats in the Senate. Suddenly, it seemed, they had an excellent opportunity to heal the internal divisions that had widened since the heyday of the Great Society.

However, the most dynamic force in the new Congress was a breed of young Democrats skeptical about the uses of federal power on which the party's success had depended from FDR to LBJ. Most of these freshly elected "Watergate babies" represented white suburbs or states with many budding entrepreneurs as well as union members. They lacked the faith that big government could solve big problems—a faith that had inspired liberals since the early twentieth century. In 1974, Gary Hart won a seat in the Senate from Colorado by running as much against the Washington establishment of his own party as against oil companies that were backing his Republican opponent. "The time is now," he thundered, "for *all* of us to rise up and take our country back from the power-hungry corrupters, the fat cats and special interest boys . . . the comfortable, complacent, backward-looking old men, many of whom inhabit the United States Senate like a private club. Now it's *our* turn!"[24]

The former campaign manager and his counterparts in the class of 1974 did advance some of the liberal issues that McGovern had highlighted during his failed run for president. Led in the House by Congressman Phil Burton from San Francisco, they scrapped the custom of naming committee chairs strictly by seniority and decreased their power to control agendas. Motivated by a historic number of female and Black representatives, they embraced such demands as equal pay for women and affirmative action—and showed more concern for protecting the environment than had older politicians from industrial towns and cities. Many of the Southern Democrats elected in 1974 made their own break with the past, too. Needing to attract Black voters to offset the white shift to the GOP, they abandoned overt appeals to racism and campaigned, like Hart, as foes of entrenched power, wherever it was lodged. What could this ambitious majority manage to accomplish if the Democrats recaptured the White House?

The answer would be a profound disappointment. Jimmy Carter won the party's 1976 nomination and then defeated President Gerald Ford by appealing, as had the Watergate babies, to the country's disgust with Washington "insiders." As a devout Southern Baptist, the governor of Georgia also gave Democrats a chance to win over a growing population of white evangelicals who, alienated by the secular cast of liberalism, had been drifting toward the GOP. Carter skillfully navigated his way through a crowded primary field that included just one contender, Senator Henry "Scoop" Jackson from Washington State, willing to call himself a liberal. The Georgian then ran a rather issue-less campaign and received barely half the popular vote. That year, thanks to post-scandal campaign finance reforms, neither major-party nominee raised much private money; both depended almost entirely on the funds provided by the millions of Americans who checked a donation box on their tax returns.[25]

Once Carter moved into the White House, the erstwhile nuclear engineer and peanut farmer proved to be an absolutely wretched politician. His campaign had promised "a government as good as its people," an enticingly hollow specimen of soft populism. Yet he had no idea how to translate even that anodyne pledge into anything resembling an attractive set of policies or a governing coalition that would support and defend them.

Instead of a coherent strategy, Carter pursued a disparate set of projects—often with little popular backing—he was convinced were necessary for the well-being of the nation and the world. He granted amnesty to draft resisters and sought to conserve energy and protect wilderness areas. He promoted human rights abroad and broke decisively with his upbringing in the Jim Crow South by vigorously enforcing the Voting Rights Act and naming African Americans to high positions in his administration. He appointed more women to significant federal jobs, from cabinet secretaries to judges, than any president before him. One of those jurists was Ruth Bader Ginsburg, whom Carter nominated to a seat on the District of Columbia Circuit in 1980.

What Carter did *not* do was advocate policies that might win the support of poor and working-class Americans buffeted by job insecurity and high inflation. Instead, he peered at social programs, old and new, through an austerity-tinted lens. Explaining that he needed "to enhance an image of fiscal responsibility," the president sought to balance the budget and opposed a national health insurance plan written by Ted Kennedy. He also signed bills to deregulate the airline and trucking industries, which even most liberals endorsed because they promised to lower prices for consumers.[26]

In sum, these moves, and the support they drew from other party leaders, signified a momentous retreat. No longer would Democrats maintain that government had an obligation to set strict rules to protect workers and demand that corporations obey them. No longer would union power be viewed as an unambiguous boon to party fortunes as well as prime evidence that Democrats were the natural home of wage earners of any race, religion, or region. The failure of "big government" to win the wars of Indochina or keep the economy from falling into a whirlpool of high prices and high unemployment turned even many liberal economists into critics of Keynesian remedies and sent them and the politicians they advised searching for quick solutions to a stubborn epidemic of stagflation that threatened to infect them all. "I'd love the Teamsters to be worse off . . . I'd love the automobile workers to be worse off," admitted Alfred Kahn, an economist and Carter administration official who argued that shielding "certain protected workers from competition" kept the free market from operating as it should. In 1979, the president appointed Paul Volcker, a former Treasury undersecretary under Richard Nixon, to head the Federal Reserve. As expected, the new chairman of the central bank waged a "war on inflation" by jacking up interest rates to levels he knew would starve many businesses of funds and throw millions of Americans out of work. Carter, who feared that vaulting prices posed the biggest threat to his reelection, let Volcker have his way.[27]

At the same time, unlike every other Democratic president before him, Carter had contempt for partisan combat and made no real attempt to build his party. In private, he scorned Robert Strauss, the DNC chair, who had organized the convention that nominated him, as one of the "big wheeler-dealer Democrats" whose power he hoped to weaken. He angered the Latino Caucus by snubbing their request to appoint members of their ethnicity to high-level positions in his administration. In the spring of 1977, Edward Roybal blasted the president's "complete lack of sensitivity to the problems of the Spanish-speaking and Latinos." Carter believed that governing the nation should be a noble enterprise that transcended efforts to gain leverage for the next election. Stuart Eizenstat, his former domestic policy adviser, has sensibly observed, "A president cannot make a sharp break between the politics of his campaign and the politics of governing if he wants to nurture an effective national coalition. This Carter not only failed to achieve—he did not want to." Walter Mondale, his own vice president, reflected, "He thought politics was sinful."[28]

To consolidate their hold over Congress and the White House, Democrats had to preserve the margin among white working-class voters they had regained after Nixon left office in disgrace. There was still no institution on their side that wielded more potential to do that than organized labor, which represented a quarter of workers in the private sector. When Carter took office, competition from manufacturers abroad and a fierce attack by anti-labor employers at home had weakened its political clout; most Democratic politicians in the South, where union density was a mere 10 percent, remained as cold to the labor movement as ever.

Labor leaders got over their internal conflicts to stress that their main goal was for Congress to enact changes in the Wagner Act that would make it easier for a majority of wage earners in a given workplace to unionize and harshly penalize companies that broke the law. Eizenstat told his boss, "It is difficult to overestimate the importance of this matter in terms of our future relationship with organized

labor . . . I think it can help cement our relations for a good while."
But Carter, who hailed from a right-to-work state, gave the idea a
decidedly lukewarm reception: "Labor Law Reform? For what is that
a euphemism?" he asked another aide. In 1978, the heavily Democratic House did finally pass a compromise reform bill. But at the
president's urging, the Senate put off its vote so the administration
could focus on getting a treaty ratified that turned over the Panama
Canal to its host country. The delay gave corporate lobbyists time to
mount an energetic campaign against the labor bill—and a filibuster
killed it. All but two of the sixteen Democrats who voted against the
legislation were Southerners.

That same year, the president and his party had another opportunity to enact a law that might both offer economic security to millions of working Americans and give them a reason to be grateful
to Democrats when they went to the polls. In 1974, Hubert Humphrey and Augustus Hawkins, a longtime Black congressman from
Los Angeles, had authored a bill to guarantee a job to every citizen
seventeen or older. If private businesses did not fill the need, the government would do so. As the unemployment rate rose to more than 8
percent, polls showed majority backing for the idea, and every Democrat who wanted to run against Gerald Ford endorsed it—except
Jimmy Carter.[29]

A year into his presidency, the measure remained popular, and a
liberal coalition spanning unions, feminists, and African American
groups lobbied for its passage. Predictably, nearly every Republican
and corporate CEO opposed it, while fears it would reduce investment and spike inflation turned many newly elected Democrats
from suburban districts against it as well. To overcome such opposition would have required the president to reverse himself and make
a zealous commitment to the cause. But to create millions of new
public jobs would have flown in the face of Carter's prime economic
goal—to control inflation by cutting the budget. So, just before the
1978 midterm election, the president signed a version of Humphrey-
Hawkins too weak to ever realize its promise. It set goals of lower
joblessness and reduced price levels for the government to meet—five
years into the future—and included no mechanism to enforce them.
The bill was, as AFL-CIO official Ken Young admitted, merely "a

symbolic step forward." After four years in control of both Congress and the executive branch, Democrats would face the voters having failed to accomplish anything of substance to soften the pain of those enduring an economy in deep crisis.[30]

## Reacting to Reaganism

In retrospect, it is astonishing that any pundit or politician believed Jimmy Carter had a chance to be reelected in 1980 or that other Democrats on the ballot could avoid going down with him. The president had failed to get Islamic militants in Iran to release fifty-two Americans they had held hostage for more than a year in the U.S. embassy in Tehran. His pro-choice stance on abortion helped stoke a revolt by evangelicals, led by Jerry Falwell's Moral Majority. And by the fall of 1980, the crisis of "stagflation" that had helped Carter defeat Gerald Ford was still battering the nation: inflation ran close to 16 percent, joblessness was more than 7 percent, and the Federal Reserve set its prime interest rate at an astonishing 21 percent.

The summer before, Carter had delivered a major address in which he counseled or rather scolded the public on how to endure such hardships: "In a nation that was proud of hard work, strong families, close-knit communities, and our faith in God, too many of us now tend to worship self-indulgence and consumption." During the Great Depression, Franklin Roosevelt had also asked Americans to sacrifice for the common good. But as the journalist E. J. Dionne, Jr., wrote, FDR "made sure that the sacrifices fell most heavily on those able to bear them" and "delivered tangible benefits to his political base." Disdainful of actions taken to gain a partisan edge, Carter had nothing to offer struggling voters but his candor.[31]

The ideological divide among Democrats hobbled his chances for victory, too. Two years before the 1980 election, Ted Kennedy was already attacking the president for attempting to trim the federal budget "at the expense of the elderly, the poor, the Black, the sick, the cities, and the unemployed." The Massachusetts senator entered the race in the fall of 1979 and quickly picked up endorsements from the United Auto Workers and several other big unions angry at

Carter for his apathy toward their legislative demands. But Kennedy was short on funds and gave no coherent reason for his challenge until he had no chance to prevail.

While easily beating his opponent, Carter could not prevent him from delivering an eloquent speech at the 1980 convention in New York's Madison Square Garden that, in ringing tones of moral capitalism, implicitly condemned Paul Volcker's decisions at the Fed as well as the administration's entire economic policy. "Let us pledge," Kennedy told the audience of delegates and liberal spectators, "that we will never misuse unemployment, high interest rates, and human misery as false weapons against inflation" and that "there will be security for all those who are now at work, and let us pledge that there will be jobs for all who are out of work."[32]

Carter's only chance to win a second term rested on the hope that Americans would view his Republican opponent as too "extremist" in his abhorrence of federal spending and too eager to humble the USSR to risk putting him in the White House. The president made no attempt to articulate a compelling vision about the future of the economy—or anything else. Ronald Reagan deftly eluded the effort to brand him as another Barry Goldwater, an unyielding zealot on the right. The former actor and union president had been a registered Democrat until 1962, had twice won landslide races for governor in the nation's largest state, and patterned his relaxed and cheerful style partly on that of FDR himself. He successfully ran as the tribune of the kind of "forgotten man and woman"—their whiteness unstated—who had hailed Roosevelt and his policies. "When Reagan spoke," reflected a biographer, "ordinary Americans did not have to make the mental translation usually required for conservative Republican speakers" at the time. "He undermined the New Deal in its own vernacular."[33]

Voters' worries about a rush to the right thus paled before Carter's failures at home and abroad. I was so disgusted by them that I cast a meaningless ballot for the nominee of the new Citizens Party, which barely a quarter million of my fellow citizens graced with our votes. Carter lost to Reagan by ten points and carried a mere six states, plus the District of Columbia. The drubbing helped the GOP gain a majority in the Senate for the first time in a quarter century. Republicans also gained more than thirty seats in the House. The margin might not have been so great if Carter had not conceded the election an hour before polls closed on the West Coast. "You guys came in like a bunch of pricks," Speaker of the House Tip O'Neill snarled at the president's liaison with Congress, "and you're going out the same way." Jimmy Carter became the first chief executive since Herbert Hoover to run for a second term and lose, badly. The parallel shocked Democrats as much as it angered them.[34]

During his eight long years in the White House, Reagan failed to transform the nation as much as he and the conservative movement from which he sprang would have liked. Beginning with firing the air traffic controllers for going on strike, Reagan did wage an effective assault on organized labor, whose numbers shrank from 21 to 16 percent of wage earners during his time in office. But with the House of Representatives still under Democratic control, most of the embattled pillars of the welfare state that liberals had erected remained intact and, in some instances, grew larger. Social Security and Medicare benefits increased, while affirmative action and the right to an abortion survived. Neither did Reagan's popularity do much to help his fellow Republicans running for state office. Democrats retained a majority of governorships throughout the 1980s and emerged from the decade with a few more legislative seats (63 percent of the total) than they had going in. On the academic front in the culture war, most professors in the liberal arts embraced the cause of racial diversity and adopted a view of the American past as a narrative of oppression as well as progress.[35]

But the popularity of the most right-wing president since Calvin Coolidge, bolstered by his powerful allies in big business and a growing number of evangelical churches, did catalyze a widening split inside the Democratic Party. "This is a single party, not a collection of squabbling interests," claimed DNC chairman Charles T. Manatt in 1981. It must have been lovely to think so. Pitched against one another were liberals who sought to revive the spirit of the Great Society and championed the progressive social movements of the 1960s and those to their right who believed the party had to shelve its faith in "big" government and exude empathy for Americans who recoiled from cultural rebellion.

The clash of ideologies inevitably led to a difference over which strategic path to follow. Each faction sought to answer the same urgent question: How should Democrats plan to defeat the conservatives who now controlled the GOP? Even in crisis, the party remained a big house where relatives of diverse demographic backgrounds, none firmly aligned with either ideological wing, lived and quarreled. And in the new world where primary voters, not insiders, decided which Democrat they wanted to be president, the media's whims and a superior organization could easily frustrate the choice of any single activist camp. Neither the liberal nor the centrist faction succeeded in nominating a candidate of its own during the 1980s. So the battle to define for whom Democrats should speak and how to put together a new majority coalition raged on.[36]

Perhaps appropriately for a party on the defensive, the most prominent leader of the Democratic left in that decade had never run for political office before. Jesse Jackson was raised by a poor single mother in South Carolina. In the early 1960s, he became a star athlete at his Black college as well as a leader of local protests against Jim Crow laws. Ordained as a Baptist minister, he rose through the ranks of the freedom movement to become an aide to Martin Luther King, Jr., whose murder at the Lorraine Motel in Memphis he witnessed with horror on the evening of April 4, 1968. Jackson then moved to Chicago and founded Operation PUSH, an organization that launched a series of boycotts against big firms like Anheuser-Busch that forced them to hire more African American workers and suppliers. "We have our civil rights, now we're fighting for our silver rights," quipped the activist-minister whom some leftists criticized for promoting Black-owned businesses as an alternative to a larger, more generous welfare state.[37]

But Jackson was also a canny observer of larger political discontents. In 1972, he chaired the Illinois delegation that gave George McGovern all its votes and left Mayor Richard J. Daley without a vote at all. As unemployment climbed during the first two years of Reagan's term, Jackson recognized there was a hunger for an inspiring alternative among Black people and white progressives alike. In 1983, he held rallies across the South to register African American voters and made contacts across the color line with left-wing organizers. As one of those organizers, Robert Borosage, later reflected, Jackson "was operating by his own intuition, and he intuitively understood . . . that blacks, or anybody, will register to vote when there's somebody running who excites them . . . He created a new reality. And he was smart enough to move into that reality." Jackson, like Adam Clayton Powell, Jr., before him, saw an opening to pressure the Democrats from both outside and inside the system at the same time.[38]

He would do so, however, on a bigger stage than Powell had ever imagined he might command. In 1984, Jackson became the first Black American to run a competitive campaign for president—a feat made possible only by the decisive role of primaries that McGovern had pioneered. Jackson rested his hopes largely on his fame and popularity among voters of his own race. Since the heyday of the freedom movement in the 1960s, African Americans had enthusiastically backed local candidates of their own, nearly every one a Democrat, who bucked the nation's rightward tilt. Members of the Congressional Black Caucus chaired six major House committees, and Black Democrats captured the mayor's office in cities both large and small. In 1983, PUSH helped register more than 150,000 new Black and Latino voters in Chicago who propelled Harold Washington to victory in the mayor's race—the first defeat in decades for the machine Richard Daley had bossed. Could this nascent coalition of racial minorities and white liberals be replicated on a national scale?

For a growing number of Democratic officials, that prospect was at best chimerical and at worst a mortal danger to the party's future. The traumas of the 1970s had convinced them that any electoral strategy that did not make economic growth a priority would fail. But Jackson was campaigning on a platform that made the Great Society seem small: it included government-funded health care for all, a jobs guarantee, raising taxes on the rich, and a sharp reduction in the defense budget. In contrast, establishment figures believed that, to win, they would have to speak to the anxieties of white middle-class voters who cared less about whether Democrats espoused policies that were "fair" to a variety of "interest groups" than whether they had a plausible notion of how to restore the kind of prosperity most

Americans had taken for granted during the quarter century after World War II. "We gradually moved from fairness to opportunity," explained strategist Al From, "because fairness meant to people, 'We're going to take from you to give to somebody else.' Opportunity meant that everybody had a chance to get ahead."[39]

The aim of these "New Democrats" was to borrow from the impulses that had fueled Reaganism in order to defeat its disciples at the polls. They did not identify as liberals, and they blamed poverty more on what Charles Robb, the former governor of Virginia, called "the spread of self-destructive behavior" by poor people than on the lack of good jobs and a steady income.[40]

Al From, the impresario of this faction, had grown up Jewish and middle-class in South Bend, Indiana. He reported briefly for a Chicago daily paper in the mid-1960s before signing up with the anti-poverty program. Its director, Sargent Shriver, sent him down to Mississippi to settle disputes among local groups that were getting federal aid and to investigate how the government's money was being spent. Evidently, that experience soured From on ambitious programs that could not live up to the lofty promises of their creators. In 1971, he embarked on a career-long mission to reinvent his party from the top down. From occupied a series of influential posts in the Senate, the Carter administration, and the Democratic Caucus in the House of Representatives. Along the way, he assembled a roster of politicians and intellectuals who agreed that the party needed a message that would honor the legacy of the New Deal while scrapping its big-spending habits and much of its leveling spirit.

Leading this charge to the cautious center were Democratic politicians from the South. Robb and such like-minded figures as Senator Sam Nunn from Georgia, Senator Dale Bumpers from Arkansas, and Governor Jim Hunt of North Carolina had all broken with the angry, race-baiting populism espoused by George Wallace. Their margins of victory came more from moderate white suburbanites and Black people than from the kind of angry voters who had fueled the "massive resistance" to civil rights in the 1960s. But when Reagan took office, Republicans boasted of having more members of Congress from the South—ten senators and forty-two representatives—than at any time since Reconstruction. Even districts filled with registered Democrats were, as Louisiana congressman Jerry Huckaby observed, "on a national level philosophically . . . more in tune with Republicans. It's just that they've been Democrats since the War between the States." Fear of further gains by the GOP in their region led New Democrats from the South to tout their plans for cutting the federal budget instead of promising that government largesse would keep flowing as it had since the Great Depression.[41]

By the mid-1980s, it was striking when one of the party's white Southern officeholders broke from the pack to point out the hypocrisy of citizens who echoed Reagan's hostility toward "big government" while continuing to reap its many benefits. One of those outliers was Ernest "Fritz" Hollings, a former governor of South Carolina first elected to the U.S. Senate in 1966. He was fond of telling an anecdote about a white constituent who embodied this myopic worldview. It is worth repeating, in full:

A veteran returning from Korea went to college on the GI Bill, bought his house with an FHA loan, saw his kids born in a VA hospital, started a business with an SBA loan, got electricity from TVA and, later, water from an EPA project. His parents, living on Social Security, retired to a farm, got electricity from REA and had their soil tested by the USDA. When his father became ill, the family was saved from financial ruin by Medicare and a life was saved with a drug developed through NIH. His kids participated in the school lunch program, learned physics from teachers trained in an NSF program and went to college with guaranteed student loans. He drove to work on the Interstate and moored his boat in a channel dredged by Army engineers. When floods hit, he took Amtrak to Washington to apply for disaster relief and spent some time in the Smithsonian museums. Then one day he got mad. He wrote his Senator an angry letter—"Get the government off my back," he wrote. "I'm tired of paying taxes for all those programs created for ungrateful people!"[42]

In the search for a candidate who could both reinvigorate the party and defeat Reagan in 1984, Democrats faced a dilemma caused by their own diversities. Visions of a fairer economy might thrill African Americans, many Latinos and Latinas, and union members. But to raise taxes to realize those plans risked losing the support of whites in the South and in middle-class suburbs everywhere. Polls continued to show, as they had since the 1930s, that the most faithful Democrats were poorer Americans of all races. Yet they voted in lower numbers than Americans with comfortable incomes. With the decline of unions, no national institution existed that had the resources and commitment to reverse that trend.

As it happened, the race for the 1984 presidential nomination featured three major candidates, each of whom championed a political approach that undercut the others. Walter Mondale had been Hubert Humphrey's protégé before serving as vice president under a centrist Southerner. This profile enabled him to claim he could bridge the gap between old liberals and New Democrats by demonstrating an earnest desire to satisfy both sides. Gary Hart adhered, in spirit, to the vow he made a decade earlier that he and other Watergate babies were not going to become "a bunch of little Hubert Humphreys." The Colorado senator denounced organized labor as a "special interest" based in a declining manufacturing sector and championed high-tech industries as the drivers of future prosperity. Finally, Jesse Jackson campaigned as an unabashed critic of the party establishment. His "Rainbow Coalition" of outsiders of all races would, he predicted, turn the nation away from Reaganism through sheer "moral force."[43]

Mondale took the prize at the convention that summer, but only after a struggle that revealed how weak a candidate he would be in the fall. The AFL-CIO endorsed him late in 1983 and donated nearly half the funds he spent in his entire campaign. But that decision gave Hart the opportunity to bash him as an "old-fashioned" politician blowing on the ashes of the New Deal order. Actually, Mondale was careful not to propose any big, expensive new federal programs. But his record gained him the support of most Northern liberals and policy makers from past Democratic administrations, while the awkward, emotionless personality he displayed on television helped make Hart's case against him.

Jackson spent most of his campaign speaking to Black audiences in churches and urban arenas. Such lines as "Hands that once picked cotton will now pick a president" inspired listeners to believe, as James Baldwin wrote, that "nothing will ever again be what it was before . . . One is not entirely at the mercy of the assumptions of this Republic." But Jackson won just four primaries, all in the South. Still, Mondale had to acquiesce to the reverend's demands for appointments and a prime-time speech at the convention, lest he alienate his African American followers.[44]

The nominee did make one major decision that defied his image as a paragon of caution and conformity. He asked Geraldine Ferraro, a forty-nine-year-old congresswoman from New York City, to join him on the ticket. Mondale hoped the pick would delight feminists in the party, win over female voters, and signal a freshness to his campaign it did not otherwise embody. Yet, soon after the convention ended, Ferraro struggled to answer reporters' questions about her family finances, including about tax returns her husband, a real estate developer, refused to release. Even so, big crowds turned out around the country to hear the animated speeches of the first woman to have a chance to win so high an office. Mondale badly needed her help; he had drawn just 38 percent of the combined votes cast in the primaries and caucuses.

The consequence in November was a dreary repeat of McGovern's debacle a dozen years before. Mondale also won but a single state (his own) as well as the District of Columbia, and his share of the popular vote was just three points higher than the percentage the South Dakota senator had received. The energetic, cash-fueled work of the labor movement did win him a healthy majority of votes from union households, and having the first woman to run on a major-party ticket slightly widened the gender gap. Nine-tenths of African Americans cast a ballot for Mondale, and their turnout was five points higher than in 1980. If anything, Jackson's run had persuaded them that, for all its shortcomings, there was only one party in America that deserved their support. But twice as many whites voted for Reagan as for Mondale; except for union members, workers did so at the same rate as did their employers. If Democrats could not find a way to narrow that margin considerably, they would never win the presidency again.

---

Two months after the 1984 election, Stanley Greenberg, a political scientist turned pollster, traveled to a white working-class county just outside Detroit, with its Black majority, to learn why Reagan had carried it by a two-to-one margin. Macomb County, heavy with active and retired members of the United Auto Workers, had begun to shift toward the GOP in presidential years; Nixon had carried it easily in 1972. But since the New Deal, no Democrat had lost so decisively as Mondale, the nominee to whom organized labor had given its all.

After conducting a series of focus groups—a technique borrowed from market research—Greenberg reported that Macomb voters burned with racial fears and resentments. They fumed against affirmative action, school busing, and violent Black criminals they accused white liberals of coddling. "Blacks constitute the explanation for their vulnerability and for almost everything that has gone wrong in their lives," wrote Greenberg. "Not being Black is what constitutes being middle class; not living with Blacks is what makes a neighborhood a decent place to live." Few of these men and women agreed with Ronald Reagan that "big government" wielded too much power over their lives. They wanted their old party to address and solve *their* economic troubles instead of lavishing its concern, at least rhetorically, on the Black poor who lived just a few miles away.[45]

In the mid-1980s, one could find such "Reagan Democrats" in metropolitan areas across the North and West. They mounted resistance to court-ordered school busing in Boston and elsewhere. Democrats in Congress and state legislatures who demonstrated empathy with the white backlash usually retained their seats or were able to win new ones. Most who had national ambitions downplayed talk about racial justice and instead scolded liberals for turning the party into what Joe Biden, a young senator from Delaware, called "a fossilized shadow of its former self." That lawmaker had first been elected in 1972 as a critic of the Vietnam War and a champion of

Black demands. But midway through his first term, Biden turned against court-ordered busing and rejected the identity of "liberal" as an electoral liability. Don't be afraid, Biden advised fellow Democrats in the 1980s, "to alter housing programs" or even "the progress of civil rights" if you hope to govern the country again.[46]

This kind of strategic thinking animated the creation of the Democratic Leadership Council in 1985. Al From founded and directed the organization, yet it would never have mattered if he had not been able to convince Biden, Gary Hart, and a bevy of other New Democrats to lend it their names and influence. In the early years of the DLC, its most prominent members were Southern moderates like Charles Robb and Al Gore, then a first-term senator from Tennessee, and Arkansas governor Bill Clinton. They wanted to move the party rightward to keep it viable in their home region. But they also believed strongly that, as From recalled, "Democrats just were not going to win by trying to put the New Deal coalition back together . . . So you had to figure out a different way to do it. Essentially what I believed is that you had to reach out to the middle class." From didn't mention the racial complexion of that targeted class, nor did he need to.[47]

He did suggest that the true raison d'être of the DLC was to gain and hold power, employing ideas palatable to a mass constituency uneasy with all that the word "liberal" had come to mean. The group issued position papers favoring a balanced budget and the development of high-tech industries, but these were largely disposable means to an end. "Like it or not," From wrote later, "a political party is defined by its presidential candidate. So our philosophy and ideas had to pass the market test . . . A market test can only come in the presidential primaries, so we needed to find a candidate." The DLC was, he boasted, "an entrepreneurial enterprise," and like any successful developer of a new business, From needed to raise capital. By 1988, he had gotten hedge-fund manager Michael Steinhardt to fund its think tank with $500,000 a year and was busily recruiting trustees, each of whom would donate at least $100,000 to the cause.[48]

Of course, such well-heeled realpolitik angered critics on the left. Jesse Jackson jibed that DLC really meant "Democrats for the Leisure Class," while Arthur Schlesinger, Jr., bashed the council for "worshipping at the shrine of the free market." Ann Lewis, director of Americans for Democratic Action, criticized the DLC for telling "business-oriented audiences" what they wanted to hear. In response, several progressive unions financed Democratic Alternatives, a voice for full employment and pay equity for women. Michael Harrington, the socialist intellectual who helped launch the new group, accused the kind of politicians who joined the DLC of thinking that Democrats "can win only if they move well to the right of their own traditions and just a bit to the left of Ronald Reagan."[49]

Such protests could not conceal a sizable discrepancy of resources and status. Not since the 1920s, when DuPont executive John Raskob bankrolled the DNC he chaired, had party leaders been so friendly to big business and the wealthy. And the lawmakers that From gathered represented states in the South and West that Democrats could not ignore if they hoped to become the majority party again. In contrast, the only voters the left could count on belonged either to a declining labor movement bottled up in the Northeast and Upper Midwest or to inward-looking networks of cosmopolitan professionals, or lived in Black and brown neighborhoods without potent machines that could guarantee a massive turnout. A progressive white populist like Jim Hightower could, on occasion, win election in a state like Texas, where conservatives were gaining. As the agricultural commissioner there, Hightower tried his best to revive the New Deal gospel with reminders that most "Middle Americans" were not embracing right-wing economic policies. They were instead "antiestablishment malcontents" incensed that "too few people control all the money and power, leaving very little for the rest of us." But no left-wing populist movement existed to back up his words.[50]

Jesse Jackson resolved to build one when he ran again for president in 1988. This time, he reached out, with the same wit and fire, to audiences all over the country who had always disliked Reaganism or felt betrayed by its champions. "Jackson could frame the issues better than any of the candidates he was running against," remembered Harold M. Ickes, the veteran Democratic operative (and son of FDR's interior secretary) who joined his staff that year. "He was a terrific candidate who did a really good job of articulating the issues that I thought should be articulated." Jackson got a standing ovation at the Montana legislature; held a rally to protest the closing of an auto plant in Kenosha, Wisconsin; and was the sole candidate to attend a gay rights march in Washington, D.C. Jackson also hired professional consultants to help run his campaign and raised $26 million, the second-highest total of any contender.[51]

To deflect the racist sentiments coursing through places like Macomb County, he sought to "whiten" his message by slamming "economic violence" in the Rust Belt and promising single-payer health care, free community college, equal pay for women, and a vast plan to build affordable housing and mass transportation. It spelled the most ambitious platform for moral capitalism any major candidate had espoused since the heyday of the New Deal. The socialist mayor of Vermont's largest city, who had spurned all previous Democratic contenders, praised Jackson as "a man who has waged the most courageous and exciting political campaign in the modern history of our nation." Twenty-seven years later, as a Vermont senator, Bernie Sanders would launch his own insurgent run for the White House.[52]

Jackson's new strategy got him closer to the prize than in 1984. He won pluralities in thirteen states and nearly seven million popular votes. But when it seemed he might actually win enough delegates to take the nomination, most white Democrats—officeholders and ordinary voters alike—got cold feet. Robert Borosage reflected, "As long as people could vote for him as sending a message to Democrats [that] we support this kind of economic populism and moral voice, they were anxious to vote for him. But as soon as he got close to actually winning the nomination, . . . people just said, 'Whoa, we're never going to do *this*.'"[53]

The DLC countered Jackson's appeal by persuading Al Gore, one of its most prominent members, to join the contest. But, in a crowded field, the senator from Tennessee gained little support from anyone except his fellow white Southerners, while Jackson was sweeping Black voters across the region. So From and his band of New Democrats had to put their single-minded quest to the side until the next quadrennial cycle.

Michael Dukakis, the party's eventual nominee in 1988, represented a compromise of sorts between the old liberalism and the centrism advocated by the DLC and others in the party establishment who sought to put the New Deal behind them. As an army veteran and the son of Greek immigrants, the governor of Massachusetts could claim to be an exemplar of the success of the ethnically inclusive order and expansive federal state built by Democrats from FDR to LBJ. But in place of the visionary rhetoric of such figures, he came over like a longtime administrator ready to tackle a big job. "This election isn't about ideology; it's about competence," Dukakis claimed in his acceptance speech. "It's not about meaningless labels; it's about American values—old-fashioned values like accountability and responsibility and respect for the truth." In polls taken soon after the convention, that appeal to a comforting, if vague, spirit of unity after eight years of right-wing governance vaulted Dukakis to a seventeen-point lead over his GOP rival, Vice President George H. W. Bush.[54]

However, a viciously effective Republican campaign soon obliterated his advantage. Bush and his ad makers condemned Dukakis for being the kind of liberal most Americans had learned to mistrust—one defined by "social issues" like crime and patriotism instead of fighting for workers and small businesses against the economic elite. They hammered him for opposing capital punishment, for vetoing a requirement that teachers lead students in reciting the Pledge of Allegiance, and, most notoriously, for furloughing from prison a Black man named Willie Horton, who then fled the state and raped a white woman. In a race where neither candidate said or did anything much to inspire voters, "going negative" was a clever strategy. With about 46 percent of the popular vote, Dukakis won but ten states, most scattered along a line that ran from New England to the Pacific Northwest. Just over half of eligible Americans cared enough to vote, the lowest share since the GOP landslide of 1924. As usual, Democrats retained their majorities in Congress and most state legislatures. But how long would that streak go on if their presidential nominees continued to be such abysmal failures?

## The Center Holds . . . Then Stumbles

In the fall of 1989, the think tank of the DLC issued a crisply worded manifesto, stuffed with data, aimed at preventing the party from losing the White House once again. Democrats, accused the authors

of "The Politics of Evasion," had been ignoring "their fundamental problems" for "years after the collapse of the liberal majority and
the New Deal alignment." In unsparing prose, William Galston and
Elaine Ciulla Kamarck, political scientists who had toiled in Mondale's hapless 1984 campaign, described three "myths" their fellow
partisans were using to explain away three crushing losses in a row:
no nominee was a genuine liberal, the party simply failed to lure
enough Americans to the polls, and Democrats still held Congress, so
no true realignment was occurring. "How can the Democratic Party
recapture the center?" asked Galston and Kamarck. Only "a frank internal debate on political fundamentals" would do. Otherwise, "Republicans will be able to convince the electorate that the Democratic
Party of 1992 is the same as the Democratic Party of 1972."[55]

Bill Clinton's victory in the next presidential contest seemed to
prove that the centrists had been right all along. Although Clinton did not become chairman of the DLC until 1990, the erstwhile
McGovern staffer had been articulating the New Democrat creed
since first being elected governor of Arkansas a dozen years before, at
the age of just thirty-one. "Every issue in Washington was obscured
by ridiculous false choices," Clinton wrote two decades later, "economy or environment; business or labor; impoverished or entitled."
His campaign for the White House would be rooted in a determination to transcend such dichotomies. Clinton would "put stale partisan rhetoric aside" and replace it "with the ideas and policies that
actually mattered to our people." He was fortunate that a fatigued
Jesse Jackson declined to run for a third time, while vowing, some-
how, to challenge party leaders who staved off egalitarian policies the
country badly needed.[56]

Clinton's triumph in 1992 depended largely on the opposition's
stumbles and misfortunes. George H. W. Bush, the incumbent, had
to contend with a recession, a major riot in Los Angeles, and a revolt
by conservatives who accused him of being a traitor to the faith of
true Reaganism. To add to Bush's misfortune, Ross Perot, a billionaire from Texas, self-financed an independent ticket that slashed into
the GOP's white male base, taking nearly a fifth of the popular vote.
For all Clinton's personal charm and command of policy, both domestic and foreign, he took a mere 43 percent of the national tally, less

than the drab Dukakis had managed. Only in a single state, his own, did the Democrat eke out a majority. But in the first three-way contest since 1968, his pluralities netted him a healthy margin in the Electoral College. Even a retrograde liberal nominee might have won that year.[57]

Larger discontents that helped explain Bush's loss as much as Clinton's victory were roiling the nation, too. In the fall of 1991, the *Philadelphia Inquirer* devoted an unprecedented twenty-five pages to a series of articles by two reporters, Donald Barlett and James Steele, who detailed a long record of greed and malfeasance on the part of big business, the rich, and their enablers in government. Bristling with an arsenal of damning charts and individual tales of woe, their book that followed a year later, *America: What Went Wrong*, documented a widening gulf between millionaires and everyone else. Like the muckrakers of the Progressive Era, the journalists deployed chapter titles like "Dismantling the Middle Class," "The High Cost of Deregulation," and "Playing Russian Roulette with Health Insurance" to alarm readers about the dire condition of those parts of the economy that mattered most to ordinary people.[58]

The authors didn't stint on criticizing politicians from both parties. The policies they condemned had largely been enacted during the last two administrations, led by Republicans. But a good many Democrats in Congress had voted for them, too. During the 1992 race, Ross Perot showed off a copy of the book, as did Bill Clinton, whose advisers turned "It's the economy, stupid" into a key slogan of his campaign. The volume sat high on bestseller lists for most of the year.

Yet once he took office, Clinton made little attempt either to address what, according to the book's authors, had gone wrong or to carry out the kind of agenda promoted by Al From and his fellow New Democrats. "The Politics of Evasion" had struck a chord among politicians and campaign consultants, but liberals remained an essential pillar of the party, and no Democratic president could ignore their preferences for change. High on that list were inequalities of race and gender. So Clinton appointed a left-wing Black professor to a top position in the Justice Department (she failed to get Senate approval), sought to allow gay men and lesbians to serve openly in the military, and appointed Ruth Bader Ginsburg, the preeminent advocate of women's rights on the job, to the Supreme Court. He also gave his wife, Hillary Clinton, the task of leading a complete overhaul of the nation's byzantine health-care system so that every citizen would be covered by insurance.

By mid-April, the worried creator of the DLC dashed off a memo to his former protégé, now residing in the White House. Al From chided Clinton, "Something about the Administration is not quite right . . . Among many moderate and conservative Democrats there is a growing feeling that you're just not dancing with the ones who brought you to the dance." The flaw in such advice was that the liberal dancers—and their voters outside the South—outnumbered the centrist chaperones. The DLC had never explained how to convince the white middle-class to see a party still rooted among unionists and racial minorities as their own.[59]

Most of the policies Clinton decided to push did backfire, severely weakening his popular standing. Top officers in the military denounced his gay rights stand; Senator Sam Nunn, a DLC member who chaired the Armed Services Committee, complained it would cause "a great deal of discomfort to an awful lot of people who are heterosexual." The resulting compromise, known as "Don't Ask, Don't Tell," made neither side happy. Clinton managed to push the North American Free Trade Agreement through Congress, although most Democrats, fearing a loss of manufacturing jobs to Mexico, voted against it. But the president's ambitious health-care initiative failed quite utterly. The plan depended on an employer mandate and was too complex to craft into an appealing message. Business groups teamed up with conservatives to damn it as a "Soviet-style scheme to bring a seventh of the economy under government control." Neither house of Congress, firmly under Democratic control, even brought the plan up for a vote.[60]

That defeat did much to end the party's dominance over the legislative branch in spectacular fashion. Republicans achieved a victory in the 1994 midterm election that one scholar accurately called "a political earthquake that will send aftershocks rumbling through national politics for years to come." They gained fifty-four seats in the House to take the reins in that chamber for the first time since riding into power on Eisenhower's coattails in 1952. More than half the GOP victors took down a Democratic incumbent—including the

Speaker of the House, Thomas Foley—while not a single Republican congressperson was defeated. The party also captured a slim majority in the Senate, which Democrats had controlled for the previous eight years. For the first time since Reconstruction, the GOP could also claim a majority of the representatives and senators from the states of the former Confederacy. The breakup of the Solid South, which had begun midway through FDR's tenure, was now complete.[61]

The GOP credited the turnover in the House to an innovative campaign devised by Representative Newt Gingrich of Georgia, the conservative ideologue who became the new Speaker. That fall, some three hundred Republican candidates had signed the "Contract with America," which nationalized the contest, promising an "end of government that is too big, too intrusive, and too easy with the public's money" and "the beginning of a Congress that respects the values and shares the faith of the American family." But, according to pollsters, more than 70 percent of voters knew nothing about the vaunted contract at all. What they did know was that Democrats, the "party of government," had failed to show that a government they ran could act efficiently and transparently to begin to fix what had gone wrong in an economy that seemed to favor the rich and well-connected over everyone else. Their disenchantment was enough to tip many seats Democrats had been winning, narrowly, over to the opposition.[62]

A week or so after the 1994 election, a lunch group of progressive activists and pollsters I frequented met inside the Capitol with Richard Gephardt, a prominent Democratic congressman from St. Louis. The pro-labor politician had mounted a brief run for president in 1988, but he would soon be accepting a demotion from leader of the House majority to the same post with the minority. At his office that day, Gephardt candidly blamed the recent political earthquake on the Democrats' own failures, then left us with a breezy note of resignation to the party's fate: "Our surveys tell us that most Americans neither consume nor wish to consume politics." The metaphor seemed a fitting end to a quarter century of frustration and internal division. A top Democrat who could joke that the battle for state power was similar to a sales effort should not have been surprised when customers rejected a familiar brand whose developers had lost their feel for how the market had changed.[63]

# 9

## COSMOPOLITANS IN SEARCH OF
## A NEW MAJORITY,
## 1994–2020

*You know what? I don't think these boys know how to win.*
—REPRESENTATIVE NANCY PELOSI, ON FELLOW DEMOCRATIC
LEADERS AFTER THE 2000 ELECTION[1]

*We measure the strength of our economy not by
the number of billionaires we have or the profits of the
Fortune 500, but by whether someone with a good idea can
take a risk and start a new business, or whether the waitress who
lives on tips can take a day off and look after a sick kid without
losing her job, an economy that honors the dignity of work.*
—BARACK OBAMA, ACCEPTING THE DEMOCRATIC
NOMINATION FOR PRESIDENT, 2008[2]

*If Democrats are now seen serving the interests of the highly
educated rather than the disadvantaged it is above all because they
never came up with an appropriate response to the conservative
revolution of the 1980s.*
—THOMAS PIKETTY, ECONOMIST, 2020[3]

## A Tale of Two States

By the middle of the 1990s, the partisan complexion of nearly every
state in the nation had altered fundamentally since the Great Depression. Those in the Deep South had begun to favor GOP presidential

nominees almost as routinely as they had once backed Democratic ones. Most New England states, once known as "rock-ribbed Republican," veered in the opposite direction and usually chose Democrats to run their legislatures, too.

Yet both California and West Virginia resisted such changes, despite the stark contrasts in their sizes and regions. The population of the Golden State had mushroomed by 500 percent since the 1930s, and its voters continued to elect mostly Republican governors, while nearly always supporting whichever nominee of either party captured the presidency. The white suburbs of Orange County, south of Los Angeles, became a thriving locus of conservative activism. At the same time, the Mountain State, whose population had grown not at all over the ensuing years, remained staunchly Democratic at every level. The only Republicans who carried the state in their runs for the White House were three incumbents—Eisenhower, Nixon, and Reagan—as they swept to national landslides.

Then both states underwent rapid electoral upheavals. In the three-way contest of 1992, Bill Clinton took California but with just 46 percent of the popular vote. Every Democratic nominee has won the state handily since then; the party also consistently garnered the lion's share of California's seats in Congress and in both houses of the state legislature. Meanwhile, 2,500 miles to the east, although most West Virginians still registered as Democrats, they voted for George W. Bush in 2000 and then by ever-increasing margins for each of his Republican successors. Midway through the Obama administration, the GOP captured the state legislature, too.

These political shifts occurred in the context of galvanic economic and cultural transformations—which Democrats responded to well in one state and helplessly witnessed transpire in the other. Such divergent fortunes reflected, in stark fashion, the party's strengths and weaknesses in the nation as a whole.

Driving the long dominance of Democrats in West Virginia had been their bond with the United Mine Workers. In 1946, Harry Truman's administration helped the union establish a free health-care system for its members, paid for by a levy on each ton of coal produced. Both the state and national parties defended the plan against attempts by coal operators to cease subsidizing it. In the pages of

UMW publications and meetings in union halls, miners—some forty thousand of whom lived in the state by the 1960s—learned that Democrats were the party that stood for higher wages, protected the right to organize, and wanted to keep them healthy, even before the passage of Medicare and Medicaid. But as the century drew to a close, mechanization of the mines and the decline of the market for coal sliced the UMW in the state to half its former size. Mass unemployment spurred a rise in drug addiction and suicide. Without the union, working-class residents no longer had a place where they could complain about their lack of economic and medical security—at least not in a way that benefited Democrats. The West Virginians who gave Donald Trump close to 70 percent of their votes in 2016 and 2020 inhabited the second-poorest state in the nation, as well as one of the whitest.

In search of solace and guidance, many residents flocked to evangelical churches. In the pews, they learned that Republicans stalwartly defended "family values" and the right to life, while Democrats were a cabal of environmentalists who wanted to ban coal mining and conspired to substitute the false gospel of multiculturalism for the word of God.[4]

California underwent quite a different makeover during the same decade. The end of the Cold War at the start of the 1990s sped up what had been a slow-moving transition to an electorate in which people of color became the majority and environmentally "clean" high-tech industry soared while manufacturing and oil production declined. Huge aircraft plants in the southern part of the state that had depended on military contracts laid off tens of thousands of well-paid workers and engineers, nearly all of them white. They "had constituted, in the good years," recalled the writer Joan Didion, "a kind of family." Many left the state in search of jobs elsewhere in the West.[5]

This skilled, native-born, largely Republican-voting workforce was replaced, gradually but decisively, by Californians new to the state and often to the nation. Formerly white neighborhoods filled up with Mexican Americans, both immigrant and native-born. Families of East and South Asian backgrounds came in large numbers, established small businesses, and sent their children to public colleges and universities. Prominent Black politicians like assembly speaker and later San Francisco mayor Willie Brown and long-serving congress-woman Maxine Waters from Los Angeles were among the party's most visible and powerful leaders, even as the percentage of African Americans in the state's population shrank. In Silicon Valley, firms spawned by young entrepreneurs like Steve Jobs and Eric Schmidt hired college-educated men and women with countercultural tastes who created products that quickly became indispensable around the world. In 1992, Bill Clinton and Al Gore wowed high-tech moguls with their knowledge of the industry and flattered them as prophets of the economic future. Since then, the Valley, once a GOP mainstay, has favored Democrats up and down the ballot. By the end of the twentieth century, whites had shrunk to a minority in California—and the two largest centers of population, Los Angeles County and the San Francisco Bay Area, had become bastions of multiethnic lib-eralism with a modernist flair.

California Democrats exploited these trends to build a new coali-tion that soon became the prevailing force in state politics. In 1994, they came out against a proposition, pushed hard by Republican governor Pete Wilson, that would have barred undocumented im-migrants from using nearly any state service—including the public schools. Proposition 187 passed easily; only in the Bay Area did most voters oppose it. But a federal judge soon struck it down for usurping federal law. And Prop 187 provoked a furious backlash by Latino voters who took out their hostility in the following years on nearly every Republican running for state or federal office. Labor activists from Mexican American communities used that passion for equity and respect to organize service workers in L.A. and elsewhere in the southern part of the state, where unions had historically languished. Their growing movement soon became nearly as vital to the success of Democratic candidates locally and statewide as the United Mine Workers had once been in West Virginia.

While party officials in California were harvesting the votes of this freshly organized segment of the working class, they also took care to express their ongoing solidarity with movements of femi-nists, gays, and lesbians who demanded the same rights that heterosexual men took for granted. In the 1970s, Democratic clubs named after such LGBT icons as Alice B. Toklas and Harvey Milk were founded in San Francisco and Los Angeles. Twenty years later, they had become institutions able to raise sizable sums and canvass for Democrats up and down the ballot.

By the early twenty-first century, the only regions of California where Republicans could still count on winning were the Central Valley, where agribusiness was king, and the lightly populated counties along the Sierra Nevada. Democrats governed nearly every city and most suburbs up and down the cosmopolitan coast—the only California most Americans knew. With large donations flowing regularly into their coffers from Hollywood and Silicon Valley, party leaders were confident they could keep the GOP at bay.

Democrats in the Golden State hoped the nation's electorate would soon head down the same path. Everywhere, swelling numbers of Black and brown working people and liberal professionals of all races would give the party an enduring majority again. Knowing the population of Latinos and Latinas had tripled in the United States since 1970 boosted their hopes. So did the growth of urban areas across the nation that tilted more decisively to Democrats in nearly every election. Surely, beamed party officials, America's evolving demography would become its political destiny.[6]

But white people without a college education remained the majority of voters in the country. And except for union members—whose numbers kept falling—most white working-class people in West Virginia and elsewhere were casting their ballots for the GOP, at least for president and, increasingly, for other offices, too. No Democratic candidate for the White House had won more than half the white vote since Johnson's landslide in 1964; only Jimmy Carter in 1976 drew as much as 40 percent of it.

As the gap between the wealthiest citizens—of both parties—and everyone else kept expanding, white working people increasingly abandoned whatever faith they had that politicians of any stripe either wanted or knew how to protect or provide good, secure jobs at decent wages. But the party led by cosmopolitan whites who largely hailed from the East or West Coast and sided, at least rhetorically,

with African Americans and recent immigrants had the more difficult task of winning back their trust.

How to regain it and construct a new governing coalition posed a
painful dilemma for national Democratic leaders, if not for their California contingent. If they made fewer promises to victims of racism
and xenophobia, they would betray their most loyal voters for uncer-
tain gain. Yet to bet their future on an emerging majority composed
mainly of people of color and educated liberals might lose elections in
the present—as well as alienate unions, the only civic institution that,
even in decline, represented millions of ordinary Americans across
racial lines. As Republicans increasingly returned to their nativist
roots, Democrats also confronted the need to defend recent immigrants, most of whom, unlike the Latinos and Latinas who helped
turn California blue, were not citizens and so could not vote.

At the turn of the twenty-first century, most Americans were not
ready to embrace the ethnocultural mélange of metropolitan California celebrated by well-educated people with professional occupations. Nor did they hanker to return to the carboniferous heyday of
states like West Virginia—dominated by whites who had little hope
for a sustained economic comeback. Democrats had no guarantee
that an effort to reconcile the new with the old America would make
them the dominant force in national politics again. Still, they had
no alternative but to try. It would take a Great Recession to produce
a vigorous set of left-wing movements that spawned a generation of
Democratic candidates who thought they had the clue to forging a
new partisan majority: mobilize working people of all races and national backgrounds behind a vision of a generous welfare state that
would also preserve the health of the planet.[7]

If biography ruled politics, the sole Democrat to hold a major leadership position through the first two decades of the twenty-first century should have offered a fruitful way to bridge or at least narrow
the nation's yawning social divide. Born in 1940, Nancy Pelosi grew

up in a world of white, churchgoing, working-class people—although her people in Baltimore, unlike most West Virginians, were Catholic not Protestant. But she made her career in San Francisco, representing perhaps the most culturally liberal and secular congressional district in America. With the rise of cybercapitalism in the 1990s, it also became one of the richest. Pelosi moved to the city in 1969, for her husband's career. She raised five children there while hosting multiple fund-raisers at their spacious home near the Golden Gate Bridge. In 1987, she won her first political race—for a safe seat in the House of Representatives. On her first day at the Capitol, just eleven other female Democrats were serving along with her. Pelosi's steadfast backing of LGBT and abortion rights and, later, her outspoken opposition to the U.S. invasion of Iraq aligned perfectly with the views of her district.

Pelosi rose steadily through the party hierarchy—from whip to minority leader—and, in 2007, became the first female Speaker in history. In that crowning election, she could count on the backing of *fifty-one* Democrats of her gender. Although the GOP took back the House four years later, the number of congresswomen from Pelosi's party kept growing. When she took possession of the Speaker's gavel again in 2019, *eighty-seven* other female Democrats had a chance to vote for her. By then, the partisan gender gap that had first opened up in the 1970s had widened to nearly 20 percent—and was critical to recapturing the House majority.

That four female Democrats did not vote for Pelosi in 2019 suggests the wisdom of Hegel's observation that increases in quantity lead to changes in quality. As the number of Democratic congresswomen expanded (while that in the GOP did not), some inevitably came to represent constituents who cringed at what one Republican operative called Pelosi's "San Francisco liberal values . . . completely removed from reality." Three of the four female Democrats who voted for someone else for Speaker in 2019 had just won close contests against GOP incumbents; during their campaigns, all vowed, if elected, not to vote for the leader of their own party.[8]

But Pelosi celebrated their victories anyway and did not take offense, at least publicly, at their refusal to support her. She may even have admired it. Ideological ardor, for her, always paled in comparison to doing what she deemed necessary to win power and hold it. Married to a wealthy investor, she was comfortable raising large donations for Democrats of any persuasion and worked harder and more successfully at that unloved task than did any of her colleagues. During the 2002 election cycle, Pelosi spent long days and nights on the road raising more than $7 million for House candidates and created two PACs of her own. Later, as Speaker of the House, she attended hundreds of events with potential donors every year. Between 2018 and 2020, she raised more than $225 million. When a staff member questioned her exhausting pace, the tireless senior citizen responded, "I don't do downtime."[9]

As a party builder, Pelosi cared less about whether a candidate agreed with her on any particular issue than whether she or he was a good fit for the district. "Pelosi doesn't begin by asking what kind of world we want," wrote the columnist Michelle Goldberg in 2020. "She asks where the votes are."[10]

Partisan pragmatism was a family tradition. Pelosi's father, Thomas D'Alesandro, Jr., was a high school dropout whose Italian heritage and New Deal politics won him five straight elections to Congress from Baltimore. "Tommy D" then served twelve years as mayor of what was a city of unionized factories and shipping firms that employed thousands of his fellow Catholics. His official accomplishments included luring a major league baseball team (which became the Orioles) to his city and establishing the Colts as Baltimore's franchise in the National Football League. Fidelity to the party of Roosevelt and Truman, bolstered by a network of some thirty local blue-collar clubs, dovetailed with attendance at the parish church.[11]

Pelosi's mother and namesake—Annunziata, known as "Big Nancy"—spent most of her days performing the kind of essential, unglamorous work to which most political women were restricted in the years before the feminist upsurge of the 1960s and '70s. At election time, Big Nancy oversaw precinct walkers and, according to her daughter's biographer, always "knew whom to call at the Housing Authority, the public hospital, or the county courthouse" for a voter who needed help. She regarded nearly every Republican as her enemy. In 1984, Big Nancy angrily rebuffed one of Ronald Reagan's staff members, who wanted her husband, long retired from politics by then, to appear with the president at an event in Baltimore. "After what he has done to poor people," she snapped, referring to Reagan, "he should not come near our house." After hanging up the phone, D'Alesandro plastered her windows with posters for Walter Mondale.[12]

"I told them this woman had vision and political skills that nobody else in Congress had," Representative John Murtha bragged about Nancy Pelosi when she became Speaker in 2007. "Don't think she's from San Francisco. She's from Baltimore." It was a flattering remark by a former marine who had represented a working-class district in Pennsylvania for thirty-five years—and whose friendship and backing Pelosi had assiduously courted. But when he said it, the white ethnic Baltimore of her youth had long since given way to a city split between poor Black residents and well-off professionals, most of them white. In the late 1960s, Thomas D'Alesandro III, Nancy's older brother, had served just a single term as mayor during a time of fierce racial conflict. He handled it so badly that he decided against running again.

When his sister first took the Speaker's gavel, the impression of Baltimore that most Americans had—if they thought about the place at all—probably came from the popular HBO series *The Wire*: a metropolis rife with menace on the streets and corruption in the police force, city hall, the longshore union, and the daily newspaper. Nancy Pelosi had made her career in the upscale, gentrifying metropoles of San Francisco and Washington, D.C. She liked to visit her old hometown, still reliably governed by Democrats, now mostly Black ones. But she devoted most of her attention to winning congressional seats in outer suburbs and small towns where sympathy for the problems of big cities ran thin.[13]

## Playing It Safe

During Pelosi's first terms in Congress, few Democratic leaders questioned the need to tack to the center to win over the prized white middle-class voters who could, they believed, make them the majority party once again. After the debacle of the 1994 midterm, Bill Clinton adopted that strategy—to win reelection and nudge the party toward embracing the business-friendly outlook of the Democratic Leadership Council—but without alienating his base among urbane liberals. In his 1995 State of the Union Address, the president seemed to embrace the conventional Beltway wisdom that the conservatives who had just taken command in Congress had also won the battle to shape public opinion. "The era of big government is over," Clinton declared. He called for "balancing the budget in a way that is fair to all Americans," a goal he said enjoyed "broad bipartisan agreement." Democrats, it appeared, would no longer abide by the Keynesian theory that budget deficits were fine as long as spending created jobs and lifted Americans out of poverty. The next year, Clinton signed a "welfare reform" bill that cut back payments to single mothers in need. By 1998, tax receipts from an economic boom had indeed made it possible for the government to balance the budget for the first time in almost three decades.

Before the president left office, he also signed the repeal of the Glass-Steagall Act, passed during the Great Depression, which had prohibited commercial banks from investing the money of their depositors on stock speculation and other risky financial ventures. The party once known for fighting for the interests of wage earners and small farmers against big business now seemed intent on rolling back nearly any regulations that made CEOs unhappy.[14]

Yet Clinton was too clever a politician to turn away from those positions dearest to his party's progressive base. While implementing neoliberal ideas about the economy, he also made a number of decisions that liberals in his party could cheer. He signed legislation— from the Family and Medical Leave Act, a higher minimum wage, and an expansion of the Earned Income Tax Credit to a doubling of federal funding for childcare—that benefited Americans with few resources and little control over their working lives. As the progressive congressman Barney Frank later wrote about Clinton and his fellow New Democrats, "Their plan was to accommodate anti-government sentiment in general while attempting to increase government in the particular."[15]

The president also appointed hundreds of liberal judges (many Black or Latino) and his two choices for the Supreme Court, Ruth Bader Ginsburg and Stephen Breyer, were stalwart defenders of abortion rights. For top posts at the Environmental Protection Agency and the National Labor Relations Board, Clinton picked officials who actually cared about protecting the environment and the rights of workers. On the other hand, he expended little effort helping organized labor regain some of its lost numbers and clout. The needs of the party's institutional bulwark thus lost out again to the pressure of corporate lobbyists. Unlike Jimmy Carter, Clinton at least had the excuse that he had to govern with a Congress led by Republicans like Newt Gingrich who would have been happier if unions did not exist at all.

In the end, Clinton's main political accomplishment was a defensive one. He won reelection easily in 1996 and thus stalled the growth of the right. Since the late 1960s, conservatives had feasted on an image of liberals as arrogant, effete, and out of touch with the problems of ordinary Americans. Clinton—with his campaign bus tours, his empathy for voters "in pain," and his praise of Americans "who work hard and play by the rules"—helped make at least a mild brand of social reformism palatable again to whites who had grown wary of the image of the party as a bastion of cosmopolitans and ghetto dwellers. His sponsorship of a crime bill that increased the number of police and boosted the incarceration of African Americans was intended to assuage their fears, although the Congressional Black Caucus backed it, too. That Clinton's second term was marked by an unemployment rate under 4 percent, coupled with low inflation and lower crime rates, further brightened the public's mood.

For such an astute politician, advocating a robust vision of moral capitalism and programs to embody it would have required a robust progressive insurgency. But those movements on the left that did exist in the second half of the 1990s were just beginning to awaken from a long spell of insularity and division. Black and Hispanic activists lacked a common agenda, and most spent their energies defending affirmative action and/or immigrant rights against right-wing attacks like that in California. Organized labor was a demoralized movement until John Sweeney of the Service Employees International Union became president of the AFL-CIO at the end of 1995, and it took the rest of the decade for him and his allies to persuade even a minority of unions to devote sizable resources to organizing new members. There was, to be sure, no shortage of liberal and radical intellectuals in the universities. But many humanists and social scientists mistook an enthusiasm for postmodern discourse theories for political insight and wrote prose only an insomniac could appreciate. The fifty thousand demonstrators who occupied the streets of Seattle in the fall of 1999 to shut down a meeting of the World Trade Organization were able to unite environmentalists and labor groups behind a shared contempt for a system that seemed to cherish no value but the bottom line. But this infant campaign for global justice failed to mature into a sustainable one.

One evening in 1996, I happened to be playing poker, badly, with a small group that included George Stephanopoulos, then one of Clinton's top aides and no friend of the DLC wing of the party. I asked him what might persuade the president to adopt more left-wing stands on economic issues. "I *wish* we had a left to push us," he replied. The conversation took place before the president's affair with Monica Lewinsky blew up the media. Besides stamping Clinton as a sexual idiot and getting him impeached, the scandal prevented the president from advancing any substantial initiatives during what remained of his second term.

Politics is fundamentally a contest between social forces, and through the Clinton years, the American left possessed neither the ideas nor the numbers to have much influence in or on the Democratic Party. Industrial labor had played that role during FDR's dozen years in power, and the Black freedom movement repeated it in the 1960s, until LBJ's escalation of the war reduced his administration to ashes.

Absent such pressure, it's not surprising that Clinton was most vocal about cultural issues that didn't directly challenge big corporations, the most powerful interests in the land. He could speak eloquently about "racial healing" and denounce gay bashing and other blatant forms of bigotry without incurring the wrath of K Street lobbyists. Such stances did help diminish the nastiness built up over the

1970s and '80s and made diversity seem an increasingly legitimate (if occasionally banal) goal of institutions, both public and private.

But to grapple seriously with the wage gap and hardcore poverty in the inner cities would have required some redistribution of wealth. To spotlight such issues in the absence of a grassroots movement and with Congress in the grip of the GOP would have taken a president willing to lose a battle that might set the stage for a later victory. Unfortunately, that is a trait few leaders of any major party have ever possessed. So Clinton used the boom of the late 1990s to put his Republican opponents on the defensive rather than to chart a humane future either for the nation or the world.[16]

During the first five years of the next presidency, a continuation of that modest, if vital, feat was all but out of the question. For Democrats, the drawn-out contest in 2000, which the conservative majority on the Supreme Court finally awarded to George W. Bush a month after Election Day, spelled an infuriating end to a frustrating race. Vice President Al Gore trudged through a campaign that pleased neither his friends in the DLC nor the liberals who had stuck by Clinton throughout his impeachment ordeal. Declaring, on occasion, that he would fight for "the people vs. the powerful," Gore strained to appeal to the party's anti-corporate tradition, disappointing New Democrats like Al From who had nurtured his career. The vice president also bewildered his pollsters by saying little about the prosperous macroeconomy. Gore's selection of Senator Joseph Lieberman, a fellow DLC stalwart, as his running mate and his reluctance to infuse his populist talk with any policies to back it up left progressives believing that if he won, Gore would be another Clinton—but without the charisma.

His drab and cloudy image helped boost the Green Party candidacy of Ralph Nader, the veteran consumer and environmental activist who vigorously attacked both parties for selling out to wealthy interests. Nader's endorsements from several progressive unions and celebrities like the comedian Bill Murray and the singer Bonnie Raitt helped him gain the admiration of left-wing college students. He won more than enough votes in Florida to throw the result in that state—and thus the nation—into doubt and turmoil.[17]

Still, after the election finally ended, Democrats had good reason to think the Republicans' return to executive power might not only be short-lived but also do little to slow their own party's emerging demographic advantage. In spite of his flaws, Gore had drawn upward of 2.5 million more popular votes than Clinton in 1996 and had consolidated his party's majorities in California and across most of the Northeast and Upper Midwest. Then, in the spring of 2001, Democrats took back control of the Senate after Jim Jeffords, a Republican senator from Vermont, announced he would caucus with the opposition party because the GOP had become more conservative than he was. That fall, a massive scandal engulfed the Houston-based Enron Corporation, a giant energy firm whose donations had done much to fuel George W. Bush's political career. The company's top executives got indicted for a plethora of financial crimes, and a planned congressional investigation would likely have driven the president's approval rating well below 50 percent.[18]

The horrific attacks of September 11 immediately dashed the Democrats' hopes and made the top Republican in the land all but invulnerable to partisan sniping. War returned to a central role in politics for the first time since the last U.S. combat troops had pulled out of Vietnam more than thirty years before. In the 2002 midterms, Republicans wrested back control of the Senate and padded their House majority by eight seats. Through the next presidential election, every Democratic politician and party official faced a choice of whether to downplay his or her misgivings about the invasions of Afghanistan and Iraq or risk being vilified as "soft on terrorism."

Liberals who, in the aftermath of the Cold War, had been arguing strenuously for shifting funds from the military to domestic needs now worried about seeming insufficiently grateful for the service of the troops in the Middle East and back home. John Kerry had burst into prominence in the early 1970s as the articulate leader of a group of Vietnam veterans who opposed a war he compared to the bloody conquest of Native Americans. In his 1971 testimony to the Senate Foreign Relations Committee, he imagined a future scenario:

"When thirty years from now our brothers go down the street without a leg, without an arm, or a face, and small boys ask why, we will be able to say 'Vietnam' and not mean a desert, not a filthy obscene memory, but mean instead where America finally turned and where soldiers like us helped it in the turning."[19]

However, Senator John Kerry began his acceptance speech at the 2004 Democratic Convention by snapping off a military salute and announcing he was "reporting for duty." The nominee then lauded his father's service as a pilot in World War II and a diplomat in Cold War Berlin before making a promise: "I will wage this war [on terror] with the lessons I learned in war"—including being candid about the intelligence used to justify it. None of this prevented the pro-Bush Swift Boat Veterans for Truth from producing slick TV ads harshly critical of his combat experience that helped defeat him that fall.[20]

While Kerry and other Democrats stuck to a cautious defense, party officials were building a well-funded, tech-savvy organization that might enable them to be more aggressive in future campaigns. To serve that end, the historic foes of Wall Street followed the example of the DLC and raised large sums from major securities and investment firms like JPMorgan Chase and Citibank. As chair of the national committee from 2001 to 2005, Terry McAuliffe—a perpetually excited protégé of the Clintons—outfitted the national party with an up-to-date computer network and email list and vowed to match or beat the level of contributions raised by his counterparts in the GOP. He also convinced unions to keep doing their part. But without the millions donated by such Hollywood producers as Haim Saban and Harvey Weinstein as well as from Wall Street, McAuliffe would have been unable to crow that "for the first time in modern history," Democrats had outraised Republicans.[21]

That unique cash advantage was the only element of partisan infrastructure the DNC chair could boast about. Since the 1970s, conservatives loyal to the party of Reagan and Gingrich had been building a formidable network of institutions to develop their ideas, recruit talented people to advance them, and ensure a steady flow of money to political figures who could turn them into law. The right had think tanks like the American Enterprise Institute and the Heritage Foundation; the Federalist Society, which nurtured future judges; and the American Legislative Exchange Council, which drafted model bills for state officeholders who aspired to weaken unions, environmental protection, and abortion rights. In 2005, Roger Ailes, a media adviser to the GOP since Nixon's 1968 campaign, took the helm at Fox Television and turned its cable channel into an unofficial and quite popular cheerleader for the party. Republican candidates who hewed to the conservative gospel also could depend on ample donations from the brothers Charles and David Koch, Las Vegas magnate Sheldon Adelson, and their billionaire ilk. They saw financing the GOP as an investment, and businesses on the right were far more likely than their Democratic counterparts to spend their money wisely—enhancing the party organization itself instead of just donating to individual candidates who might lose their races.[22]

Some Democrats did try to redress the structural imbalance. In 1995, a group of liberal lawyers founded the American Constitution Society as a foil to the Federalist Society. In 2002, several veterans of the Clinton administration launched the Center for American Progress (CAP) to supply their party with the type of intellectual and agitational resources that the Heritage Foundation and the AEI gave to theirs (notwithstanding CAP's claim to be "an independent nonpartisan policy institute"). In addition, advocacy groups for progressive causes such as the NAACP, the Sierra Club, EMILY's List, and the Human Rights Campaign funneled their donations almost exclusively to Democrats. But these fragmented efforts articulated no common vision or policy agenda for the party as a whole. During a period of economic growth whose benefits went disproportionately to the rich, Democrats had nothing to offer the average family whose income did not increase at all. The consequence, as had been true since the downfall of the Great Society, was that it was easier to say what most Democrats opposed than what they stood for.[23]

For the midterm election of 2006, playing it safe was enough. George W. Bush had transformed himself from a strong-willed commander in a righteous conflict into the mismanager of two stalemated wars in the Mideast, as well as a fumbler of vital aid to the residents of New Orleans, most of them Black, whose city was devastated by flooding in the wake of Hurricane Katrina. In 2005, the president had also floated the idea of turning Social Security into a private program, a notion that quickly sank under the weight of mass outrage both inside and outside the Washington Beltway.

So in 2006, Democrats essentially asked Americans to do no more than reject Bush's record of incompetence. Nancy Pelosi employed her political savvy and fund-raising prowess to claw back a House majority for a party whose message was designed to alienate as few voters as possible. Together with Harry Reid, the minority leader of the Senate, she concocted a six-point platform that inoffensively called for "Real Security at Home and Overseas," "Affordable Health Care," and "Honest Leadership and Open Government." Unlike with the GOP's Contract with America a dozen years earlier, Democratic leaders did not insist that candidates run on its promises. "They have made a conscious decision to focus on Republican weakness, and it may turn out to be the right decision," commented GOP strategist Frank Luntz. "But it means nobody knows what they're going to do."[24]

To manage the campaign, the leaders appointed Senator Chuck Schumer of New York and Congressman Rahm Emanuel from Chicago—who seldom let progressive ideals get in the way of their hunger for personal and partisan success. Emanuel, who had served in the Clinton White House, fashioned an image of himself as a free-cursing "Rahmbo" who scoffed at the "liberal theology" he claimed had driven his party to defeat in the past. When possible, he recruited military veterans with moderate views to flip Republican-held seats and used his connections in the financial world to help them raise the necessary cash. As a Harvard undergraduate, Schumer had campaigned for Eugene McCarthy in 1968. But in Congress he avoided siding with left-wing causes and voted, along with a slim majority of his Democratic colleagues, to authorize the 2003 invasion of Iraq. The senator also did legislative favors for Wall Street investment firms that furnished him with ample campaign funds in return.[25]

Midterm voters during a president's second term usually turn against the incumbent's party, but the result in 2006 was better than most Democrats had expected. Their party recaptured narrow control of both houses of Congress, as well as a majority of executive offices in states across the nation. Capitalizing on the failed governance of a party that did not believe in a strong government (except for national security) restored majorities that Democrats had once taken for granted. How they intended to use that power while keeping intact a broad coalition led by coastal cosmopolitans was a different matter entirely.

## A Rebellion of Unrealized Expectations

During the following decade, that decision increasingly became one Democratic insiders would not be able to make on their own. With mounting size and strength, an insurgency on the left set forth an ambitious array of policies and inspired candidates to defy the centrist logic that had reigned supreme in the party since the end of the 1980s. On the campaign trail, to have opposed the invasion of Iraq from the beginning (as did Barack Obama) turned from a liability into a badge of wisdom. Democratic activists young and old sympathized with movements that called for racial justice, same-sex marriage, a doubling of the national minimum wage, and rights for undocumented immigrants. "Economic equality," a new term for a vision as old as the party itself, quickly became a demand shared by activists in all those movements, although it was a priority only for some. Senator Bernie Sanders, an avowed socialist long dismissed by the mass media and the leaders of a party he caucused with but did not join, won millions of votes in two competitive races for the Democratic nomination. By 2020, the combined effort of these movements had nudged the policies of the party further to the left than at any time since George McGovern's campaign raised and dashed progressive hopes almost fifty years earlier.

Popular insurgencies had moved Democrats in analogous ways before. In the 1890s, the Populists did much to fuel William Jennings Bryan's dozen years of party leadership. The uprising of labor in the 1930s was essential to the making of a new majority party. And the Black freedom movement gradually convinced national Democrats to abandon their racist traditions, although that meant losing most white Southerners, their most reliable voting bloc. Unlike those lefts, the one that emerged in the early twenty-first century shared no unified identity, constituency, or set of demands. But its activists and favorite officeholders did share something vital with their ideological progenitors: a persistent animus toward big business and its political enablers, along with a determination to gain rights and power for ordinary working Americans, however defined.

The desire for a moral capitalism that would both emulate and transcend that championed by the makers of the New Deal and the Great Society did not immediately transform the leadership of the party at either the state or national level. Most tribunes of the Democratic left continued to emerge from the same well-educated, culturally modernist milieu that had spawned ADA, the McGovern campaign, and Jesse Jackson's Rainbow Coalition. But by the end of the Obama administration, it was they and not their centrist adversaries who were largely calling the party's ideological tune. In 2011, the Democratic Leadership Council, that well-funded entrepreneurial body Bill Clinton had once chaired, declared bankruptcy and promptly went out of business.

What made this reversal of fortunes possible was the shock and mass pain caused by the Great Recession. Progressives had been constructing popular websites, holding Netroots conferences, and staffing campaigns for like-minded candidates since the late 1990s. They shared the conviction of Minnesota senator Paul Wellstone—"I represent the Democratic wing of the Democratic Party." (A former college professor and state chair of Jesse Jackson's final campaign, Wellstone died in a plane crash in 2002.) But the collapse of the American financial system in the fall of 2008, which quickly rippled around the globe, won countless new converts to the old, still sturdy, hostility to banks and investment houses that manipulated other people's money to make big profits and ended up wrecking the lives of millions.[26]

Ironically, the Democrat who took best advantage of this crisis rarely echoed the populist rage about the economic calamity that animated his party's new left. Before he became a politician, Barack Obama had shared that class-aware, moral perspective and sought ways to implement it both in theory and in practice. He worked as a community organizer in parts of Chicago wracked by the loss of good jobs. In 1991, he co-wrote a manuscript with his friend Bob

Fisher arguing that the party could win back a majority by espousing universal programs that delivered "long-term, structural change, change that might break the zero-sum equation that pits powerless Blacks [against] only slightly less powerless whites." But in 2004, while running for the U.S. Senate, Obama introduced himself to a national audience with a keynote speech at the Democratic National Convention that warned "those who are preparing to divide us, the spin masters, the negative ad peddlers" that "there is not a liberal America and a conservative America—there is the United States of America." He spoke with soothing elegance for a revival of patriotic bipartisanship without suggesting what that unity of feeling might accomplish in the unlikely event that it actually occurred.[27]

In 2008, most liberals in his party, and even leftists outside it, put aside any doubts they had about his potential to shake up the · nation for good. On election night, Bob Dylan happened to be giving a concert in Minneapolis, the city where he began his career half a century earlier singing at a radical coffeehouse. "I was born in 1941," Dylan told the audience in his sandpapery voice. "That was the year they bombed Pearl Harbor. I've been living in darkness ever since. It looks like things are going to change now."[28]

Most of his fellow Americans on the broad left could second that emotion. Nearly seventy million voters had just chosen an eloquent, hip, youngish man of biracial parentage with a background as an anti-apartheid activist, community organizer, and opponent of the Iraq war to govern their country. Not since FDR's race in 1936 had a Democratic nominee united such an avid progressive coalition behind a victorious campaign. That the first African American president belonged to a party that, for most of its history, had explicitly preached and practiced white supremacy graced Obama's win with a spirit of redemption. Outside the South, he even won a majority of the white vote.

Of course, most Black Americans greeted Obama's election as a day of jubilee. On the night of his victory, I was a guest commentator on an African American radio station broadcasting from a suburb of Washington, D.C. On the same show was a conservative Black pundit who had just voted for John McCain. But as the decisive states were tallied, he began to tear up, with relief and perhaps joy. "I am so happy to be with my brothers tonight," he confessed. "This just might be the best moment of my mother's whole life." Just before Inauguration Day, Congressman John Lewis, an icon of the Black freedom movement, exulted, "Barack Obama is what comes at the end of that bridge in Selma."[29]

I fully shared their enthusiasm. In the fall of 2006, I wrote a rave review of *The Audacity of Hope*, Obama's book-length teaser for the campaign to come. Just before the first primaries, I helped organize a group called Historians for Obama. Our statement of support declared "our country is in serious trouble" and listed multiple reasons—from the wealth gap and the lack of national health insurance, to global warming and an "inept and arrogant" foreign policy. To us, Obama was clearly "the candidate best able to address and start to solve these profound problems." As cosmopolitan academics, our zeal was certainly enhanced by knowing that, if elected, Obama would not only be the first Black president; he would also be the first one with two parents who had earned graduate degrees and, like their son, pursued professional and politically conscious careers. That this man might launch another New Deal, this time a firmly anti-racist one, was an audacious hope indeed.[30]

That it did not come to pass was due both to Obama's flaws as a politician and to the resistance he had to overcome. On the one hand, this exponent of bridging partisan divisions believed too much in his ability to win over Republican officeholders and too little in their ideological desire and electoral need to humble and defeat him and his party. "We are about to find out," a shrewd Democratic activist commented privately soon after Obama took office, "whether this country can be governed by consensus."[31]

The new president compounded a naïve faith in his powers of persuasion with a failure to rally popular support behind the initiatives he and the Democratic Congress took to restore prosperity. During his first year in office, as unemployment climbed to 10 percent and housing foreclosures kept rising, the president spent little time explaining to hard-pressed Americans how the massive Recovery Act and rescues of the big auto companies he signed were helping them.

That reluctance contrasted sharply with the behavior of his New

Deal predecessor. Franklin D. Roosevelt delivered his first Fireside Chat on the radio just eight days after he took office in 1933. That straightforward, reassuring message about why he had declared a bank holiday elicited thousands of grateful letters. A young mother named Myra King Whitson wrote from Houston, "Our radio seemed to bring you to us in person—there is a deep happiness—a feeling that we have a real share in our government, and that our government is making our welfare its chief concern." FDR made such chats a hallmark of his long tenure, and he and his wife, Eleanor, also regularly left Washington to speak with hard-luck farmers and workers.[32]

During his 2008 campaign, Obama did shower voters with eloquent empathy. On election night, he declared, "If this financial crisis taught us anything, it's that we cannot have a thriving Wall Street while Main Street suffers." But, during his first term, he immersed himself in designing policies that could pass Congress and generally refrained from attacking either the bankers who had caused the crisis or the Republicans who had let them do it. "He posed as a progressive and turned out to be counterfeit," charged Cornel West, perhaps the president's most prominent Black critic. "We ended up with a Wall Street presidency . . . He's just another neoliberal centrist with a smile and a nice rhetorical flair."[33]

Yet Obama's left-wing detractors also ignored obstacles that would have confronted any serious reformer who moved into the White House near the start of an economic crisis severe enough to be compared to the Great Depression. "Black Man Given Nation's Worst Job," quipped *The Onion* a day after the election. When FDR took office more than three years following the stock market crash, no one blamed him for the millions of unemployed or the thousands of banks in danger of collapsing. Obama had to weather the inevitable decline of the economy and so reaped less credit from the slow recovery that followed. If Roosevelt had been elected in, say, 1930, he surely would have struggled mightily to enact the programs that became keystones of the modern liberal state.

Neither should one dismiss the reforms that Obama and Congress did manage to pass when Democrats held a majority in Congress during the first two years of his administration. The economic stimulus plan, the Affordable Care Act ("Obamacare"), the Dodd-Frank regulation of high finance, and the beginning of a serious effort to stall and reverse global warming were bold, politically fraught attempts to solve some of the nation's—and one of the world's—most serious problems. If these were the acts of a neoliberal in the pocket of Wall Street, the Republicans who blasted Obama as a dangerous "socialist" failed to get the message.

The GOP treated the Speaker of the House to an equal helping of vehemence after she played a vital role in passing the most significant expansion of the welfare state in almost half a century. Had Pelosi not insisted that Obama stick to his campaign promise to enact a law providing all citizens with access to health-care coverage—a goal Ted Kennedy called "above all, a moral issue"—the president would likely have agreed to endorse a more limited bill that covered only children. Rahm Emanuel, then his chief of staff, preferred that option to what he feared would be a repeat of the Hillarycare debacle of fifteen years before.[34]

Debating what became Obamacare did eat up much of the time of Congress and the attention of the media during the president's first term in office. Every Republican lawmaker in both chambers, emboldened and/or pressured by rank-and-file conservatives in the new Tea Party movement, was prepared to vote against it. To secure enough support in the House, Speaker Pelosi had to anger other feminists in her caucus who wanted to require that insurers cover abortions as well as birth control. The contentious, often confusing battle dragged on for more than a year and helped drive public approval of the bill below 40 percent. "We have to just rip the Band-Aid off and have a vote," Pelosi told her members in March 2010. On the first day of spring, the House passed the Affordable Care Act with just seven votes to spare. Obama signed it two days later.[35]

That narrow victory might have stirred the president to explain to Americans, on screen or in person, how the bill would provide security to their health without breaking their personal budgets. He also could have touted the steadily improving economy that the funds appropriated by the Democratic Congress had made possible. Instead he stayed in the capital, where he struggled, vainly, to make a grand deal with Republicans to keep Social Security solvent by trimming benefits.

Earlier, Democrats close to Obama had flubbed another excellent opportunity to capitalize on the excitement his campaign had generated. In 2009, aides put together a plan to enlist his army of supporters in a new party-building enterprise: they would register new voters, back local candidates, and more. But internal squabbles and an inattentive president reduced Organizing for America to an offshoot of the DNC. As such, it "deployed the campaign's vast email list to hawk coffee mugs and generate thank-you notes to Democratic members of Congress," according to a journalist who studied its history. The consequence of these failures, bemoaned the journalist and historian Eric Alterman, was that Americans who had backed Obama so enthusiastically in 2008 seldom "got to hear the values he professed as a candidate given voice by the president they helped elect." One of the most inspiring Democratic candidates in history thus committed one of the cardinal errors in politics: he dispirited and demobilized his base.[36]

In 2010, without that zealous support, Democrats suffered one of the worst midterm losses in their history. Republicans depicted the president as the leader of a party driving America to a "socialism" that would take wealth from the hardworking many and lavish it on a feckless minority. The only response the governing party made to this viciously effective, if quite false, attack was a good-natured desire, as Obama's campaign adviser David Axelrod put it, to bring "people together around commonsense solutions to stubborn problems" and "doing business in the light of day so the American people could see how decisions were being made, and participate in them." Republicans gained sixty-three seats to retake the majority in the House; they also took close to seven hundred seats in state legislatures from Obama's party. Although Democrats still carried the urban electorate, their recent gains in rural redoubts were all but wiped out. After leaving the White House, Obama admitted his political failure: the midterm debacle "proved that—whether for lack of talent, cunning, charm or good fortune—I'd failed to rally the nation, as FDR had once done, behind what I knew to be right."[37]

If GOP voters in 2010 had not nominated for the Senate several Tea Party favorites, including one who opposed both the fluoridation of tap water and the separation between church and state, and another who bragged she had "dabbled into witchcraft," their party would likely have captured the upper house, too. With less controversial nominees, Republicans completed that task four years later.

In between those defeats for his party, however, Obama won his own race for reelection with surprising ease. In 2012, he had the good fortune to run against Mitt Romney, whose career in private equity made him a perfect foil in the wake of the severe recession that could be credibly blamed on financiers like himself. Democratic consultants made ads that pummeled the GOP nominee's firm, Bain Capital, for making big profits by laying off wage earners. And Obama found his populist voice again; he delivered speeches attacking "you're-on-your-own" economics and the plague of inequality that resulted from it. Democrats took Senate seats in Wisconsin, Ohio, and Massachusetts by echoing those arguments—and added a strong pro-union message. Yet when Obama left office, neither he nor his fellow Democrats had articulated an identity or strategy that might turn the party into a force equipped not just to win a given election but to define, once again, what politicians could do to help ordinary people harmed by elites and structures of the economy they did not elect and could not, by themselves, control.

---

That task fell, by default, to insurgents critical of a president whose election in 2008 nearly all of them had cheered. In one sense, the left that thrived during the Obama years and kept growing after Donald Trump's election in 2016 differed from its progenitors who had forced the party to alter its mission and build a new majority. Unlike labor's "new millions" in the 1930s, the Black freedom movement of the 1960s, or the anti-war movement later that decade, the newest American left—led largely by children of professionals facing a precarious future—rallied around no single issue that united its parts and inspired its growth. Proponents of Black Lives Matter, the Green New Deal, and a more robust union militancy applauded one another's demands while organizing separately. Notwithstanding their diverse passions, nearly all activists agreed that decades of conservative thinking and policy, under presidents and congresses of both parties, had turned the United States into a meaner nation in which the rich invariably got their way. Equality—in all its meanings—was their common desire.

First came the Occupy Wall Street uprising. In September 2011, several dozen radicals began camping out in Zuccotti Park near Wall Street in lower Manhattan. They declared themselves the representatives of the 99 percent of the people against the 1 percent who ruled the global economy and whose reckless investment schemes had brought on the Great Recession. Within days, the group in the renamed Liberty Park swelled into the thousands. Soon, protesters inspired by their example were occupying parks and other locations in dozens of other cities and towns; thanks to blanket media coverage, "economic inequality" suddenly became as inescapable an issue as civil rights had been during the 1960s.[38]

However, unlike that anti-racist movement, Occupy really did express the sentiments of most Americans, if not quite 99 percent of them. A poll that November reported that 60 percent of the public "supported government efforts to reduce disparities in wealth"; another survey taken that same month found that the same proportion of registered voters agreed it was necessary "to reduce the power of major banks and corporations" and give neither "financial aid to corporations" nor "provide tax breaks to the rich." For decades, union officials and left-wing Democrats had been demanding changes in a status quo that favored the wealthy. But it took a protest by a group composed in the main of young, middle-class anarchists without steady jobs to make a big dent in what the historian Steve Fraser had grimly dubbed "the Age of Acquiescence."[39]

Labor leaders and many urban Democrats were quick to endorse the uprising. Local unions supplied the encampments with food and other resources. Police broke up the protests later that winter. But in the wake of the demonstrations, the Service Employees International Union, the largest private-sector union in the country—organized one-day strikes among fast-food workers for a wage of $15 an hour; the demand quickly became part of the arsenal of every progressive organizer and a plank in the party's platform in 2016.

Leading Democrats proclaimed their sympathy for Occupy, too.

In October 2011, Nancy Pelosi told ABC News, "I support the message to the establishment, whether it's Wall Street or the political establishment and the rest." When the stimulus bill was passed in 2009, Americans thought, she said, that "there would be capital available and Main Street would benefit from the resources that went largely to Wall Street." She added, "That didn't happen. People are angry."[40]

With her statement, the former (and future) Speaker of the House was also sending a warning to the White House: harness this wave of economic discontent, or it may pull you under. In the latter months of 2008, Obama had the good fortune to be running in the midst of an economic debacle and had the ardent backing of every major union in the country. In his acceptance speech in Denver, he set aside his bent for compromise to blame the "old, discredited Republican philosophy" of "trickle-down economics" for causing millions of Americans to lose their jobs, their homes, and their ability to pay credit card bills and college tuition. But once in office, he made no attempt to get Congress to enact the Employee Free Choice Act, labor's main legislative priority. He also remained silent in 2011 when the GOP governor and legislature in Wisconsin slashed collective bargaining rights for most public workers in what had long been a bastion of unionism. As an uprising rather than a movement, Occupy was not equipped to survive for long. But Pelosi was telling the president that neglecting its appeal would be an act of political malpractice.

Black Lives Matter was even more impossible to ignore. Young African Americans who had celebrated Obama's election but quickly realized that he would, or perhaps could, do little to dismantle racist practices made criminal justice their primary target. As the journalist Jelani Cobb observed, "Until there was a Black Presidency it was impossible to conceive of the limitations of one." BLM protesters rallied first in the summer of 2013 after a Florida jury acquitted a neighborhood watchman for killing Trayvon Martin, an unarmed Black teenager, on the streets of a gated community. Over the next three years, the protests grew, in decentralized fashion, from smartphone to smartphone and city to city, as the murders of individual Black men and women were caught on amateur videos and viewed everywhere.[41]

In a trajectory familiar from the Black freedom movement of the 1960s, activists moved swiftly from protesting specific outrages— lack of civil and voting rights then, police killings now—to a bold assault on the norms and structures of American society itself. The three young individuals who launched the original BLM presence on social media proudly identified themselves as "queer Black women" and insisted the new freedom movement "affirm the lives" of African Americans of all genders, sexualities, and national origins. Their language testified to the remarkable legitimacy and influence the cause of LGBTQ rights and identity had gained in the early years of the twenty-first century. The trio of organizers roundly condemned both "hetero-patriarchal society" and a "narrow" Black nationalism of the past that had taken those norms for granted.[42]

To have an African American as president gave the new Black movement both a sense of hope and a target on which to train its frustrations with the slow pace of change. Many lashed out at Obama and other members of the Black elite, in and out of government, for preaching to young African Americans in poor communities a gospel of "respectable" speech and dress instead of enacting policies that would give them a good education and secure jobs at living wages.[43]

At the same time, the enthusiasm for Obama's presidency, which never flagged among most African Americans, did help gain the Black left a nationwide audience for the first time in decades. Organizers of mass protests could point to the gap between Obama's rhetoric about racism and his lack of progress in combating the suffering it caused. A month after Martin's murder, the president declared, "If I had a son, he'd look like Trayvon . . . When I think about this boy, I think about my own kids." But Obama also made clear that he would not do more to address and remedy the problems of African Americans than he would for the concerns of other citizens. Black Lives Matter thus became the latest progressive movement to advance by challenging a president who either did not, or could not, fulfill his promises—instead of having to combat one, like Ronald Reagan, who had no sympathy at all with its cause.[44]

During Obama's presidency, the most successful movement on the broad left was one with no explicit connection to class or racial equality, although it still rose in tandem with those movements. The

LGBTQ activists who pressed for legalizing same-sex marriage managed to turn an extension of the sexual freedom espoused by cultural rebels in the 1960s into a demand for equal protection of the law, one that became difficult for anyone but religious fundamentalists to resist. Four years after Obama had been elected in 2008 as an opponent of gay marriage, he changed his mind or, more likely, decided to help increase the speed at which the winds of politics were already blowing. In June 2015, by a single vote, the Supreme Court, in *Obergefell v. Hodges*, agreed, and marriage equality became the law of the land.[45]

That triumph was not merely the result of an increased tolerance of sexual diversity in American culture; it depended on a shrewd strategy that LGBT activists, nearly all of them Democrats, carried out with persistence and an acute sense of how to shift public opinion their way. In the 1990s, gay rights attorneys filed suit in liberal states like Hawaii and Vermont where they could establish precedents. Then they challenged the Defense of Marriage Act, signed by President Bill Clinton, and were able to convince Obama's Justice Department not to defend the law in court. Accompanying these legal maneuvers was a change of message: instead of talking about marriage as a "right," the movement's literature stressed that same-sex couples wanted to get married for the same reasons that straight couples did: for "love and commitment." That helped break down the resistance of people who had bridled at the idea of overturning a legal norm as old as civilization itself.[46]

Although Barack Obama's gradual "evolution" toward backing same-sex marriage frustrated its supporters, his change of position accelerated the pace of their victory. The president's new stance immediately became that of his party. It helped win over Black churchgoers as well as bind most young people of all races to the Democrats—when they bothered to vote. By 2015, it had become inconceivable that the administration would side with the four conservative justices who dissented from the landmark ruling.

The clearest evidence that a mostly young left was thriving inside Obama's party emerged during the final year of his presidency—in the extraordinary campaign for the Democratic nomination by an independent senator in his seventies who had often criticized the president for not following through on his progressive promises. Bernie Sanders received 43 percent of the vote in his 2016 run for the nomination and drew a majority of votes cast by people of all races under thirty years old. His popularity was a testament both to his personal authenticity and to the hunger for radical change stoked by the larger upsurge of the left. It went largely unnoticed that most progressives who rallied to Sanders had earlier backed Obama as a politician who evoked the same ethos of a social movement. Their disenchantment with the incumbent whetted their desire for a candidate who would never cease waving the banner of fundamental change.

By the time he announced his run for president, Sanders had spent more than half a century advocating for an agenda that would turn the United States into a social-democratic nation—Finland with a lot more people and much warmer summers. His rhetoric had rarely altered from his time as mayor of Burlington in the 1980s to his campaign for the White House more than thirty years later. Although socialism was his ultimate goal, the policies Sanders championed were steps on the road to a markedly more egalitarian, but still capitalist, society. He bashed billionaires for corrupting democracy and gave strong support to unions and public health insurance—while paying somewhat less attention to racial injustice and the degradation of the environment.

Inevitably, this stance led Sanders to attack Obama during the first term. "I think that there are millions of Americans who are deeply disappointed in the president," he claimed in 2011, "who believe that with regard to Social Security and a number of other issues, he has said one thing as a candidate and is doing something very much else, who cannot believe how weak he has been . . . in negotiating with Republicans." In the summer of 2016, after losing the nomination to Hillary Clinton, Sanders refreshed his critique: "After Obama became president," Sanders told an interviewer, "he severed his ties with the grassroots that got him elected."[47]

Despite losing the nomination in 2016, Sanders and his followers wielded a good deal of influence over a party the senator never actually joined. Hillary Clinton seconded the Vermont senator's opposition to the Trans-Pacific Partnership trade agreement backed by

President Obama and embraced his call for a big boost in the minimum wage, debt-free tuition in public colleges, and a reversal of the 2010 Supreme Court ruling in the *Citizens United* case, which allowed corporations to spend unlimited amounts on campaigns so long as they did not coordinate with efforts by the candidates themselves. As a result, the platform adopted by the Democratic Party in 2016 leaned further leftward than any since the days when party leaders were proud to wear the liberal label. "More than anyone else," commented the progressive journalist Harold Meyerson, "Bernie created the current American left, but just as much, by running for president, he revealed its existence—surprising the nation, surprising the left, surprising himself."[48]

## Dumping Trump and Beyond

Donald Trump's shocking 2016 victory and his appalling performance as president accelerated the leftward shift among Democrats that had been building over the previous decade. Social movements that stirred under Obama now took to the streets and the media with a fury directed at a president who routinely mocked them and scorned their discontents. Participants identified themselves with the Resistance—a name borrowed, consciously or not, from the Europeans who had battled fascism during the Second World War with words and weapons.

A day after the 2017 inauguration, some three million people packed the Washington Mall and several million others thronged cities around the country in a Women's March, animated by Trump's misogynistic words and actions. Largely spontaneous protests soon broke out against the administration's ban on travelers from much of the Muslim world. Environmental activists horrified by the president's dismissal of climate change developed a sweeping agenda for a Green New Deal, which quickly became the favored environmental program for progressives both inside and outside the Democratic Party. Then, in May 2020, a Minneapolis policeman murdered a Black man named George Floyd by kneeling on his neck for more than nine minutes; a witness video of the event spurred the largest mass protests in U.S. history. They were the first demonstrations for racial justice in which white people outnumbered African Americans.

The grassroots fervor helped produce an impressive institutional gain for the left, as well. Democratic Socialists of America, a marginal group composed mainly of veteran radicals since its founding in 1982, mushroomed from 6,000 members to nearly 100,000 during the five years between Sanders's initial run for president and the election of 2020. There had not been so large a socialist organization in the United States since the eve of World War I. After the 2020 contests, some 101 DSA members held office around the country, all in progressive districts and cities. Four were members of Congress, double the number the old Socialist Party was able to elect a century earlier.[49]

The wisest decision these freshly minted socialist politicians made came at the start of their primary campaigns: to run as Democrats in places where the party's nominee was nearly certain to win. Abandoning the quixotic dream of a consequential third party made it possible to achieve something of unprecedented significance: to embed a dynamic social democratic movement inside the heart of one of the two major parties. In the mid-1960s, the Black freedom movement and organized labor had worked together to compel politicians to enact the landmark programs of the Great Society. But their leaders did not describe themselves as "democratic socialists" (although key actors like Martin Luther King, Jr., Bayard Rustin, and Walter Reuther privately did).

The standout figure among the new generation on the realistic left was Alexandria Ocasio-Cortez, a charismatic young activist from New York City who had interned for Senator Ted Kennedy while in college. Her family's Puerto Rican background and her fluency in Spanish, along with her knack for skewering conservatives on social media, helped make her a symbol of the multiracial millennials who had staged and marched in big protests against the Trump administration. Ocasio-Cortez—the ubiquity of whose nickname, AOC, signaled her renown—had organized for Sanders during the 2016 campaign and then became one of his leading surrogates in the next one. The Women's March was her first national demonstration; naturally, she livestreamed it on her Facebook page.

Yet AOC's larger and more potent left did not come close to winning the 2020 Democratic presidential nomination for the candidate it favored. As in every quadrennial contest between a progressive and a more centrist Democrat since McGovern's run in 1972, the latter took the prize. Despite his passionate young admirers, the proud socialist from Vermont failed to increase his base of support from the previous race against Hillary Clinton. In 2020, Sanders drew no more than 40 percent in any state, except his own, even after he was one of the last two contenders in the race. The horrifying prospect of a second Trump term persuaded more Democrats to vote for Joe Biden as the safer, more familiar, more electable choice instead of the man who championed proposals like Medicare for All and the Green New Deal, which had the potential to transform their lives and the nation. Older African American voters were particularly vital to Biden's triumph. For them, the ideology and policy preferences—even the race of a candidate—meant less than which one had the best chance to win a general election they believed Black people could not afford to lose.

For all its fire, the nomination battle obscured a troubling continuity that had plagued the party since it lost its dominant place in American politics half a century before. Democrats still had trouble articulating with force and clarity what kind of economy they believed in and how it would benefit most people who worked for somebody else and struggled to remain in a middle class whose shrinking politicians bemoaned.

Of course, every major candidate for president hawked a few ideas meant to address the manifestly unequal society they aspired to govern. Joe Biden called for "stronger labor laws and a tax code that rewards [the] middle class." Sanders demanded higher taxes on billionaires and, in an echo of the long-forgotten Humphrey-Hawkins bill, jobs for every able-bodied adult. Massachusetts senator Elizabeth Warren offered a slew of plans that included giving employees seats on corporate boards and breaking up giant firms like Facebook and Amazon. California senator Kamala Harris urged a big tax cut for ordinary families and "stricter penalties for companies that cheat their workers."

A majority of Americans, according to polls, supported most if not all these proposals. Yet neither Biden nor the Democrats he defeated articulated a larger vision, slogan, or even fresh name that would animate and tie together such worthy ideas. Neither the New Freedom nor the New Deal had achieved all its goals—and each had taken the continuation of a racist order for granted. But under the leadership of Woodrow Wilson and Franklin Roosevelt, the party rallied behind a common vision of uplifting working people and humbling the wealthy, and most voters recognized that, whether or not they endorsed it.

The muddle for Democrats in the twenty-first century stemmed in part from their dual and somewhat contradictory ambitions: to empower and raise the living standards of working people and to humble the big corporations that dominated the marketplace for a wide range of vital products and services. One could lambaste a behemoth like Walmart or Amazon for setting its own rules and squeezing out competition as well as for paying poor wages and resisting attempts by their workers to organize unions. But how many voters would be willing to pay higher prices and spend more time searching for what they wanted or needed to buy from a plethora of smaller firms in the same industry? In terms that William Jennings Bryan and Franklin Roosevelt would have cheered, the economist and journalist David Dayen denounced, in 2020, "this age of plutocrats . . . of soaring inequality and broken democracy, this age of middle-class despair and sawed-off ladders to prosperity."[50] Yet the age when small proprietors could thrive if government kept their giant competitors in check may have passed.

During Obama's tenure, Democrats did succeed in enacting one notable policy that embodied an ethical ideal analogous to that which had helped turn Social Security and Medicare and, once, the Wagner Act into nearly indestructible pillars of the welfare state. The Affordable Care Act fell quite short of fulfilling the promise "that health care should be a right and not a privilege," and the torturous process of passing and implementing it gave Republicans the opportunity to wrest back control of the House in 2014 and make gains in the Senate. Yet like the landmark entitlement programs of the New Deal and Great Society, Obamacare soon gained acceptance and then popularity. Most Americans quickly came to believe that every citizen was entitled to have regular medical care, whether or not they could afford it. All Democrats thus embraced a principle that every mass party in other industrial nations had long taken for granted. In the midterm contests of 2018, they turned it into a campaign weapon: candidates who ran on "strengthening Obamacare" won enough seats long held by Republicans, most in suburban districts, to enable their party to wrest back control of the House.

---

For Democrats, the election of 2020 spelled relief instead of deliverance from the dilemma of how to build an enduring new majority. Joe Biden won the presidency with more than half the popular vote and took two states—Arizona and Georgia—that no nominee of his party had carried for more than two decades. For the seventh time in the last eight presidential contests, more Americans favored a Democrat than his or her rival from the GOP.

Turnout was remarkably high on both sides. The Democratic ticket of Joe Biden and Kamala Harris won in excess of fifteen million more votes than had Hillary Clinton and Tim Kaine in the previous quadrennial contest. It was the greatest such leap of support for a major party since 1932, when Franklin D. Roosevelt received nearly eight million more votes in his landslide victory than had Alfred E. Smith in his lopsided loss to Herbert Hoover four years before.

However, the swing voters who rejected Donald Trump did not rush to embrace Joe Biden's party. The Democrats lost eleven seats in the House and failed to take a single state legislative chamber away from the GOP. With surprising wins in two January runoff elections in Georgia, Democrats did gain a tie in the Senate—which Harris, the new vice president and the first woman to hold that job, had the power to break. But the electorate remained as closely divided as it had been since the end of the New Deal order, decades before.

The coalition that vanquished Donald Trump was also virtually the same one that had narrowly failed to defeat him in 2016. Majorities of college-educated people of all races from large metropolitan areas and of Black and Hispanic working people were enough to carry the popular vote and turn just enough red states blue to win the presidency. Most Democrats inhabited thriving, if quite unequal, hubs of high-tech and finance that, since the 1990s, had fueled growth for the many and huge profits for the few. But enough white Americans still lived in rural areas and towns dependent on such older industries as agriculture, manufacturing, and mining to make the GOP competitive in races for Congress and the presidency; due to the natural bias of both the Electoral College and Senate toward rural states, that could remain so for decades to come. The United States has lacked a dominant party since the early 1970s. The partisan standoff had lasted longer than any such period in the nation's history, and it showed no signs of ending.[51]

The COVID-19 pandemic, whose first cases in the United States appeared in January 2020, did give Democrats a splendid opportunity to argue with unusual confidence that only an expansion of public power could protect and advance the common welfare. As during earlier mass traumas, such as the Civil War and the Great Depression, the disease and the quarantine, which shut down countless businesses and threw millions out of work, turned state action from a debatable option into an urgent necessity. On the eve of the 2020 election, Joe Biden had begun to compare the task before him if he won with that which Franklin Roosevelt faced when he took power in 1933. On a visit to the Georgia town where FDR had often retreated to soothe his paralyzed legs, the Democratic standard-bearer said, "This place, Warm Springs, is a reminder that though broken, each of us can be healed. That as a people and a country, we can overcome a devastating virus. That we can heal a suffering world. That yes, we can restore our soul and save our country."[52]

During his first year in office, Biden sought, with strong backing from most Democrats, to enact legislation that emulated those New Deal programs that benefited all but the wealthiest Americans. But his adversaries in the GOP did their best to make the old curses against "big government" potent once again. Whether Biden and his party could pass a durable reform agenda depended on whether they could repeat another achievement of FDR's, one Democrats had not accomplished since 1934: to increase their congressional majorities in the first midterm election after retaking the White House.

As an institution, the twenty-first-century party could have equipped itself better to advance its goals. With the demise of the tightly organized machines that dispensed patronage and rewarded loyalty, Democrats at the state and local levels had to rely on dedicated volunteers whose numbers and enthusiasm waxed and waned with each election cycle. The ease with which individual candidates could use technology to appeal directly to voters also weakened the party structures that remained. At the national level, the DNC became something of an empty shell. The perpetual task of winning or holding seats in Congress and the states fell to the DCCC, the DSCC, and the DLCC—acronyms that obscured the labors of thousands of managers, consultants, publicists, programmers, and canvassers serving candidates for the House, the Senate, and state legislatures whose ambitions often outstripped their political skills. The cosmopolitan denizens of this "vast Washington-centric Blob," as one scholar dubbed it, ensured the party would give strong backing to abortion rights, marriage equality, and racial justice.[53] But as winners in the meritocratic lottery, most professional Democrats had less contact with those who lived on often meager paychecks, and tended to feel less urgency about highlighting solutions to the economic inequality their candidates ritually condemned in speeches.

In the intensely combative environment of Trump's years in power, Democrats were fortunate not to have to go into battle armed solely with the party's official apparatus. In the progressive corner of civil society blossomed a welter of organizations that advocated versions of moral capitalism and were adept at the quotidian business of running campaigns or providing eager supporters to them. There was Indivisible, founded after the 2016 election. By the start of the next presidential campaign, it boasted some five thousand local chapters, at least one in each congressional district. All were committed to achieving "economic justice" and other reforms. There was Fair Fight, created by Georgia state representative Stacey Abrams before her 2018 run for governor to combat voter suppression by Republicans and sign up new voters, particularly young ones of color. Abrams lost that race, in part because her opponent found ways to disenfranchise many Blacks in the state. But because she and her allies screwed up their anger and went on to register nearly 800,000 Georgians, Joe Biden carried the state two years later, while the party's Senate candidates—a Black minister and a Jewish filmmaker/ journalist—won their races and flipped control of the upper chamber. Older single-issue groups like the Sierra Club, Planned Parenthood, and the NAACP donated to and worked to elect their favored candidates as well. But the fresh troops of the Resistance provided the party with the élan of a social movement combined with a zeal to carry out the practical duties ward bosses performed in a bygone era.[54]

At the same time, Democratic activists could not perceive their institution as akin to a social movement. The job of a political party in a democratic system is to win elections and then pressure officeholders to carry out policies their voters desire. In contrast, social movements exist to articulate alternative policies and make strong moral pleas for a single issue or more. Their job is not to win over a majority, but to persuade the minority who identify with them to change the way power works.

Still, Democrats would benefit from stoking the impulse behind every successful movement: a sense of common purpose toward a worthy end, of solidarity among its loyalists and empathy toward Americans who need and deserve a more equitable society. The greater the number who can be mobilized to fight intelligently and strategically on their own behalf, the closer the nation will come to achieving that end.

———— ◦ ————

Out in Nevada, a singular union provided a model of sorts for Democratic success. On election night in 2018, a throng of workers, clad in bright red shirts with the name of their local etched in thick black letters, half walked, half marched through the ridiculously wide corridors of Caesars Palace on the Las Vegas Strip. The members of Culinary Workers Union Local 226 laughed and chatted; occasionally, one would start chanting, "We vote, we win!" and his or her comrades would keep the slogan going. They were headed for a ballroom at the hotel that resembled a gargantuan parody of the Roman Forum to watch the returns come in.

When the secretary of state's office finally released the tally, the union chant got quickly transformed into reality. By convincing margins, voters elected Democrats to every statewide office but one, as well as three out of Nevada's four congressional seats; they also ousted the incumbent Republican senator in the year's only Democratic gain in the upper chamber (my son was the challenger's campaign manager). Democrats increased their already healthy majorities in the legislature, too, and Nevada became the first state with more women than men in such a body.

Without Local 226, some or all those victories may not have been possible. The union—which represented some fifty-seven thousand workers who served guests in Vegas with food and drink, cleaned their rooms, and carried their bags—was a formidable electoral machine in Clark County, home to three of every four Nevadans. The union held regular political education sessions for its members and rented buses to transport them to the polls. In the contracts it signed with hotels, it even won the right for members to take a two-month leave from their jobs to campaign.

When Democrats carried Clark by 10 percent or more, the white rural Republican base could not muster enough votes to defeat them. In the teeth of the pandemic that pushed most of its members into unemployment, Local 226 repeated that performance in 2020. Its members knocked on more than half a million doors and again lifted Democrats to victories up and down the ballot.[55]

Local 226 was a model of multiculturalism in action. Its members hailed from more than 170 countries and spoke more than forty different languages. A majority were Latinos or Latinas, and most were women. As the 2020 census reported, they belong to the fastest-growing demographic group in the nation.

The expansive local helped thousands of workers to prepare for the citizenship exam; it also ran a pharmacy where members and their families filled their prescriptions—for free. The union thus projected an image of immigrants from south of the border that differed markedly from that put forth by the left, which saw them largely as victims of nativist bigotry, or the right, which cursed them as job stealers or criminals. These were immigrants who won power on the job and knew how to use it to defend their political interests.

Unions like this, filled with workers who spoke with foreign accents as well as regional ones, had been critical to creating the New Deal order. In the 1930s and '40s, the CIO broke the resistance of anti-union employers in the auto, steel, longshore, and electrical industries *and* turned once solidly Republican states like Ohio, Pennsylvania, and Michigan into strongholds of pro-labor Democrats.

Heavy manufacturing has long been in decline in the United States and, with it, the working-class institutions that once made it possible for men and women with only a high school education or less to have a secure job that paid decent wages. But the men and women in Las Vegas hotels who made beds, cleaned rugs, and cooked and served meals and drinks were engaging in as socialized a form of labor as bolting a fender on a Chevrolet or tending a blast furnace.

As in the strong industrial unions of the past, Local 226 gave its members a sense of being part of a community of people who did not just work together. They also taught one another the stakes of local and national politics and spent many hours fanning out around Nevada to elect men and women who, they believed, would protect and advance their needs. That meant endorsing and working for every Democrat who won his or her nomination, whether they echoed the social-democratic ideology of Bernie Sanders or the practiced moderation of Harry Reid, the state's former senator, who arranged the match between union and party almost twenty years before, when Democrats were a minority in Nevada.

The Democratic Party, as during the heydays of the New Deal and the Great Society, can taste victory consistently only if its activists, candidates, and officeholders debate their differences without one side denouncing or seeking to purge another. It would help if Democrats everywhere, wage earners or not, emulated what the members of Local 226 accomplished in their workplaces and neighborhoods. Just as the Republicans could not tout themselves the "Christian party" if they did not have thousands of evangelical churches on their side, so Democrats will not become a "working-class party" or true "party of the people" unless they help build and support strong institutions of ordinary Americans to become potent forces in a broader coalition. Durable groups composed of those who aspire to be what Walt Whitman called the collective "equalizer of his age and land" remain essential to turning back the determined challenge of an opposition that, under Donald Trump, doubted the very legitimacy of democratic rule—whether with a lowercase or an uppercase "d." We organize, we vote, and we win.[56]

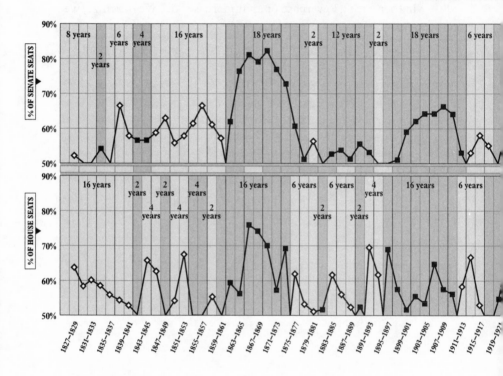

# HOUSE OF REPRESENTATIVES: 1827–2023

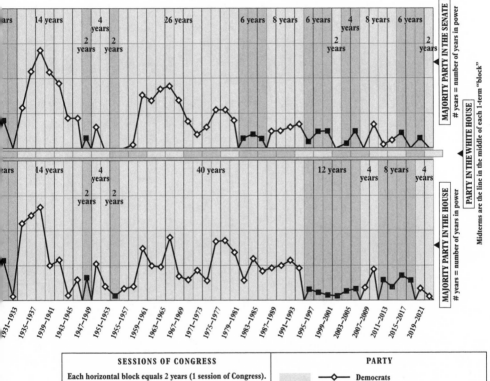

| SESSIONS OF CONGRESS | PARTY |
|---|---|
| Each horizontal block equals 2 years (1 session of Congress). On the scale, every other session of Congress is shown (i.e., 2009–2011 is all of 2009 and 2010, newly elected take office in January 2011) | ◇ Democrats  ■ Anti-Jacksonians / Whigs (1829–1855) Republicans (1855–present) (others not shown) |

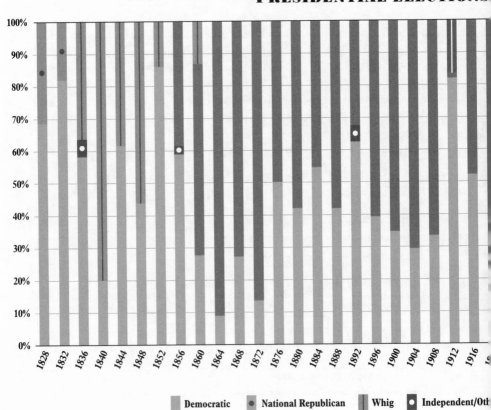

| | | | |
|---|---|---|---|
| ▉ Democratic | ● National Republican | ▉ Whig | ◯ Independent/Oth |

# ELECTORAL RESULTS BY PARTY

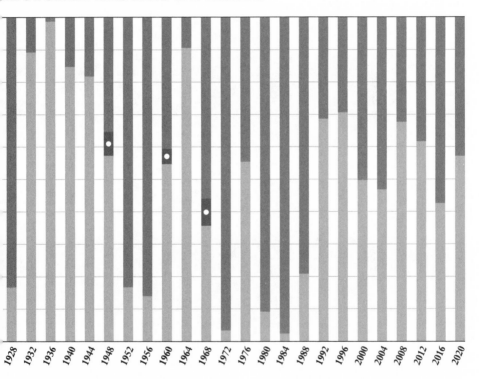

Republican ▌▌ Progressive

This chart does not reflect faithless electors whose votes did not influence the outcome.

# NOTES

## PREFACE: TO PROMOTE THE GENERAL WELFARE

1. "Barbara Jordan, Politician, 1936–1996," Great Texas Women, texaswomen .housing.utexas.edu/pdfs/jordan.pdf.
2. Reid J. Epstein and John Eligon, "Biden Said, 'Most Cops Are Good.' But Progressives Want Systemic Change," *The New York Times,* August 19, 2020, www.nytimes.com/2020/08/19/us/politics/democrats-biden-defund -police.html.
3. James Wood, "It's Still Mrs. Thatcher's England," *The New Yorker,* December 22, 2019, www.newyorker.com/magazine/2019/12/02/its-still-mrs -thatchers-britain.
4. Michael Tomasky, *If We Can Keep It: How the Republic Collapsed and How It Might Be Saved* (New York: Liveright, 2019), 53.
5. Lizabeth Cohen, *Making a New Deal: Industrial Workers in Chicago, 1919– 1939* (Cambridge, UK: Cambridge University Press, 1990), 285–86; Joe Kennedy III, "A Call to Moral Capitalism," *American Prospect,* February 14, 2019, prospect.org/economy/call-moral-capitalism/.
6. "Remarks by the President on the Economy in Osawatomie, Kansas, December 6, 2011," obamawhitehouse.archives.gov/the-press-office /2011/12/06/remarks-president-economy-osawatomie-kansas; Chris Cillizza, "Bernie Sanders Wants to Get Rid of Billionaires. All of Them," CNN, www.cnn.com/2019/09/24/politics/bernie-sanders-ultra-wealth -tax-billionaires/index.html; "Elizabeth Warren Lays Out Plan to Fight Coronavirus at Houston Town Hall," *ABC13 Eyewitness News,* March 4, 2020, abc13.com/politics/elizabeth-warren-addresses-coronavirus-at -houston-town-hall/5972608; Abigail Johnson Hess, "Biden Promises to Be 'the Most Pro-Union President'—and Union Members in Congress Are Optimistic," CNBC, December 2, 2020, www.cnbc.com/2020/12 /01/biden-promises-to-be-the-most-pro-union-president-and-rep.html.
7. Richard Hofstadter, *The Age of Reform: From Bryan to F.D.R.* (New York: Vintage, 1955), 18.
8. Herbert Croly quoted in Lewis L. Gould, *The First Modern Clash over Federal Power: Wilson versus Hughes in the Presidential Election of 1916* (Lawrence: University Press of Kansas, 2016), 56.
9. Like most historians of the subject then and since, Kent focused on presidents and presidential contests. Frank R. Kent, *The Democratic Party: A*

*History* (New York: Century, 1928), 3; Jill Lepore, *Mansion of Happiness: A History of Life and Death* (New York: Knopf, 2012), xi.

10. Jeffrey M. Jones, "Support for U.S. Third Political Party at High Point," Gallup, February 15, 2021, news.gallup.com/poll/329639/support-third -political-party-high-point.aspx.

11. George H. Sabine, introduction to *Freedom and Responsibility in the American Way of Life*, by Carl Becker (New York: Knopf, 1945), xxxi.

### PROLOGUE: A USEFUL MYTH

1. Thomas Jefferson quoted in James Morone, *Republic of Wrath: How American Politics Turned Tribal, from George Washington to Donald Trump* (New York: Basic Books, 2020), 9.

2. Thomas Jefferson quoted in Merrill Peterson, *Thomas Jefferson and the New Nation* (New York: Oxford University Press, 1975), 931. Jefferson made the statement in an attempt to soothe a conflict within the ranks of his own faction.

3. "FDR Dedicates Jefferson Memorial," UPI, April 13, 1943, www.upi .com/Archives/1943/04/13/FDR-dedicates-Jefferson-Memorial/4891523 584554.

4. Richard Hofstadter, *The American Political Tradition and the Men Who Made It* (New York: Knopf, 1948), 42. Hofstadter also wrote, "The mythology that has grown up around Thomas Jefferson is as massive and imposing as any in American history." Ibid., 28. After the political and cultural changes wrought by the Black freedom movement, that, at least, is no longer true.

5. William Jennings Bryan to Mary Foy, letter quoted in Michael Kazin, *A Godly Hero: The Life of William Jennings Bryan* (New York: Knopf, 2006), xv.

6. Thomas Jefferson quoted in Alexander Keyssar, *Why Do We Still Have the Electoral College?* (Cambridge, MA: Harvard University Press, 2020), 29.

7. First Inaugural, www.presidency.ucsb.edu/documents/inaugural-address -20. Thomas Jefferson to Levi Lincoln, letter quoted in Stanley Elkins and Eric McKitrick, *The Age of Federalism: The Early American Republic, 1788–1800* (New York: Oxford University Press, 1993), 754.

8. Gary J. Kornblith and John M. Murrin, "The Dilemmas of Ruling Elites in Revolutionary America," in *Ruling America: A History of Wealth and Power in a Democracy*, ed. Steve Fraser and Gary Gerstle (Cambridge, MA: Harvard University Press, 2005), 57; Danielle Allen quoted in Ezra Klein, "The Radicalism of the American Revolution—and Its Lessons for Today," *Vox*, July 3, 2020, www.vox.com/2020/7/3/21311294/declaration-of -independence-fourth-of-july-american-revolution-the-ezra-klein-show.

9. For the most complete record of results and turnout, see Curtis Gans

with Matthew Mulling, *Voter Turnout in the United States, 1788–2009* (Washington, D.C.: CQ Press, 2011). The best history of suffrage is Alex Keyssar's *The Right to Vote: The Contested History of Democracy in the United States*, rev. ed. (New York: Basic Books, 2009).

10. Kornblith and Murrin, "The Dilemmas of Ruling Elites in Revolutionary America," 43.

11. Alben Barkley quoted in Caroline Heller, "Political Appropriations and the Construction of the Jefferson Icon in the United States Congress, 1924–1943," *Current Objectives of Postgraduate American Studies* 15, no. 1 (2014), 14.

12. "Howard W. Smith," Wikipedia, en.wikipedia.org/wiki/Howard_W ._Smith.

13. Franklin D. Roosevelt, "Address at the Groundbreaking for the Thomas Jefferson Memorial, Washington, D.C.," December 15, 1938, www.presidency.ucsb.edu/documents/address-the-groundbreaking-for -the-thomas-jefferson-memorial-washington-dc.

14. Surprisingly, two years before Alexandria Ocasio-Cortez was elected to Congress, she toured the memorial and remarked, "Jefferson is one of my all-time favorite presidents. Lincoln is my all-time bae for sure, but as a writer and philosopher it is pretty hard to compare anyone to Jefferson." Quoted in David Freedlander, *The AOC Generation: How Millennials Are Seizing Power and Rewriting the Rules of American Politics* (Boston: Beacon Press, 2021), 55.

### 1. CREATING THE DEMOCRACY, 1820–1848

1. Martin Van Buren, from an 1856 letter, quoted in Jean H. Baker, *Affairs of Party: The Political Culture of Northern Democrats in the Mid-Nineteenth Century* (Ithaca, NY: Cornell University Press, 1983), 131.

2. Unnamed source quoted in Donald B. Cole, *Martin Van Buren and the American Political System* (Princeton, NJ: Princeton University Press, 1984), 34. The second description comes from Henry B. Stanton (husband of Elizabeth Cady Stanton), ibid., 430.

3. *The Autobiography of Martin Van Buren*, ed. John Clement Fitzpatrick. Published as the *Annual Report of the American Historical Association for the Year 1918* (Washington, D.C.: U.S. Government Printing Office, 1920), 7.

4. James Madison, *Federalist No. 10*, November 27, 1787, Constitution Society, constitution.org/1-Constitution/fed/federal10.htm.

5. Martin Van Buren, in *The Albany Argus*, c. 1824, quoted in Richard Hofstadter, *The Idea of a Party System: The Rise of Legitimate Opposition in the United States, 1780–1840* (Berkeley: University of California Press, 1970), 251; *Autobiography of Van Buren*, 125.

6. Martin Van Buren, "Thoughts on the Approaching Election in New York," quoted in Gerald Leonard, "Party as a 'Political Safeguard of

Federalism': Martin Van Buren and the Constitutional Theory of Party Politics," *Rutgers Law Review* 54 (Fall 2001): 247.

7. J. M. Opal, *Avenging the People: Andrew Jackson, the Rule of Law, and the American Nation* (New York: Oxford University Press, 2017), 140.

8. John S. Bagg, editor of the *Detroit Free Press*, quoted in William Gerald Shade, *Banks or No Banks: The Money Issue in Western Politics, 1832–1865* (Detroit: Wayne State University Press, 1972), 124.

9. Matthew Costello, "The Enslaved Households of President Martin Van Buren," White House Historical Association, November 27, 2019, www .whitehousehistory.org/the-enslaved-households-of-martin-van-buren#: ~:text=As%20Van%20Buren%20studied%20law,later%20than%20July %204%2C%201827.

10. Walt Whitman, "To a Locomotive in Winter," first published in 1876, whitmanarchive.org/published/LG/1881/poems/269.

11. For a brilliant interpretation of how and why the franchise was expanded in antebellum America, see Alex Keyssar, *The Right to Vote: The Contested History of Democracy in the United States*, revised edition (New York: Basic Books, 2009), 22–60. As late as the early 1840s, seven overwhelmingly rural states still allowed voice voting. Joel H. Silbey, *The American Political Nation, 1838–1893* (Stanford, CA: Stanford University Press, 1991), 144. Alexis de Tocqueville quoted in William E. Gienapp, "'Politics Seem to Enter into Everything': Political Culture in the North, 1840–1860," in *Essays on American Antebellum Politics, 1840–1860*, ed. Stephen E. Maizlish and John J. Kushma (College Station: Texas A&M University Press, 1982), 16. On the limits of political enthusiasm in the period, see Glenn C. Altschuler and Stuart M. Blumin, *Rude Republic: Americans and Their Politics in the Nineteenth Century* (Princeton, NJ: Princeton University Press, 2000).

12. For the number of officials, see Marvin Meyers, *The Jacksonian Persuasion: Politics and Belief* (Stanford, CA: Stanford University Press, 1957), 241. The quote is from *The Albany Argus* in 1824. Silas Wright quoted in Michael Wallace, "Changing Concepts of Party in the United States: New York, 1815–1828," *American Historical Review* 74, no. 2 (December 1968): 458; Charles Sellers, *The Market Revolution: Jacksonian America, 1815–1846* (New York: Oxford University Press, 1991), 111.

13. James Kent quoted in Meyers, *Jacksonian Persuasion*, 239, 242.

14. Martin Van Buren quoted in Meyers, *Jacksonian Persuasion*, 247. Daniel Tompkins, a Van Buren ally who was president of the convention, pitched the same argument in terms that mingled patriotism with class consciousness: "Property, when compared with our other essential rights, is insignificant and trifling. Life, liberty, and the pursuit of happiness, not of property, are set forth in the Declaration of Independence as cardinal objects . . . How was the late war [of 1812] sustained? Who filled the ranks of your armies? Not the priesthood, not the men of wealth not

the speculators . . . And yet the very men who were led on to battle had no vote to give for their commander-in-chief . . . We give to property too much influence. It is not that which mostly gives independence. Independence consists more in the structure of the mind and in the qualities of the heart. We should look to the protection of him who has personal security and personal liberty at stake." Quoted in George Bancroft, *Martin Van Buren to the End of His Public Career* (New York: Harper and Brothers, 1889), 83–84.

15. Erastus Root quoted in Edwin G. Burrows and Mike Wallace, *Gotham: A History of New York City to 1898* (New York: Oxford University Press, 1999), 514. See the debate about Black suffrage in Nathaniel H. Carter and William L. Stone, *Reports of the Proceedings and Debates of the Convention of 1821, Assembled for the Purpose of Amending the Constitution of the State of New York* (Albany: E. and E. Hosford, 1821), 183–95.

16. Keyssar, *Right to Vote*, 44.

17. Wallace, "Changing Concepts of Party," 470n57; Van Buren, *Autobiography*, 401.

18. Anonymous New York state senator, 1824, quoted in Wallace, "Changing Concepts of Party," 488; Martin Van Buren quoted in Edward M. Shepard, *Martin Van Buren* (1888; rev. ed., Boston: Houghton, Mifflin and Company, 1899), 453.

19. Martin Van Buren, *Inquiry into the Origin and Course of Political Parties in the United States* (1867), quoted in Thomas M. Coens, "The Formation of the Jackson Party, 1822–1825" (PhD dissertation, Harvard University, 2004), 284; J. Fenimore-Cooper, *A Letter to His Countrymen* (New York: John Wiley, 1834), 99.

20. Van Buren, *Autobiography*, 185.

21. Cole, *Martin Van Buren and the American Political System*, 97.

22. Andrew Jackson Donelson and Andrew Jackson quoted in Robert V. Remini, *Andrew Jackson and the Course of American Freedom, 1822–1832* (New York: Harper & Row, 1981), 95–96.

23. "The Theft of the Presidency" is the title of the chapter on the 1824 election in Remini, *Andrew Jackson and the Course of American Freedom*, 74–99. On the similar views of Clay and Adams, see David S. Heidler and Jeanne T. Heidler, *Henry Clay: The Essential American* (New York: Random House, 2010), 179–80.

24. Andrew Jackson quoted in Opal, *Avenging the People*, 120.

25. John Quincy Adams quoted in Remini, *Andrew Jackson and the Course of American Freedom*, 110.

26. Martin Van Buren to Thomas Ritchie, January 13, 1827, quoted in Joel H. Silbey, *Martin Van Buren and the Emergence of American Popular Politics* (Lanham, MD.: Rowman and Littlefield, 2002), 50; Martin Van Buren to Andrew Jackson, September 14, 1827, typescript in Series 7, Van Buren Papers, Library of Congress.

27. Only in the elections of 1920 and 1924 did less than half the eligible voters cast a ballot.

28. Richard Hofstadter quoted in Donald B. Cole, *Vindicating Andrew Jackson: The 1828 Election and the Rise of the Two-Party System* (Lawrence: University Press of Kansas, 2009), 185; James Parton quoted ibid., 184; William Leggett quoted in Russell Hanson, *The Democratic Imagination in America: Conversations with Our Past* (Princeton, NJ: Princeton University Press, 1985), 128.

29. William L. Marcy quoted in Remini, *Andrew Jackson and the Course of American Freedom*, 347.

30. I have drawn these numbers from Richard R. John's splendid history, *Spreading the News: The American Postal System from Franklin to Morse* (Cambridge, MA: Harvard University Press, 1995), 3. Jacksonian loyalist quoted ibid., 240.

31. On "regular voters" not caring about who benefited from patronage, see Gienapp, "'Politics Seem to Enter into Everything,'" 52.

32. "Postage Rates for Periodicals: A Narrative History," U.S. Postal Service, about.usps.com/who-we-are/postal-history/periodicals-postage-history .htm. On circulation, see John, *Spreading the News*, 4.

33. On Jackson's appointment of editors, see Donald B. Cole, *A Jackson Man: Amos Kendall and the Rise of American Democracy* (Baton Rouge: Louisiana State University Press, 2004), 117. Jabez Hammond quoted in Silbey, *American Political Nation*, 54.

34. Elbert B. Smith, *Francis Preston Blair* (New York: Free Press, 1980), 46.

35. Francis Blair quoted in Erik McKinley Eriksson, "The Establishment and Rise of the *Washington Globe*: A Phase of Jacksonian Politics" (master's thesis, University of Iowa, 1921), 34. For Blair's profit, see ibid., 26.

36. *Washington Globe*, June 13, 1831; *Washington Globe*, May 19, 1832; quoting the *Kentucky Republican*, *Washington Globe*, May 23, 1832. On the influence of the *Globe*, see Smith, *Francis Preston Blair*, 46–47.

37. Stephen Skowronek, *Presidential Leadership in Political Time: Reprise and Reappraisal*, 3rd ed. (Lawrence: University Press of Kansas, 2020), 35.

38. Van Buren, *Autobiography*, 625.

39. Andrew Jackson, "July 10, 1832: Bank Veto," University of Virginia, Miller Center, Presidential Speeches, millercenter.org/the-presidency /presidential-speeches/july-10-1832-bank-veto.

40. Thomas Hart Benton quoted in Smith, *Francis Preston Blair*, 66.

41. Van Buren, *Autobiography*, 628.

42. *The Cincinnati Enquirer* quoted in Stephen E. Maizlish, *The Triumph of Sectionalism: The Transformation of Ohio Politics, 1844–1856* (Kent, OH: Kent State University Press, 1983), 1.

43. Martin Van Buren, "March 4, 1837: Inaugural Address," University

of Virginia, Miller Center, Presidential Speeches, millercenter.org/the -presidency/presidential-speeches/march-4-1837-inaugural-address.

44. Martin Van Buren quoted in Silbey, *Martin Van Buren*, 117, 118.

45. Some middle-class women who backed the Whigs were active in abolitionism, the temperance movement, religious charities, anti-prostitution crusades, and other "benevolent activities" that Democrats tended to avoid or criticize. See Elizabeth R. Varon, *We Mean to Be Counted: White Women and Politics in Antebellum Virginia* (Chapel Hill: University of North Carolina Press, 1998).

46. For a thoughtful, vivid description of the Whig campaign, see Michael F. Holt, *The Rise and Fall of the American Whig Party: Jacksonian Politics and the Onset of the Civil War* (New York: Oxford University Press, 1999), 105–13. On the origin of "O.K.," see ibid., 111.

47. The letter from William L. Marcy et al., dated October 20, 1842, can be found in the Hathaway Family Papers, Rare Books Collection, Cornell University Library. Thanks to the library staff for locating and sending me a copy. Lincoln's plan is copied in Silbey, *American Political Nation*, 53.

48. For details on state officeholders, see "Political Party Strength in New York," Wikipedia, en.wikipedia.org/wiki/Political_party_strength_in _New_York; and "Political Party Strength in Ohio," Wikipedia, en .wikipedia.org/wiki/Political_party_strength_in_Ohio. For turnout, see Gienapp, "'Politics Seem to Enter into Everything,'" 18. For changes in partisan vote totals, see Holt, *Rise and Fall of the American Whig Party*, 141–43.

49. In all the Ohio elections held between 1832 and 1853, Democrats averaged 48.9 percent of the vote against 47.3 percent for their opponents. Kenneth J. Winkle, *The Politics of Community: Migration and Politics in Antebellum Ohio* (Cambridge, UK: Cambridge University Press, 1988), 176.

50. Ohio Democrats quoted in Maizlish, *Triumph of Sectionalism*, 6, 8.

51. William Leggett quoted in Meyers, *Jacksonian Persuasion*, 200; *Democrat* quoted in Jerome Mushkat, *Tammany: The Evolution of a Political Machine, 1789–1865* (Syracuse, NY: Syracuse University Press, 1971), 172.

52. John O'Sullivan, "The Great Nation of Futurity," *United States Democratic Review* 6, no. 23 (November 1839): 426–30.

53. Walt Whitman, "Andrew Jackson," *Brooklyn Daily Eagle and Kings County Democrat*, June 8, 1846, reprinted in *The Collected Writings of Walt Whitman: The Journalism*, vol. 1, *1834–1846*, ed. Herbert Bergman (New York: Peter Lang, 1998), 407.

54. Silbey, *American Political Nation*, 259. The population of seventeen million in 1840 was about 5 percent of today's number. The federal budget in 2016 was just under $4 trillion—or about two hundred times larger than that in 1840. Silas Wright quoted in John Arthur Garraty, *Silas Wright* (New York: Columbia University Press, 1949), 31.

55. Sean Wilentz, "The Bombshell of 1844," in *America at the Ballot Box: Elections and Political History*, ed. Gareth Davies and Julian E. Zelizer (Philadelphia: University of Pennsylvania Press, 2015), 37.

56. Andrew Jackson to Benjamin F. Butler, Van Buren's convention manager, quoted in Remini, *Andrew Jackson and the Course of American Democracy*, 504.

57. Andrew Jackson quoted in Remini, *Andrew Jackson and the Course of American Democracy*, 511, 516.

58. For context, see Adam Rothman, "The 'Slave Power' in the United States, 1783–1865," in *Ruling America: A History of Wealth and Power in a Democracy*, ed. Steve Fraser and Gary Gerstle (Cambridge, MA: Harvard University Press, 2005), 64–91. The congressman was George Rathbun from Auburn, New York; quoted in Eric Foner, *Free Soil, Free Labor, Free Men: The Ideology of the Republican Party before the Civil War* (New York: Oxford University Press, 1970), 61. For the brief text of the Wilmot Proviso, see www.mtholyoke.edu/acad/intrel/wilmot.htm.

59. Martin Van Buren, "The Barnburner Manifesto," issued in April 1848, quoted in Silbey, *Martin Van Buren*, 194.

## 2. TO CONSERVE THE WHITE MAN'S REPUBLIC, 1848–1874

1. Stephen A. Douglas to August Belmont, December 25, 1860, in *Letters of Stephen A. Douglas*, ed. Robert W. Johannsen (Urbana: University of Illinois Press, 1961), 505.

2. Quoted in Jean H. Baker, *Affairs of Party: The Political Culture of Northern Democrats in the Mid-Nineteenth Century* (Ithaca, NY: Cornell University Press, 1983), 257. The meeting was held on November 28, 1863.

3. *The Pilot* quoted in Timothy J. Meagher, *The Lord Is Not Dead: A History of Irish Americans* (New Haven: Yale University Press), forthcoming.

4. Samuel Cox quoted in Joel H. Silbey, *The American Political Nation, 1838–1893* (Stanford, CA: Stanford University Press, 1991), 215.

5. I borrow the term "egalitarian whiteness" from David A. Bateman, Ira Katznelson, and John S. Lapinski, *Southern Nation: Congress and White Supremacy after Reconstruction* (Princeton, NJ: Princeton University Press, 2018).

6. "Autobiographical Sketch, September 1, 1838," in Johannsen, *Letters of Stephen A. Douglas*, 57.

7. On Belmont's mansion, which was later demolished: Tom Miller, "The Lost August Belmont Mansion—No. 109 Fifth Avenue," *Daytonian in Manhattan*, April 18, 2016, daytoninmanhattan.blogspot.com/2016/04/the-lost-august-belmont-mansion-no-109.html. Belmont may have been the model for Julius Beaufort, the immoral character who flaunts his wealth in Edith Wharton's 1920 novel *The Age of Innocence*, which is based on Manhattan high society during the Gilded Age.

8. Belmont's religious affiliations after he moved to the United States are somewhat in doubt. He may have converted to Christianity before his marriage ceremony, which was held in 1849 at a fashionable Episcopalian church on Fifth Avenue in Greenwich Village. But he doesn't appear to have attended services afterward. Belmont's political adversaries quoted in Irving Katz, *August Belmont: A Political Biography* (New York: Columbia University Press, 1968), 19, 144.

9. August Belmont quoted in *Letters, Speeches, and Addresses of August Belmont* (privately printed, 1890), 141.

10. Lewis Cass quoted in Joshua Lynn, "Preserving the White Man's Republic: The Democratic Party and the Transformation of American Conservatism" (PhD dissertation, University of North Carolina–Chapel Hill, 2016), 32.

11. Barnburner Manifesto, written in the winter of 1848 by Martin Van Buren with help from his son John Van Buren and Samuel Tilden, quoted in Sean Wilentz, *The Rise of American Democracy: Jefferson to Lincoln* (New York: W. W. Norton, 2005), 615.

12. With a fortune of $200,000, Van Buren was already a wealthy man when he stepped down from the presidency in 1841. Edward M. Shepard, *Martin Van Buren* (1888; rev. ed., Boston: Houghton, Mifflin, 1899), 450.

13. Robert W. Johannsen, *Stephen A. Douglas* (New York: Oxford University Press, 1973), 533.

14. Stephen A. Douglas to Thomas Settle, quoted in Michael Todd Landis, *Northern Men with Southern Loyalties: The Democratic Party and the Sectional Crisis* (Ithaca, NY: Cornell University Press, 2014), 35; Stephen A. Douglas to editor of *Washington [D.C.] Union*, March 19, 1852, in Johannsen, *Letters of Stephen A. Douglas*, 243.

15. Nathaniel Hawthorne, *The Life of Franklin Pierce* (Boston: Ticknor, Reed, and Fields, 1852), 111.

16. Stephen A. Douglas quoted in Johannsen, *Stephen A. Douglas*, 421.

17. Francis Blair quoted in Johannsen, *Stephen A. Douglas*, 423.

18. Johannsen, *Stephen A. Douglas*, 453–54.

19. James Buchanan quoted in Jean H. Baker, *James Buchanan* (New York: Henry Holt, 2004), 86.

20. Eric Foner, *Free Soil, Free Labor, Free Men: The Ideology of the Republican Party Before the Civil War* (New York: Oxford University Press, 1970), 149, 177; for the record of corruption, see James McPherson, *Battle Cry of Freedom: The Civil War Era* (New York: Oxford University Press, 1988), 225–26.

21. Stephen A. Douglas, May 1857, quoted in Johannsen, *Stephen A. Douglas*, 569; ibid., 571.

22. Abraham Lincoln quoted in Eric Foner, *Politics and Ideology in the Age of the Civil War* (New York: Oxford University Press, 1980), 47; partisans quoted in Michael F. Holt's meticulous study, *The Election of 1860:*

*"A Campaign Fraught with Consequences"* (Lawrence: University Press of Kansas, 2017), 51.

23. An unnamed delegate quoted in Holt, *The Election of 1860*, 62.

24. Stephen A. Douglas to August Belmont, marked "Private," May 22, 1860, in Belmont Family Papers, Columbia University Rare Books and Manuscripts.

25. *The New York Times* quoted in Holt, *Election of 1860*, 129.

26. Stephen A. Douglas, "Let the People Rule," speech, July 31, 1860, stephen adouglasassociation.com/uploads/speeches/people_rule.pdf; *Montgomery Daily Advertiser* quoted in Johannsen, *Stephen A. Douglas*, 791. A Republican editor in Hartford lampooned Douglas's itinerant campaigning under the title "'BOY' LOST": "He is about five feet nothing in height, and about the same in diameter the other way. He has a red face, short legs, and a large belly . . . Talks a great deal, and very loud; always about himself. He has an idea that he is a candidate for the Presidency." Quoted in Johannsen, *Stephen A. Douglas*, 781.

27. August Belmont letter, quoted in Katz, *August Belmont*, 77.

28. Stephen A. Douglas quoted in Johannsen, *Stephen A. Douglas*, 868.

29. Nathaniel Hawthorne, "Earth's Holocaust," 1844. Later collected in Hawthorne's *Mosses from an Old Manse*, vol. 2 (New York: Wiley and Putnam, 1846).

30. Stephen A. Douglas, in one of his debates with Abraham Lincoln during the race for the U.S. Senate, quoted in Baker, *Affairs of Party*, 185.

31. Lewis Cass quoted in John Gerring, *Party Ideologies in America, 1828–1996* (Cambridge, UK: Cambridge University Press, 1998); the Democrat quoted in Lynn, "Preserving the White Man's Republic," 94.

32. Unnamed Democrat quoted in Rebecca Edwards, *Angels in the Machinery: Gender in American Party Politics from the Civil War to the Progressive Era* (New York: Oxford University Press, 1997), 21.

33. The New York figure comes from Edwin G. Burrows and Mike Wallace, *Gotham: A History of New York City to 1898* (New York: Oxford University Press, 1999), 743.

34. See Frank Towers, "American (Know-Nothing) Party," in *The Princeton Encyclopedia of American Political History*, ed. Michael Kazin, Rebecca Edwards, and Adam Rothman (Princeton, NJ: Princeton University Press, 2010), 1:23–25.

35. Protestant merchant quoted in Meagher, *The Lord Is Not Dead*. In 1856, Stephen Douglas married a much younger woman, Adele Cutts, who had been raised Catholic. A priest conducted the ceremony. But nativist critics do not seem to have attacked him for that. His first wife, a Protestant, had died three years before.

36. Theodore Parker quoted in Meagher, *The Lord Is Not Dead*; *Pittsburgh Catholic*, March 1855, quoted ibid.

37. Mike Walsh quoted in Sean Wilentz, *Chants Democratic: New York City and the Rise of the American Working Class* (New York: Oxford University press, 1984), 330, 333.

38. John Sherman quoted in Silbey, *American Political Nation,* 170.

39. George Pendleton quoted in Thomas S. Mach, *"Gentleman George" Hunt Pendleton: Party Politics and Ideological Identity in Nineteenth-Century America* (Kent, OH: Kent State University Press, 2007), 69; Jennifer Weber, *Copperheads: The Rise and Fall of Lincoln's Opponents in the North* (New York: Oxford University Press, 2006), 4.

40. Horatio Seymour quoted in Weber, *Copperheads,* 67.

41. *Chicago Times* article quoted in Weber, *Copperheads,* 39.

42. Dayton disciple of Clement Vallandigham quoted in Frank L. Klement, *The Limits of Dissent: Clement L. Vallandigham and the Civil War* (Lexington: University Press of Kentucky, 1970), 106.

43. Samuel Cox quoted in David Lindsey, *"Sunset" Cox: Irrepressible Democrat* (Detroit: Wayne State University Press, 1959), 69; Samuel Sullivan Cox, *Eight Years in Congress, from 1857 to 1865* (New York: D. Appleton, 1865), 6. For a pithy statement of Cox's views on war and abolition, see his speech in the House on the conscription bill in early 1863, in Cox, *Eight Years in Congress,* 310.

44. Clement Vallandigham quoted in Joel H. Silbey, *A Respectable Minority: The Democratic Party in the Civil War Era, 1860–1868* (New York: W. W. Norton, 1977), 103.

45. Ambrose Burnside's order quoted in Weber, *Copperheads,* 95, from which I have also taken the description of Vallandigham's arrest and the immediate reaction to it.

46. Horatio Seymour quoted in Weber, *Copperheads,* 96.

47. Clement Vallandigham quoted in Leon Friedman, "The Democratic Party, 1860–1884," in *History of U.S. Political Parties,* vol. 2, *1869–1910: The Gilded Age of Politics,* ed. Arthur M. Schlesinger, Jr. (New York: Chelsea House, 1973), 890; trooper quoted in Chandra Manning, *What This Cruel War Was Over: Soldiers, Slavery, and the Civil War* (New York: Knopf, 2007), 100. On the 1863 vote for governor, see "1863 Gubernatorial Election," 78Ohio, 78ohio.org/1863-gubernatorial-race. Vallandigham even failed to carry Montgomery, his home county.

48. The quote about Horatio Seymour is taken from a Philadelphia paper in 1868. William C. Harris, *Two Against Lincoln: Reverdy Johnson and Horatio Seymour, Champions of the Loyal Opposition* (Lawrence: University Press of Kansas, 2017), 3.

49. Quoted in Meagher, *The Lord Is Not Dead.* The fullest account of the event is Iver Bernstein's *The New York City Draft Riots: Their Significance for American Society and Politics in the Age of the Civil War* (New York: Oxford University Press, 1990).

50. Horatio Seymour and *World* editorial quoted in Bernstein, *The New York City Draft Riots*, 50; George T. McJimsey, *Genteel Partisan: Manton Marble, 1834–1917* (Ames: Iowa State University Press, 1971), 49.

51. August Belmont, address given on September 17, 1864, in *Letters, Speeches, and Addresses of August Belmont*, 142.

52. "1864 Democratic Party Platform," August 29, 1864, The American Presidency Project, www.presidency.ucsb.edu/ws/index.php?pid=29578.

53. *Chicago Tribune*, September 1864, quoted in Katz, *August Belmont*, 144.

54. George McClellan to August Belmont, October 30, 1864 (year assumed; McClellan noted only the day and month on his letter), Belmont Family Papers.

55. Seymour quoted in Silbey, *Respectable Minority*, 149.

56. Alfred Connable and Edward Silberfarb, *Tigers of Tammany: Nine Men Who Ran New York City* (New York: Holt, Rinehart, and Winston, 1967), 153; *The New York Times*, July 2, 1868, 8.

57. August Belmont, speech to the Democratic National Convention, July 4, 1868, in Belmont, *Letters, Speeches, Addresses*, 185–86; *World*, April 1868, quoted in Silbey, *Respectable Minority*, 199.

58. Ohio partisans quoted in Samuel deCanio, *Democracy and the Origins of the American Regulatory State* (New Haven, CT: Yale University Press, 2015), 69.

59. *Cincinnati Daily Enquirer*, June 30, 1867, quoted in Chester McArthur Destler, "The Origin and Character of the Pendleton Plan," *Mississippi Valley Historical Review* 24, no. 2 (September 1937): 176.

60. Democratic Party delegates quoted in Stewart Mitchell, *Horatio Seymour of New York* (Cambridge, MA: Harvard University Press, 1938), 423; "1868 Democratic Party Platform," July 4, 1868, The American Presidency Project, www.presidency.ucsb.edu/ws/index.php?pid=29579.

61. *Louisville Daily Courier* quoted in David W. Blight, *Race and Reunion: The Civil War in American Memory* (Cambridge, MA: Harvard University Press, 2001), 101. On terror against Black voters, see Eric Foner, *Reconstruction: America's Unfinished Revolution, 1863–1877* (New York: Harper & Row, 1988), 343.

62. Democrats, Clement Vallandigham, and August Belmont quoted in Lawrence Grossman, *The Democratic Party and the Negro: Northern and National Politics, 1868–92* (Urbana: University of Illinois Press, 1976), 23, 25, 26.

63. William Smith, "Declaration of Independence from the Sale of the Democratic Party Made by the Barnacles to Horace Greeley at the Cincinnati Convention," August 24, 1872, digitized pamphlet in Georgetown University Library, accessed via *Sabin Americana: History of the Americas 1500–1926* (Gale, Cengage Learning), www.gale.com/c/sabin-americana-history-of-the-americas-1500-1926.

64. *The Cincinnati Enquirer* quoted in Nicolas Barreyre, *Gold and Freedom:*

*The Political Economy of Reconstruction* (Charlottesville: University of Virginia Press, 2015), 205.

65. *Buffalo Advertiser* quoted in David W. Blight, "The Civil War and Reconstruction Era, 1845–1877: Lecture 26 Transcript," History 119, Open Yale Courses, openmedia.yale.edu/projects/iphone/departments /hist/hist119/transcript26.html; *World*, November 9, 1874, quoted in Schlesinger, *History of U.S. Political Parties*, 948.

66. Nashville newspaper quoted in Blight, "The Civil War and Reconstruction Era, 1845–1877."

### 3. BOSSES NORTH AND SOUTH, 1874–1894

1. John Kelly, in *The Irish-American*, November 17, 1877, quoted in Terry Golway, *Machine Made: Tammany Hall and the Creation of Modern American Politics* (New York: Liveright, 2014), 124.

2. *Tammany Times*, August 26, 1893, 3. This sentence was often printed close to the masthead of the paper.

3. "The Shell Manifesto" quoted in William J. Cooper, Jr., *The Conservative Regime: South Carolina, 1877–1890* (Baltimore: Johns Hopkins University Press, 1968), 167.

4. Edward L. Ayers, *The Promise of the New South: Life After Reconstruction* (New York: Oxford University Press, 1992), 38.

5. Theodore Roosevelt, "Machine Politics in New York City," *The Century* 33, no. 1 (November 1886): 74, 76. On the popularity of the "machine" metaphor, see James J. Connolly, *An Elusive Unity: Urban Democracy and Machine Politics in Industrializing America* (Ithaca, NY: Cornell University Press, 2010), 54–56.

6. For a splendidly detailed and shrewd narrative of how the major parties ran politics in this period, see Mark Wahlgren Summers, *Party Games: Getting, Keeping, and Using Power in Gilded Age Politics* (Chapel Hill: University of North Carolina Press, 2004). On the disenfranchisement of Black voters, see Alexander Keyssar, *The Right to Vote: The Contested History of Democracy in the United States*, rev. ed. (New York: Basic Books, 2009), 83–93.

7. On the Republican skew of these new states, see Summers, *Party Games*, 131–34.

8. *World*, January 5, 1869, quoted in George T. McJimsey, *Genteel Partisan: Manton Marble, 1834–1917* (Ames: Iowa State University Press, 1971), 135.

9. Samuel Tilden, 1871, quoted in Jerome Mushkat, *The Reconstruction of the New York Democracy, 1861–1874* (Rutherford, NJ: Fairleigh Dickinson University Press, 1981), 185.

10. William G. Riordon, *Honest Graft: The World of George Washington Plunkitt* (1905; repr. St. James, NY: Brandywine Press, 1994), 53–54.

11. New York's thirty-five electoral votes were 19 percent of a majority in

1876; its thirty-seven electoral votes decreased slightly to 16 percent by 1896. Between 1872 and 1912, only one nominee who did not carry New York was elected president: Rutherford B. Hayes in 1876, who lost the national popular vote.

12. "The Story of a Busy Life," *The New York Times*, June 2, 1886, times machine.nytimes.com/timesmachine/1886/06/02/103116054.html?page Number=1.

13. Mark Wahlgren Summers, *The Gilded Age, or, The Hazard of New Functions* (Upper Saddle River, NJ: Pearson, 1997), 182. These references to Kelly's early life come mostly from his only scholarly biography: Arthur Genen, "John Kelly: New York's First Irish Boss" (PhD dissertation, New York University, 1971). A journalist who was a friend of Kelly's also wrote a hagiographic account that dwells on his career before he became boss: James Fairfax McLaughlin, *The Life and Times of John Kelly: Tribune of the People* (New York: American News, 1885).

14. Genen, "John Kelly," 22.

15. For a succinct description of Kelly's organization, see Genen, "John Kelly," 51–55.

16. Riordon, *Honest Graft*, 71.

17. Riordon, *Honest Graft*, 163–65. As a rising politician in Boston during the Gilded Age, John Fitzgerald, John F. Kennedy's maternal grandfather, had a similarly hectic schedule. Frederik Logevall, *JFK: Coming of Age in the American Century, 1917–1956* (New York: Random House, 2020), 23–24. *Irish World* quoted in Eric Foner, "Class, Ethnicity, and Radicalism in the Gilded Age: The Land League and Irish-America," in *Politics and Ideology in the Age of the Civil War* (New York: Oxford University Press, 1980), 165. For a similar description of "the duties of an Assembly District leader" from the mid-1880s, see William M. Ivins, *Machine Politics and Money in Elections in New York City* (New York: Harper & Brothers, 1887), 11–14.

18. *Evening Express*, July 30, 1879, quoted in Genen, "John Kelly," 208; John Kelly, in *New York World*, November 5, 1875, quoted ibid., 128. The figure of $7.50 is cited in Daniel Czitrom, *New York Exposed: The Gilded Age Police Scandal That Launched the Progressive Era* (New York: Oxford University Press, 2016), 87. For a lower figure ($5) and other details on the costs of elections in the city during Kelly's heyday, see Ivins, *Machine Politics and Money in Elections in New York City*.

19. This was Kelly's second marriage. His first wife had died a decade earlier. On Tammany's support for the Land League, see Foner, "Class, Ethnicity, and Radicalism in the Gilded Age," 165–66. On the percentage of Irish Americans in the city population, see Genen, "John Kelly," 31.

20. See the description of the parade in Genen, "John Kelly," 164–65.

21. Sven Beckert, *The Monied Metropolis: New York City and the Consolida-*

*tion of the American Bourgeoisie, 1850–1896* (Cambridge, UK: Cambridge University Press, 2001), 220–24.

22. Newspapers and George McNeill quoted in Genen, "John Kelly," 182; Golway, *Machine Made*, 122; Beckert, *Monied Metropolis*, 223–24.

23. Golway, *Machine Made*, 124.

24. William Allen White quoted in Alfred Connable and Edward Silberfarb, *Tigers of Tammany: Nine Men Who Ran New York* (New York: Holt, Rinehart, and Winston, 1967), 208.

25. Henry George speech, October 5, 1886, quoted in *Henry George's 1886 Campaign*, prepared by Louis F. Post and Fred C. Leubuscher (1887; repr. New York: Henry George School, 1961), 20–29.

26. The twenty-eight-year-old Theodore Roosevelt was also on the mayoral ballot as the Republican nominee. He scorned Tammany but despised the Union Labor Party for seeking to set "one class of citizens against all other classes." Quoted in Edward T. O'Donnell, *Henry George and the Crisis of Inequality: Progress and Poverty in the Gilded Age* (New York: Columbia University Press, 2015), 213.

27. Martin Shefter, "The Electoral Foundations of the Political Machine: New York City, 1884–1897," in *The History of American Electoral Behavior*, ed. Joel Silbey, Allan G. Bogue, and William H. Flanigan (Princeton, NJ: Princeton University Press, 1978), 284.

28. Edwin G. Burrows and Mike Wallace, *Gotham: A History of New York City to 1898* (New York: Oxford University Press, 1999), 1108.

29. *Tammany Times*, July 30, 1893, 5.

30. On assessments for various offices, see Ivins, *Machine Politics and Money in Elections in New York City*, 54–57. In the 1880s, about $700,000 (equivalent to about $16 million today) was spent on a typical New York City election by all sides. Morton Keller, *Affairs of State: Public Life in Late Nineteenth Century America* (Cambridge, MA: Harvard University Press, 1977), 542. In 2013, Bill DeBlasio spent about the same amount on his own campaign for mayor.

31. Richard Croker, "Tammany Hall and the Democracy," *North American Review* 154, no. 423 (February 1892): 225, 227–28.

32. Wade Hampton III quoted in Rod Andrew, Jr., *Wade Hampton: Confederate Warrior to Southern Redeemer* (Chapel Hill: University of North Carolina Press, 2008), 297.

33. Wade Hampton III, speech, *The New York Times*, July 28, 1868, 5.

34. For Hampton's testimony, see Andrew, *Wade Hampton*, 363–64.

35. Francis Davie quoted in Andrew, *Wade Hampton*, 381.

36. Black South Carolinian and Wade Hampton III quoted in Eric Foner, *Reconstruction: America's Unfinished Revolution, 1863–1877* (New York: Harper & Row, 1988), 574; Cooper, *The Conservative Regime*, 23.

37. Wade Hampton III quoted in Cooper, *The Conservative Regime*, 71.

38. On the eight-box law, see www.scencyclopedia.org/sce/entries/eight-box -law.

39. On the violent history of Edgefield County, see Fox Butterfield, *All God's Children: The Bosket Family and the American Tradition of Violence* (New York: Knopf, 1995).

40. Robert Chandler quoted in Stephen Kantrowitz's fine biography, *Ben Tillman and the Reconstruction of White Supremacy* (Chapel Hill: University of North Carolina Press, 2000), 76.

41. Quoted in Kantrowitz, *Ben Tillman*, 113–15.

42. Benjamin Tillman quoted in Cooper, *Conservative Regime*, 167; Charles J. Holden, "'Is Our Love for Wade Hampton Foolishness?': South Carolina and the Lost Cause," in *The Myth of the Lost Cause and Civil War History*, ed. Gary W. Gallagher and Alan T. Nolan (Bloomington: Indiana University Press, 2000), 69. That summer, Hampton, perhaps to remind white voters about his central role in overthrowing "radical" rule, wrote an article for a national magazine that accused the Republican Party of a "senseless advocacy of universal suffrage" that allowed both "ignorant, uneducated Blacks" and the "scum of European nations" to vote. He also advocated colonizing all American Blacks "to some other land." Wade Hampton III, "The Race Problem," *The Arena* 2 (July 1890): 137–38.

43. Benjamin Tillman quoted in Francis Butler Simkins, *Pitchfork Ben Tillman: South Carolinian* (1944; repr. Columbia: University of South Carolina Press, 2002), 169–71.

44. Benjamin Tillman quoted in Kantrowitz, *Ben Tillman*, 150.

45. Benjamin Tillman quoted in Kantrowitz, *Ben Tillman*, 131.

46. Lewis L. Gould, "Grover Cleveland," in *The Reader's Companion to the American Presidency*, ed. Alan Brinkley and Davis Dyer (Boston: Houghton Mifflin Harcourt, 2000), 257. The best recent study of Cleveland's political ideas and deeds is Richard E. Welch, Jr., *The Presidencies of Grover Cleveland* (Lawrence: University Press of Kansas, 1988).

47. During the Civil War, Cleveland hired a substitute to be drafted in his place, but because he had to take care of his widowed mother, his later political opponents refrained from attacking his lack of a military record. He was the only president from 1869 to 1901 not to have served in the Union Army.

48. Allan Nevins, *Grover Cleveland: A Study in Courage* (New York: Dodd, Mead, 1932), 119, 125.

49. Grover Cleveland, "Veto Message," February 16, 1887, www.presidency .ucsb.edu/documents/veto-message-237; Welch, *Presidencies of Grover Cleveland*, 99.

50. Summers, *Party Games*, 190.

51. On the confrontation in Chicago, see Golway, *Machine Made*, 138–39. The Nast cartoon appeared in the July 19, 1884, issue of *Harper's Weekly*.

52. Cleveland also received support from five activists in the Woman Suffrage

Party of New York, including Delia Stewart Parnell, mother of the future Irish nationalist hero Charles Parnell. They claimed Cleveland had told them that he would sign "any woman suffrage measure we could get the Legislature to pass." Clarence S. Lozier, M.D., et al. to "Good Friend," October 12, 1884, Grover Cleveland Papers, Library of Congress, Roll 2.

53. Grover Cleveland's tariff message, December 1887, quoted in Welch, *Presidencies of Grover Cleveland*, 87.

54. Grover Cleveland quoted in Nevins, *Grover Cleveland*, 439.

55. "Big" Tim Sullivan quoted in Richard F. Welch, *King of the Bowery: Big Tim Sullivan, Tammany Hall, and New York City from the Gilded Age to the Progressive Era* (Albany: State University of New York Press, 2008), 39.

56. Grover Cleveland, speech to a special session of Congress, August 8, 1893, University of Virginia, Miller Center, Presidential Speeches, miller center.org/the-presidency/presidential-speeches/august-8–1893-special -session-message.

57. Benjamin Tillman quoted in Simkins, *Pitchfork Ben Tillman*, 314.

### 4. THE PROGRESSIVE TURN, 1894–1920

1. William Jennings Bryan, speech at Tammany Hall, quoted in William J. Bryan, *The First Battle: A Story of the Campaign of 1896* (Chicago: W. B. Conkey, 1896), 510.

2. William Jennings Bryan quoted in John Gerring, *Party Ideologies in America, 1828–1996* (Cambridge, UK: Cambridge University Press, 1998), 207.

3. Woodrow Wilson, acceptance speech, quoted in Lewis L. Gould, *The First Modern Clash over Federal Power: Wilson versus Hughes in the Presidential Election of 1916* (Lawrence: University Press of Kansas, 2016), 90.

4. William Jennings Bryan and the Railroad, railroads.unl.edu/student _projects/nsanderson/speeches/Trip2/Sept7_Chicago,IL.html.

5. Eugene V. Debs quoted in Michael Kazin, *A Godly Hero: The Life of William Jennings Bryan* (New York: Knopf, 2006), 64; William Allen White quoted ibid., 72.

6. *Chicago Daily Tribune*, November 4, 1908, 3. To illustrate the story, the paper's editorial cartoonist sketched three images of Bryan as the drunk and Uncle Sam as the enforcer.

7. Silas Bryan quoted in Kazin, *A Godly Hero*, 5.

8. William Jennings Bryan quoted in Kazin, *A Godly Hero*, 148, 147.

9. These details and others from Bryan's life and career are taken from Kazin, *A Godly Hero*.

10. William Jennings Bryan quoted in Lawrence F. Prescott, *Living Issues of the Campaign of 1900: Its Men and Principles* (Denver, CO: Western Book, 1900), 2:6–7. William James to Francis Boott, September 15, 1900, in *The Correspondence of William James*, vol. 9, *July 1899–1901*, ed. Ignas K.

Skrupskelis and Elizabeth M. Berkeley (Charlottesville: University of Virginia Press, 2001), 303. In 1896, Theodore Roosevelt, who was on the left of his party, was nevertheless so hostile to Bryan and his allies that he charged them with plotting a "social revolution" and called the Democratic campaign a "preposterous farrago of sinister nonsense" emitted by an "amiable and windy demagogue." Quoted in Paolo E. Coletta, "Will the Real Progressive Stand Up?: William Jennings Bryan and Theodore Roosevelt to 1909," *Nebraska History* 65 (1984): 17.

11. Richard Hofstadter, *The American Political Tradition and the Men Who Made It* (New York: Knopf, 1948), 137. Hofstadter was describing Wendell Phillips, the abolitionist who, after the Civil War, became a champion of labor unions.

12. *Richmond Times*, 1898, quoted in Michael Perman, *Struggle for Mastery: Disfranchisement in the South, 1888–1908* (Chapel Hill: University of North Carolina Press, 2001), 15.

13. Charlestown *News and Courier* quoted in Perman, *Struggle for Mastery*, 104.

14. Reporter quoted in Dewey W. Grantham, *Southern Progressivism: The Reconciliation of Progress and Tradition* (Knoxville: University of Tennessee Press, 1983), 115. On turnout, see Alex Keyssar, *The Right to Vote: The Contested History of Democracy in the United States* (New York: Basic Books, 2009), 95–96, and David Bateman, Ira Katznelson, and John S. Lapinski, *Southern Nation: Congress and White Supremacy after Reconstruction* (Princeton, NJ: Princeton University Press, 2018), 211–13.

15. C. Vann Woodward quoted in Bateman, Katznelson, and Lapinski, *Southern Nation*, 244.

16. Tom Watson, *The People's Party Campaign Book 1892* (repr. New York: Arno, 1975), 26.

17. Tom Watson quoted in C. Vann Woodward, *Tom Watson: Agrarian Rebel* (New York: Macmillan, 1938), 409.

18. Woodward, *Tom Watson*, 411, 438; Zachary Smith, "Tom Watson and Resistance to Federal War Policies in Georgia During World War I," *Journal of Southern History* 78 (May 2012): 311; "Why Bryan Will Never Be President," editorial, *Watson's Jeffersonian Magazine*, 1909, 17.

19. As one political scientist puts it, "Elements of the radical West had to be incorporated [by 1912] into virtually any winning Democratic coalition, so that a truly conservative Democracy was no longer as viable as it had been." Alan Ware, *The Democratic Party Heads North, 1877–1962* (New York: Cambridge University Press, 2006), 130.

20. Mike Wallace, *Greater Gotham: A History of New York City from 1898 to 1919* (New York: Oxford University Press, 2017), 129. In 1905, the year before it vowed to fight the "criminal combinations of capital," Tammany had engaged in massive fraud to defeat William Randolph Hearst's campaign for mayor.

21. William Howard Taft quoted in Kazin, *A Godly Hero*, 159.

22. Kazin, *A Godly Hero*, 187, 190. The New York delegation, controlled by Tammany Hall but not hostile to Wall Street, voted for Bryan's resolution, too. As he did so, Boss Murphy looked over at August Belmont, Jr., and quipped, "Now Auggie, listen to yourself vote yourself out of the convention." Quoted ibid., 188.

23. Woodrow Wilson to H. S. McClure, April 9, 1910, quoted in David Sarasohn, *Party of Reform: The Democrats in the Progressive Era* (Jackson: University Press of Mississippi, 1989), 119–20.

24. Woodrow Wilson, *The New Freedom: A Call for the Emancipation of the Generous Energies of a People* (New York: Doubleday, Page, 1913), www .gutenberg.org/files/14811/14811-8.txt.

25. "1912 Democratic Party Platform," June 25, 1912, The American Presidency Project, www.presidency.ucsb.edu/documents/1912-democratic -party-platform. On the GOP's reaction to the Adamson Act, see Gould, *The First Modern Clash over Federal Power*, 95–97.

26. *The Sun* quoted in Elizabeth Sanders, *Roots of Reform: Farmers, Workers, and the American State, 1877–1917* (Chicago: University of Chicago Press, 1999), 249.

27. For "egalitarian whiteness," see Bateman, Katznelson, and Lapinski, *Southern Nation*, 217ff.

28. William Jennings Bryan, *Under Other Flags: Travels, Lectures, Speeches* (Lincoln, NE: Woodruff Collins Printing, 1904), 73.

29. Walter Lippmann quoted in Ronald Steel, *Walter Lippmann and the American Century* (Boston: Little, Brown, 1980), 24.

30. Herbert Croly quoted in Arthur S. Link, *Wilson: The New Freedom* (Princeton, NJ: Princeton University Press, 1956), 151.

31. Melvyn Dubofsky, *The State and Labor in Modern America* (Chapel Hill: University of North Carolina Press, 1994), 54–56.

32. William Howard Taft quoted in Arthur S. Link, *Wilson: Confusions and Crises, 1915–1916* (Princeton, NJ: Princeton University Press, 1964), 325. Taft later became a colleague of Brandeis's on the Supreme Court.

33. Colorado Democrat quoted in Link, *Wilson: Confusions and Crises*, 362; "1916 Democratic Party Platform," June 4, 1916, The American Presidency Project, www.presidency.ucsb.edu/documents/1916-democratic -party-platform.

34. Frederic C. Howe quoted in Michael McGerr, *The Decline of Popular Politics: The American North, 1865–1928* (New York: Oxford University Press, 1986), 163.

35. Sarasohn, *Party of Reform*, 212.

36. Wilson's speech to Congress, April 2, 1917, www.americanyawp.com /reader/21-world-war-i/woodrow-wilson-requests-war-april-2-1917.

37. Claude Kitchin quoted in Michael Kazin, *War Against War: The American*

*Fight for Peace, 1914–1918* (New York: Simon & Schuster, 2017), 183; William Stone quoted ibid., 146.

38. *New York World* quoted in Kazin, *War Against War,* 271; Tom Watson quoted in Zachary Smith, "Tom Watson and Resistance to Federal War Policies in Georgia during World War I," *Journal of Southern History* 78, no. 2 (May 2012): 311.

39. Woodrow Wilson quoted in A. Scott Berg, *Wilson* (New York: Simon & Schuster, 2013), 657. During the twentieth century, every major war into which a Democratic administration led the nation hurt the party's electoral prospects, at least in its immediate aftermath. Republicans gained seats in Congress and took the White House by running against Harry Truman's stalemate in Korea and Lyndon Johnson's failed promise to win the war in Vietnam. Even the glow of victory in World War II under a Democratic administration soon faded, as Republicans took control of Congress in 1946 and put Truman on the defensive with charges that he allowed Communists like Alger Hiss to hold high posts in the government.

40. "39 Labor Leaders Out for Harding," *The New York Times,* October 31, 1920, E13.

41. William Jennings Bryan quoted in Kazin, *A Godly Hero,* 268.


5. IT'S UP TO THE WOMEN, 1920–1933

1. "Booms Mrs. Catt for Presidency," *The New York Times,* February 15, 1920, timesmachine.nytimes.com/timesmachine/1920/02/15/118262309.html?pageNumber=8.

2. Eleanor Roosevelt, "Women Must Learn to Play the Game as Men Do," *Red Book Magazine* 50 (April 1928): 78–79, 141–42, Eleanor Roosevelt Papers Project, George Washington University, Columbian College of Arts and Sciences, erpapers.columbian.gwu.edu/women-must-learn-play-game-men-do.

3. Frances Perkins, "Gov. Smith, the Great Humanitarian," *The Bulletin* (Women's National Democratic Club), October 1928, 6.

4. For a summary of the Democrats' performance in state elections, see Alan Ware, *The Democratic Party Heads North, 1877–1962* (New York: Cambridge University Press, 2006), 150. On the DNC's woes, see Jo Freeman, *A Room at a Time: How Women Entered Party Politics* (Lanham, MD: Rowman & Littlefield, 2000), 87.

5. William Jennings Bryan, criticizing New York governor Al Smith's effort to relax enforcement of the Volstead Act in 1923, quoted in Robert A. Slayton, *Empire Statesman: The Rise and Redemption of Al Smith* (New York: Free Press, 2001), 201. It was John Higham who coined the term "the tribal Twenties" in his classic work *Strangers in the Land: Patterns of American Nativism, 1860–1925* (New Brunswick, NJ: Rutgers University Press, 1955), 264.

6. Eleanor Roosevelt, *It's Up to the Women* (1933; repr. New York: Nation Books, 2017), 217.

7. Elisabeth Israels Perry, *Belle Moscowitz: Feminine Politics and the Exercise of Power in the Age of Alfred E. Smith* (New York: Oxford University Press, 1987), 74–75. Born in 1877, Belle Lindner first married Charles Israels, who committed suicide in 1911. She then married Henry Moscowitz, a fellow social worker, in 1914. To avoid confusion, I refer to her throughout this chapter by the name she used when she became a prominent Democrat.

8. Oral History of Frances Perkins, part 1, session 1, Oral History Research Office, Columbia University, 1952, transcript, 126.

9. Kristin Downey, *The Woman Behind the New Deal: The Life of Frances Perkins, FDR's Secretary of Labor and His Moral Conscience* (New York: Nan A. Talese, 2009), 28, 27.

10. Roosevelt, *It's Up to the Women*, 173; Pauline Newman quoted in Nancy F. Cott, *The Grounding of Modern Feminism* (New Haven, CT: Yale University Press, 1987), 127.

11. "Women Members by Congress, 1917–Present," U.S. House of Representatives, History, Art & Archives, history.house.gov/Exhibitions-and-Publications/WIC/Historical-Data/Women-Members-by-Congress.

12. Emily Newell Blair, *Bridging Two Eras: The Autobiography of Emily Newell Blair, 1877–1951*, ed. Virginia Jeans Laas (Columbia: University of Missouri Press, 1999), 200; Downey, *The Woman Behind the New Deal*, 45.

13. Blair, *Bridging Two Eras*, 196, 160.

14. Blair, *Bridging Two Eras*, 223.

15. Blair, *Bridging Two Eras*, 222. The WDNC's publication was originally named *The Fortnightly Bulletin* and renamed *The Bulletin* when it became a much longer and monthly magazine in 1926. To avoid confusion, I have called it simply *The Bulletin* throughout this chapter.

16. In the early 1920s, the Women's Division of the DNC also issued a well-illustrated, smoothly written pamphlet designed to aid women new to politics: "So You're Going to Hold a Meeting!," WNDC Papers, Manuscript Division, Library of Congress, box 113.

17. *The Bulletin*, May 26, 1923, 1; September 15, 1923, 1, 3; August 4, 1923, 4.

18. Kristi Andersen, *After Suffrage: Women in Partisan and Electoral Politics Before the New Deal* (Chicago: University of Chicago Press, 1996), 7, 83.

19. William Gibbs McAdoo quoted in David Burner, *The Politics of Provincialism: The Democratic Party in Transition, 1918–1932* (1968; repr. Cambridge, MA: Harvard University Press, 1986), 114.

20. "1924 Democratic Party Platform," June 24, 1924, The American Presidency Project, www.presidency.ucsb.edu/documents/1924-democratic-party-platform.

21. Willian Jennings Bryan quoted in Michael Kazin, *A Godly Hero: The Life of William Jennings Bryan* (New York: Knopf, 2006), 284.

22. Blair, *Bridging Two Eras*, 301; H. L. Mencken, "Mr. Davis' Campaign," October 13, 1924, in *On Politics: A Carnival of Buncombe*, ed. Malcolm Moos (Baltimore: Johns Hopkins University Press, 1956), 115.

23. Mencken, "Mr. Davis' Campaign," 114.

24. *The Bulletin*, July 26, 1924, 2; the leaflet can be found in the WNDC Papers, box 113. In line with this sentiment, the headline on a postcard the club mailed out near the end of the campaign urging women to vote for Davis read "A Call to Duty." Ibid.

25. Unnamed biographer quoted in John F. McClymer, "Of 'Mornin' Glories' and 'Fine Old Oaks': John Purroy Mitchel, Al Smith, and Reform as an Expression of Irish American Aspiration," in *The New York Irish*, ed. Ronald H. Bayor and Timothy J. Meagher (Baltimore: Johns Hopkins University Press, 1996), 379.

26. Frances Perkins quoted in Downey, *The Woman Behind the New Deal*, 40.

27. Al Smith quoted in Downey, *The Woman Behind the New Deal*, 77.

28. Oral History of Frances Perkins, part 2, session 1, transcript, 38, 39, 43, 47.

29. The film, titled *Mr. Potato*, was widely viewed both "in private gatherings and movie theaters." Perry, *Belle Moscowitz*, 143.

30. Frances Perkins quoted in Perry, *Belle Moscowitz*, 153.

31. Oliver H. P. Garrett, "Profiles: A Certain Person," *The New Yorker*, October 9, 1926, 26, 27.

32. Perry, *Belle Moscowitz*, 149.

33. Eleanor Roosevelt quoted in Blanche Wiesen Cook, *Eleanor Roosevelt*, vol. 1, *The Early Years, 1884–1933* (New York: Penguin, 1993), 195.

34. Roosevelt, "Women Must Learn to Play the Game as Men Do."

35. Roosevelt, "Women Must Learn to Play the Game as Men Do."

36. Burner, *Politics of Provincialism*, 179–216.

37. Perry, *Belle Moscowitz*, 199; Slayton, *Empire Statesman*, 281.

38. Robert Chiles, *The Revolution of '28: Al Smith, American Progressivism, and the Coming of the New Deal* (Ithaca, NY: Cornell University Press, 2018), 3; "Text of Hoover's Speech on Relation of Government to Industry," *The New York Times*, October 23, 1928, 2, timesmachine.nytimes .com/timesmachine/1928/10/23/95636170.html?pageNumber=2.

39. My argument in this paragraph is indebted to the details and analysis in Chiles, *Revolution of '28*.

40. Perkins, "Gov. Smith, the Great Humanitarian"; Blair, *Bridging Two Eras*, 325, 323. On Ross's ordeal, see Teva J. Scheer, *Governor Lady: The Life and Times of Nellie Tayloe Ross* (Columbia: University of Missouri Press, 2005), 139–40.

41. Slayton, *Empire Statesman*, 251, 287; Downey, *The Woman Behind the New Deal*, 92. Because of his opposition to the Klan, several Black newspapers in the North did endorse Smith, as did the Black nationalist leader Marcus Garvey. But Smith received about the same small percentage of

the African American vote as had the two other Democratic nominees in the 1920s. See Slayton, *Empire Statesman*, 288–90; Chiles, *Revolution of '28*, 122–23. A friendly history of the Democrats published in 1928 included this observation: "It is to-day difficult to find in any party many intelligent and candid men who believe that unrestricted Negro suffrage was justified at the time, that it has worked for the benefit of either race, or that it ever will be beneficial to the country of [*sic*] the people as a whole." Frank R. Kent, *The Democratic Party: A History* (New York: Century, 1928), 228–29.

42. The anti-Catholic insult was coined by a female Pentecostal bishop, Alma White, a supporter of the KKK. Quoted in Slayton, *Empire Statesman*, 316.

43. For a nuanced interpretation of this phenomenon, see Jerome M. Clubb and Howard W. Allen, "The Cities and the Election of 1928: Partisan Realignment?," *American Historical Review* 74, no. 4 (April 1969): 1205–20.

44. On the work of the little-known Bernice Secrest Pyke, see Paul C. Taylor, "The Entrance of Women into Party Politics" (PhD dissertation, Harvard University, 1966), 470–83; quotation on 479.

45. H. L. Mencken, Nov. 12, 1928, quoted in Chiles, *Revolution of '28*, 179.

46. Al Smith quoted in Cornelius P. Cotter and John F. Bibby, "Institutional Development of Parties and the Thesis of Party Decline," *Political Science Quarterly* 95, no. 1 (Spring 1980): 4.

47. Belle Moscowitz, interview with *The New York Telegram*, December 31, 1928, quoted in Perry, *Belle Moscowitz*, 205.

48. Emily Newell Blair quoted in Kathryn Anderson, "Practicing Feminist Politics: Emily Newell Blair and U.S. Women's Political Choices in the Early Twentieth Century," *Journal of Women's History* 9, no. 3 (Fall 1997): 50–72; Nellie Tayloe Ross, "Woman Powers of the Democratic Party," *The Bulletin*, March 1931, 10.

49. Frances Perkins, *The Roosevelt I Knew* (New York: Penguin, 1946), 32.

50. Roosevelt, *It's Up to the Women*, 175.

### 6. AN AMERICAN LABOR PARTY? 1933–1948

1. Herbert Hoover quoted in Joan Hoff Wilson, *Herbert Hoover: Forgotten Progressive* (Long Grove, IL: Waveland Press, 1975), 212.

2. Louise Overacker, "Labor's Political Contributions," *Political Science Quarterly* 54, no. 1 (March 1939): 56.

3. Ed Crump to Senator Kenneth McKellar (D-Tenn), May 29, 1944, quoted in Lyle W. Dorsett, *Franklin D. Roosevelt and the City Bosses* (Port Washington, NY: Kennikat Press, 1977), 41.

4. George Washington was elected unanimously twice, in 1789 and 1792, and just one elector cast his vote for someone besides James Monroe in

1820. But no true parties existed in the eighteenth century, and Monroe had no organized opposition.

5. The many thousands of letters Americans wrote to FDR in response to his Fireside Chats provide some of the most nuanced evidence of their attitudes toward him. For a rich sample, see Lawrence W. Levine and Cornelia R. Levine, *The People and the President: America's Conversation with FDR* (Boston: Beacon Press, 2002). Quote from Eleanor Roosevelt on 559.

6. "1936 Democratic Party Platform," June 23, 1936, The American Presidency Project, www.presidency.ucsb.edu/documents/1936-democratic -party-platform; "Franklin Roosevelt's Re-Nomination Acceptance Speech (1936)," The American Yawp Reader, www.americanyawp .com/reader/23-the-great-depression/franklin-roosevelts-re-nomination -acceptance-speech-1936.

7. John L. Lewis quoted in David Plotke, *Building a Democratic Political Order: Reshaping American Liberalism in the 1930s and 1940s* (Cambridge, UK: Cambridge University Press, 1996), 171. Labor organizations as a whole spent $770,218 in the campaign; the United Mine Workers donated $469,870. Overacker, "Labor's Political Contributions," 59.

8. Factory worker quoted in William E. Leuchtenburg, *Franklin D. Roosevelt and the New Deal, 1932–1940* (New York: Harper & Row, 1963), 189.

9. "*NRLB v. Jones & Laughlin Steel Corp.*," Wikipedia, en.wikipedia.org /wiki/NLRB_v._Jones_%26_Laughlin_Steel_Corp.

10. Daniel Schlozman, *When Movements Anchor Parties: Electoral Alignments in American History* (Princeton, NJ: Princeton University Press, 2015), 51.

11. Richard Hofstadter, *The Age of Reform: From Bryan to F.D.R.* (New York: Vintage, 1955), 308.

12. "Commonwealth Club Address: Franklin D. Roosevelt, September 23, 1932," Teaching American History, teachingamericanhistory.org/library /document/commonwealth-club-address.

13. Lizabeth Cohen, *Making a New Deal: Industrial Workers in Chicago, 1919–1939* (Cambridge, UK: Cambridge University Press, 1990), 286.

14. Mary Dreier to J. Joseph Huthmacher, May 1962, box 324, folder 5, Robert F. Wagner Papers, Georgetown University Library, Washington, D.C.

15. Robert F. Wagner quoted in *The New York Times*, July 6, 1937, in Schlozman, *When Movements Anchor Parties*, 59. On Wagner's support for racial justice, see his letter to Walter White, head of the NAACP, October 23, 1938, Wagner Papers, box 324, folder 27.

16. Joseph Schlossberg quoted in Steven Fraser, *Labor Will Rule: Sidney Hillman and the Rise of American Labor* (New York: Free Press, 1991), 95.

17. "Transcript of National Labor Relations Act (1935)," Our Documents, www.ourdocuments.gov/doc.php?flash=false&doc=67&page=transcript.

18. Journalist and reporter quoted in J. Joseph Huthmacher, *Senator Robert F. Wagner and the Rise of Urban Liberalism* (New York: Atheneum,

1968), 108; Sidney Hillman quoted in Irving Bernstein, *Turbulent Years: A History of the American Worker, 1933–1941* (Boston: Houghton Mifflin, 1970), 75. Wagner converted to Catholicism in 1946.

19. Sidney Hillman and Harold Ickes quoted in Fraser, *Labor Will Rule*, 358, 445.

20. John J. Raskob, March 1934, quoted in Frederick Rudolph, "The American Liberty League, 1934–1940," *American Historical Review* 56 (October 1950), 19.

21. Daniel Scroop, *Mr. Democrat: Jim Farley, the New Deal, and the Making of Modern American Politics* (Ann Arbor: University of Michigan Press, 2006), 123–24.

22. Molly Dewson quoted in Susan Ware, *Beyond Suffrage: Women in the New Deal* (Cambridge, MA: Harvard University Press, 1981), 45. On Norton, see David L. Porter, *Mary Norton of New Jersey: Congressional Trailblazer* (Madison, NJ: Fairleigh Dickinson University Press, 2013).

23. Dorsett, *Franklin D. Roosevelt and the City Bosses*, 107.

24. Michael P. Weber, *Don't Call Me Boss: David L. Lawrence, Pittsburgh's Renaissance Mayor* (Pittsburgh: University of Pittsburgh Press, 1988), 81; David Lawrence quoted ibid., 79.

25. David Lawrence quoted in Richard C. Keller, "Pennsylvania's Little New Deal," *Pennsylvania History* 29, no. 4 (October 1962): 405. State Republicans actually coined "Little New Deal" as a jibe, but Democrats soon adopted the term.

26. Black journalist quoted in Nancy Weiss, *Farewell to the Party of Lincoln: Black Politics in the Age of FDR* (Princeton, NJ: Princeton University Press, 1983). For vote totals in cities with large Black populations, see ibid., 206–207.

27. John Brophy, March 1938, quoted in Eric Schickler, *Racial Realignment: The Transformation of American Liberalism, 1932–1965* (Princeton, NJ: Princeton University Press, 2016), 59.

28. Sidney Hillman, August 1936, quoted in Schickler, *Racial Realignment*, 55. There were exceptions, of course. For example, Josephus Daniels had inflamed the disenfranchisement of Black North Carolinians at the end of the 1890s from his editorship of the state's highest-circulation newspaper. He continued to defend that end, if not the violent tactics employed. But as FDR's ambassador to Mexico, Daniels was a staunch defender of the Spanish Loyalists, and he backed Henry Wallace's renomination as vice president at the 1944 Democratic convention.

29. Publicist quoted in Fraser, *Labor Will Rule*, 398.

30. Josiah Bailey quoted in Devin Caughey, *The Unsolid South: Mass Politics and National Representation in a One-Party Enclave* (Princeton, NJ: Princeton University Press, 2018), 83; Martin Dies, Jr., quoted in *Congressional Record*, 75th Congress, 2nd session (1937), 82:1404. See "Martin Dies Jr.," Wikipedia, en.wikipedia.org/wiki/Martin_Dies_Jr.

31. Lyndon Johnson quoted in Caughey, *Unsolid South*, 138–39. Just 28 percent of the respondents in the Gallup poll favored going in a "more liberal" direction, and only 41 percent of Democrats. But those who identified as "lower income" were almost evenly split on the question. George H. Gallup, *The Gallup Poll: Public Opinion, 1935–1971*, vol. 1, *1935–1948* (New York: Random House, 1972), 109.

32. Claude Pepper and William Allen White quoted in Alan Brinkley, *The End of Reform: New Deal Liberalism in Recession and War* (New York: Knopf, 1995), 141.

33. "1940 Democratic Party Platform," July 15, 1940, The American Presidency Project, www.presidency.ucsb.edu/documents/1940-democratic -party-platform.

34. John L. Lewis quoted in Fraser, *Labor Will Rule*, 446; San Francisco Council quoted in Bruce Nelson, "Unions and the Popular Front: The West Coast Waterfront in the 1930s," *International Labor and Working-Class History*, no. 30 (Fall 1986): 73. Wagner gave a nationally broadcast speech rebutting Lewis's address, too, and received many letters praising it from such government officials as Henry Wallace and from ordinary voters alike. See Wagner Papers, box 408, folder 12.

35. Samuel Lubell quoted in Nelson, "Unions and the Popular Front," 73–74; "President's Victory: Its Meaning," *United States News*, November 15, 1940, in Wagner Papers, box 408, folder 14.

36. Susan Levine, "In WWII, Patriotism Unified a Nation," *The Washington Post*, May 23, 2004, www.washingtonpost.com/archive/local/2004/05 /23/in-wwii-patriotism-unified-a-nation/a605dcd6-f2da-42e0-ae00-83 d990429aba/?utm_term=.2e36a10004fc.

37. Unnamed Republican congressman quoted in David Brody, *In Labor's Cause: Main Themes on the History of the American Worker* (New York: Oxford University Press, 1993), 181.

38. Paweł Laider and Maciej Turek, "The Smith-Connally Act: 57 Stat. 163 (1943)," Basic Documents in Federal Campaign Finance Law, CambridgeCore, January 2018, www.cambridge.org/core/books/basic -documents-in-federal-campaign-finance-law/smithconnally-act-57-stat -163-1943/7E03B46B32739E5AD42EAD7D6C5E1AD7; Brinkley, *End of Reform*, 217.

39. On payment of poll taxes, see William H. Riker, "The CIO in Politics, 1936–1946" (PhD dissertation, Harvard University, 1948), 310. Riker does not mention the race of the recipients, but the inability to pay poll taxes was just one of the obstacles facing Southern Blacks who tried to exercise the franchise.

40. Franklin D. Roosevelt, "State of the Union Message to Congress, January 11, 1944"; CIO Political Action Committee, "The People's Program for 1944," copy in author's possession.

41. Fraser, *Labor Will Rule*, 515.

42. Limerick quoted in Fraser, *Labor Will Rule*, 527.

43. According to William Riker, the CIO spent $1.56 million, the AFL just $236,000, and other labor groups, $416,000. Riker, "CIO in Politics," 130–31. About half the total was spent on the presidential ticket. FDR quoted in Fraser, *Labor Will Rule*, 535.

44. Orson Welles quoted in Levine and Levine, *The People and the President*, 560.

45. Plotke, *Building a Democratic Political Order*, 197.

46. Nelson Lichtenstein, *The Most Dangerous Man in Detroit: Walter Reuther and the Fate of American Labor* (New York: Basic Books, 1995), 231.

47. Lichtenstein, *The Most Dangerous Man in Detroit*, 246.

48. See Robert Taft's 1947 speech on the Taft-Hartley Act, posted on You-Tube, www.youtube.com/watch?v=ZJZvlCRxYHI; Murray quoted in Plotke, *Building a Democratic Political Order*, 237.

49. On Truman's private belief that Taft-Hartley "was essentially a good and needed law," see Robert H. Zieger, *The CIO, 1935–1955* (Chapel Hill: University of North Carolina Press, 1995), 275. For the veto message, see Harry S. Truman, "Veto of the Taft-Hartley Labor Bill," June 20, 1947, National Archives, Harry S. Truman Library and Museum, www.trumanlibrary.gov/library/public-papers/120/veto-taft-hartley-labor-bill.

50. Robert Wagner quoted in Huthmacher, *Senator Robert F. Wagner and the Rise of Urban Liberalism*, 338, 337.

51. Clark Clifford, "Memorandum for the President," November 19, 1947, Clark Clifford Papers, Political File, Harry S. Truman Presidential Library.

52. Gallup, *The Gallup Poll*, vol. 1, *1935–1948*, 724–25.

53. *The Nation*, June 28, 1947, 1 (editorial).

54. Harry Truman quoted in Sean J. Savage, *Truman and the Democratic Party* (Lexington: University Press of Kentucky, 1997), 136. On the railway tour and the strategy of the campaign more generally, see the narrative by the DNC's head of publicity that year: Jack Redding, *Inside the Democratic Party* (Indianapolis: Bobbs-Merrill, 1958).

55. Anthony Leviero, "Truman Humble in Pledging Service to American People," *The New York Times*, November 4, 1948; Redding, *Inside the Democratic Party*, 143. Together Dewey and Thurmond actually received a majority of the popular votes in the South. For a succinct statistical breakdown of the 1948 results, see Savage, *Truman and the Democratic Party*, 138–43.

56. James L. Sundquist, *Dynamics of the Party System: Alignment and Realignment in the United States*, rev. ed. (Washington, D.C.: Brookings Institution Press, 1983), 424. The class gap in 1948 was a whopping 44 percent.

57. A. H. Raskin quoted in Fraser, *Labor Will Rule*, 573.

### 7. FREEDOM AND FRAGMENTATION, 1948–1968

1. Hubert Humphrey speaking for the minority civil rights plank at the 1948 Democratic National Convention in Philadelphia, americanrhetoric .com/speeches/huberthumphrey1948dnc.html.

2. "(1955) Congressman Adam Clayton Powell, Jr., 'Speech on Civil Rights,'" BlackPast, www.blackpast.org/african-american-history/speeches-african -american-history/1955-adam-clayton-powell-jr-speech-civil-rights.

3. "Love Me, I'm a Liberal," released on the album *Phil Ochs in Concert*, Elektra Records, 1966.

4. George C. Wallace quoted in Stephen Smith and Kate Ellis, "Campaign '68: George C. Wallace, Powerful Third-Party Candidate," *APM Reports*, n.d., features.apmreports.org/arw/campaign68/d1.html.

5. "Text of the Recorded Speech of Senator Barkley as the Democratic Convention Keynoter," *The New York Times*, July 13, 1948, timesmachine .nytimes.com/timesmachine/1948/07/13/85254625.pdf.

6. Hubert H. Humphrey, "1948 Democratic National Convention Address," July 14, 1948, American Rhetoric, americanrhetoric.com /speeches/huberthumphey1948dnc.html.

7. Scott Lucas quoted in Arnold A. Offner, *Hubert Humphrey: The Conscience of the Country* (New Haven: Yale University Press, 2018), 3.

8. Hubert H. Humphrey, *The Education of a Public Man: My Life and Politics*, ed. Norman Sherman (Garden City, NY: Doubleday, 1976), 115.

9. *The Washington Post*, July 15, 1948, 1. I have borrowed the metaphor of a "ticking time bomb" from Steve Fraser's book *Mongrel Firebugs and Men of Property: Capitalism and Class Conflict in American History* (New York: Verso, 2019), 161.

10. "US Real GDP Per Capita by Year," www.multpl.com/us-real-gdp-per -capita/table/by-year; Maurice Isserman and Michael Kazin, *America Divided: The Civil War of the 1960s*, 5th ed. (New York: Oxford University Press, 2015), 11, 8.

11. "Everywhere in Europe it was the parties of the Left which were seen as best suited to carry out social reforms, to fight for them against vested interests, to make them a political priority, and to resist the inevitable compromises longer and more determinedly than others." Donald Sassoon, *One Hundred Years of Socialism: The West European Left in the Twentieth Century*, new ed. (London: I. B. Tauris, 2014), 139.

12. Lyndon Johnson quoted in John Gerring's excellent study, *Party Ideologies in America, 1828–1996* (Cambridge, UK: Cambridge University Press, 1998), 237.

13. V. O. Key quoted in the magisterial study by Nelson Lichtenstein, *State of the Union: A Century of American Labor* (Princeton, NJ: Princeton University Press, 2002), 147. Meany quoted ibid.

14. Adam Clayton Powell, Jr., *Keep the Faith, Baby!* (New York: Trident Press, 1967), 243.

15. Adam Clayton Powell, Jr., *Adam by Adam: The Autobiography of Adam Clayton Powell, Jr.* (New York: Dial Press, 1971), 74; Adam Clayton Powell, Jr., quoted in Edward J. Blum, "'A Third Force': The Civil Rights Ministry of Congressman Adam Clayton Powell, Jr.," in *Faithful Republic: Religion and Politics in Modern America*, ed. Andrew Preston, Bruce J. Schulman, and Julian E. Zelizer (Philadelphia: University of Pennsylvania Press, 2015), 90.

16. Neil Hickey and Ed Edwin, *Adam Clayton Powell and the Politics of Race* (New York: Fleet Publishing, 1965), 294.

17. Adam Clayton Powell, Jr., quoted in Charles V. Hamilton, *Adam Clayton Powell, Jr.: The Political Biography of an American Dilemma* (New York: Atheneum, 1991), 105.

18. Wil Haygood, *King of the Cats: The Life and Times of Adam Clayton Powell, Jr.* (Boston: Houghton Mifflin Harcourt, 1993), 211.

19. I am quoting the familiar lines from FDR's 1936 acceptance speech and the title of the 1958 book by the liberal economist John Kenneth Galbraith.

20. Melvyn Dubofsky, *The State and Labor in Modern America* (Chapel Hill: University of North Carolina Press, 1994), 209.

21. On the 1949 Detroit mayor's race, see Thomas J. Sugrue, *The Origins of the Urban Crisis: Race and Inequality in Postwar Detroit* (Princeton, NJ: Princeton University Press, 1996), 82–84; Nelson Lichtenstein, *The Most Dangerous Man in Detroit: Walter Reuther and the Fate of American Labor* (New York: Basic Books, 1995), 306–308.

22. Richard Hofstadter, "From Calhoun to the Dixiecrats," *Social Research* 16, no. 2 (June 1949): 150.

23. Devin Caughey, *The Unsolid South: Mass Politics and National Representation in a One-Party Enclave* (Princeton, NJ: Princeton University Press, 2018), 135, 136. This paragraph draws on my 2019 review of this book and others on Southern politics: Michael Kazin, "The Southern Paradox," *The Nation*, February 21, 2019, www.thenation.com/article/democratic-party-in-the-south-review-bateman-katznelson-lapinski-caughey.

24. The Democratic colleague was Carl Vinson, whom Rivers succeeded as chairman of the committee in 1965. William V. Moore, "Rivers, Lucius Mendel," *South Carolina Encyclopedia*, www.scencyclopedia.org/sce/entries/rivers-lucius-mendel.

25. See the classic study of this group by James Q. Wilson, *The Amateur Democrat: Club Politics in Three Cities* (Chicago: University of Chicago Press, 1962).

26. Arthur Schlesinger, Jr., quoted in Steven M. Gillon, *Politics and Vision:*

*The ADA and American Liberalism, 1947–1985* (New York: Oxford University Press, 1987), 63.

27. Conservative newspaper and Nashville minister quoted in Gillon, *Politics and Vision*, 78, 77.

28. Eleanor Roosevelt in 1956 and Adlai Stevenson in 1946 quoted in Richard Henry, *Eleanor Roosevelt and Adlai Stevenson* (New York: Palgrave Macmillan, 2010), 18, 19.

29. Adlai Stevenson quoted in Henry, *Eleanor Roosevelt and Adlai Stevenson*, 27.

30. Adlai Stevenson quoted in John Bartlow Martin, *Adlai Stevenson of Illinois: The Life of Adlai E. Stevenson* (Garden City, NY: Doubleday, 1976), 689.

31. Eleanor Roosevelt quoted in Martin, *Adlai Stevenson of Illinois*, 39, 42. On the use of "egghead," see ibid., 640.

32. A Gallup poll taken in late July, right after both parties had held their conventions, found that 41 percent considered themselves Democrats, 34 percent Republicans, and 25 percent Independents. George H. Gallup, *The Gallup Poll: Public Opinion*, vol. 2, *1949–1958* (New York: Random House, 1972), 1079.

33. "1952 Democratic Party Platform," July 21, 1952, The American Presidency Project, www.presidency.ucsb.edu/documents/1952-democratic -party-platform; Gerring, *Party Ideologies*, 234.

34. Gallup, *The Gallup Poll*, vol. 2, *1949–1958*, 1077. The CIO-PAC waged an active effort for the entire Democratic ticket, but a survey of UAW members in Detroit that year found that 40 percent either opposed the union's activity in politics or did not state a definite opinion about it. Robert H. Zieger, *The CIO, 1935–1955* (Chapel Hill: University of North Carolina Press, 1995), 309.

35. Hubert Humphrey quoted in Offner, *Hubert Humphrey*, 101.

36. John Bartlow Martin, *Adlai Stevenson and the World* (Garden City, NY: Doubleday, 1977), 122.

37. John F. Kennedy quoted in Gilbert C. Fite, *Richard B. Russell, Jr., Senator from Georgia* (Chapel Hill: University of North Carolina Press, 1991), 334. The video Kennedy narrated: "The Pursuit of Happiness," given on August 13, 1956, is posted on YouTube. The platform: "1956 Democratic Party Platform," August 13, 1956, The American Presidency Project, www.presidency.ucsb.edu/documents/1956-democratic-party -platform.

38. Haygood, *King of the Cats*, 215; *The New York Times*, October 12, 1956, 26. Roy Wilkins, the executive director of the NAACP, had earlier considered backing Eisenhower, too, but backed off after Eleanor Roosevelt threatened to resign from the organization's board.

39. Adlai Stevenson quoted in Martin, *Adlai Stevenson and the World*, 361; "Black Vote for President," FactCheck.org, cdn.factcheck.org /UploadedFiles/Black_Vote_Pres.jpg.

40. See the analysis of the 1956 race in Michael Barone, *Our Country: The Shaping of America from Roosevelt to Reagan* (New York: Free Press, 1990), 283–300.

41. Arthur Schlesinger, Jr., writing in his journal, quoted in Henry, *Eleanor Roosevelt and Adlai Stevenson*, 81.

42. Sean McCann, "'Investing in Persons': The Political Culture of Kennedy Liberalism," in *The Cambridge Companion to John F. Kennedy*, ed. Andrew Hoberek (Cambridge, UK: Cambridge University Press, 2015), 64, 60.

43. Walter Reuther quoted in Lichtenstein, *The Most Dangerous Man in Detroit*, 349.

44. The only major bill related to organized labor passed by the new Congress elected in 1958 was the Landrum-Griffin Act of 1959, which placed restrictions on the conduct of internal union elections and finances, an effort to prevent abuses in the Teamsters and a few smaller unions a unions earlier revealed in congressional hearings.

45. Paul Butler quoted in Sam Rosenfeld, *The Polarizers: Postwar Architects of Our Partisan Era* (Chicago: University of Chicago Press, 2018), 53.

46. Julian E. Zelizer, *The Fierce Urgency of Now: Lyndon Johnson, Congress, and the Battle for the Great Society* (New York: Penguin, 2015), 35. One Democrat who opposed the civil rights bill was Nellie Tayloe Ross, the former governor of Wyoming. Then in her nineties, she was living in Washington, D.C., and voiced a fear of Black crime. Teva J. Scheer, *Governor Lady: The Life and Times of Nellie Tayloe Ross* (Columbia: University of Missouri Press, 2005), 212–13.

47. "John F. Kennedy: Civil Rights Address," June 11, 1963, American Rhetoric, www.americanrhetoric.com/speeches/jfkcivilrights.htm.

48. For the relevant polls, see George H. Gallup, *The Gallup Poll: Public Opinion*, vol. 3, *1959–1971* (New York: Random House, 1972), 1837–38, and "Public Opinion on Civil Rights: Reflections on the Civil Rights Act of 1964," Roper Center for Public Opinion Research, 2014, ropercenter.cornell.edu/public-opinion-civil-rights-reflections-civil-rights-act-1964.

49. The exception was Ralph Yarborough from Texas, a liberal stalwart, who won reelection that fall running against a wealthy Republican who attacked him for his support of the bill, saying, "The new Civil Rights Act was passed to protect 14 percent of the people. I'm also worried about the other 86 percent." The Republican's name was George Herbert Walker Bush. Sean Sullivan, "George H. W. Bush Embodied the Republican Party's Decades-Long Struggle with Race," *The Washington Post*, December 4, 2018, www.washingtonpost.com/politics/george-hw-bush-embodied-the-republican-partys-decades-long-struggle-with-race/2018/12/04/1268ab08-f73b-11e8-8c9a-860ce2a8148f_story.html.

50. Fannie Lou Hamer quoted in Offner, *Hubert Humphrey*, 201; Hubert Humphrey quoted in Michael E. Parrish, *Citizen Rauh: An American*

*Liberal's Life in Law and Politics* (Ann Arbor: University of Michigan Press, 2010), 173.

51. Lyndon Johnson quoted in Offner, *Hubert Humphrey*, 195.

52. John McCormack quoted in Hamilton, *Powell*, 372.

53. Adam Clayton Powell, Jr., quoted in Thomas J. Sugrue, *Sweet Land of Liberty: The Forgotten Struggle for Civil Rights in the North* (New York: Random House, 2008), 297.

54. The song that condemns the violence of the state's white authorities was released in 1965. Phil Ochs, "Here's to the State of Mississippi," Genius .com, genius.com/Phil-ochs-heres-to-the-state-of-mississippi-lyrics.

55. For a chronological record of key polls on race relations and the civil rights movement, see "iPoll Search Results," Civil Rights Movement Archive, www.crmvet.org/docs/60s_crm_public-opinion.pdf. The first Gallup poll that showed approval of LBJ's job performance under 50 percent was in June 1966. Gallup, *Gallup Poll*, vol. 3, *1959–1971*, 2011. On the "declining salience" of the issue of race, see Doug McAdam, *Political Process and the Development of Black Insurgency, 1930–1970* (Chicago: University of Chicago Press, 1982), 197–201.

56. George Wallace quoted in Michael Kazin, *The Populist Persuasion: An American History*, 2nd rev. ed. (Ithaca, NY: Cornell University Press, 2017), 237.

57. Martin Luther King, Jr., "Beyond Vietnam," speech, April 4, 1967, www .americanrhetoric.com/speeches/mlkatimetobreaksilence.

58. Hubert Humphrey in April 1966, quoted in Offner, *Hubert Humphrey*, 243.

59. The official Democratic slogan was "All the Way with LBJ." On the Port Huron statement, see Michael Kazin, "The Port Huron Statement at Fifty," *Dissent* 59, no. 2 (Spring 2012): 83–89.

60. Carl Oglesby, "Let Us Shape the Future," Students for a Democratic Society (SDS) Document Library, November 27, 1965, www.sds-1960s .org/sds_wuo/sds_documents/oglesby_future.html.

61. Labor officials quoted in Peter B. Levy, *The New Left and Labor in the 1960s* (Urbana: University of Illinois Press, 1994), 49. The three unions were the International Longshore and Warehouse Union; United Electrical, Radio and Machine Workers of America; and the International Union of Mine, Mill and Smelter Workers.

62. Gus Tyler quoted in John Quirk, "The Liberal Split: ADA and LBJ," *Commonweal*, March 1, 1968, 643. Thanks to Daniel Schlozman for sharing this quote with me from his unpublished book, coauthored with Sam Rosenfeld.

63. Bayard Rustin, "Reflections on the Death of Martin Luther King, Jr.," in *Time on Two Crosses: The Collected Writings of Bayard Rustin*, 2nd ed., ed. Devon W. Carbado and Donald Wiese (New York: Cleis Press, 2015), 194–95.

64. Michael A. Cohen, *American Maelstrom: The 1968 Election and the Politics of Division* (New York: Oxford University Press, 2016), 276.
65. Richard J. Daley quoted in Isserman and Kazin, *America Divided*, 231. White quoted in Cohen, *American Maelstrom*, 279.
66. Hubert H. Humphrey, "Address Accepting the Presidential Nomination at the Democratic National Convention in Chicago," August 29, 1968, The American Presidency Project, www.presidency.ucsb.edu/documents /address-accepting-the-presidential-nomination-the-democratic-national -convention-chicago-2. The only partial exception to the rule about a divided party going down to defeat was the Democratic convention in 1948, although most Southern Democrats did not join the walkout by segregationist delegates from Alabama and Mississippi.
67. George Wallace quoted in Michael Kazin, *The Populist Persuasion: An American History*, rev. ed. (Ithaca, NY: Cornell University Press, 2017), 237.
68. Lichtenstein, *The Most Dangerous Man in Detroit*, 428.
69. Arthur Schlesinger, Jr., quoted in Offner, *Hubert Humphrey*, 217.
70. Bob Moses quoted in Parrish, *Citizen Rauh*, 173–74. On the pattern of the vote on open housing, see Raymond E. Wolfinger and Fred I. Greenstein, "The Repeal of Fair Housing in California: An Analysis of Referendum Voting," *American Political Science Review* 62, no. 3 (September 1968), 758–59.
71. Lichtenstein, *The Most Dangerous Man in Detroit*, 425.

#### 8. WHOSE PARTY IS IT? 1969–1994

1. Quoted in Thomas Ferguson and Joel Rogers, *Right Turn: The Decline of the Democrats and the Future of American Politics* (New York: Hill and Wang, 1986), 5.
2. Jesse Jackson, "1988 Democratic National Convention Address," July 19, 1988, American Rhetoric, www.americanrhetoric.com/speeches /jessejackson1988dnc.htm.
3. James Carville, a key Clinton strategist, hung a sign with these words in the campaign headquarters. It soon became a popular catchphrase for the entire campaign. politicaldictionary.com/words/its-the-economy-stupid.
4. Thomas Byrne Edsall, *The New Politics of Inequality* (New York: W. W. Norton, 1984), 33.
5. Only 13 percent of delegates to the 1968 convention were women, just 5 percent were Black, and only 3 percent were under thirty. Kathryn J. McGarr, *The Whole Damn Deal: Robert Strauss and the Art of Politics* (New York: Public Affairs, 2011), 99. According to Harold M. Ickes, a longtime adviser to Democratic campaigns and presidents, until the aftermath of the 1968 convention, "There was no cohesive set of delegate selection rules at the national level. In a number of cases, I actually

have a memo . . . about the process by which delegates were selected to the national convention. And in a number of cases, state chairmen just selected them. They selected them one or two years in advance. So there was no set of cohesive rules like what we know now." Author phone interview with Ickes, June 2020. Thanks to Sophia Zahner for her transcription.

6. George McGovern quoted in Thomas J. Knock, *The Rise of a Prairie Statesman: The Life and Times of George McGovern* (Princeton, NJ: Princeton University Press, 2016), 410–11.

7. The figure of 20 percent comes from the best single analysis of the impact of the reform commission: David Plotke, "Party Reform as Failed Democratic Renewal in the United States, 1968–1972," *Studies in American Political Development* 10, no. 2 (Fall 1996), 239.

8. For a summary of the guidelines, see Byron E. Shafer, *Quiet Revolution: The Struggle for the Democratic Party and the Shaping of Post-Reform Politics* (New York: Russell Sage Foundation, 1983), 541–45.

9. McGarr, *The Whole Damn Deal*, 99.

10. This phenomenon rippled through congressional elections, too. In 1978, spending in the "average" House race rose to more than $200,000, the equivalent of about $800,000 in 2020. Alan Ware, *The Breakdown of Democratic Party Organization, 1940–1980* (Oxford, UK: Oxford University Press, 1985), 175.

11. Quoted in Sam Rosenfeld, *The Polarizers: Postwar Architects of Our Partisan Era* (Chicago: University of Chicago Press, 2018), 171.

12. David S. Broder, "Sen. McGovern Opens '72 Race for President," *The Washington Post*, Jan 19, 1971, A1. The story headlined "U.S. Confirms 1st GNP Drop in 12 Years" appeared on the front page just to the right of the report on the senator's entry into the race.

13. Gary Hart quoted in Bruce Miroff, *The Liberals' Moment: The McGovern Insurgency and the Identity Crisis of the Democratic Party* (Lawrence: University Press of Kansas, 2007), 176; Christopher Lydon, "Celebrities Rally Around McGovern," *The New York Times*, April 2, 1972, A28. McGovern quoted in Miroff, *The Liberals' Moment*, 126.

14. McGovern quoted in Jefferson Cowie, *Stayin' Alive: The 1970s and the Last Days of the Working Class* (New York: New Press, 2010), 87. On the disconnect between views of the war and of anti-war protesters, see E. M. Schreiber, "Anti-War Demonstrations and American Public Opinion on the War in Vietnam," *British Journal of Sociology* 27, no. 2 (June 1976), 225–36.

15. James Reston quoted in Rick Perlstein's vivid narrative, *Nixonland: The Rise of a President and the Fracturing of America* (New York: Scribner, 2008), 651.

16. Bella Abzug and Shirley MacLaine quoted in Miroff, *The Liberals' Moment*, 208. McGovern delegates did endorse such feminist demands as equal pay for women and government-funded childcare.

17. George Meany quoted in Taylor E. Dark, *The Unions and the Democrats: An Enduring Alliance* (Ithaca, NY: ILR Press, 1999), 88.
18. On the making of the larger political identity, see Benjamin Francis-Fallon, *The Rise of the Latino Vote: A History* (Cambridge, MA: Harvard University Press, 2019). For the 1972 platform, see "1972 Democratic Party Platform," July 11, 1972, The American Presidency Project, www .presidency.ucsb.edu/documents/1972-democratic-party-platform.
19. George McGovern, "Address Accepting the Presidential Nomination at the Democratic National Convention in Miami Beach, Florida," July 14, 1972, The American Presidency Project, www.presidency .ucsb.edu/documents/address-accepting-the-presidential-nomination-the -democratic-national-convention-miami.
20. Jean Westwood quoted in Cowie, *Stayin' Alive*, 166.
21. Pauline Kael quoted in James Wolcott, "The Fraudulent Factoid That Refuses to Die," *Vanity Fair*, October 23, 2012, www.vanityfair.com /culture/2012/10/The-Fraudulent-Factoid-That-Refuses-to-Die.
22. Democrats held a lead of thirteen points among white voters and an overwhelming lead among Black ones. Paul R. Abramson, John H. Aldrich, and David W. Rohde, *Change and Continuity in the 1992 Elections* (Washington, D.C.: CQ Press, 1994), 229.
23. Robert Strauss quoted in McGarr, *The Whole Damn Deal*, 131.
24. Gary Hart quoted in Patrick Andelic, *Donkey Work: Congressional Democrats in Conservative America, 1974–1994* (Lawrence: University Press of Kansas, 2019), 17.
25. The following section on Carter's presidency is adapted, in part, from my review-essay, "The President Without a Party," *The Nation*, July 30–August 6, 2018.
26. On Jimmy Carter's domestic programs, see Stuart Eizenstat, *President Carter: The White House Years* (New York: Thomas Dunne Books, 2018), and Kai Bird, *The Outlier: The Unfinished Presidency of Jimmy Carter* (New York: Crown, 2021).
27. Alfred Kahn quoted in Zachary D. Carter, *The Price of Peace: Money, Democracy, and the Life of John Maynard Keynes* (New York: Random House, 2020), 480. Kahn headed the agency in charge of deregulating the airlines.
28. Jimmy Carter quoted in McGarr, *Whole Damn Deal*, 239; Roybal quoted in Francis-Fallon, *The Rise of the Latino Vote*, 323; Eizenstat, *President Carter*, 2; Mondale quoted in Steven M. Gillon, *The Democrats' Dilemma: Walter F. Mondale and the Liberal Legacy* (New York: Columbia University Press, 1992), 201.
29. On the politics of the Humphrey-Hawkins bill, see Andelic, *Donkey Work*, 72–91, and Stein, *Pivotal Decade*, 190–92. In 1946, Congress had passed a Full Employment Act that, despite its name, did not include a federal commitment to achieve that goal.

30. Ken Young quoted in Andelic, *Donkey Work*, 89.
31. Jimmy Carter, "Energy and the National Goals: A Crisis of Confidence," July 15, 1979, American Rhetoric, www.americanrhetoric.com /speeches/jimmycartercrisisofconfidence.htm (video); E. J. Dionne, Jr., *Why Americans Hate Politics* (1991; repr. New York: Simon & Schuster, 2004), 141.
32. Ted Kennedy, "1980 Democratic National Concession Address," August 12, 1980, American Rhetoric, www.americanrhetoric.com/speeches /tedkennedy1980dnc.htm.
33. Lou Cannon, *Reagan* (New York: Putnam, 1982), 88; Jefferson Cowie, *The Great Exception: The New Deal and the Limits of American Politics* (Princeton, NJ: Princeton University Press, 2016), 187.
34. Tip O'Neill quoted in John A. Farrell, *Tip O'Neill and the Democratic Century* (Boston: Little, Brown, 2001), 536. John Anderson, a former liberal Republican congressman, ran as an independent that year and received 6.6 percent of the popular vote, most in areas that normally voted Democratic.
35. For the totals, see Fred Barnes, "Dream On: The Republican Realignment Quest," *The New Republic*, January 23, 1989, 9.
36. Charles T. Manatt quoted in Andelic, *Donkey Work*, 147.
37. Jesse Jackson quoted in Marcia Chatelain, *Franchise: The Golden Arches in Black America* (New York: Liveright, 2020), 216.
38. Robert Borosage, quoted in Marshall Frady, *Jesse: The Life and Pilgrimage of Jesse Jackson* (New York: Random House, 1996), 306–307.
39. "Interview 1 with Al From," April 27, 2006, William J. Clinton Presidential History Project, University of Virginia, Miller Center, transcript, 10, millercenter.org/the-presidency/presidential-oral-histories/al-oral-history 2006.
40. Charles Robb, in 1986, quoted in Al From, *The New Democrats and the Return to Power* (New York: St. Martin's Press, 2013), 73.
41. Jerry Huckaby quoted in Jonathan Bartho, "Reagan's Southern Comfort: The 'Boll Weevil' Democrats in the 'Reagan Revolution' of 1981," *Journal of Policy History* 32, no. 2 (2020), 219.
42. Thanks to David Rudd, Hollings's longtime aide, for sharing this quote. The date is unknown, but it was sometime in the middle of Reagan's term.
43. Gary Hart quoted in Dionne, *Why Americans Hate Politics*, 270; Jesse Jackson quoted in Adolph L. Reed, Jr., *The Jesse Jackson Phenomenon* (New Haven: Yale University Press, 1986), 9.
44. James Baldwin quoted in Frady, *Jesse*, 370.
45. Stanley B. Greenberg, "Report on Democratic Defection," April 15, 1985, quoted in Thomas Byrne Edsall and Mary D. Edsall, *Chain Reaction: The Impact of Race, Rights, and Taxes on American Politics* (New York: W. W. Norton, 1991), 182.
46. Joe Biden quoted in Paul Taylor, *See How They Run: Electing the President*

*in an Age of Mediaocracy* (New York: Knopf, 1990), 100. On Biden's political evolution, see Evan Osnos, *Joe Biden: The Life, the Run, and What Matters Now* (New York: Scribner, 2020).

47. "Interview 1 with Al From," 14.
48. From, *The New Democrats and the Return to Power*, 103, 57; Kenneth S. Baer, *Reinventing Democrats: The Politics of Liberalism from Reagan to Clinton* (Lawrence: University Press of Kansas, 2000), 137.
49. Jesse Jackson, Arthur Schlesinger, Jr., and Ann Lewis quoted in Baer, *Reinventing Democrats*, 81; Michael Harrington, "Will Democrats Self-Destruct?," *The New York Times*, October 9, 1986, A35.
50. Jim Hightower quoted in Robert Kuttner, *The Life of the Party: Democratic Prospects in 1988 and Beyond* (New York: Viking, 1987), 202.
51. Author phone interview with Harold M. Ickes, June 2020.
52. Bernie Sanders quoted in Michael Kruse, "What Jesse Taught Bernie About Running for President," *Politico*, March 15, 2019, www.politico .com/magazine/story/2019/03/15/bernie-sanders-2020-race-jesse-jackson -1988-presidential-campaign-225809.
53. Robert Borosage quoted in Frady, *Jesse*, 394.
54. "The Democrats in Atlanta: Transcript of the Speech by Dukakis Accepting the Democrats' Nomination," *The New York Times*, July 22, 1988, www.nytimes.com/1988/07/22/us/democrats-atlanta-transcript -speech-dukakis-accepting-democrats-nomination.html.
55. William Galston and Elaine Ciulla Kamarck, "The Politics of Evasion: Democrats and the Presidency," September 1989, Progressive Policy Institute, 2, 19, 20, www.progressivepolicy.org/wp-content/uploads/2013 /03/Politics_of_Evasion.pdf.
56. Bill Clinton, foreword to From, *The New Democrats*, x.
57. If Perot had not run, it's unclear which of the major-party candidates—if either—his voters would have chosen. But he did win roughly a quarter of both working-class white men and of white men overall—two groups that had been moving toward the Republicans since 1972.
58. Donald L. Barlett and James B. Steele, *America: What Went Wrong?* (Kansas City, MO: Andrews McMeel, 1992).
59. From, *The New Democrats*, 196. From's memo was written on April 17, 1993.
60. Sam Nunn quoted in Robert O. Self, *All in the Family: The Realignment of American Democracy Since the 1960s* (New York: Hill and Wang, 2012), 412; John Micklethwait and Adrian Woodridge, *The Right Nation: Conservative Power in America* (New York: Penguin, 2004), 109.
61. Gary C. Jacobson, "The 1994 House Elections in Perspective," *Political Science Quarterly* 111, no. 2 (Summer 1996), 203. In 1994, Republicans took twenty-one Southern House seats away from the opposition party, to gain a regional majority of sixty-six to fifty-nine, and four new Senate seats there, to achieve a margin of thirteen to nine. Michael Nelson,

"Redividing Government: National Elections in the Clinton Years and Beyond," in *42: Inside the Presidency of Bill Clinton*, ed. Michael Nelson, Barbara A. Perry, and Russell L. Riley (Ithaca, NY: Cornell University Press, 2016), 45.

62. "The Republican 'Contract with America' (1994)," Oxford University Press, global.oup.com/us/companion.websites/9780195385168/resources/chapter6/contract/america.pdf.

63. Author's recollection. To my knowledge, no one recorded the conversation.

**9. COSMOPOLITANS IN SEARCH OF A NEW MAJORITY, 1994–2020**

1. Nancy Pelosi to Representative George Miller, a longtime ally, after speaking at a retreat of party leaders, quoted in Molly Ball, *Pelosi* (New York: Henry Holt, 2020), 80.

2. Barack Obama, "Barack Obama's Acceptance Speech," *The New York Times*, August 28, 2008, www.nytimes.com/2008/08/28/us/politics/28text-obama.html.

3. Thomas Piketty, *Capital and Ideology*, trans. Arthur Goldhammer (Cambridge, MA: Harvard University Press, 2020), 834.

4. On the rise of evangelical politics in the state, see Michael Tomasky, "West Virginia," in *These United States: Original Essays by Leading American Writers on Their State Within the Union*, ed. John Leonard (New York: Nation Books, 2003), 475–84.

5. Joan Didion, *Where I Was From* (New York: Knopf, 2003), 135.

6. Sylvia Manzano, "Latinos in the Sunbelt: Political Implications of Demographic Change," in *Sunbelt Rising: The Politics of Space, Place, and Region*, ed. Michelle Nickerson and Darren Dochuk (Philadelphia: University of Pennsylvania Press, 2011), 342.

7. See graph in Piketty, *Capital and Ideology*, 820. As Piketty documents, nearly every social-democratic and labor party in Western and Central Europe had the same problem: gaining votes among the college educated and citizens from non-white backgrounds while steadily losing the support of the native-born white working class.

8. "Pelosi Is the Star of GOP Attack Ads, Worrying Democrats," *The Washington Post*, August 9, 2018, www.washingtonpost.com/powerpost/pelosi-is-the-star-of-gop-attack-ads-worrying-democrats-upbeat-about-midterms/2018/08/09/f85a2474-9b43-11e8-8d5e-c6c594024954_story.html.

9. Ball, *Pelosi*, 93. On the amount raised during the 2020 cycle (in which the party lost seats), see Nicholas Fandos, "Leader of Impeachment Ponders Life After Trump," *The New York Times*, November 19, 2020.

10. Michelle Goldberg, "Madame Speaker," *The New York Times Book Review*, May 31, 2020, 39.

11. For a rich description and analysis of Baltimore's evolution during the

middle decades of the last century, see Kenneth D. Durr, *Behind the Backlash: White Working-Class Politics in Baltimore, 1940–1980* (Chapel Hill: University of North Carolina Press, 2003).

12. Big Nancy D'Alesandro quoted in Ball, *Pelosi*, 3–4.

13. John Murtha quoted in Marc Sandalow, *Madam Speaker: Nancy Pelosi's Life, Times and Rise to Power* (New York: Modern Times, 2008), 191.

14. William Jefferson Clinton, "State of the Union Address," January 23, 1996, clintonwhitehouse4.archives.gov/WH/New/other/sotu.html. The following paragraphs on the Clinton administration are adapted, in part, from Michael Kazin, "Good Bill," *Mother Jones*, September–October 2000.

15. Barney Frank, *Frank: A Life in Politics from the Great Society to Same-Sex Marriage* (New York: Farrar, Straus and Giroux, 2015).

16. This paragraph and the preceding three are adapted from Kazin, "Good Bill."

17. On the DLC's disenchantment with Gore, see Al From Oral History, Miller Center, University of Virginia, 2006, part 2, 37. millercenter.org /the-presidency/presidential-oral-histories/al-oral-history-2006.

18. On Jeffords's switch of parties, news.bbc.co.uk/2/hi/americas/1350305 .stm; on Enron, Richard A. Oppel, Jr., and Don van Natta, Jr., "Enron's Collapse: The Relationships; Bush and Democrats Disputing Ties to Enron," *The New York Times*, January 12, 2002, www.nytimes .com/2002/01/12/business/enron-s-collapse-the-relationships-bush-and -democrats-disputing-ties-to-enron.html.

19. John Kerry, "Vietnam Veterans Against the War Statement by John Kerry to the Senate Committee of Foreign Relations," April 23, 1971, The Sixties Project, www2.iath.virginia.edu/sixties/HTML_docs/Resources /Primary/Manifestos/VVAW_Kerry_Senate.html.

20. John F. Kerry, "Address Accepting the Presidential Nomination at the Democratic National Convention in Boston," July 29, 2004, The American Presidency Project, www.presidency.ucsb.edu/documents /address-accepting-the-presidential-nomination-the-democratic-national -convention-boston.

21. Terry McAuliffe, with Steve Kettmann, *What a Party!: My Life Among Democrats, Presidents, Candidates, Donors, Activists, Alligators, and Other Wild Animals* (New York: Thomas Dunne Books, 2007), 374. On the party's courtship with high finance, see Jacob S. Hacker and Paul Pierson, *Winner-Take-All Politics: How Washington Made the Rich Richer— And Turned Its Back on the Middle Class* (New York: Simon & Schuster, 2010), 223–52.

22. Hacker and Pierson, *Winner-Take-All Politics*, 179.

23. Center for American Progress, "About," n.d., www.americanprogress .org/mission.

24. For the platform, "New Direction—Six for '06," see Nancy Pelosi, with

Amy Hill Hearth, *Know Your Power: A Message to America's Daughters* (New York: Doubleday, 2008), 118. Frank Luntz quoted in Margaret Talev and Kevin G. Hall, "Democrats' 'Six for '06' Short on Specifics," *Spokesman-Review*, October 29, 2006, www.spokesman.com/stories/2006/oct/29/democrats-six-for-06-short-on-specifics.

25. On Rahm Emanuel, see Rick Perlstein, "The Sudden but Well-Deserved Fall of Rahm Emanuel," *The New Yorker*, December 31, 2015, www.newyorker.com/news/daily-comment/the-sudden-but-well-deserved-fall-of-rahm-emanuel.

26. On the struggle of progressives for influence in the party between 2004 and 2008, see Matt Bai, *The Argument: Inside the Battle to Remake Democratic Politics* (New York: Penguin, 2008). This section on Obama and his administration is partly adapted from Michael Kazin, "Criticize and Thrive: The American Left in the Obama Years," in *The Presidency of Barack Obama*, ed. Julian E. Zelizer (Princeton, NJ: Princeton University Press, 2018), 246–60.

27. "Barack Obama's Remarks to the Democratic National Convention," *The New York Times*, July 27, 2004, www.nytimes.com/2004/07/27/politics/campaign/barack-obamas-remarks-to-the-democratic-national.html. Obama quotations from the unpublished manuscript "Transformative Politics," in the forthcoming book by Timothy Shenk, *The Golden Line: The People, the Powerful, and the American Political Tradition* (New York: Farrar, Straus and Giroux, 2022).

28. Bob Dylan quoted in https://www.newyorker.com/news/george-packer/dylan-on-obama.

29. John M. Broder and Monica Davey, "Celebration and Sense of History at Chicago Party," *The New York Times*, November 5, 2008, www.nytimes.com/2008/11/05/us/politics/05chicago.html. Lewis quoted by David Remnick, "The President's Hero," *The New Yorker*, February 2, 2009: www.newyorker.com/magazine/2009/02/02/the-presidents-hero.

30. The text of the statement and those who signed it: "Historians for Obama," *History News Network*, April 21, 2008, hnn.us/articles/44958.html. Conservatives ridiculed Obama for those same attributes: Victor David Hanson labeled him "a distant, cool, rather narcissistic yuppie . . . who has not a clue about the lives of the middle and working classes," while Charles Krauthammer called him a kingpin of "the arrogant elites" who have an "undisguised contempt for the great unwashed."

31. Anonymous source, private conversation with author, 2009.

32. Myra King Whitson quoted in Lawrence W. Levine and Cornelia R. Levine, *The Fireside Conversations: America Responds to FDR During the Great Depression* (Berkeley: University of California Press, 2010), 2–3.

33. Cornel West interview with Thomas Frank, *Salon*, August 24, 2014.

34. Ball, *Pelosi*, 186.

35. Ball, *Pelosi*, 192.

36. Micah Sifry, "Obama's Lost Army," *New Republic*, February 9, 2017, newrepublic.com/article/140245/obamas-lost-army-inside-fall-grassroots -machine; Eric Alterman, *Kabuki Democracy: The System vs. Barack Obama* (New York: Nation Books, 2011), 4.

37. David Axelrod, *Believer: My Forty Years in Politics* (New York: Penguin, 2015), 426; Barack Obama, *A Promised Land* (New York: Crown, 2020), 594.

38. For a list of and documents from occupations in the United States and abroad, see #Occupy Archive, occupyarchive.org/items.

39. Polls quoted in Todd Gitlin, *Occupy Nation: The Roots, the Spirit, and the Promise of Occupy Wall Street* (New York: It Books, 2012), 37. Steve Fraser, *The Age of Acquiescence: The Life and Death of American Resistance to Organized Wealth and Power* (New York: Little, Brown, 2014).

40. Nancy Pelosi quoted in Jessica Desvarieux, "Pelosi Supports Occupy Wall Street Movement," ABC News, October 8, 2011, abcnews.go.com/Politics /pelosi-supports-occupy-wall-street-movement/story?id=14696893.

41. Jelani Cobb, "The Matter of Black Lives," *The New Yorker*, July 27, 2020 (originally published in 2016), 20.

42. "Herstory," Black Lives Matter, Blacklivesmatter.com/herstory. The three women are Alicia Garza, Patrisse Cullors, and Opal Tometi.

43. See Fredrick C. Harris, "The Rise of Respectability Politics," *Dissent*, Winter 2014, 33–37.

44. For a left-wing critique of Obama's presidency that understands his enduring appeal, see Keeanga-Yamahtta Taylor, *From #BlackLivesMatter to Black Liberation* (Chicago: Haymarket Books, 2016), 135–52.

45. Becky Bowers, "President Barack Obama's Shifting Stance on Gay Marriage," *PolitiFact*, May 11, 2012, www.politifact.com/truth-o-meter /statements/2012/may/11/barack-obama/president-barack-obamas-shift -gay-marriage.

46. Most of this paragraph is based on David Cole, *Engines of Liberty: The Power of Citizen Activists to Make Constitutional Law* (New York: Basic Books, 2016), 15–93.

47. Bernie Sanders quoted in Evan McMorris-Santoro, "The Obama Campaign Remembers 2012 Very Differently Than Bernie Sanders," *Buzzfeed*, November 8, 2015, www.buzzfeed.com/evanmcsan/the-obama-campaign -remembers-2012-very-differently-from-bern?utm_term=.wbreRG11q# .lhaM07yyZ; Bernie Sanders quoted in Eric Bates, "Bernie Looks Ahead," *New Republic*, November 2016, 31.

48. Harold Meyerson, "Still the Man Who Will Change America," *American Prospect*, April 8, 2020, prospect.org/politics/bernie-sanders-still-the-man -who-will-change-america.

49. Peter Dreier, "The Number of Democratic Socialists in the House Will Soon Double. But the Movement Scored Its Biggest Victories Down Ballot," *Talking Points Memo*, December 11, 2020, talkingpointsmemo.com

/cafe/number-democratic-socialists-congress-soon-double-down-ballot
-movement-scored-biggest-victories.

50. David Dayen, *Monopolized: Life in the Age of Corporate Power* (New York:
The New Press, 2020), 2.

51. In the 2020 election, Biden carried 84 percent of the counties with the
largest share of voters who had college degrees. Until the 1992 election,
Democrats had never carried even a majority of such places before.

52. Joe Biden quoted in Charlotte Alter, "How Joe Biden Is Positioning
Himself as a Modern FDR," *Time*, October 28, 2020, time.com/5904569
/joe-biden-fdr.

53. Daniel Schlozman, "Beltway Blues," *Dissent*, Summer 2018, 17, www
.dissentmagazine.org/article/beltway-blues-democrats-coalition-defining
-party.

54. On the politics of Indivisible, see "Indivisible's Core Advocacy Issues,"
Indivisible, indivisible.org/core-advocacy-issues; Joan Walsh, "Indivisible Is Working Hard to Live Up to Its Name," *The Nation*, August 27,
2019, www.thenation.com/article/archive/indivisible-resistance-grassroots
-election-2020; Stacey Abrams quoted in Kenneth Quinnell, "Black
History Month Profiles: Stacey Abrams," AFL-CIO, February 27,
2020, aflcio.org/2020/2/27/Black-history-month-profiles-stacey-abrams.

55. Savanna Strott and Tabitha Mueller, "Polls Show How Latino Voters
Helped Drive Biden Win in Nevada, Though Trump Gained Ground
Since 2016," *Nevada Independent*, November 16, 2020, thenevadainde
pendent.com/article/polls-show-how-latino-voters-helped-drive-biden-win
-in-nevada-though-trump-gained-ground-since-2016.

56. Walt Whitman, *Complete Poetry and Collected Prose* (New York: Library
of America, 1982), 8–9. This section on Local 226 is adapted from my
article "There Is Power in This Union," *Dissent*, November 8, 2018,
www.dissentmagazine.org/blog/nevada-democrats-culinary-union-226
-midterms. For an excellent, sober analysis of the limits of labor influence
under the Biden administration, written just before the inauguration,
see Rich Yeselson, "Union Power After the Election," *Dissent*, November 25, 2020, www.dissentmagazine.org/online_articles/union-power
-after-the-election.

# GOOD READING

A single life would not be enough time to read all or even most studies that have been written about the history of the world's oldest mass political party. But among the books I have managed to read about the topic, here are some of those I found to be most enlightening.

### GENERAL WORKS

Cobble, Dorothy Sue. *For the Many: American Feminists and the Global Fight for Democratic Equality.* Princeton, NJ: Princeton University Press, 2021.

Cowie, Jefferson. *The Great Exception: The New Deal and the Limits of American Politics.* Princeton, NJ: Princeton University Press, 2016.

Erie, Stephen P. *Rainbow's End: Irish-Americans and the Dilemmas of Urban Machine Politics, 1840–1985.* Berkeley: University of California Press, 1988.

Fraser, Steve, and Gary Gerstle, eds. *Ruling America: A History of Wealth and Power in a Democracy.* Cambridge, MA: Harvard University Press, 2005.

Gerring, John. *Party Ideologies in America, 1828–1996.* Cambridge, UK: Cambridge University Press, 1998.

Gerstle, Gary. *Liberty and Coercion: The Paradox of American Government.* Princeton, NJ: Princeton University Press, 2015.

Kazin, Michael, Rebecca Edwards, and Adam Rothman, eds. *The Princeton Encyclopedia of American Political History.* 2 vols. Princeton, NJ: Princeton University Press, 2010.

Kent, Frank R. *The Democratic Party: A History.* New York: Century, 1928.

Keyssar, Alexander. *The Right to Vote: The Contested History of Democracy in the United States,* rev. ed. New York: Basic Books, 2009.

———. *Why Do We Still Have the Electoral College?* Cambridge, MA: Harvard University Press, 2020.

Parmet, Herbert S. *The Democrats: The Years After FDR.* New York: Macmillan, 1976.

Schlozman, Daniel. *When Movements Anchor Parties: Electoral Alignments in American History.* Princeton, NJ: Princeton University Press, 2015.

Silbey, Joel H. *The American Political Nation, 1838–1893.* Stanford, CA: Stanford University Press, 1991.

Skowronek, Stephen. *Presidential Leadership in Political Time: Reprise and Reappraisal,* 3rd ed. Lawrence: University Press of Kansas, 2020.

Witcover, Jules. *Party of the People: A History of the Democrats.* New York: Random House, 2003.

## FROM THE BEGINNING THROUGH THE CIVIL WAR

Altschuler, Glenn C., and Stuart M. Blumin. *Rude Republic: Americans and Their Politics in the Nineteenth Century.* Princeton, NJ: Princeton University Press, 2000.

Baker, Jean H. *Affairs of Party: The Political Culture of Northern Democrats in the Mid-Nineteenth Century.* Ithaca, NY: Cornell University Press, 1983.

Bridges, Amy. *A City in the Republic: Antebellum New York and the Origins of Machine Politics.* Cambridge, UK: Cambridge University Press, 1984.

Cole, Donald. *Martin Van Buren and the American Political System.* Princeton, NJ: Princeton University Press, 1984.

Foner, Eric. *Politics and Ideology in the Age of Civil War.* New York: Oxford University Press, 1980.

Hofstadter, Richard. *The Idea of a Party System: The Rise of Legitimate Opposition in the United States, 1780–1840.* Berkeley: University of California Press, 1970.

Johannsen, Robert W. *Stephen A. Douglas.* New York: Oxford University Press, 1973.

John, Richard R. *Spreading the News: The American Postal System from Franklin to Morse.* Cambridge, MA: Harvard University Press, 1995.

Katz, Irving. *August Belmont: A Political Biography.* New York: Columbia University Press, 1968.

Manning, Chandra. *What This Cruel War Was Over: Soldiers, Slavery, and the Civil War.* New York: Knopf, 2007.

Meyers, Marvin. *The Jacksonian Persuasion: Politics and Belief.* Stanford, CA: Stanford University Press, 1957.

Peterson, Merrill. *Thomas Jefferson and the New Nation.* New York: Oxford University Press, 1975.

Remini, Robert V. *Andrew Jackson and the Course of American Freedom, 1822–1832.* New York: Harper & Row, 1981.

———. *Andrew Jackson and the Course of American Democracy, 1833–1845.* New York: Harper & Row, 1984.

Silbey, Joel H. *A Respectable Minority: The Democratic Party in the Civil War Era, 1860–1868.* New York: W. W. Norton, 1977.

Weber, Jennifer. *Copperheads: The Rise and Fall of Lincoln's Opponents in the North.* New York: Oxford University Press, 2006.

Wilentz, Sean. *The Rise of American Democracy.* New York: W. W. Norton, 2005.

Wood, Gordon S. *The Radicalism of the American Revolution.* New York: Knopf, 1992.


## FROM RECONSTRUCTION THROUGH THE 1920S

Anderson, Kristi. *After Suffrage: Women in Partisan and Electoral Politics Before the New Deal.* Chicago: University of Chicago Press, 1996.

Ayers, Edward L. *The Promise of the New South: Life After Reconstruction*. New York: Oxford University Press, 1992.

Barreyre, Nicolas. *Gold and Freedom: The Political Economy of Reconstruction*. Charlottesville: University of Virginia Press, 2015.

Bateman, David, Ira Katznelson, and John S. Lapinski. *Southern Nation: Congress and White Supremacy after Reconstruction*. Princeton, NJ: Princeton University Press, 2018.

Blight, David W. *Race and Reunion: The Civil War in American Memory*. Cambridge, MA: Harvard University Press, 2001.

Burner, David. *The Politics of Provincialism: The Democratic Party in Transition, 1918–1932*. 1968. Reprint, Cambridge, MA: Harvard University Press, 1986.

Chiles, Robert. *The Revolution of '28: Al Smith, American Progressivism and the Coming of the New Deal*. Ithaca, NY: Cornell University Press, 2018.

Connable, Alfred, and Edward Silberfarb. *Tigers of Tammany: Nine Men Who Ran New York*. New York: Holt, Rinehart, and Winston, 1967.

Edwards, Rebecca. *Angels in the Machinery: Gender and Party Politics from the Civil War to the Progressive Era*. New York: Oxford University Press, 1997.

Freeman, Jo. *A Room at a Time: How Women Entered Party Politics*. Lanham, MD: Rowman & Littlefield, 2000.

Grant, Keneshia. *The Great Migration and the Democratic Party: Black Voters and the Realignment of American Politics in the 20th Century*. Philadelphia: Temple University Press, 2020.

Hofstadter, Richard. *The Age of Reform: From Bryan to F.D.R.* New York: Vintage, 1955.

Kantrowitz, Stephen. *Ben Tillman and the Reconstruction of White Supremacy*. Chapel Hill: University of North Carolina Press, 2000.

Overacker, Louise. *Money in Elections*. New York: Macmillan, 1932.

Perman, Michael. *Struggle for Mastery: Disfranchisement in the South, 1888–1908*. Chapel Hill: University of North Carolina Press, 2001.

Perry, Elisabeth Israels. *Belle Moscowitz: Feminine Politics and the Exercise of Power in the Age of Alfred E. Smith*. New York: Oxford University Press, 1987.

Sanders, Elizabeth. *Roots of Reform: Farmers, Workers, and the American State, 1877–1917*. Chicago: University of Chicago Press, 1999.

Sarasohn, David. *Party of Reform: The Democrats in the Progressive Era*. Jackson: University Press of Mississippi, 1989.

Summers, Mark Wahlgren. *Party Games: Getting, Keeping, and Using Power in Gilded Age Politics*. Chapel Hill: University of North Carolina Press, 2004.

Ware, Alan. *The Democratic Party Heads North, 1877–1962*. New York: Cambridge University Press, 2006.

## THE NEW DEAL ORDER, 1930S–1970S

Bird, Kai. *The Outlier: The Unfinished Presidency of Jimmy Carter*. New York: Crown, 2021.

Brinkley, Alan. *The End of Reform: New Deal Liberalism in Recession and War.* New York: Knopf, 1995.

Cohen, Lizabeth. *Making a New Deal: Industrial Workers in Chicago, 1919–1939.* Cambridge, UK: Cambridge University Press, 1990.

Francis-Fallon, Benjamin. *The Rise of the Latino Vote: A History.* Cambridge, MA: Harvard University Press, 2019.

Fraser, Steve. *Labor Will Rule: Sidney Hillman and the Rise of American Labor.* New York: Free Press, 1991.

———, and Gary Gerstle, eds. *The Rise and Fall of the New Deal Order, 1930–1980.* Princeton, NJ: Princeton University Press, 1989.

Gillon, Steven M. *Politics and Vision: The ADA and American Liberalism, 1947–1985.* New York: Oxford University Press, 1987.

Hamilton, Charles V. *Adam Clayton Powell, Jr.: The Political Biography of an American Dilemma.* New York: Atheneum, 1991.

Haygood, Wil. *King of the Cats: The Life and Times of Adam Clayton Powell, Jr.* Boston: Houghton Mifflin Harcourt, 1993.

Huthmacher, J. Joseph. *Senator Robert F. Wagner and the Rise of Urban Liberalism.* New York: Atheneum, 1968.

Katznelson, Ira. *Fear Itself: The New Deal and the Origins of Our Time.* New York: Liveright, 2013.

Levine, Lawrence W., and Cornelia R. Levine. *The People and the President: America's Conversation with FDR.* Boston: Beacon Press, 2002.

Lichtenstein, Nelson. *The Most Dangerous Man in Detroit: Walter Reuther and the Fate of American Labor.* New York: Basic Books, 1995.

Miroff, Bruce. *The Liberals' Moment: The McGovern Insurgency and the Identity Crisis of the Democratic Party.* Lawrence: University Press of Kansas, 2007.

Offner, Arnold A. *Hubert Humphrey: The Conscience of the Country.* New Haven, CT: Yale University Press, 2018.

Plotke, David. *Building a Democratic Political Order: Reshaping American Liberalism in the 1930s and 1940s.* Cambridge, UK: Cambridge University Press, 1996.

Rosenfeld, Sam. *The Polarizers: Postwar Architects of Our Partisan Era.* Chicago: University of Chicago Press, 2018.

Schickler, Eric. *Racial Realignment: The Transformation of American Liberalism.* Princeton, NJ: Princeton University Press, 2016.

Scroop, Daniel. *Mr. Democrat: Jim Farley, the New Deal, and the Making of Modern American Politics.* Ann Arbor: University of Michigan Press, 2006.

Shafer, Byron E. *Quiet Revolution: The Struggle for the Democratic Party and the Shaping of Post-Reform Politics.* New York: Russell Sage Foundation, 1983.

Sugrue, Thomas J. *The Origins of the Urban Crisis: Race and Inequality in Postwar Detroit.* Princeton, NJ: Princeton University Press, 1996.

Ware, Susan. *Beyond Suffrage: Women in the New Deal.* Cambridge, MA: Harvard University Press, 1981.

Weiss, Nancy. *Farewell to the Party of Lincoln: Black Politics in the Age of FDR.* Princeton, NJ: Princeton University Press, 1983.

Wilson, James Q. *The Amateur Democrat: Club Politics in Three Cities.* Chicago: University of Chicago Press, 1962.

Zelizer, Julian. *The Fierce Urgency of Now: Lyndon Johnson, Congress, and the Battle for the Great Society.* New York: Penguin, 2015.


## A DIVIDED PARTY IN A DIVIDED NATION, 1980S–2020

Alterman, Eric. *Kabuki Democracy: The System vs. Barack Obama.* New York: Nation Books, 2011.

Andelic, Patrick. *Donkey Work: Congressional Democrats in Conservative America, 1974–1994.* Lawrence: University Press of Kansas, 2019.

Baer, Kenneth S. *Reinventing Democrats: The Politics of Liberalism from Reagan to Clinton.* Lawrence: University Press of Kansas, 2000.

Bai, Matt. *The Argument: Inside the Battle to Remake Democratic Politics.* New York: Penguin, 2008.

Ball, Molly. *Pelosi.* New York: Henry Holt, 2020.

Dionne, E. J. *Why Americans Hate Politics.* 1991. Reprint, New York: Simon & Schuster, 2004.

———. *Code Red: How Moderates and Progressives Can Unite to Save Our Country.* New York: St. Martin's Press, 2020.

Freedlander, David. *The AOC Generation: How Millennials Are Seizing Power and Rewriting the Rules of American Politics.* Boston: Beacon Press, 2021.

Hacker, Jacob S., and Paul Pierson. *Winner-Take-All Politics: How Washington Made the Rich Richer—And Turned Its Back on the Middle Class.* New York: Simon & Schuster, 2010.

Kuttner, Robert. *The Life of the Party: Democratic Prospects in 1988 and Beyond.* New York: Viking, 1987.

Masket, Seth. *Learning from Loss: The Democrats, 2016–2020.* Cambridge, UK: Cambridge University Press, 2020.

Piketty, Thomas. *Capital and Ideology.* Trans. Arthur Goldhammer. Cambridge, MA: Harvard University Press, 2020.

Reed, Adolph L., Jr. *The Jesse Jackson Phenomenon: The Crisis of Purpose in Afro-American Politics.* New Haven, CT: Yale University Press, 1986.

## ACKNOWLEDGMENTS

I have led a fortunate life in many ways, not the least of which is to have friends and colleagues as generous as they are wise. If Dan Gerstle had not raised the idea of this book with me five years ago, it probably would not exist. Dan's father, the great historian Gary Gerstle, then gave the entire manuscript a sharp, judicious critique.

Other fine scholars and writers read individual chapters or offered excellent advice about how to understand such a sprawling, daunting subject. Thanks, in particular, to Mike Amezcua, Katherine Benton-Cohen, Dorothy Sue Cobble, Lizabeth Cohen, Maurice Jackson, Chandra Manning, Joseph McCartin, John McNeill, Jaime Sanchez, Jr., Tim Shenk, and Julian Zelizer.

At the Institute for Advanced Study at Princeton, I got to spend a pleasurable and productive year of writing—and to stroll through the beautiful forest that sits right on campus. Michael Walzer made that fellowship possible and has been a mentor since my college years—and, more recently, as my fellow co-editor at *Dissent*. At the School of Social Science, Didier Fassin, Joan Scott, and Axel Honneth were splendid hosts and brilliant critics. Denise Brennan and other fellows provided fresh ideas and hours of companionship.

The talks I gave and the suggestions I received from the Friends of the IAS; at Cornell University, where I gave the Carl Becker Lectures; and at Ohio State University were invaluable in nudging me to think past the narrative trees to contemplate the shape of the thematic forest. Up in Ithaca, Larry Glickman treated me with kindness and enthusiasm.

My reviews and essays about Democrats for *The Nation* and *The New Republic* forced me to start writing about the party's history while I was still learning about it. There can be no magazine editors in the nation more adept than David Marcus, Laura Marsh, and Chris Lehmann. At *The New York Times*, Clay Risen helped me think about the meaning of Bernie Sanders; at *The New York Review of Books*,

Emily Greenhouse and Prudence Crowther did the same for John F. Kennedy. And thanks to the late Richard Ben Cramer, the title of whose fine book about the 1988 campaign inspired the title of this one.

Harold M. Ickes and David Rudd know more about the modern Democratic Party than I will ever learn, so I was fortunate they agreed to let me interview them. Sophia Zahner transcribed those interviews and also compiled a rich variety of images from which I could choose. Jeffrey Ngo spruced up my endnotes.

At FSG, Alexander Star has been an editor sublime. Not only were his suggestions for framing and revision prompt and *always* on the mark; he deployed his deep knowledge of history to get me to think more carefully about the arguments I wanted to make. Ian Van Wye, Alex's assistant, was just as helpful in giving me advice about publishing details—and in keeping me on deadline.

Alex and Ian worked with a brilliant team to turn my ungainly Word files into a real book. Janet Renard provided a precise copyedit, Songhee Kim an elegant design, and Gregg Kulick an image for the jacket that evokes bravura campaigns, past and present. Nancy Elgin skillfully managed the production editorial process.

Out by the Pacific, Sandy Dijkstra showed once again what an exceptional agent she is. From shaping an appealing proposal to negotiating a great deal, she combines candor with a bottomless appetite for good writing. And her line "Michael, one cannot assume interest" remains the best and pithiest advice about the craft I have ever received.

No fortune can be sweeter than to belong to a family whose members freely point out my flaws while conveying their unbounded love. Watching and hearing about Danny's essential work for contemporary Democrats inspired me to write this history; he is a fount of essential information and shrewd, realistic takes. Maia cares as much about good prose as she does about becoming a fine actor. They both bring more joy to my life than I can ever express. In Barb and Jake, my children have found delightful mates who take care of them and make them happy. My sister, Kate, writes the most supportive messages any writer (or brother) could want. I only wish she and her wife, Lynne, did not live so far away. Maggie the schnoodle would prefer some Cheerios or cheese to being thanked in a book. But I would be a lonelier fellow if she did not lie near me as I read and type, search and worry.

Beth remains the smartest, most moral, most generous, and kindest woman I have ever known. Forty-five years after we met, I still cannot believe how lucky I am to share my life with her.

# INDEX

A NOTE ABOUT THE AUTHOR

Michael Kazin is a professor of history at Georgetown University and the editor emeritus of *Dissent*. His books include *War Against War: The American Fight for Peace, 1914–1918*; *American Dreamers: How the Left Changed a Nation*; *The Populist Persuasion: An American History*; and *A Godly Hero: The Life of William Jennings Bryan*. He is a member of the American Academy of Arts and Sciences and the editor of *The Princeton Encyclopedia of American Political History*.